My health remains good, &c
At Courtenar, and I am not
disappointed about a Room
that is promised me. I shall
open my Ey__ here about the
1st of August.

I expect daily to get a
little from Mr Gregory, and as
soon as I do, I will write
you again.

I am exceedingly pained to
learn that my missionary plan
has thrown your out, &
also your son Charly; but
I hope in the end you
will not be losers. I trust
you will find something
profitable to turn your
hands to in meantime.

Remember me kindly to your
good wife and little
Bry, I am affectionate Brother
your Cathie

THE LETTERS

OF GEORGE CATLIN

AND HIS FAMILY

Here is a fresh perspective on one of the unique characters in the history of western America. Despite George Catlin's great reputation, and the appearance of at least three biographies since 1948, virtually nothing is known of his personal life. This book provides the missing information.

Nearly two hundred recently discovered personal letters are used as the basis for recounting the fortunes of the Catlin family. Focusing on George and his activities, the author gives a detailed account of this typical Yankee family caught up in the western excitement that pervaded America in the years between the Battle of New Orleans and Appomattox.

The fourteen Catlin children were all born in western Pennsylvania—an area to which their father migrated from his native Connecticut. As members of a transplanted New England patriarchy, they were prepared for the world with a modicum of Calvinistic piety, with as much formal education as their backwoods environment could provide, and with a continuing stream of advice from the domineering old Federalist who was their father.

The correspondence between Putnam Catlin and his children, and among themselves, reflects with remarkable fidelity the major preoccupations of their era. The chronic lack of money, the obsessive pursuit of success and self-improvement, the chimera of western opportunity with its hazards of land speculation, and the rustic's fascination with the more sophisticated urban centers of the Atlantic seaboard and Europe—all find expression in their letters.

Most importantly, the letters provide a hitherto unverified dimension to the Catlin clan's most distinguished member—George. Writing to the family in Pennsylvania, he describes the travail of his famous trip to the Indian pipestone quarries in the Dakotas. Later he and his wife Clara tell of their life in London and their adventures on the continent. And finally there is a first-hand account of George's later years in Brussels, written by his younger brother Francis, who visited him there when he was no longer the social lion of the salons of London and Paris.

MARJORIE CATLIN ROEHM is the granddaughter of George Catlin's youngest brother, and an accomplished amateur portraitist.

UNIVERSITY OF CALIFORNIA PRESS

THE LETTERS

OF GEORGE CATLIN

AND HIS FAMILY

A Chronicle of the American West

MARJORIE CATLIN ROEHM

BERKELEY AND LOS ANGELES 1966

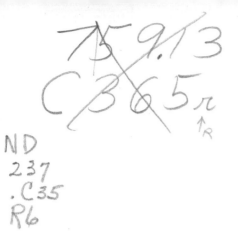
UNIVERSITY OF CALIFORNIA PRESS
BERKELEY AND LOS ANGELES

CAMBRIDGE UNIVERSITY PRESS
LONDON, ENGLAND

To my grandchildren
Lindsey, Craig, and Rod Stevenson

PREFACE

THIS BOOK is based upon nearly two hundred letters written by members of the Catlin family. None of them has ever been published or even accessible to George Catlin's biographers. Much has been written about this artist who became famous for his paintings and writings of the North American Indians; however, his biographers have always commented on the fact that few personal letters from him were to be found, and that nothing, aside from vital statistics, was known about the family in which he was raised. No one has known what sort of son, brother, husband, or father he was. Thomas Donaldson said of him: "No man of his station or who had done so much, left so little from which to give a correct account of his private life." [1]

This old family correspondence, spanning more than half a century, includes thirty-five letters from George, and thirty-one letters written to him by members of his family. [2] They take the reader from a country village in Pennsylvania to Florida, to England, to Belgium, and to Wisconsin Territory in the untamed wilderness.

It has been said that George never mentioned the births of his children; never spoke of his brothers and sisters. His letters tell of them all. The Catlins were a closely knit family. George was a warmhearted man, a generous and dutiful son and brother. Despite his years in sophisticated European cities, he dreamed of some day settling down

[1] *The George Catlin Indian Gallery*, Annual Report of . . . the Smithsonian Institution, 1885 (Washington: The Institution, 1886), p. 717.

[2] For a list of the letters see Appendix I.

vii

in a country town with his beloved wife and "little chubs"; a dream that never came true.

For lack of information, George's biographers have had to skirt certain periods in the artist's life. For instance, what really happened to George in the summer of 1836? Finding a bill for the rent of a church in Buffalo, New York, dated August 1, 1836, plus a bill for advertising his exhibit in the city at that time, would naturally lead one to believe that George had his first "big city" exhibition there that summer. He did not, although he planned to. Nothing has been known of the confusion and worry that filled those summer and fall months of 1836. It is all told in letters from both George and his father, providing a revealing chapter in the artist's life, and showing an almost monomaniacal streak in his character.

What was George doing in Belgium between 1868 and his return to the United States in 1871? It was known that his brother Francis paid him a visit, but that is all. Sixteen long letters from George to Francis, written in Brussels, together with a hitherto unknown diary kept by Francis during his two months' visit there, give a vivid picture of a deaf old man living in a silent world with pet mice for company, and still working! His bitterness against Henry Schoolcraft shows up many times in Francis' diary, but the artist's troubled past had in no way destroyed his faith in the future value of his works— nor had it dimmed the flame of his fantastic optimism and self-confidence.

My father was Francis Eugene Catlin, third son of Francis Putnam Catlin, who was the youngest of the fourteen children born to Putnam and Polly Catlin. My grandfather came to live with my parents shortly after their marriage, and left all his possessions with them when he died in 1900. For many years these letters lay in a little old trunk, tucked away in attics. In the days of my grandfather letters were not hastily written, to be read quickly and then discarded. They were the only means of communication, and were saved to be read over and over again. Times were hard, postage expensive, so when father Putnam wrote to one of his children he gave the current news of the whole family, thus keeping one in touch with them all. The result is that the over-all continuity is surprisingly good.

As there are so many letters in this collection from George to his father, and vice versa, I believe Francis took possession of those which his father had saved. (Francis was the only child at home when Putnam died.) As for George's letters from members of the family, they must have been sent to Francis by the artist's daughters. Although nineteen years younger than his brother George, he was very close to the artist from 1868 until the latter's death in 1872. George had told him that all his correspondence, from childhood on, was in a box stored with his original paintings in Philadelphia. No doubt it was delivered to his daughters when the Indian gallery was donated to the Smithsonian Institution in 1879.

With the aid of a magnifying glass and patience, I have copied all these letters, many torn, cracked and faded with age. It is possible to include only a portion of them here, but I have used them all to tell the story of George Catlin and his family. There has been no attempt to "butter up" any of its members; no deletions to cover their frailties. Omissions are made only because the material was of limited interest or to avoid repetition. The letters are now in the Bancroft Library of the University of California, at Berkeley.

The letters have been copied as they were written. Those from Putnam, until late in life, were extremely well written. However, punctuation, aside from commas and dashes, was not considered too important at that time, and capitals were strewn about very carelessly. Because of high postage rates, the sheets were generally covered with small writing from one edge to the other, seldom allowing any waste of paper for paragraphing. I have noticed a wider space sometimes left between sentences, which I have accepted as meaning the end of a paragraph, allowing me to "break" a page at intervals. Francis Catlin's diary, however, was a personal, pencil-scribbled account of his trip, made up of many disconnected notes, abbreviations, and dashes. For easier reading I have spelled out the abbreviated words, and added a few commas and periods, but not enough to destroy the "tone" of the diary.

All biographers of George Catlin must necessarily get their information about his journeys from the artist's own accounts. Since his books are easily available, and I mean here to direct attention to other members of his family, I have given but brief summaries of his expeditions into Indian country.

George's portrait of his father shows a fine-looking, stern-faced gentleman. Putnam Catlin could have been one of the outstanding personalities in the early history of our country, but he never lived up to his potential. He was seemingly content to be a big frog in the smallest puddle available, and let the world float along without his aid or interference.

His exceptionally well-phrased letters appear to have been written by a man whose philosophy of life had brought him a consciousness of great success. I believe he tried to imbue in his sons the ambition he himself lacked—either that, or to create in their minds the image of as great a man as he believed himself to be. His letters are worthy of special attention.

Polly Catlin, mother of fourteen children, had but two interests in life: her family and her Bible. She was particularly concerned over the health and morals of her brood, always "full of fears," but hoping for the best. Her infrequent letters are very poorly written, but intensely interesting. She used many colloquial expressions of that day; and she had a sense of humor, which Putnam lacked.

George wrote in a delightful, chatty manner—as, perhaps, he talked. His words seem to flow gracefully over the page in an interesting, descriptive conversation. He was the most gifted member of the family. His brothers Julius and James had artistic ability, and Julius might have made a name for himself had he lived. George was also endowed with an extra supply of ambition and optimism—two qualities necessary for success. However, he was completely lacking in business sense. George spoke of financial matters in practically every letter. He was never solvent, but there was always a pot of gold waiting around the next corner.

George was no paragon, but although he had many faults, his morals or integrity have never been questioned. He was a gentleman, and attracted men of intellect and culture. He had a personality that drew people to him wherever he went. His life was as colorful as his palette, a mad whirl of activity and adventure. Bernard DeVoto said of him: "He was an extraordinary man, a man with a certain greatness in him; his work is notable and his life was picturesque." [3]

Because of his greater importance, I have given the most space to George, including all of his letters in their entirety. As personal letters, they will shed light on his character, and fill in many gaps and dates in his life. However, he came from a vigorous and interesting American family, who lived out their lives in the nineteenth century, in the years of tremendous growth and excitement in a rough new country. There is drama in their letters, and some of that drama is tragedy. There are pages stained with the writer's tears, and brave letters extolling the beauties of the western prairies, minimizing the poverty, the loneliness and heartbreak that belonged to the West. It is all here in these letters; in the life of George Catlin and his family.

---

[3] Bernard De Voto, *Across the Wide Missouri* (Boston: Houghton Mifflin Company, 1947), p. 393.

ACKNOWLEDGMENTS

As NOTED ABOVE, this book is made up, for the most part, of unpublished family letters I have placed in the Bancroft Library. I have included a few letters obtained through the generosity of public institutions. For copies of such letters, and permission to print them, I express my thanks to the New-York Historical Society, the Missouri Historical Society, and the Historical Society of Pennsylvania. I thank the State Historical Society of Wisconsin for permission to quote portions of an article published by that Society.

I also wish to acknowledge generous help received from Margaret Gleason, State Historical Society of Wisconsin; Priscilla Knuth, Oregon Historical Society; Lucy B. Gardner, Historical Society of Montrose, Pennsylvania; Louise C. Roloson, Melbourne, Florida; and Mrs. Bernard Lien, Easton, Minnesota.

I am indebted to my good friend Edgar L. Morphet, of the University of California, for urging me to "do something" with the old family correspondence; I have had a wonderful time digging deep into the lives of my ancestors. I have a very warm feeling for all at the Bancroft Library, and will ever be grateful to George P. Hammond, Director of the Library from 1946 to 1965, and to Dale L. Morgan, its Editor, for their personal friendship, interest, and advice. To Lloyd G. Lyman, Assistant Director of the University of California Press, whose criticism and encouragement truly made this book possible, I say "thank you" with all my heart.

Last, but certainly not least, I wish to applaud my husband,

ACKNOWLEDGMENTS

Harold Roehm, whose unlimited patience in living with a "writing woman" was nothing short of a miracle.

MARJORIE CATLIN ROEHM

Berkeley, California

FOREWORD

SINCE Bernard DeVoto's *Across the Wide Missouri* appeared in 1947, we have seen a major renaissance in popular and scholarly esteem for the artists of the early West. This revaluation has extended beyond their paintings as art to the function of this art as social documentation and reportage upon the wonderfully varied Western landscape.

DeVoto noted that Catlin was the first painter of the West, or at least, the first painter who had any effect. He also observed that it was hard to make dependable statements about Catlin on the basis of what had been written up to that time. "And this is a pity, for he was an extraordinary man, a man with a certain greatness in him; his work was notable and his life was picturesque. Purely as an adventure story his biography would be fascinating and historians, whether of our society or of our art, would find him richly significant."

In 1948 Loyd Haberly served up Catlin's life as the fascinating adventure story DeVoto had envisioned. His *Pursuit of the Horizon* was a readable work that was also undocumented, unindexed, and rather too uncritical. Since then Catlin has preoccupied the art historian Harold McCracken, who devoted a chapter to the "Dean of Western Artists" in *Portrait of the Old West* (1952), then addressed himself to a much more thorough study, *George Catlin and the Old Frontier* (1959). Marvin C. Ross also made a contribution with an introduction to *George Catlin, Episodes from* "Life Among the Indians" *and* "Last Rambles," a 1959 reworking of two lesser-known books by the artist. Now, from Mrs. Marjorie Catlin Roehm, the granddaughter of George's youngest brother, Francis, we have a wholly fresh approach to Catlin's life, a book that offers a novel and badly needed perspective on both the artist and the age he typified.

The heart of Mrs. Roehm's book is a magnificent family archive made up of 174 letters addressed to or written by various members of the clan, from 1798 to 1870, supplemented by such Catlin letters as have been preserved in institutional collections. This personal archive had been completely unknown to students of Catlin's life; it consists of letters by George's father and mother, by the artist and his wife Clara, and by brothers, sisters, nieces, nephews, and various in-laws, to say nothing of such unlooked-for records as Francis Catlin's 1868 diary of a visit with his aging but undefeatable brother in Brussels. This collection of family papers had come down through the generations in classical fashion, preserved in an old trunk stowed away in the attic of various Catlin homes.

By now we have heard much—rather too much, perhaps, because in too narrow a compass—of George Catlin as the first really accomplished painter to portray the Plains Indians in their own country, as the man who in a sense fathered American ethnology. Catlin created his own legend by correspondence to newspapers, exhibitions of his astonishing Indian Gallery, and numerous books, especially his *Letters and Notes on the Manners, Customs, and Condition of the North American Indians,* first published in London and New York in 1841. It has been difficult to perceive clearly the realistic features of the landscape in Catlin's life, beyond the shimmering mirage of the legend, though the general outline has been evident enough.

Catlin was a promising young lawyer, born in the Susquehanna Valley of northern Pennsylvania, who found himself possessed of an artistic bent beyond resisting. He transformed himself into an accomplished and successful painter who would deserve a place in the annals of American art for his portraits alone. But the American Indians captured his imagination after he painted a Seneca notable, Red Jacket, in 1826. Overcome by a Rousseauian vision of the red man who must dwell in noble simplicity beyond the circle of corruption that surrounded civilization, Catlin conceived the idea of visiting the Western frontier to record on canvas the lives and aspect of the Indians to be found there. In 1830 he achieved something in the way of a preliminary reconnaissance, visiting St. Louis, Prairie du Chien, and Cantonment Leavenworth. Then in 1832 he came back to establish the foundation on which he erected a career.

He was given the opportunity to ascend the Missouri to Fort Union on the steamboat *Yellowstone*, the first steamboat voyage to the mouth of the Yellowstone; and he then paddled back down the river in a canoe with just two companions, stopping off at various Indian villages and cramming notebooks and sketchbooks with what he saw, freshly observed and graphically reported. In 1834 he accompanied the Dragoons on their historic march to the Comanche country, and in 1836 he visited the Red Pipestone Quarry in Minnesota. (He brought back specimens of the material from which the Indians fashioned ceremonial pipes; the mineral was named Catlinite and is still so known.) These were the field researches that gave authority and substance to Catlin's dream of a great Museum of the American Indian, the walls of which would be covered with hundreds and thousands of paintings and artifacts, authentic beyond all question.

The Indian Gallery Catlin created and began to display was a popular and critical success; but he was a half-century, at least, ahead of his time; Congress could not quite be brought to the point of glorifying that recurrent inconvenience, the American Indian. Catlin was now in some measure, and remained for the rest of his life, a prisoner of his own great dream. Like most successful artists, he was something of an exhibitionist, with a showman's talent. The enormous financial and emotional investment he had made in his Indian Gallery required him to take it to London, and later to the Continent, always hoping that he could dispose of it advantageously —but preferably to the United States government, to be preserved as a national treasure. Along the way he gave England what might be described as her first Wild West shows, more than forty years before Buffalo Bill took his first exhibition on the road. Adversity overtook him; he lost his wife and came to know what the debtor's prison looked like; he embarked upon extraordinary new travels that took him to South America and the Pacific Coast of North America; and he died in 1872 at the age of 76, working away until just a few weeks before his death. (As it turned out, his Indian Gallery came to the Smithsonian Institution finally, as a gift from the heirs of another man. The collection has been preserved there since 1879, and was the basis of a major exhibition in the summer of 1965, the paintings having been cleaned, restored, and hung in much the fashion Catlin had once displayed them, massed for best effect, and grouped tribally.)

Mrs. Roehm has not altered this story. It is her shift in emphasis that gives her book so much charm. In previous books about the artist, Catlin's family have emerged pretty much the "stick-men" critics have sometimes belabored in Catlin's hastier sketches. Now they come out of the shadows into full daylight, rounded human beings because allowed to speak in their own voice. With great skill Mrs. Roehm has made the family letters themselves the basic fabric of her book. As she says, the continuity is surprisingly good. Large as was the family, complex as were their interests, scattered as they were by time and economic circumstance, they kept track of one another through their letters; and these letters afford us a rich insight into American life, from George Washington's era to that of Ulysses S. Grant. Although the book necessarily revolves around the most famous member of the Catlin family, all the others have their place; this would be a notable work if it contained nothing more than the letters dealing with the financial downfall of George's sister Eliza and her husband Anson Dart after the Panic of 1837, and their struggle afterward to establish themselves on the Wisconsin prairies.

No ancestor-worshiper, Mrs. Roehm provides a bridging text and commentary upon the letters that is continuously perceptive, shrewd in its insights, alertly critical, and delightful in general. I have had the pleasure of seeing her shape this book through a great many drafts, each much improved over the last, and now I take satisfaction in seeing it go forth to the world, readjusting all our ideas about the Catlin family and affording us a new vantage point for contemplating the American society of which they were so characteristic a product.

Dale L. Morgan

CONTENTS

PART ONE: THE EARLY YEARS
1643–1829

1643–1788: Origin of the Catlins—Prologue to the Great Migration—1787–1817: Wilkes-Barre, Ona-qua-gua Valley, Hopbottom and the birth of fourteen children—1817–1830: Montrose and the liquor problem—Letters to George at law school—Putnam chooses a career for Julius—Law versus the paint brush—A war veteran seeks a job—The death of Lynde—The weaving of a dream—The artist takes a wife—Julius and tragedy.

PART TWO: INDIAN COUNTRY
1830–1837

1830–1832: The pulse of the nation—Putnam has his worries—St. Louis and the beginning of the Great Adventure—Letters from Great Bend—A problem is solved—1832: A trip on the Yellowstone to the Upper Missouri—1833: Putnam writes Francis on the correct use of capital letters—The story of John Catlin—1834: In the land of the Comanches—1835: Letters from the family—Up the Mississippi.

PART THREE: HIGHLIGHTS AND SHADOW
1836–1840

1836: George and Clara lose their first child—George decides to take a trip—A disrupted exhibit in buffalo—Where is George?—Where the red pipe-stone came from—1837: Land speculation and Anson Dart—Francis goes to Pensacola—A quick sketch of the Catlin family—1838:

A Wild West show in New York—Francis decides to go to sea—George receives praise but no offers—Family letters—1839: Family correspondence—George says farewell to America.

PART FOUR: PALACES AND PIONEERS
1840–1842

1840: An artist in London-Town—Anson Dart is in difficulty—Clara arrives in London—Eliza prepares for the Wilderness West—News of the pioneers—London has its dull season—Eliza writes about Green Lake—1841: Francis is told what to bring to Wisconsin—Letters from London—George publishes his book on the North American Indians—News from the pioneers

PART FIVE: WAR-WHOOPS AND TRAGEDY
1842–1845

1842: Letters from George, Eliza and Richard—The death of a patriarch; the end of an era—"Poor Henry" and the Bankrupt Law—George goes to Liverpool—The Dart Family writes to Clara—1843: War-whoops in London—The Darts urge George and Clara to come to Wisconsin—Letters from Henry and Mary—Eliza writes her mother—George writes to his mother—Francis disappoints the Darts—1844: Letters from Anson, George and Polly—The death of Polly—Letters from Mary, Henry and Eliza—More war-whoops in London

PART SIX: THE SKY FALLS DOWN
1845–1864

1845–1853: The Darts expect a visit from George and Clara—Tragedy in Paris—A change in the life of the pioneers—More tragedy in Paris—The axe falls—The "Harpies" gather for the kill—1850–1861: Oregon Territory; Anson Dart and a census report—A vagabond artist—Letters from Wisconsin—1861–1864: The tale of the pioneers comes to a close

CONTENTS

PART SEVEN: THE WANDERER RETURNS
1860–1869

1860–1868: George the optimist picks up his pen again—1868: George tells Francis to come to Bruxelles—Francis Catlin's diary on his trip to Belgium—

PART EIGHT: THE LONG ROAD HOME
1869–1900

1869: "Push it Francis, Push it!"—The outlines and Mr. Steele— 1870: The glitter of illusion—A clutch at straws—1871: The end of the road

PART ONE: THE EARLY YEARS

1643–1829

1643–1788: Origin of the Catlins; Prologue to the Great Migration; 1787–1817: Wilkes–Barre, Ona-qua-gua Valley, Hopbottom and the birth of fourteen children   1817–1830: Montrose and the liquor problem; Letters to George at law school; Putnam chooses a career for Julius; Law versus the paint brush; A war veteran seeks a job; The death of Lynde; The weaving of a dream; The artist takes a wife; Julius and tragedy.

Thomas Catlin came to America in 1643. Lineal descendants: John, Samuel, John
Eli (b. 1773; d. 1820) m. Elizabeth Wey
Putnam (b. 1764; d. 1842) m. Polly Sutton (b. 1770; d. 1844)

Charles m. Amanda Burr
b. 1790
d. 1832

Theodore
Theodosia
James

Clara
b. 1792
d. 1809

Juliet*

Henry m. Mary Grubb
b. 1791
d. 1863

several children

m. Eliza ?

several children

George m. Clara Gregory
b. 1796
d. 1872

Elizabeth Wing
Clara Gregory
Victoria Louise
George

Eliza m. Anson Dart
b. 1798
d. 1866

George
Gertrude*
Putnam
Mary
Richard
Elizabeth
Julius*
Charles

James m. Abigail Sayre
b. 1800
d. 1847

seven children

Mary m. Asa Hartshorn
b. 1802
d. 1848

Thomas
Horace

Julius
b. 1804
d. 1828

Lynde
b. 1806
d. 1824

Sally*

Richard m. Darwina Barstow
b. 1809
d. 1874

Anna*
Lizzy*

John
b. 1812
d. 1834

Francis m. Elizabeth DuBois
b. 1815
d. 1900

George*
Clara*
Charles
Francis
Fred

m. Mary Weed Tolbert

William Weed

* Died young

Origin of the Catlins

T H E R E   W A S a close bond between George Catlin and his father; a relationship built on respect and understanding. George could not have been a tractable child. The self-will displayed in his later years would indicate a defiant lad. Yet he was greatly influenced by Putnam's early teaching; and as long as his father lived, George craved his approval. Even middle-aged, during his first flush of success in London, his letters showed an almost childish desire for his father's praise.[1]

Putnam Catlin was an aristocratic despot in his family. In the early 1800's youth was notably rebellious, and only a tight grasp on the reins of authority could ensure a father that his son would bring honor to his name. Putnam's wife, Polly, brought up the two daughters, but the boys were his business, and he made it a full-time job. Each son must be able to "make a good report of himself," obey the Commandments, and respect the name of Catlin. A review of his early years shows the forces which shaped *his* life, to which he, in turn, tried to make his sons conform.

Putnam was born in Litchfield, Connecticut, in 1764, the only son of Eli Catlin and Elizabeth Wey. Catlin is a notable English name, and no doubt it gave him some feeling of superiority in the backwoods villages where he spent his life.[2] Add to this a rigid Puritan heritage, and you have a good index to Putnam Catlin's character.

---

[1] George, in London, strutted with his pen when he wrote his father of his triumphs—of the applause he received when he lectured: "At the end of every sentence, it was 'hear, hear,' & loud & repeated cheers." He was an excited provincial who wanted his father to come to London where he could proudly show him the sights of the great city—"it will be the greatest feate & féte of my life." Another time he wrote: "to think that, from a little go-to-the-mill-boy I have worked my way across the Atlantic, & at last into the Palace & presence of the Queen of England, and received from her own lips her thanks for the interesting information which I have given her."

[2] The Catlins had been seated near Rochester, County of Kent, England, ever since the Norman Conquest. Reynold de Catlyn, one of the followers of William

The little elm-shaded town of Litchfield was a county seat which became famous for the men it produced. Ethan Allen, Oliver Wolcott, and Lyman Beecher all came from Litchfield. Judges Tapping Reeve and James Gould practiced law in the village, and in it later established their famous law school—the first of its kind in America.

The leaders of the town were decidedly intellectual, but there was a powerful bias among those whose forebears had settled the town, and they practically built a fence around it to keep out undesirables. The early New Englanders were followers of John Calvin, and the dogma of that great theologian was still a harsh thread in the fabric of their daily life. Congregationalism was their faith, and the ministers exerted a great influence in the community. Politically, the town was predominantly Federalist.

The husband was lord of the manor, and his wife and children obeyed him without question. Home discipline was strict, and idleness was sin. However, the boy Putnam was encouraged to listen to his elders' conversations when kinsmen and neighbors gathered around the family hearth. Idle chitchat was not exchanged. Life was a serious business. The affairs of the township and nation were discussed, or the minister's last sermon would be carefully analyzed. Putnam's contact with these people naturally left its mark.

A son's education was of great importance.[3] A three-year-old

---

the Conqueror, is mentioned in the Domesday Book as possessing "two knights fees" of land in Kent County. Various individuals of the family had been honorably employed in the service of the kings of England and other European powers. The Arms now borne by the family were granted to Sir Robert Catlin for great gallantry at the Battle of Agincourt, 1415. Another person of consequence was "Sir Robert Catlin," Lord Chief Justice of Kings Bench in the reign of Queen Elizabeth, 1558.

Thomas Catlin was one of three brothers who came to America from England in 1643. He settled in Hartford, Connecticut. Around 1730 one of his descendants moved west to Litchfield, where George Catlin's grandfather, Eli Catlin, was born.

[3] The education of girls in the average family was considered frivolous. They were taught to read and write and do simple sums. What more did they need? Girls married in their middle teens if they were lucky, so all they needed to know

should be able to read. In fact, this was a good age to start Latin lessons, the language so necessary for the professions from which a gentleman might choose: theology, law, and medicine. A child's day was spent in study and chores around the home. Play time? That was idleness, and therefore sinful. Boys became men at sixteen, paid taxes, and joined the militia. A carefree boyhood was something Putnam never had.

Putnam's father was one of the first who answered General Washington's call for volunteers. He was commissioned a lieutenant on January 2, 1776.[4] In March, 1777, when he was only thirteen, Putnam enlisted as a fifer in the same company. He remained in the army until the close of the war in 1783.

As a member of the gentry Putnam was expected to choose a profession. He began "reading law" with the distinguished Uriah Tracy in the fall of 1783, and passed the Connecticut bar examination in 1786.

---

was how to catch a husband, manage a house, and raise a family. In wealthier homes, if a girl showed interest in study, she might be given a better education, but it wasn't forced. All mothers, rich or poor, wanted to see their daughters married, and it wasn't a good idea for a wife to be too well educated. This Calvin-tinted belief in male superiority was carried into Putnam's marriage, and even showed faintly in his son George's attitude toward his wife Clara. Clara was his mental equal, and he loved her, but he showed little consideration for her wishes. *He* was king, and Clara meekly followed behind him.

[4] In *The George Catlin Indian Gallery*, Annual Report of . . . the Smithsonian Institution, 1885 (Washington: The Institution, 1886), p. 702, Thomas Donaldson mistakenly says that Eli Catlin enlisted as lieutenant in the Second Connecticut Regiment in January, 1777, for Eli's commission states that "Eli Catlin, Gentleman," was commissioned as "first lieutenant of Captain Nath'l Tuttle's Company in the nineteenth Regiment of foot commanded by Colonel Charles Webb." It was dated January 1, 1776, and signed by John Hancock, President of the Second Continental Congress.

Prologue to the Great Migration

W H I L E P U T N A M was reading law in Litchfield, the great American surge west was beginning. Under British restrictions on settlement, the pre-Revolutionary settlers in Connecticut had accepted the old-country tradition of permanency of location, where the family seat was the home of one generation after another. Thomas Catlin had settled there in 1643, and for over one hundred and fifty years Connecticut had been home to his descendants. It took a war to shake them loose.

With independence and freedom from the restrictions on settlement in the old Northwest Territory, the fever to go west hit the New England settlers with the force of an epidemic, and it was the Connecticut Yankees who broke the path to the new frontier. They were not the older men or the well-to-do inhabitants, but the younger generation, impatient and dissatisfied with the prospect of scratching a living from the rocky soil. One ox cart after another, piled with pots, pans, and babies, departed for the Promised Land, leaving many deserted villages behind them.

Putnam wanted to try his wings, but he did not have the ambition for too long a flight.[5] He had heard a great deal about the beautiful Wyoming Valley in Pennsylvania. The state legislature had just organized Luzerne County, and had chosen the little town of Wilkes-Barre for its county seat. This was just the place for a young lawyer, and Putnam was admitted as an attorney during the first term of Court in Wilkes-Barre, May 28, 1787.

---

[5] No doubt Putnam considered his move from Connecticut to Pennsylvania quite a daring expedition. Later he told his son Francis, "You will see clearly that every young man will have to rise on his own merit, and it should be so—when I was 22 years old I sallied off to the west among strangers and had to cater for myself."

Wilkes-Barre, Ona-Qua-Gua Valley, Hopbottom, and the birth of fourteen children

W I L K E S - B A R R E was named for two distinguished Englishmen who supported the rights of the American colonies during the Revolution. The town was located nearly in the center of the Wyoming Valley, on the Susquehanna River. Putnam with his background and legal ability made many friends. Among them was Colonel Timothy Pickering, who came to Wilkes-Barre about the same time, as a special representative of the state government to organize the new county of Luzerne.[6] Putnam evidently did well as a young lawyer. His judgment was respected, and he was active in politics as an ardent Federalist.

The young attorney now wanted a wife and home of his own, and when his eyes fell on pretty, nineteen-year-old Polly Sutton in her Quaker bonnet, he knew he need look no further. Polly was the daughter of James Sutton who fought the Indians in the Pennsylvania backwoods during the Wyoming massacre of 1778. Both Polly and her mother were briefly captured by the savages. Polly's playmate, five-year-old Francis Slocum, was carried off by the Indians and later adopted by the Miami tribe. Polly was one of a large family, and, judging by her later letters, she had little education.[7]

---

[6] Colonel Timothy Pickering had been Quartermaster General of the United States Army for four years during the Revolutionary War, and then became both Secretary of State and of War during Washington's administration. Later he was elected Representative to Congress from his home state, Massachusetts.

[7] Perhaps Putnam had been instructed by his parents before he left home as to the type of wife he should select: a pleasant-looking, even-tempered woman, healthy, and capable of managing his home and raising his children. Education? Unimportant. Putnam should make all decisions.

Polly may have learned to read and write along with her children. That she seemed to have little difficulty in spelling the harder words showed she made good use of Noah Webster's famous "Spelling Book." One finds many words in her letters scratched out and rewritten correctly. In this collection her few letters

Polly and Putnam were married in 1789, the year George Washington became President of the United States.

Within the next twelve years spent in Wilkes-Barre, their children, Charles, Henry, Clara, Juliet, George, Elizabeth (Eliza), and probably James were born.[8]

Putnam was an eloquent speaker, often called upon to deliver addresses for or against a political policy which was under dispute, concerning the county, state, or national government. In the spring of 1798 Putnam played a prominent part at a county meeting, speaking in defense of the President's foreign policy. His address was unanimously agreed to by the members, and President John Adams sent his letter of gratitude to Putnam. When George Washington died on December 14, 1799, Putnam received an invitation to a funeral oration to be given in the great man's memory.

In 1800 or 1801 Putnam bought a farm forty miles from Wilkes-Barre in the beautiful Ona-qua-gua Valley in Broome County, New York.[9] It has been said that failing health influenced him to give up his general law practice and try the role of country squire.[10] It must have been a hard journey, transporting furniture, farm implements, personal belongings, and six or seven children over the narrow Indian trails to their new home.

George Catlin, many years later, wrote this about his childhood: "My father's plantation in the picturesque little valley of the Ona-quagua, on the banks of the Susquehanna River, hemmed in with huge mountains on either side, was the tapis on which my boyish days

---

were addressed to her youngest son, Francis, often with a humorous apology for her mistakes. She generally added a note to Putnam's letters to Francis, but never to those he wrote to George. It is possible that she did not wish to display her ignorance before her well-educated older son.

[8] Charles was born in 1790, Henry in 1791, Clara in 1792, Juliet (who died in infancy) in 1794, George in 1796, Eliza in 1798, and James in 1800.

[9] Biographers of George Catlin have placed the date of his father's move to Ona-qua-gua Valley in New York state as 1797. In view of the preceding documents this date is wrong. Putnam must have lived in Wilkes-Barre until sometime in 1800 or 1801.

[10] Donaldson, *The George Catlin Indian Gallery*, p. 703.

were spent, and rife with legends of Indian lore. This picturesque and insignificant little valley, which at that time had acquired no place in history, having been settled but a few years, nevertheless had its traditions of an exciting interest as the rendezvous of Brant, the famous and terrible Mohawk chief, and his army, during the frontier war in which the Wyoming massacre took place. The plows in my father's field were daily turning up Indian skulls or Indian bones, and Indian flint arrow-heads." [11]

Travelers through the valley always stopped at the farm, knowing they would receive a warm welcome from the Catlins.[12] Old settlers, soldiers, hunters and trappers sat at the supper table or gathered around the fireplace, and the children, wide-eyed, would listen to the exciting tales that were told about the redskins. Members of the Oneida tribe were often seen in the valley, and they would be friendly toward a little boy with his gun or fishing pole. They must have left a colorful picture in George's mind; and childhood impressions are lasting.

Putnam's family was steadily increasing. Five more children were born in the ten years spent here: Mary (1802), Julius (1804), Lynde (1806), Sally (1807), and Richard (1809). Sally lived but a month, and here sixteen-year-old Clara died. Death came so easily in those days; no wonder Polly spoke of being "full mournful" at times.[13]

About 1810 Putnam sold his farm in the valley and moved to

---

[11] George Catlin, *Last Rambles Amongst the Indians of the Rocky Mountains and the Andes* (New York: D. Appleton and Company, 1867), pp. 9–10. Published in London by Sampson Low, Son and Marston, 1868.

[12] Donaldson, *The George Catlin Indian Gallery*, p. 704.

[13] "Planned parenthood" was an unknown concept in that day; a baby a year was the accepted fact. Children were numerous but infant mortality great, which doubtless accounts for so little mention of the small fry in the old letters. Death took so many that there was a superstitious fear about speaking of any child too favorably. "One mustn't make an idol of a child" was often said to a mother who showed unnecessary affection for her little one. To do so was inviting disaster. Children were treated impartially, and if they reached their teens and chances for their survival looked promising, the parents could begin to plan for their future.

another at Hopbottom, Pennsylvania.[14] He had been given the land in payment for acting as agent for a large tract in that district. Putnam's mother had died, and his father, Eli Catlin, had come from Litchfield to make his home with his son.

It was probably here in Hopbottom that Polly Catlin became a Methodist. She was born a Quaker, but like so many other Americans in the post-Revolutionary years, she was profoundly influenced by the excitement of the Great Revival and the preaching of John Wesley.[15]

The names of two more children were now added to the big family Bible, John (1812) and Francis (1815). Charles, the oldest of this enormous brood, was twenty-five when the fourteenth child was born. He was practicing law in Wilkes-Barre, and courting a young school teacher, Amanda Burr, whom he married the following year. George, still in his teens, taught in a little one-room schoolhouse one winter, where the teacher was hired for three months at the fine salary of eight dollars a month.

In 1811 the county of Luzerne was divided, and Susquehanna County was established with Montrose its county seat. In 1813 Putnam was admitted to the bar in Susquehanna County, and the following year was elected a representative in the legislature of Pennsylvania.[16]

---

[14] Hopbottom, named for the hops that once grew so profusely in that area, was first called Tioga, then Waterford, later changed to Hopbottom, and still later, in 1825, to Brooklyn. This last name stuck.

[15] An amusing bit of gossip tells that in 1804 Hopbottom was visited by a couple of itinerant Methodist preachers. As a result, there was quite a religious revival that lasted nearly a year, and "Hoppingbottom" was the name given the place by outsiders, because of the leaping and shouting by which the converted exhibited their spiritual joy. The houses gave so little privacy that people were accustomed to retire into the woods to pray. One hunter said there were so many people praying that they frightened the deer away. (Emily C. Blackman, *History of Susquehanna County, Pennsylvania* [Philadelphia: Claxton, Remsen and Haffelfinger, 1873], pp. 137–138.)

[16] The announcement to Putnam of his election was as follows: "We the subscribers return Judges for the Counties of Luzerne, Susquehanna and

Montrose and the liquor problem

THE CATLIN FAMILY moved again in 1817; this time to Montrose, just a short distance from Hopbottom. Montrose was a pretty little village in one of the most fertile sections of Susquehanna County, surrounded by deep woods and numerous small lakes. Not many years earlier the only roads leading to the place were Indian trails. Its population in 1817 was about two hundred.

Here the Catlin family made their home until 1831.[17] Putnam was elected Judge of Common Pleas, was cashier of the Silver Lake Bank when it was first organized, and treasurer of the Milford and Owego Turnpike for seven or eight years. When the Susquehanna Academy was established at Montrose, Putnam was appointed one of its trustees.

It was said of him, "Though he had an aristocratic bearing, he was yet truly affable, and easily approached. He would say, 'I shall always have enough.' The poor were never turned away from his door, and would take the clothing which Mrs. Catlin thought still serviceable, and give it to the children of others more needy. He encouraged young men to clear land for him; and though it was then the custom to give cattle or 'truck' as payment for work, he would pay to each from two to three dollars in cash, that they might be able to

---

Bradford, after casting up the votes of said Counties at the house of Cyrus Avery on the 18th day of October, 1814, do certify that you are elected a member of Assembly for said Counties. Witness our hands and seals the day & year above mentioned.

George Miller [seal]
James Frim [seal]
Jonathan Gerny [seal]

[17] Biographers of George Catlin have said that Putnam moved from Montrose to Great Bend in 1821. Putnam's letter to George, dated January 21, 1831, mentioned that he had just moved to Great Bend. Previous letters from Putnam (from 1817 through 1831) were written from Montrose.

expend some on holidays. Even as late as 1825, for a whole summer's work, a farm hand received but $10, in cash, the rest in produce." [18]

Putnam was a close friend of Dr. Robert Rose, perhaps the leading benefactor in the early development of Susquehanna County. It was largely due to his energy and enthusiasm that the first agricultural society in the county was organized in 1820, with Putnam Catlin vice president.[19] This was a very important activity, giving much prestige to its members. One object of the society was to encourage the people to raise more stock, and produce less wheat for whiskey. Transportation of wheat itself was difficult, but the shipment of whiskey barrels was comparatively easy, besides being far more remunerative.

The leading men of the county were alarmed, however, over the growing intemperance among the population. They were particularly aroused over conditions in Montrose, the county seat, although this problem was not just local. Drinking intoxicants was universal in that day; a total abstainer was rare indeed. It is said that nearly as much whiskey was consumed for drinking purposes as water. The early settlers needed it. They were poor, most of them, and often lonely with no near neighbors. The bottle on the kitchen shelf was a necessity second only to shelter and food for the family. Times grew better, worries grew less, but the bottle remained. Laborers wouldn't take a job if a jug was not placed within reach. The genteel little lady in the big house wouldn't think of being without it if she had guests. However, the first temperance society in the United States had been formed in Putnam's home town, Litchfield, Connecticut, in 1789, when several hundred farmers pledged not to give any strong liquors to workmen on their lands.

In Montrose, there was too much whiskey being made and sold, too many distilleries running full tilt, too many unlicensed taverns, inns, and tippling houses, and deacons ran the distilleries. Several ministers were merchants and saw nothing wrong in selling Bibles or liquor. When approached on the subject the good men indignantly

---

[18] Blackman, *History of Susquehanna County*, p. 130.
[19] *Ibid.*, p. 504.

replied that they had families to support, and if some of the people in Montrose drank too much it certainly was not their fault. There was nothing backstage about the business; it was all carried on open and aboveboard, a custom and condition of the time.[20]

In 1828 a number of men from all parts of the county met in Montrose to form a temperance society. During court that year the Grand Jury resolved to abolish their usual custom of drinking liquor while in session. Laborers accustomed to their handy jug were given cider instead. They kicked up a row but it did them no good.[21]

Letters to George at law school

REARING AND EDUCATING nine sons was not an easy task, particularly when times were hard and money scarce. Farm life was beneficial to Putnam's health, but not to his pocketbook. His income had to be stretched to the limit to cover the needs of his family. However, it was still possible to "live off the land," so the Catlins were fairly comfortable.

Education in backwoods villages began in a one-room schoolhouse —and often ended there. Well-to-do parents sent their sons to local academies for further study, and possibly to college. Loyd Haberly says that George attended the academy at Wilkes-Barre.[22] If so, it is likely that his older brother, Charles, went there also.

Whatever education the nine Catlin boys received was supplemented by their father's wide range of knowledge. He was an avid student of philosophy, history and biography, and often recited long

---

[20] From later letters by Putnam it can be assumed that two of his sons were not able to overcome their love for the bottle.

[21] Blackman, *History of Susquehanna County*, pp. 557–570.

[22] Loyd Haberly, *Pursuit of the Horizon: A Life of George Catlin, Painter & Recorder of the American Indian* (New York: The Macmillan Company, 1948), p. 15.

passages from the classics. Proud of his heritage and the name he bore, Putnam dreamed of each son in an honored profession. A legal career held the greatest prestige in Putnam's estimation, possibly because he had been a respected member of the bar himself for so many years.

Charles, the eldest son, passed the bar examinations at Wilkes-Barre in 1814. Henry, the next, showed no particular aptitude for anything. A good-natured fellow, he seemed perfectly willing to take life as it came, and hope for the best.

The third son, George, was Putnam's concern. He was a handsome young man, with personality and intelligence. Putnam, perhaps, had seen in him a future statesman, and started early to direct the lad's education for such a career.

George's delay in entering law school (he was past twenty) can be ascribed to either Putnam's lean purse or George's apathy toward a legal career. The latter seems more credible. George had already shown a definite talent in portraiture; he had done some beautiful miniatures on ivory. The fact that he took time out from his law studies to paint an oil portrait of Judge Tapping Reeves showed his attraction to a paintbrush. Certainly Putnam must have been aware of his son's ability along that line, but he did not see painting as a career for a man with George's background and intelligence. Putnam was a very persuasive orator, and evidently he convinced his son that father knew best.

Charles had received his law education at Wilkes-Barre, but nothing was too good for George. Regardless of the expense, he entered the famous Litchfield Law School in July, 1817, at the age of twenty-one.

While in Litchfield, George received the following letters from his father and brother Charles:

Wilkes Barre July 12th 1817

Dear Brother—
Your letter of the 5th never came to my hand until this

moment, and already Mr. Overton is preparing a letter for you to Gould.

We have no news here—Amanda is well and doing well—her sister Mrs. Marsh from York State is here—& Marilla. Edw'd Overton is reading with us again—Bridge here going on well. I will write you soon again—and more fully—Will you be a man—a Lawyer—or a poor lazy devil like me?

I shall now read hard to be as good a lawyer when you return as yourself—

Your affectionate Brother
Charles Catlin

Montrose, 4 Aug't, 1817

My dear Son,

Your letter of 20th July informing me of your arrival at L and the arrangements made for your improvement was very gratifying to me particularly as I learn you are in health and well pleased with the prospects afforded you. You are now placed more favorably for study & the improvement of your mind than you could be at any other place in the United States. And the encouragement given me in your letter that you are resolved to profit what you can by it, is very pleasing to me. The gratitude you express and the tenderness you reciprocate, evinces the continuation of that filial regard and reverence that I have always seen in you.

I call on you now, while so far removed from me and the family you love, to recollect the advice I have so often and so pressingly given you, as to moral conduct & principles, which I need not repeat, for, while you remember me, you must remember my instructions. Let no temptations whatever allow you to stray from the path of virtue, and strict propriety of conduct. When allurements to vice assault you, instantly think of me, think of home, think of your sisters, your brothers—think of yourself, and you will escape every snare.

Preserve your health as your first care, dont neglect this at any time, prescribe rules for the government of your time, make study as agreeable as you can and make all the proficiency in your power, at the same time make yourself as composed and happy as you can, in the anticipation of the honors and the profits awaiting the industrious and successful candidates for the profession. You would desire to gratify me—then let me hear a good account of you—your situation is truly responsible, there are many anxious wishes for you wafted in every western breeze. You will find many friends & I have no doubt that you will be very well contented in Litchfield. I have not time to write what I could wish. I will write you often. But I would have you frequently sit down and imagine that I am present lecturing and admonishing you, and let it be a substitute for a long letter, such as I should write.

Henry has not yet arrived, and I know not but he is yet waiting in Balto for his money. I am very anxious for his return. James and part of the family are obliged to wait his return and still remain at the Bend.

My new business [Montrose bank] keeps me constantly employed here, and will be fatiguing and full of care. The family are all well at this time, I had a letter from Charles this day. John Seelye is in his grave, Mrs. Morgan also, the latter much lamented. I am in usual health but I am apprehensive that such close confinement will not agree well with my health. Thomas Welles is now with us in the absence of James, I want James every day. I will now inclose you 40 dollars and wait an opportunity of sending you more.

It is not particularly necessary now that I write you an introductory letter, since Mess'rs Mallery & Overton have written. You will have received one letter from me.

Make my respects to enquiring friends. Tell major Seymour his negroes in Lawsville will all starve, and what is more they'l cultivate nothing on his land but briers. Negroes and Indians were never intended for farmers; it will be best that Sharp be coaxed to give up his contract, and let some good man take the land on lease or purchase.

Your sister Eliza will go down next week to stay a few weeks with Amanda while Charles goes the circuit, afterwards she thinks of visiting Danbury.

Yours affectionately
Putnam Catlin

Charles, six years older and a married man with an established law practice, felt it his duty also to advise the young student:

Wilkes Barre Nov. 27th 1817

Dear Brother—

Your letters of enquiries came duly to hand and would have received an answer immediately but for the hurry of a two weeks court. I have (it is too true) been unpardonably neglectful in omitting to write you per promise, but I trust you know me too well to attribute it to any other than the common reason—"I will write tomorrow" which never comes.

I hope and trust, however that you have found an interest in your studies—which will occupy your attention to such a degree as to have little room for letter writing—Every days experience shows me the folly of having let slip too many hours which if again possessed would be devoted to severe study. The Literary world is becoming every day more creditable—and more difficult of entrance—and the mind of ardent youth must be deliberately directed—and uniformly bent on its subjects—or civick honours will but ridicule.

Horace advises to every ardent & lawful undertaking—that the principal step is the "Nunc tempus"—and who ever keeps the nunc tempus before him as his motto has done much toward accomplishing his object.

He also says—"dimidium facti qui cepit habet"—he has finished who has begun—This is very true in many things—and particularly in your pursuits. When you have laid aside all pretentions to importance which is natural to youth—and no more see a handsome leg—a genteel carriage or fellow—when you have abandoned girls & wine—and when your mind has taken "french leave" as it should of every thing but your subjects of law—why then you "have begun"—and then you have the "dimidium facti." Never forget this, for a few years will attest its truth.

Department of news—

Well uncle George—we have a fine boy—whose name is Theodore—three days old. P. Catlin is "Grandady!" Amanda is doing very well. . . .

We have no quail here I believe this fall—at least I have seen none. I have been out but one day hunting, and then killed 12 pheasants & black squirrels, 2 plover and a wild turkey.

Edward Overton is at home again hunting &c. I have moved office into my front room where I live—more convenient in cold weather—I shall start for Susque'a County tomorrow—and when there, shall conclude whether I move there or not—probably I may. . . .

In haste your
affectionate Brother
Charles Catlin

Charles again wrote George the following January third, saying: "I have the promise of a few minutes only to write you—and improve it in wishing you a 'happy new year' and a profitable one. We are all well here—and jogging along in the old form—and raving at the 'hard times'—and the last war which produced them—'We must have Canada' and 'protect seamans rights'—we lost the one and abandoned the other—and our country rues—and will rue it." Charles moved his little family to Montrose that fall, writing "Wilkes-Barre is stupid, and can never rise while the inhabitants are poor and bankrupt. Montrose is growing very fast and everything about it is cheering." But these were the years following the War of 1812—money was hard to come by, and employment difficult to obtain.

Putnam wrote to George again on January 21, 1818. George was doing well; keeping pace with his classmates, most of them students from colleges in the east and the south. Putnam wrote:

My dear George,

I am momently expecting Charles, according to appointment. He was to bring Amanda & son, but there has been no snow near Wilkesbarre this winter. Henry & his wife were to meet them here; Charles will have to come alone.

It affords me great satisfaction to hear that you are well, and regularly pursuing your studies; but I am very desirous of seeing you & cannot feel fully reconciled to such long absence; there are many things I wish to impress on your mind, which I cannot well express in a letter. I ought, however, to be content if you are well and happy, although I am deprived of your society, provided I may be assured you are doing well; that is, cheerful, contented, studious, and above all of good moral character, & gaining fast a reputation, which will not only insure you success in your course, but will afford your friends and relatives that high satisfaction which their partiality for you deserves.

To become a Lawyer you must study closely a number of years to come; and to make a tollerably decent essay in the outset so as not to despair of yourself, you will have to be assiduous for the whole time that can be allowed you; a little time mispent now will defeat the whole plan.

I fear you have too much writing to perform it will encroach on your hours for reading and reflection, and what is still worse, if you are in the habit of writing in an ill posture, it will injure your side or breast so that you will never recover of it; by all means take care of that—never lean against the table.

You must accustom yourself to public speaking and study that kind of oratory and logic which is suited to the Bar, you will have excellent examples before you, & will I hope deserve and experience the aid of gentlemen near you who will kindly afford you a helping hand. It is an arduous struggle you have to encounter, but the prize before you is of immense value. I hope, my dear George you are thoughtful and industrious & will make the best efforts to succeed handsomely.

If you have not already learnt to apportion your time to good advantage, & to have a perfect command of yourself so as to give up all trifles, and every purpose except that of improving your mind, it will have been to little purpose that you have placed yourself at school.

I often regret that you had not began earlier, & I sometimes fear, that placed as you now are in the midst of finished scholars who have enriched their minds with all the sciences, you will feel below the point of emulation; but that must not be; let emulation be excited, & let your ambition and your genius bear you forward determined not to to bother hindmost, remembering always, you have but a short time left to prepare for the stage of action.

I wish I could promise you a second year in Litchfield; it will not be well in my power; you must therefore get as much legal science as possible while there, and attend to other studies on your return.

Your year will soon be rounded, and you will return to the family circle where all will be overjoyed to meet you. In the meantime our ardent prayers are offered to Heaven for your health and happiness.

I remain my dear Son
most tenderly yours
Putnam Catlin

Charles has just arrived and goes to Wayne Court, & will return to attend Susq Court next week, all well at Wilkesbarre. . . . P. S. I shall send you some money by private opportunity which offers this week. there is some risque by mail.

On August 10, 1818, Charles wrote George from Wilkes-Barre:

I am here attending Court—and have just received a line

from Father requiring me in obedience to your letter to forward you a certificate of your clerkship in my office. This you know will be done immediately and with much pleasure. I hope and believe you are well qualified to undergo the strictures of a Committee.

I expected your return in August inst., and intended to have had you admitted at our Court at Montrose holden or to be holden on Monday the 31st. But if you can be admitted in Connecticut in Sept, perhaps it will be well—We are all very anxious to see you—and promise ourselves much pleasure in a chit-chat with G. Catlin, Esq! . . .[23]

Putnam chooses a career for Julius

WITH GEORGE launched in the legal profession, Putnam turned his attention to the next two sons. He had no money for further education. James was a very likable fellow, a "go-getter" who would try his hand at many different vocations before he settled down, but his father knew he would eventually find his place in the business world.

Julius, however, only fifteen years old in 1819, posed a problem. Like George, he was charming, intelligent, and talented in the arts.

---

[23] There is some confusion regarding when and where George was admitted to the bar. Donaldson (*The George Catlin Indian Gallery*, p. 706) says that George returned to Pennsylvania in 1819, "where he entered upon the study and then the practice of law in the courts of Luzerne and adjoining counties." Blackman (*History of Susquehanna County*, p. 47) gives a list of lawyers in Susquehanna County, with George Catlin mentioned as having passed the bar at "Wilkesbarre (?)" in December, 1818. Charles' letter indicates George was admitted to the bar in Connecticut in September, 1818. He could have been accepted later at Wilkes-Barre.

George, no doubt, had helped him with his painting, and Julius idolized his elder brother.

Because we have later facts to draw from, it can be inferred, with little stretching of the imagination, that Putnam decided that his young son must be sent away to school before George influenced the boy regarding the future. Putnam wanted Julius to study for a professional career, but an empty purse was the drawback. His agile brain finally found an answer: West Point. It wasn't difficult to stir excitement in a youthful mind with glowing pictures of military life, and the glory and honor which naturally would follow. In writing a business letter to his good friend, Colonel Timothy Pickering, Putnam added a request that the colonel intercede for him in obtaining an appointment to the Military Academy for his son Julius. The colonel was very glad to oblige him.[24]

Julius Catlin was admitted to West Point in 1820. He graduated as a cadet from Pennsylvania in 1824, was appointed lieutenant in the first U. S. Infantry, and was sent to serve on the rugged western frontier.

Law versus the paint brush

FOR A FEW YEARS George dutifully practiced law, but in a most desultory fashion. No doubt his desire to please his father outweighed (for a time), the fact that he was completely uninterested in his work.

Many years later he wrote: "During this time (while practicing law from 1820 to 1823) another and stronger passion was getting the advantage of me, that for painting, to which all of my love of pleading soon gave way; and after having covered nearly every inch

[24] See Appendix II.

of the lawyer's table (and even encroached upon the judge's bench) with penknife, pen and ink, and pencil sketches of judges, jurors, and culprits, I very deliberately resolved to convert my law library into paint pots and brushes, and to pursue painting as my future, and apparently more agreeable profession." [25]

Philadelphia was then the most successful commercial city in the new nation. Before the railroads joined the North and South together, it was the meeting ground for the two sections of the country. It was also a cultural center, and its academy of art, founded by Charles Willson Peale in 1805, attracted the country's leading artists.

With the daguerreotype and camera still in the future, portraiture was enjoying its heyday—as essential as the furniture in public buildings, and a mark of distinction in private homes. When George Catlin arrived in Philadelphia in 1823, Thomas Sully, John Nagle, Rembrandt Peale, and others were there. It did not take long for the lawyer-turned-painter to be accepted as a worthy associate. The miniatures he had brought with him showed his ability. He soon received commissions for portraits. In February, 1824, he was made a member of the Academy of Fine Arts: the honor bestowed because of his exquisite watercolor miniatures on ivory. This distinction naturally led to more and better commissions, and the name of George Catlin became very well known.

Undoubtedly Putnam regretted his son's decision to give up the law, but the latter's rapid success in Philadelphia could not help but make him realize that George had chosen the right path. His later letters showed his undisguised pride in this son and the honor he was bringing to the Catlin name.

---

[25] Donaldson, *The George Catlin Indian Gallery*, p. 706.

I N 1 8 2 0 , Putnam Catlin, then fifty-six, and needing to augment his slim income, sought an appointment to one of the county offices as Register or Chief Clerk. Several of his influential friends wrote glowing letters in his behalf to Joseph Heister, Governor of Pennsylvania. Nothing came of it. Putnam tried once more, in 1827, to obtain a political appointment; this time in the New York Custom House. Most of his children were now located in the state of New York, and he and Polly wished to be nearer to them. Once again good friends wrote strong recommendations for him, speaking of his great capacity for business, and his unquestioned character, integrity and honor. Putnam, himself, wrote to his friend, Abra Bradley, Assistant Postmaster General. The following letter was Putnam's retained copy of his plea to Mr. Bradley, which explains several careless omissions.

Montrose Pa May 11 1827

Dear Sir,

In January last, I made application for an appointment in the Custom house department in New York, to Jonathan Thompson the Collector of that Port. I presented to Mr. Thompson at that time recommendatory letters from L. Catlin [Lynde Catlin, uncle of Putnam] & George Griffen Esquires copies of which I here inclose. I had a short conversation with the Collector, and learnt that the Secy Mr. Rush, left the appointments generally to him the collector, and that there were on the roll of applicants about 400 names, that he was usually governed by the date of application, unless particularly advised from the head of the department at Washington. At that time, I took the liberty of addressing a letter to my friend Mr. Miner of Congress, who with another member from this district, made a letter to the Secy in my favour inclosing copies of the letters of Mr. L. Catlin

& Geo Griffen. Mr. Miner has since written to me advising that I persevere in my application but did not mention having asked the aid of your influence, I therefore venture to tax your friendship probably for the last time. You know well my history, even from our earliest school days, & ever since—that for the last forty years I have resided in the interior of Penna without patrimony patronage or pension; you have counted my fourteen children, and you know that I supported my revolutionary father in my family for more than thirty years after he had grown old and poor in the service of his country. You will now learn, that my family is now scattered, and I would leave this rough country and follow part of my children to the city, provided I could find suitable employment there, for the short remnant of active life my pretensions to office I admit are humble, and I therefore waited till my superiors have all, as I think been provided for in some way, my age is now 62 years, that of the officers and soldiers generally, not less than 70, for I was not 19 at the close of the war, and though one of the youngest of the survivors, I may expect but a very few years more of active life. It must be now well understood and admitted by all, that the revolutionary soldiers who served to the close of the war, have some equitable claim on their country for the last four years service although the Congress in their deliberations on the subject for the last two years have unfortunately, not been able exactly to adjust.

I inclose also, a copy of my discharge from the army signed by General washington which I have preserved and which I shall value highly while I live.

You see, my friend, that I am not ashamed at this time to show that I carried my pack and acted an humble part in that revolution (considering my youth, and that my father was a commissioned officer in the same war) for, "Honor & shame from no condition rise" &c.

I will not intrude further on your time, than to observe, I am aware how difficult it is at this time to obtain an appointment, &

that I may not succeed without the interposition of your friendship and kind office in speaking of me to the Secy of the Treasury or perhaps to the President as the political father of our country, if I may be permited to think of such patronage. I certainly could not expect it, only, as being one of the last of that army, that ever will apply for an active office under the Government. Mr. Thompson the Collector at New York is well acquainted with the gentlemen who have given me letters to him, and you know their respectibility too well to believe them capable of recommending any person to an office for which they might think him unfit.

I must beg your pardon for giving you this trouble, and do cheerfully submit the whole to your friendship and better judgment. And am very truly dear Sir your obedient and humble servant

Putnam Catlin

Abra Bradley Esquire.

This was, indeed, a most humble plea to a life-long friend, but it was not granted. Regardless of the letters from prominent men extolling his virtues, Putnam could not land even a small county appointment. Something beside his age must have held him back. It may have been that his touch of arrogance—a "holier than thou" attitude—outweighed his capabilities. A more obvious reason is that Putnam Catlin was first a Federalist, later a Whig. From the time of Jefferson's administration the public offices were controlled by the National Republicans, afterward called the Democratic Party. Putnam later wrote George: "My application for the Prothy's office has failed as perhaps might have been expected, & for the reasons you mentioned, or perhaps I was suspected of Anti-masonry. It matters not which—I am not sorry I made the application, for I have learnt how these matters are conducted at Harrisburg." George's reasons were not given. There was no further comment on the subject.

The death of Lynde

PUTNAM CATLIN was sixty years old in 1824, and Polly was fifty-four. Eleven of their fourteen children were living. Henry had married Mary Grubb; James wed Abigail Sayre. Mary had been courted and won by Asa Hartshorn, a local watchmaker and lay minister; while Eliza had set up housekeeping with Anson Dart, a Montrose druggist.

Dart was a personable young man with a quick mind, although his letters show a lack of schooling. Born in Vermont, he had come to Montrose about 1816 to try his luck. He and Eliza soon moved to New York City, where according to his son Richard, he became a druggist, and imported from France the first ounce of quinine brought to America.[26]

The older children were now leaving home, but so far they had settled near enough to enable Putnam to advise and "hold council" with them when he deemed it necessary. Still living at home were the four young sons, Lynde, Richard, John, and Francis. In 1824 Lynde, just eighteen, died. Putnam's letter to George telling of the boy's death was one of intense anguish.

Sunday morn July 25 1824

My dear Son

This letter brings you the afflictive and heart rending intelligence of the death of your brother Lynde he breathed his last about one o'clock P.M. on Saturday the 24, the tenth day after he received the hurt. We thought his case dangerous, but did not think his exit would be so sudden. If you had come in the Saturday stage you could only have mingled your tears with

---

[26] *Settlement of Green Lake County*, Wisconsin State Historical Society Proceedings, 1909. (Madison, Wis.: published by the Society, 1910), p. 259, fn. 12.

ours at the funeral—the corpse is to be interred at five o'clock this afternoon.

He had during his sickness a great deal of pain which he bore with great fortitude & had every possible attention paid to him. We are deeply afflicted in this loss, we knew his integrity and guileless disposition and we loved him most tenderly—but his suffering is at an end and we must be submissive. we must now look to the living—every loss of this kind should tend to make us love each other better.

Do not my dear son, in any degree, reproach your self for not coming on Saturday, we all think you did right under the circumstances. nor do I think you should put your self to inconvenience to come over on Tuesday next, though we should be happy to see you when you can best come, though it must be before you return to the city—you will have no need of going to Saratoga or the Falls I must expect you to return this way.

My own health is not very good & dont know if I shall be able to accompany miss Cook as far as Owego. She will now be very anxious to return to her mother, & if you should not be able to come home in the tuesday stage, she will probably take the friday stage & some of us will accompany her. We think you will hardly leave Owego till the last of the week; but you will write by return mail and let us know.

we did not write you how dangerous your brother was, or perhaps you would have come at all hazards on Saturday—but it would have been unavailable—as you could only have seen his corpse, therefore I repeat it you should give yourself no uneasiness on account of not coming. Neither should you or I indulge immoderate grief—Let us cherish a sweet remembrance of his virtues and be silent.

While I have been writing an examination has been made by the Surgeon to find the cause of his complaint—who reports there was no stone or calcula in the bladder, the bladder was in a state of inflamation, adhered to the pelvis in the lower part, and very much contracted, the inner coat almost entirely destroyed, and left in a raw state. no urine in the bladder of consequence, nor could it contain more than a gill. No remedy could ever be applied to recover the bladder, the patient might have lived for years (without the accident) but must always have been miserable, and for years past he must have felt pain on every motion, to which habit must have reconciled him. The accident was the immediate cause of his death—by producing inflamation & fever. The Surgeon says his friends should not wish him back to drag out a miserable existence with the incurable complaint—hence the [illegible] overcast his mind and countenance, which [illegible] in vain tried to dissipate.

I think my dear George you should not come home [torn] but write me, and let Nancy come over on [torn] or Friday. I have written you see in great haste because I am much agited.

I am more than ever your affectionate [torn]

Putnam [torn]

The weaving of a dream

GEORGE CATLIN'S popularity and orders for portraits had grown rapidly. He was at his best with watercolor miniatures, but also was developing his own technique in oils. His reputation had spread to Boston, New York and Baltimore. By 1826 he was well established in his career, and although he was happy whenever he held a paint-brush in his hand, he had the feeling that he was once again on a well-trod road with nothing new or exciting around the corner.

George was not a sit-downer—he was always aquiver with energy. This feeling of unrest was given no sedative by the era in which he was living. The papers were filled daily with accomplishments that only yesterday had been a dream. Optimism and a glorious spirit of adventure prevailed during the opening of the unknown West.

George, without a doubt, felt this push. Perhaps it made him realize that he would never make a "big noise" as a mere portrait painter; he had too much competition. He could not abandon his paintbrush, but there must be *something* in the wide field of art that would make him pick up that tool with never-ending delight and excitement—and also bring recognition to the name of George Catlin.

Many years later he wrote of this period of frustration: "my mind was continually reaching for some branch or enterprise of the arts, on which to devote a whole life-time of enthusiasm; when a delegation of some ten or fifteen noble and dignified-looking Indians, from the wilds of the 'Far West,' suddenly arrived in the city, arrayed in all of their classic beauty—with shield and helmet—with tunic and manteau —tinted and tasseled off, exactly for the painter's palette!" These Indians were on their way to Washington on treaty business. They were not like those seen along the eastern shores, dirty and ignorant, corrupted by civilization. These were proud, clear-eyed men who roamed the plains far from the white man's influence, and who truly represented the first inhabitants of this country. They walked slowly, with the poise of royalty, and as they passed the artist in their gorgeous tribal robes, George had his inspiration—The American Indian. . . . "And the history and customs of such a people, preserved by pictorial illustrations, are themes worthy the lifetime of one man, and nothing short of the loss of my life shall prevent me from visiting their country, and of becoming their historian." [27]

Very little was known about these first Americans, so rapidly being shoved into oblivion by the greed of the white men for their lands and furs. The Indians who lived even on the fringe of civilization were tainted—they had forgotten the laws of their tribes and tried to emulate the white people to whom they had at first looked up. They were drunken and dirty, they stole and plundered. These were the

---

[27] George Catlin, *Letters and Notes on the Manners, Customs, and Conditions of the North American Indians* . . . (2 vols.; London: published by the author, 1841), I, 2.

Indians most whites knew. They were completely ignorant of the true red man. George's mission in life would be to enlighten them. By traveling into Indian country, visiting many tribes, he would live with them and get to know them. He would paint them and their villages, and write about their customs and beliefs. With pen and paintbrush he would leave for future generations a true history of the first Americans. As Thomas Donaldson says: "It was a high and noble ambition, worthily conceived and most faithfully executed." [28]

It is surprising that this impetuous fellow did not pack up his paints and leave immediately on his quest. Fortunately, he had sense enough to realize that it would take money to make these expeditions, and that he would have to stick to portrait painting for a while. He had plenty of orders to fill, but he left the painting of fat jowled men or simpering females if any western Indians appeared. In Buffalo, in 1826, he painted an exceptionally fine portrait of Red Jacket, the old Seneca warrior. Colonel William Stone, editor of the *New York Commercial Advertiser*, and a great friend and admirer of the artist, wrote a very complimentary article about this portrait.

In the meantime, George's favorite brother, Julius, had graduated from West Point, and was now stationed at Cantonment Gibson in Arkansas. The two had kept in close touch. No doubt George wrote Julius of his plans for the future, suggesting that his younger brother join him and collect natural history specimens to accompany his Indian collection. The artist may have known of his brother's unhappiness in the role of soldier—when Julius resigned his commission in September, 1826, he joined George in New York.

Among the old letters are five notes from Julius to George, written in the summer of 1828 (see pp. 35–36). Julius was then twenty-four, with four years of military training and two years of hard frontier service behind him. In reading these letters, written in delicate, spidery script, and with a most whimsical manner of expression, one wonders why his father chose the military road for him to follow, for

---

[28] Donaldson, *The George Catlin Indian Gallery*, p. 710.

there could have been no potential soldier in Julius' make-up. If the stubborn Puritan had dreams of a general in the family, he was to be disappointed. Judging from these few notes to George, army life had not made a scratch on the surface of the young man's personality—Julius was born a dreamer, an artist, and a poet.

Putnam's reaction to Julius' severance from the army is not on record. He may have blamed George; but, on the other hand, George was doing well and he was proud of him. Putnam's father, Eli, had died in 1820, at the age of eighty-seven. This narrow-minded Puritan, who believed in a son's complete subjection to his father's will, had no doubt greatly influenced Putnam in the rearing of his children. With Eli gone, Putnam still continued to "advise and counsel," but his letters show respect for each son's opinions.

The artist takes a wife

GEORGE CATLIN continued painting portraits, and saved his money. He was thirty-two in 1828, and so far had paid little attention to women, but now he fell in love. Clara Gregory was just twenty, beautiful, and from a well-to-do family of Albany, New York. Her brother was Dudley Gregory of New Jersey, later mayor of Jersey City. The couple were married in Albany on May 10, 1828. Putnam must have been overjoyed; now certainly there should be no hunting out of wild Indians in George's future. On May 30 he wrote the happy pair from Montrose, addressing the letter to George Catlin, Artist, Courtlandt St. N. York:

> My dear George and my dear Clara,
>   Most sincerely do I *wish you much joy*. And all of our family here join me heartily on this occasion of sending to both of you, our kindred and most affectionate salutations.

A letter from Mr. Dart as well as the papers, announced your marriage, and I hasten to address you with my approbation.

We returned from our journey last evening; it was extended to the falls by the way of Lewistown Queenston, &c. You will be disappointed as well as Eliza in not having at this time a visit from your mother. She could not summon courage enough to go round by Albany & New York, particularly as Miss Cook could not make it convenient to accompany her. Such is unfortunately the state of her nerves, that on a journey, through fear of casualties, she suffers almost continually having an unavoidable dread of steamboats. To confirm her fears, there was some confusion on the Cayuga new boat on our passage home, by reason of a breach of one of the conductors of steam, so that the ladies were driven out of the cabin by the entrance of hot water. Nobody was hurt, neither was there any danger in fact, the machine was repaired in about two hours, and took us very safely to Ithaca. I was very sorry that the accident happened while she was on board, for I had taken such pains to persuade her that she would be as safe as in a church. I took Francis with us, and we had nothing to do but wait on your mother and make the journey comfortable and pleasant for her.

Burr [Charles' son] and Nancy returned with us, so that we have now something of a family. But your mother agrees to come down in the stage by and by, provided you cannot make it convenient to come up with your Lady and visit us.

Charles, on notice, came down and met us at Lockport. We found Henry and his family very well. We found them industrious, cheerful and happy. On our return we met James and his little family at Grant's, on his way to Lockport, but we had only time to shake their hands and bless them.

My own health is as good as usual, which I must now try to preserve, on account of the pension late granted by my country for youthful service, more especially, that I may visit my children now and then, which is now the only earthly pleasure I may promise myself.

33

I will anticipate seeing you very happy as a husband, with a wife looking over your shoulder, encouraging and admiring the arts, rather than leading you by the heart-strings into the fashionable mazes of luxury and dissipation. You will now be more happy and composed, what is the world now to you? In your room, and in your little parlour by your own fireside you will find contentment and solace, no where else. I cannot express the desire I now have to see you, and that we all have.

In regard to our journey, I was much pleased with the route, and we made it very comfortable. We ascended Queenston Heights, and the monument, from the top of which Frank [Francis] and I viewed a part of Lake Ontario and the fine extensive country on every side, took lodgings at Brown's in preference to Forsythe's, viewed the Falls from table rock, went down the steps, passed under the rock to the sheet of water, contented to stop there. We could not cross the ferry to the American side, because old Charon, in making a new road to his ferry, had blown the rocks & piled them, so that at that time there was no passing with comfort. I intended seeing the other side, and crossing the Island Bridge.

Take good care of Clara and love her as much as you please. It is written "Thou shalt not worship any graven image," but it is nowhere written thou shalt not idolize your wife. Your sister Mary almost envies Eliza the privilege she has of embracing Clara.

I suppose Julius is now at Easton, but will shortly be in the city and take his room. You must not be surprised if I should contrive some business that would bring me to the city in the course of a month or two.

Remember us to all our folks in the city.

Yours affectionately
P. Catlin

Julius—and tragedy

ENTHUSIASTIC over George's dream, Julius Catlin was planning to join him on his venture into the Indian country. George would paint Indians and he would gather specimens. Evidently he also had quite a talent for miniature painting, because he was able to employ himself in this profession while waiting for George to say, "Let's go!"

Julius wrote to George in New York, from Easton, Pennsylvania, on May 27, 1828:

Dear Brother,

I write to you again in consequence of my great anxiety to receive the cases for which I wrote in my last letter. I have painted a number of pictures, but the persons do not offer to pay me yet—I suppose they will not until I fix on a day to leave—there are three or four who will not at any rate pay me until I get the cases, that I may deliver the pictures, for which reason I did not enclose you the money, fearing that the *little* I have *not*, might be in requisition before I get more. I have no one sitting at present, am waiting only to get the cases for what I have done. I think, if you will give them in charge to the Steward of the Brunswick boat, he will take the trouble to leave them with suitable directions, at the Stage office, then, to be sent by a passenger.

Do you not think my memory is improving? When I left the city last, I left nothing, *with the exception of all my clothes!!*

Your affectionate brother Julius

Morristown—the day it was mal'd 1828
[on envelope: June 5]

Dear Geo.

I arrived at this place yesterday morning from Easton, and here will I be pen ink and paper at least for two weeks or three.

I have got a truly pleasant room, and have my meals with a gentleman and his wife, who is but little longer a husband than yourself; "snug as three in a bed," tho' in different rooms! He is a fine fellow, and lugs some twenty of a day into my room, and his loquacity has already prevailed over the indifference, or parsimony of some, who have promised to sit. Potter, miniature painter, a good one, now dead, painted at 21 at this place, and had so much to do, that he was under the awful necessity of augmenting his price to drive them off!! All tell me, I am safe for a month or two, and that the unusual proportion of pretty girls (sweet creatures) are more than ordinarily fond of miniatures (their own) and some have engaged to take the chair, and as the weather is anything but dry, (a murrain on it) the sign may not fail. If letters come for me please to direct them to Morristown. If you can send me a couple or three cases, of size I sent in my last but one letter, I wish you would, for I have engaged to send them immediately on to Easton. I am not yet paid for what I painted there, but in part, and a part of little or nothing, is not much.

Your affectionate brother
Julius Catlin

On the sixth of June Julius wrote George: "I am careless not to mention more wants in one letter. I write to you today for some ivory, which I want very much. I have hardly a piece left that will answer for anything else than a picture of a corncrib. I this morning received an invitation from a French gent & lady to accompany them to their seat, a few miles from town, spend a week, and paint four miniatures, to which I consent! and will leave in the morning in a carriage which they will send for me! They are vastly rich and accomplished, speak french exclusively, and can hardly be understood when they attempt to speak English, so you will know how I am for the week to come. . . ."

In the spring of 1828 George Catlin had painted a portrait of Governor De Witt Clinton. The Franklin Institute of Rochester,

New York, asked him to copy the portrait for them. George finished the painting in September, and asked Julius to deliver it to the Institute. The errand ended in tragedy—Julius was drowned.

According to his obituary, printed in the *Rochester Daily Advertiser* on September 22, 1828, Julius met his death while swimming in the Genesee River, or was first struck senseless by the fisherman who had seen his costly "watch establishment." [29]

Young Julius was buried in Rochester with no friend or relative present at his funeral. It would be many days before a letter could reach George, who would then have to write the terrible news to his parents. In an old notebook, Putnam copied his son's obituary, also a poem, "The Stranger's Burial," written by a young man in Rochester, which appeared in the *Rochester Republican* the day after the burial.

---

[29] See Appendix III.

PART TWO: INDIAN COUNTRY

1830–1836

1830–1832: The pulse of the nation; Putnam has his worries; St. Louis and the beginning of the Great Adventure; Letters from Great Bend; A problem is solved   1832: A trip on the *Yellowstone* to the Upper Missouri   1833: Putnam writes Francis on the correct use of capital letters; The story of John Catlin   1834: In the land of the Comanches   1835: Letters from the family; Up the Mississippi.

The pulse of the nation

PUTNAM CATLIN was sixty-six in the spring of 1830, and much had happened to him, and to his country, during the three decades since he had come to the Wyoming Valley with knee breeches, silver buckles, cocked hat, and a law degree.

New York had overtaken Philadelphia and Boston to become the first city with a population of 250,000. Business was booming, but transportation was the big stumbling block to further progress, despite the rapid development of turnpikes, canals and steamboats. It took twenty-five hours to make the 270 miles from Boston to New York; and one had to change stages five times. From Baltimore to Louisville was a journey of over six days by stage and steamboat.

Until the building of the railroads, commerce between the North and South was carried by the rivers. Before the steamboats made their welcome appearance, the dugout, keelboat, flatboat and pirogue carried their cargoes of furs, lumber, flour, pork, "hoop-poles and punkins" down the "Mississip" and the Missouri. When traders reached their destination, the boat would be sold or restocked for northern trade, and slowly, with much puffing and sweating, poled back up the river against the powerful current. It was hard going, and generally took eight or nine months to make the round trip.

The steam locomotive was the obvious answer to transportation problems, but a development of this kind required much financing, and it was hard to persuade men of wealth that a railroad would ever pay. The first American-built locomotive, the "Tom Thumb," made its maiden run on the New Baltimore & Ohio tracks in August, 1830. At times it reached the terrifying speed of eighteen miles an hour! Within the next ten years the "iron horse" passed the experimental stage, and the way was opened to tie the country together.

As the Western movement swept on, ships from Europe brought thousands of immigrants to our ports, looking for a life denied them in their own countries. New highways and canals carried them to the wilderness. The Great Lakes became a trading route. Between 1827 and 1837 more than 300,000 people crossed the Mississippi, and the sound of the axe and the smoke from brush fires declared the taming of the territories that would soon become Arkansas, Missouri, and Iowa.

During these thirty years Putnam had fathered fourteen children. Nine were still living, but only two were now at home—John and Francis, still in their teens. One by one his sons were breaking away. It must be remembered that the family had been raised under the strict discipline of both the father and grandfather. Eli had lived with them until the four elder sons were grown. It was natural for them to want to order their own lives, make their own decisions in a vastly changed world; a world far removed from the placid existence of their parents, watching the years go by.

Putnam has worries

MANY NEW ENGLANDERS, particularly those whose forebears had been of the landed gentry in Europe, did not have the "push" of the pioneers who had come to this country to better themselves. They wanted their share of the worldly goods, but did not extend themselves to get it. Putnam reflected this conservative element. He had had many opportunities in his earlier years to make money; other settlers around him, with far less education and intelligence, were now men of wealth and property. Putnam was seemingly content to be known just as a gentleman "with an aristocratic bearing," although he carried a comparatively empty purse all his life.

George Catlin inherited his father's unaggressive attitude toward money-making. Both James and Richard made wise investments in land during the 1830's, and the latter made land speculation more or less his career, becoming a very wealthy man. It is strange that

George, the most venturesome and optimistic of the sons, was not excited over the land-buying mania then sweeping the country.[1]

The year 1830 brought Putnam worry and heartbreak over two of his sons—George and Charles. Neither had accepted his advice. Charles' case was tragic.

Intemperate drinking in Montrose has already been discussed. In spite of (or in defiance of) Putnam's sermons on the evils of liquor, Charles' fondness for the bottle had finally ruined his business and family life. Other homes had been broken up for the same reason, but that made it no easier for the proud old gentleman who had always held his head high and expected his children to do the same. No doubt this was the main reason for Putnam's desire to leave Montrose (see p. 45); Charles' behavior and the disgrace of a divorce in the family had brought shame to a good name.

With George the situation was less acute, but worrying to his father. George had been very ill following the death of Julius, blaming himself for sending him on the errand that had ended so tragically. George was not a robust man: the Catlin family seemed to have a tendency toward lung trouble, often referred to in their letters. "The consumption," of course, was a common ailment in those days, the cause of many deaths. George did not have to stay north because of his work, so the winters of 1828 and 1829 he and Clara had gone south, and with health regained he continued painting, saving money, and planning for his big adventure.

George was well aware of the opposition to his plans, but it made

---

[1] Thomas Donaldson says that George Catlin knew nothing of the methods of acquiring money either by speculation or investment, so he was always poor. What money he had, he made by his art or his publications, which, judiciously handled, should have made him a competence. George was frequently in Chicago during the 1830's—at a time when the investment of a few hundred dollars in real estate would have made him a wealthy man, and when his brother-in-law, Dudley Gregory, would have gladly invested for him in Chicago had George suggested it. George, however, was interested in Indians, not land or wealth. See *The George Catlin Indian Gallery*, Annual Report of . . . the Smithsonian Institution, 1885 (Washington: The Institution, 1886), p. 711.

not a whit of difference to him. He was a stubborn man. He made friends easily and kept them; he had moral honesty and solid integrity, and his letters clearly show his deep affection for his parents and wife. However, he, George Catlin, came first in any consideration. His excessive egotism was perhaps his worst fault. He was also impetuous, deciding on a minute's notice to do something that called for serious contemplation. But he acted first, and reasoned later—often to his sorrow. Clara would have many trying days ahead of her, for George, in spite of his devotion, acted for his own interest, always.

Right then he was making his plans for his journeys into the Indian country. Years later he wrote: "I had fully resolved—I opened my views to my friends and relations, but got not one advocate or abettor. I tried fairly and faithfully, but it was in vain to reason with those whose anxieties were ready to fabricate every difficulty and danger that could be imagined, without being able to understand or appreciate the extent or importance of my designs, and I broke with them all,—from my wife and aged parents,—myself my only advisor and protector." [2]

If Putnam had any idea that George would be leaving for St. Louis in the spring of 1830, he made no mention of it when he wrote to his son on February 15. The letter sounds as if Putnam still had hopes that he could head him off:

Dear George,

It was with great pleasure I read last evening your letter of the 7 instant for I had for several weeks [been] desirous of and expecting to hear from—not knowing whether you had removed to Washington or remained at Richmond. I can well conceive that both you and Clara must in many respects have had a pleasant winter. I could wish it might also have been a profitable one, & I do hope it will prove so as you may dispose of your

---

[2] George Catlin, *Letters and Notes on the Manners, Customs, and Conditions of the North American Indians . . .* (2 vols.; London: published by the author, 1841), I, 3.

work. And I imagine it will be your policy to get it off your hands as early as practicable on some accounts, particularly that you may employ your time on new works. I had seen in Colo. Stone's paper the eulogium on Red Jacket & the compliments paid you. I hasten to say we are all at this time well. I had a very comfortable time in returning from Harrisburg after remain there a week. My application for the Prothy's office has failed as perhaps might have been expected, & for the reasons you mentioned, or perhaps I was suspected of Anti-masonry. It matters not which—I am not sorry I made the application, for I have learnt how these matters are conducted at Harrisburg.

Mr. Dart has purchased a property in Weston on the head waters of the Mohawk 5 miles above Rome to which he will remove in March or April, and is very solicitous that I should go into the neighborhood. Which I think might suit me if it should be possible to sell here. I can have little inducement to remain here or in Penna unless the projected National Railroad from N Y to the Mississippi Valley should be realized. I shall apprise you of any movement I shall fix on. I fear however I cannot effect a sale of any property here for half its value.

I wrote to Charles last week informing him that Amanda had obtained her decree of Divorcement at Harrisburg Common Pleas, which I think is well for both of them. I flatter myself it will have a favorable effect on his mind. I have reason to believe he has become temperate and in a better way of maintaining himself. His two little sons remain with us, Amanda and the daughter are at Oxford.

James is at Lockport near Henry with a drug & grocery shop, but he writes discouragingly of the place, as unfortunately, that town is divided by the Locks and the lower town (so called) have the location of the Bank and the Albany Land Co have thrown in so many goods as to destroy the trade on the rock, as they are selling below the N Y price—says although he has built a house, he shall remove in the spring. This is unfortunate indeed for poor James. . . .

I am sorry to hear there are so many Artists before you in Washington but I imagine you may have work in Richmond still. I am as anxious as ever to hear of your fame and success as an artist. On your own account, on Clara's, on mine, & your country's, continue to make every possible exertion—persevere and do not get discouraged. I have so much patriotism—enlarged patriotism, as to pray fervently that the Constitution formed may be adopted by Virginia.[3] Present me most affectionately to Clara, and all send love to her and to yourself. Clara must write to us. . . .

P. Catlin

St. Louis and the beginning of the Great Adventure

WHEN GEORGE jumped from the stage in St. Louis in the spring of 1830, he must have felt as if he were stepping into another world. This was the "Gateway to the West," a booming, noisy river town of nearly ten thousand souls of many nationalities. The street was full of people. Dignified men with well-trimmed whiskers and tall beaver hats rubbed elbows with trappers in dirty leather shirts and leggings. Soldiers walked briskly along the narrow cobbled street, and the drabness of the town was cut by the vivid colors of the Indian robes as the stately men of the plains and prairies strode silently past on their moccasined feet.

St. Louis was headquarters for the western armies as well as for fur companies, their trappers, and traders. General William Clark was Superintendent of Indian Affairs, and he alone held the key to the

---

[3] The Virginia Constitutional Convention of 1829–1830 was in session while George was in Richmond, and he was commissioned to paint a composite picture of this group of eminent men.

Indian country. No one could travel there without his permission. He was responsible for the whole western territory and its Indian population.

It was to Clark's headquarters that Catlin made his way. In Washington he had obtained the necessary letters of introduction to General Clark and the men in charge of the trading posts on the Missouri River. These military and trading posts at strategic points along the river afforded fair protection from the Indian. Western America was not a safe country for the tenderfoot.

Clark apparently was glad to meet the slightly built, eager-faced young man, laden with knapsack, bulging portfolio, and rolls of canvas. Catlin later wrote: "My works and my design have been warmly approved and applauded by this excellent patriarch of the Western world; and kindly recommended by him in such ways as have been of great service to me." [4]

In the summer of 1830 General Clark had to make a trip up the Mississippi to Fort Crawford, a military post at Prairie du Chien. There he was to attend councils with representatives of the Iowas, Missouris, Sauks, and Foxes. It was at one of these councils that the last-named tribe, represented by a Sauk chief, Kee-o-Kuk, sold their land in northern Illinois to the United States commissioners, and consented to move west of the Mississippi River. Another Sauk chief, Black Hawk, fought against this treaty to which he and his followers had given no consent. He said the white men had forced it upon his tribe, and he refused to move from his home and the sacred bones of his ancestors. His followers were many, and the dispute would not be ended until the Black Hawk War two years later.

Since Clark knew that these council meetings would be long drawn-out affairs, and that the chiefs would be decked out in their very best clothes, he invited Catlin to come along and get started on his paintings. The artist needed no second invitation.

Catlin painted rapidly all the time he was in Indian country. He had to. He could not take the time to make "finished" paintings; he

---

[4] George Catlin, *Letters and Notes*, II, 30.

would need hundreds for his museum-to-be. It was the main characteristics he was after: the face, a true likeness of his subject and how it might differ from that of another tribe; the clothes painted faithfully to preserve tribal individuality, either on the spot, or, with his copious notes giving minute detail, finished when he arrived home. Hands he practically ignored, giving them but crude strokes of his brush. There has been much criticism on this point, and also on the proportions of some of his figures in group pictures. He just did not take the time to consider such matters before he splashed the paint on the canvas. When not painting he was filling one notebook after another with remarks on each tribe, notes that later would be carefully written in detail.

The tireless artist made another trip that year with Clark to Cantonment Leavenworth on the lower Missouri. This military post was established in 1827 to protect the Santa Fe Trail. Already Indian emigrants from Illinois and Michigan were settled within twenty or thirty miles of the fort, and there was a Kickapoo village but four miles away. Here Catlin was able to prepare more paintings, of Shawnees, Iowas, Delawares, Sauks and Foxes, and the Kickapoos.

The Missouri River was the most important river to the fur trade. Along its banks posts were plentiful. They were built, used for a time, and then abandoned for another site.

During that year (1830) George met many of the leading men of the American Fur Company whom he would see again along the Missouri: Pierre Chouteau, who directed the affairs of the company at St. Louis; Kenneth McKenzie, chief trader for the division of the company based at Fort Union; and Major John Dougherty, U. S. agent for the Pawnees, Otoes and Iowas. Major Benjamin O'Fallon, until recently Indian agent on the Missouri, now lived near St. Louis. Catlin evidently gave or sold him several of his paintings, for the famous traveler, Prince Maximilian of Wied-Neuwied, wrote of seeing them in O'Fallon's home when entertained there in 1833. Prince Paul of Württemberg, who had first come to this country in 1823, was back again. He visited the Mandans on the upper Missouri in the spring of 1830, then returned to St. Louis. No doubt Catlin met him, and received much information about the tribe he was so eager to visit.

George was not idle a moment. He needed money, and to acquire it he was dependent on his paint brush and pen. It is said that in whatever town he happened to be, regardless of the length of his stay, he would hang out his shingle: "Portraits Painted." He painted a portrait of General Clark, and received commissions from other important personages in St. Louis.

In the fall of 1830 he returned to Washington, but the first of January, 1831, found him back in St. Louis. He returned to Philadelphia in the early summer.[5] In a year and a half George had made a fine beginning for his Indian gallery. And the next year he would go up the wide Missouri to the mouth of the Yellowstone!

Letters from Great Bend

P u t n a m , Polly, and sixteen-year-old Francis had now moved to Great Bend, Pennsylvania (about fifteen miles from Montrose), where Putnam owned some property. This pretty little village with a population of eight hundred, was located at a bend in the winding Susquehanna River, just below the New York boundary.

Putnam's letter to George, dated January 21, 1831, contains so much news of the family members, and of his move to Great Bend, that it is probable he had not written to George since his letter dated Montrose, February 15, 1830. Was it because his son had gone into

---

[5] George evidently intended returning home in a couple of months, because Putnam said in his letter of June 23, 1831: "You gave me reason to expect you in April and we were disappointed." However, in this same letter Putnam wrote that he had received George's letter of June 14, and would look forward to seeing him and Clara in July.

Indian country against his advice? There is a feeling of constraint in this letter, completely absent in his next.

During the months George was away, Clara spent the time "visiting around" with friends and relatives. George was showing no consideration for his young wife. Putnam expressed his disapproval in this letter.

Great Bend Jany 21 1831

Dear George,

I write you now to speak of our friends here, as Dart, Hartshorn, and families have this moment left us. The former arrived two days since, the latter met him here yesterday. You may easily imagine that this has been a pleasant meeting, tomorrow or next day we shall again meet them at Montrose, and extend the visit. To us, such meetings are indeed interesting, since we certainly have but little time on earth left us, and our only interest and happiness in this world is to see & hear from our dear, but scattered children. On such occasions we do not neglect to call the family roll, and speak and feel much about the dear absentees.

Eliza had written to Clara, but has not received an answer, inviting her to meet her here, or at Hartshornes if possible and convenient. We can hardly conceive how you can well bear the separation for the winter, or that you can both be contented, nor are we certain whether Clara is at this time at New York or Albany. We shall remain uneasy till we hear more from you as to your final arrangement & views, and the result of your Southern labours and travels, as well as your present encouragement—and whether you have heard from France the reception of your picture, whether engraved. Do not, my dear son believe we can feel indifferent or disinterested in any degree, about your reputation, your interest and your comfort.

The health of your mother, & my own, is as usual, and our activity as well as can be expected at the age 66 years; being fixed in one of my houses here very comfortably. Not having been able to sell my farm, and not willing to return to it I came here to repair the large house & fit it for a female Seminary, in which I think I shall succeed so far as to have the school commence the first of April under the direction of a scientific Clergyman & his Lady; in doing this, it will give this place a start, and make my buildings & lots more valuable. The children all approve of my course.

My ultimate object would be, to sell out here if possible and remove to Western, near Rome in Oneida County, where Dart has located, and there assemble some of my scattered family. James has removed from Lockport to Seneca falls near the Cayuga bridge, Richard has commenced a little drug store at Lockport without funds, and I feel much anxiety for them, the former although every way worthy has not hitherto been successful, and the latter equally worthy, has been too anxious to commence I fear too early in business. Charles is also there engaged in a little school which is all I can say of him. Henry will hold his office another year & perhaps be reelected; he is worthy and respected but he has a large family on his hands, his wife having mainly lost her sight. John is clerk in a store at Hopbottom—a worthy & promising young man, Francis is now with me. Your two sisters are in good health and have equally attentive and excellent husbands. In writing to you or my other children I can say little more than speaking about the others of the family—it is all in fact that concerns me in this world and so it will be to the last.

I have been disappointed in not having a letter from Clara, and in not hearing from you since you returned to Washington. Our member Stevens has been home this winter but I did not see him.

Your sisters, and all here, charged me to present them in my letter, most affectionately to you.

I shall hope to hear from you soon, and remain, my dear son

very affectionately
Putnam Catlin

The following letter from Putnam was addressed "George Catlin, Esq.—Artist—New York." From this letter it can be assumed that George was in New York on June 14, or expected to be there within a few days.

Geo Catlin Esquire

Great Bend June 23 1831

My dear Son

Having this moment received your letter of 14th instant I set down thus promptly to answer it, anxious you should know how happy I am in hearing of your health and welfare.

You must consider me the same anxious parent I have always been, though now I have not a child near me. I have even spared Francis the last, for he is with Richard at Western near Dart's.

My family consists of your mother a servant girl and a boy of 12 years old to wait on us, and we have at present 2 boarders, vis, the Presbyterian Clergyman and your cousin Miss Bedford who attends the school opposite. I live in the Henry house, the female school is in the Bowes house, both houses have been thoroughly repaired this spring, so that our situation is indeed very pleasant.[6] The school commenced in April & has now about

---

[6] The old homes were often called by the name of the original owner, but no "Mr. Henry" can be found among the early settlers of Great Bend. However, the "Bowes house," generally called the "white house" in these letters, was where George Catlin planned some day to live. He loved the little village and the big old house that had been known as the "Bowes Mansion," said to be rich in early historical associations. Built in 1805 by an Englishman, Joseph Bowes, it had been used as a residence and general store; later it was a church, and then a hotel. How it came into Putnam's hands is not known, but he had repaired it, and the house was now a seminary for young ladies. The school didn't last long. In the summer of 1832 Putnam called his son James home to manage it until someone could be found to replace the "scientific clergyman" who fled after a scandal in which he played a leading part. The following year the students were dismissed.

50 pupils, two churches have been lately erected within a few rods of my buildings, and a new bridge is building across the Susquehanna,[7] all which serve to render our location very tollerable, and, if my memory is correct, you had always a partiality to this spot.—At any rate, we now think it very fine, and as a rail road from Ithica to N Y through this way, is contemplated, it will become more interesting.

You gave me reason to expect to see you in April and we were disappointed. I have written to Clara twice without answer. I believe she is now at Albany, or perhaps with Eliza. I should have written again to you if I had known how to direct a letter for I confess I had become quite uneasy on your acct as you did not write. I am now quite easy and will anticipate much pleasure in seeing you once more with us. You may expect to find us in tollerable health, but broken with years and cares. I have sold my farm for half its value & glad to get rid of it. My old friend M. B. Wallace has, somewhat unceremoniously, left us in the lurch which has and will make me trouble.

It gives me comfort to learn that although you have had troubles & embarrassment you are in no degree discouraged. I had feared that my last letter might have hurt your feelings, it was far from my intentions to do so. Your explanation is satisfactory & you will derive self-confidence, in overcoming such things by strenuous exertions. I thank Heaven that your health has been so far spared, and hope as the hot season has arrived you can leave the south without being further exposed to that climate. Clara must grow impatient to see you. I think you will

---

[7] The old adage "if at first you don't succeed, try, try again," was amply illustrated by the early settlers who were so determined to span the Susquehanna. The first bridge was finished in 1814, and destroyed by an ice freshet in 1822. It was rebuilt that summer, destroyed again by a freshet in 1831. It was now being rebuilt, and would withstand the elements until 1846, when it would break down again. But the settlers would be wiser by that time, and a covered bridge finally solved the problem. Until that time, whether or not the bridge would hold was the leading topic of conversation every spring.

find her at Albany, then you can come by Newburgh, or round by Rome & Dart's.

Richard has recently opened a store at Dart's place, your brother James has a little drug store at Seneca falls 2 miles west of Cayuga Bridge, Henry remains in Lockport. Charles is in Buffalo, I trust somewhat reformed. Your brothers Henry and James have become professing Christians & zealous as well as Richard.

There is no entertainment on earth for me, so joyous as will be the meeting of you at this place and at the time you promise, here you and our dear Clara may repose with us (it may, and probably will be for the last time) with those whose affections you know to be unaffected, strong, natural and enduring, here you can for awhile take leave of the cares and anxieties of fashionable life, & here, narrate your travels, and communicate your views to those who above all, have the deepest interest in your comfort happiness and fame. Mr. Hartshorn & your brother John, intend to be at Darts about the 10th of July, they may happily meet you there if you should take that circuit from Albany.

I trust you will not fail to bring with you your brushes and painting apparatus, as you will where ever you go have many calls, & feel justified in making a long visit.

In having expended a few hundred dollars in repairing my buildings here, they will be more saleable by far, and I may incline to sell out & remove to Oneida County to live near some of my children—about which, and other interesting matters, we will take sweet counsel together when we meet here.

May kind Heaven preserve us till we have such meeting.

I am dear George your affectionate parent P. Catlin Your mother desires to be most affectionately remembered.

IN 1871 George Catlin prepared an itinerary of his journeys in search of Indian subjects. Concerning the year 1833 he wrote: "In the summer of 1833 I ascended the Platte to Fort Laramie, visiting the two principal villages of the Pawnees, and also the Omahas and Ottoes, and at the Fort saw a great number of Arapahos and Cheyennes, and rode to the shores of the Great Salt Lake, when the Mormons were yet building their temple at Nauvoo, on the Mississippi thirty-eight years ago." [8]

This statement created a problem for his biographers, because there was no documentary evidence to support it. True, his collection contained portraits of some of the tribes he mentioned having visited on this expedition, but his *Letters and Notes* gave no report of this trip, which, if made, would top all others in importance.

Finally, Harold McCracken found indisputable evidence that George spent the year 1833 in Cincinnati, Ohio.[9] It was then thought that the artist might have made the mountain trip in 1831. Catlin's itinerary for that year was brief: "In 1831, I visited with Governor Clark, the Konzas [Kansas], and returned to Saint Louis.[10] Judging from Putnam's letter of June 23, 1831, this would be all George could have accomplished in the length of time he was away from home.

Dale L. Morgan, an authority on the American fur trade, says that Catlin's trip to the Rocky Mountains in the 1830's must be regarded as fiction. "There was no Fort Laramie until 1834. The Mormons were not then building their temple on the Mississippi at Nauvoo;

---

[8] Donaldson, *The George Catlin Indian Gallery*, p. 475.

[9] Harold McCracken, *George Catlin and the Old Frontier* (New York: The Dial Press, 1959), pp. 130–131.

[10] Donaldson, *The George Catlin Indian Gallery*, p. 425.

they were not expelled from Missouri until the winter of 1838–1839, and only began their temple in 1841." [11]

_____

[11] Dale Morgan writes me: "To my way of thinking there is little question that George was drawing the long bow, or letting his enthusiasm as a showman get the better of him, in ever intimating that he visited the Laramie River, Great Salt Lake, etc. His offhand remark placed this in a context of 1833, but even if conclusive documentation on his whereabouts that year had not come to light, I would not have accepted the historicity of such a trip. For one thing, it would have been a tremendous experience for him, and he would have exploited it to the full, as he did his Missouri River voyage of 1832, and his experiences with the Dragoons in 1834; it would also have left some deposit in his drawings and Indian portraits, no one of which shows that he ever laid eyes on mountain Indians (other than the Crows encountered at the Missouri River posts in 1832), or in any way reflects the remarkable scenery of the Rockies, which would have added much to his public exhibitions.

"These considerations, which apply to 1833, are even more forcible applied to 1831. For one thing, he would have to apply for a license to enter the Indian country. Such a letter of application, and the official letter of authorization, exists for 1832, but not for 1831. Even more conclusive, he would have found no opportunity for making such a visit to the mountains in 1831. That was the year when everything went haywire for all the companies. Thus Thomas Fitzpatrick came down to the States in the spring of 1831 to arrange for a new outfit for the Rocky Mountain Fur Company, but found on his arrival at the frontier that Smith, Jackson, and Sublette had just left for Santa Fe. He started out after them, accompanied their party to New Mexico, and finally, in the late summer of 1831, took a pack party north from Taos to resupply his firm. Again, Fontenelle & Drips had gone to the mountains in 1830. They returned to the States in the late summer of 1831. In the fall of 1831 Andrew Drips turned back to the mountains with a new outfit, but under severe winter conditions had to stop somewhere in the Laramie region and winter there. So Catlin could not have accompanied a Fontenelle & Drips party in 1831. Etienne Provost took a party from Fort Union to Green River in the spring and summer of 1831, to resupply William Henry Vanderburgh, but he did not go all the way to Great Salt Lake. It is inconceivable that Catlin accompanied him. The only other party that went to the mountains in 1831 was the Gantt & Blackwell party, which split up and wintered by detachments on the Laramie and on waters draining into the Yampa. No members of this party went on to Great Salt Lake. What all this boils down to is that if George made any mountain trip in 1831, he went practically alone, though an absolute greenhorn, and came back practically alone, a proceeding

In 1871 George was seventy-five years old, and his life had been full of adventure. When making out an itinerary for all of his trips into Indian country he probably couldn't remember that he stayed "home" in 1833. Perhaps he had planned to make the mountain trip at some time, and had made notes of what tribes he would visit.

A trip on the Yellowstone to the Upper Missouri

GEORGE WAS BACK in St. Louis early in 1832. Pierre Chouteau had invited him to voyage up to Fort Union on the American Fur Company's new steamboat, the *Yellowstone*. This would be its second trip. The year before, it had ascended the Missouri as far as Fort Pierre, and now it would attempt the entire two-thousand-mile run to the mouth of the Yellowstone River.

The boat was to leave on March 26, which gave the artist time to paint any impressive looking Indians around St. Louis before he left. It is possible that this is when he painted the portraits of two of the Flathead Indians who had come to General Clark for information on the "white man's Bible." Their queries were instrumental in bringing many missionaries into the Far West, including Marcus Whitman, who, in 1836, established his well-known mission in the Columbia River Valley.

The *Yellowstone* finally steamed off with a full cargo and a motley array of characters leaning over the rails of the noisy, puffing craft. Besides Catlin and Chouteau, Major John F. A. Sanford, sub-agent for the Mandans, Minnetarees and Crows, was on board with a delegation of Assinaboins returning from Washington. The rest was a colorful melange of French-Canadian trappers and river men in dirty,

unprecedented and inconceivable. Impossibility piles upon impossibility; and we have to conclude that no such mountain trip was ever made."

smelly Indian shirts and leggings, and equally smelly half-breeds to do menial jobs at the fort.

Hiram Martin Chittenden, in his account of the fur trade of the Far West, writes of this momentous occasion, "In several respects the voyage of the *Yellowstone* in 1832 has been a landmark in the history of the West. It demonstrated the practicability of navigating the Missouri by steam as far as to the Yellowstone with a strong probability that boats could go on to Blackfoot country. Among the passengers was the artist Catlin, whose works have given added celebrity to the voyage." [12]

The trip up the muddy, swirling Missouri was an adventure in itself. Because of the constant undermining of the river banks, not only large branches, but huge tree trunks, logs, and bushes constituted a deadly menace to anything in their path, for they were not always visible in the coffee-colored water. Prince Maximilian, who made this same trip the following year, said that many times the boat was stopped to enable the crew to cut away some of the dangerous obstructions below the surface in order to get the boat through. Once a very large branch forced its way into the cabin before it broke off. No wonder the boat was moored to the shore when night came! Daylight was needed to steer the craft through the ever-changing channel with its constant flow of debris and undetected sandbars.

When more fuel was needed, the boat would be moored to the shore in a wooded area, and the wood-cutters would get busy. This delay would be a good chance to bring some extra food aboard; in this way waterfowl, deer, antelope, and eventually buffalo were added to the menu.

In its sluggish progress up the river the *Yellowstone* passed by the Indian villages of the Kansas, Sauks, Iowas, Omahas, Otoes, and Poncas, and Catlin made notes about them, as he planned to paddle a canoe back to St. Louis, stopping where he pleased.

When the steamboat was within two hundred miles of Fort Pierre,

---

[12] Hiram Martin Chittenden, *American Fur Trade of the Far West* (3 vols.; New York: F. P. Harper, 1902), I, 338.

it ran onto a sandbar. As it might have to sit there for weeks waiting for a sufficient rise in the water, Chouteau sent a number of men off on foot to the fort. Catlin, hearing that a large party of Sioux were encamped there, grabbed his knapsack, portfolio, and rifle and joined them. A good cure for "weak lungs" might be a two-hundred-mile trek in Indian moccasins, trying to keep up with a company of half-breeds whose lives were spent in just this way. However, the journey was worth the aches and pains, for when they neared the fort, George saw a great number of the Sioux tipis, Indians on horseback and afoot, countless children and dogs, and a blaze of color in every direction. The artist had a glorious time splashing the same colors on canvas until the boat arrived.

Next to Fort Union, Fort Pierre was the most important fur post on the river. It was the successor of Fort Tecumseh, which had been built in the 1820's for the Columbia Fur Company. In 1827 this company merged with the American Fur Company. The fort finally became so undermined that it had to be replaced, and the new post, named for Pierre Chouteau, had just been completed. The old fort was abandoned, as usual, and this one was built a half mile back from the rushing river, and three miles above the mouth of the Teton (Bad River), near present Pierre, South Dakota.

The fort was the main depot for the Sioux trade, and its manager was William Laidlaw, a good-natured Scotchman. The fort was built in the usual manner. It was formed in the shape of a large quadrangle, surrounded by eighteen-foot pickets placed closely together. The one large gate was guarded by a well-placed cannon. At diagonally opposite corners of the "wall" were two blockhouses with mounted cannon, and on their roofs were galleries from which one could see the prairie for miles around. Inside the outer enclosure, following the wall on three sides, were the stores and living quarters for the fort's personnel. A large space in the enclosure was for the Indians who came to trade. Even the horses had stables within the walls of the fort. They were taken out to the prairie each morning and carefully guarded, for the best of Indians couldn't resist stealing a horse.

The number of people in every fort was considerable. Besides the clerks, trappers, and interpreters, were the French-Canadian engagés, mostly married to Indian women.

This was the country of the Sioux, the most populous of the Plains Indians, and therefore the most powerful and the most feared. Divided into several branches, they roamed the plains from the upper Mississippi and Missouri to the base of the Rocky Mountains. They followed the buffalo and had no permanent home.

An interesting thing happened to George at Fort Pierre. He had been painting portraits one after another, the Sioux braves patiently standing in a row awaiting their turn, as much heavy protocol was used in forming the line. To hurry it up, the artist painted one chief in profile. A surly, disgruntled warrior who thought he should have been placed further ahead in the line, made the remark that only half the face was painted because there was nothing on the other side. Angry words flew back and forth, and finally the two warriors reached for their guns. The "profiled" Indian was killed. It was lucky that the *Yellowstone* was ready to leave the fort. It got underway at once.

Now the boat was puffing along in the beautiful country of the high Missouri. Occasional Indian villages appeared along the river banks, and great herds of buffalo and elk were to be seen on the green velvet carpet of the prairie. This was the true Indian country, largely unspoiled by civilization.

After three months of hard going, the *Yellowstone* reached its destination, Fort Union. It was now the fifth of June, and the prairie around the fort, which was perched on a rise, was dotted with Indian tipis. This was a rendezvous for many tribes in the area who gathered here to trade, sometimes making the trip from miles away, pitching their tents and going to housekeeping. Enemy tribes would appear and settle down not far away. The Fort was a peace zone. That was the law, and it was obeyed. The Crows and the Blackfeet were the deadliest of foes on the open prairie, but here they sometimes joined in games and amusements, chatted and laughed together.

This was the part of the country that Catlin wanted to visit; here were truly primitive Indians. He would paint the mighty and predatory Crows and Blackfeet, the Assiniboins and Ojibways, and by canoe he would visit the villages of the Mandans and Minnetarees, about two hundred miles down the river.

Fort Union was the American Fur Company's most important and best equipped trading post, built in 1829. This was the Assiniboin country, a tribe that lived on both sides of the Canadian border and did most of its trading with the British posts. The American Fur Company wanted their trade, and also that of the Blackfoot tribe who claimed the richest beaver land in the country. They had refused to have any dealings with the Americans until 1830, and even now trade was on a very precarious footing.

Kenneth McKenzie, a Scot, managed Fort Union. Two other trading posts had recently been established for the American Fur Company: Fort Cass, two hundred miles from Fort Union up the Yellowstone River, and Fort McKenzie, three hundred miles up the Missouri at the mouth of the Marias.

Fort McKenzie (formerly Piegan, later Benton) was managed by Major D. D. Mitchell, and situated well inside the Blackfoot country. This was an extremely hostile and warlike tribe, numbering around fifty thousand before the smallpox epidemic of 1837. A handsome, proud, and haughty people, they followed the buffalo on both sides of the Rockies, and were enemies of the Americans, and all other tribes, particularly the Crows.

Fort Cass was completed in 1832, and Samuel Tulloch put in charge, to trade with the Crows, a tribe given various reputations by travelers into the Far West. Thomas Farnham, who took the land route to the Pacific coast in 1839, but did not actually visit the Crow country, said that they were the most arrant rascals in the mountains, murder and robbery their principal employments. Prince Maximilian saw them in 1833, and said they were the proudest of the Indians; although they despised the whites, they did not kill them, but often plundered them. Bernard DeVoto has said that although they fought all Indians, had bad morals, and were thieves, they were friendly, and in many ways the most notable and interesting of the Plains Indians.

All the Indians on the upper Missouri lived well, as the country was bountifully stocked with buffalo. Having to hunt for their food, they were more at home in the saddle than on foot; superb riders, who with bow and arrow or lance killed their buffalo while riding at full speed.

Catlin later wrote: "The several tribes of Indians inhabiting the regions of the Upper Missouri . . . are undoubtedly the finest looking, best equipped, and most beautifully costumed of any on the Continent . . . they are all entirely in a state of primitive wildness, and consequently are picturesque and handsome, almost beyond description . . . As far as my travels have yet led me into the Indian country, I have more than realized my former predictions that those Indians who could be found most intirely in a state of nature, with the least knowledge of civilized society, would be found to be the most cleanly in their persons, elegant in their dress and manners, and enjoying life to the greatest perfection. Of such tribes, perhaps the Crows and Blackfeet stand first; and no one would be able to appreciate the richness and elegance (and even taste too), with which some of these people dress, without seeing them in their own country. I will do all I can, however, to make their looks as well as customs known to the world; I will paint with my brush and scribble with my pen, and bring their plumes and plumage, dresses, weapons, &c., and everything but the Indian himself, to prove to the world the assertions which I have made above." [13]

The Indians, on the whole, were wary of having their portraits painted. Superstition ruled their lives; the medicine men predicted premature death for any who submitted to such a strange practice— one's soul might leave the body and go into the painted one! When Catlin told them that he was bestowing an honor upon them, vanity overcame the fears of a sufficient number for the artist to paint—in fact, he was glad the "honor" was not great enough to convince more than a minority, for he hadn't the time to paint them all, and if one thought himself slighted there might be trouble.

---

[13] George Catlin, *Letters and Notes*, I, 23.

Catlin filled canvas after canvas, not only portraits, but Indians in groups, playing games, dancing, and hunting the buffalo. Day after day his brushes were dipped into the bright reds, yellows, and blues for their fantastic costumes and head-gear, and at night he filled notebooks with information about each tribe.

After a month's painting in and around Fort Union, the jubilant artist hired two trappers to help him paddle a canoe down the Missouri to St. Louis. He was anxious to visit the villages of the Mandans, who, instead of following the buffalo over the prairies, waited until they came within shooting distance of their homes. This did not create too much of a hardship as they lived in the heart of the buffalo country. There were times, however, when the buffalo went far afield, and extended their visiting too long. This would mean acute hunger for the tribe. The Mandans raised maize, pumpkins, and squashes, and dried the wild fruit, but buffalo meat was the main item on their menu, and a prolonged lack of it would bring forth the Buffalo Dance, their plea to the Great Spirit to bring the animals back to the soup pots. The ceremony never failed, for the dance did not end until scouts reported that the buffalo were returning. When one dancer wearied, another took his place; the dance could go on for months.

The Mandan Indians had been known since explorers visited them in the 1730's. Here Lewis and Clark spent the first winter on their trek to the Pacific. The tribe was peaceable and very friendly toward the whites. Having previously lived at various other sites on the river, they were now situated in two villages a mile or so apart, near present Bismarck, North Dakota. Fort Clark, named for General William Clark, was built for trade with the Mandans in 1831. This post was of great importance to the fur company. James Kipp was its director, and John F. A. Sanford, the sub-agent, made periodic visits to it.

The Mandans lived in mud huts, the tops of which were slightly rounded and made firm enough for the inmates to use as sun porches. On a clear day they would be covered with laughing Indians, children and dogs, drying skins, sleds, snow-shoes, and other articles that perhaps had lain there for months and would remain until needed again.

Catlin's brush was busy from dawn to dusk, and then exchanged for a pen. He wrote that the Mandans were perhaps one of the most ancient tribes in North America, and that their traditions and strange customs made them a peculiar and distinct race. They were not all dark complexioned; many had white skin, and a great many of them, including children, had silvery white hair. They were intelligent people, some showing much talent in music and art; and were more advanced in their manufactures than other tribes.

Because of his ability to put quickly the likeness of a subject on canvas, George acquired great prestige. Portraiture was something the natives had never seen before, and what George could do with his paint brush was "medicine" (magic). He was given the name of "great medicine white man," and allowed to sit in at the council meetings of their chiefs and medicine-men. Thus he came into possession of a good deal of information he could not have obtained otherwise. He was permitted to watch tribal ceremonies rarely witnessed by white men; particularly the religious torture ceremony "O-Kee-pa," an annual rite that if not seen, would be hard to believe.

Prince Maximilian of Wied Neuwied, with the Swiss artist, Charles Bodmer, spent the winter of 1833–34 in the Mandan villages. Maximilian was gathering material for his book on North America, with Bodmer along to make sketches and paintings to illustrate it. Mr. Kipp, clerk in charge of Fort Clark, told him about this pagan rite of the Mandans. He had seen it, and said that George Catlin had witnessed it the year before, and had sent a fine description of it to Colonel Stone's *The Commercial Advertiser* in New York. As this rite was a very important piece of data, Maximilian obtained the article and had incorporated it into his forthcoming German publication. Unfortunately, this particular article was eliminated in the English publication of the book.

In late summer of 1832, Catlin paddled his canoe back to St. Louis, painting more Indians on the way. On his arrival he found Black

Hawk, the Sauk chief, imprisoned with some of his followers at Jefferson Barracks, about ten miles from the town. His war against the treaty his tribe had made with the white men had failed. Catlin painted his portrait, as well as one of Kee-o-Kuk, who was at the fort to speak in behalf of the members of the tribe. George went home to Clara late in the fall of 1832, and learned that his brother Charles had died in September.

There are no letters from Putnam in 1832. Very likely he and Polly locked their doors and closed the shutters—and waited for the news that their son had been scalped by the Indians.

1832 was not only George Catlin's *big* year; it was also his best, so far as his Indian paintings are concerned. He had not yet completed his study of the American Indian; he still had more journeys to make. But nowhere else would he find red men so "paintable" as those who hunted the buffalo between the Missouri River and the Rocky Mountains. They could not be equaled in stature, dignity, or dress. These were the paintings that George copied over and over again; the paintings that showed the world the first Americans, and how they lived before the white men came. George came home with joy in his heart, and hundreds of paintings and Indian artifacts for the museum he was so certain would be established to hold them.

One can but wonder what those trappers and traders in the wilderness thought of Catlin, the artist. Many of them were scum: dirty, drunk, illiterate, and immoral. They lived in a land without laws. Money was their god; murder not uncommon. Squaws were plentiful; many lived at the forts, and their half-breed children played in and out of the enclosures. The fur traders certainly did not give the Indians a favorable impression of the lordly white race.

Catlin must have been hated, laughed at, and sneered at, many times. Here was a man who neither drank nor smoked. He did not want a squaw, and he waxed poetic over a sunset on the prairies. Worst of all, he glorified a race of men that others regarded as "God-damned thieving Indians."

Chittenden wrote: "It will ever be a source of poignant regret among the millions of those who helped despoil him [the Indian] of his country, and who look with pity upon a fate which they were powerless to avert, that there could not have been reserved in all this vast continent a true home for the Indian—a place where he could have led the life he used to lead when he chased the deer and buffalo, trapped the cunning beaver, and made war upon his enemies. Such was the life for which alone he was fitted, and we have yet to see any departure from it that has not resulted disastrously to his race." [14]

Putnam writes Francis on the correct use of capital letters

W ITH G EORGE safely back in civilization and planning to stay put for the year, his parents breathed easily once more. Great Bend was a little village of white houses and picket fences, where the streets were filled with swirling dust in the summer, and mud, frozen ruts, or snow the rest of the year. Two churches had been built across the road from the Catlins', and their bells on a Sunday morning must have had a friendly sound to these two quiet people approaching their seventies. If there was any variety in their life Putnam never wrote of it. It is highly possible that although Putnam was friendly to all, he had too much reserve to exchange idle badinage with others. Polly, on the other hand, would thoroughly enjoy the weekly sewing circle and the friends who dropped in for a cup of tea. She doubtless had her flower garden to attend to, while, since Putnam wrote Francis about haying and harvest, he evidently had a small farm on the Henry property (or was speaking for the town as a whole).

On July 26, 1833, Putnam wrote to eighteen-year-old Francis who was working in Lockport, New York, and living with his oldest brother Henry and wife Mary. This was the first time he had been away from his parents for any length of time, and his father felt the

---

[14] Chittenden, *American Fur Trade of the Far West, II,* 835.

necessity of carrying on the boy's training by mail. This was the only son over whom he still had control, and he wasn't going to lose it! He wrote:

Dear Francis,

I have received your letter of 2nd July but found some difficulty in reading some part of it. Your imitation of your brother's hand, is pleasing enough as it shows your power of varying your style of writing but it will for some time be more difficult to be read. I notice that a great proportion of your words have *Capitals* which is no ornament, and is against the rules— you will recollect that the pronoun *I, proper names* of persons & places, & the *beginning of sentences* are only to have capitals; and you will observe that all the letters should appear in the words, as distinct as possible in excellent writing which you can easily conform to by a little care in forming your style or manner of writing. It will be important to you to get early into a good habit of writing, which you can easily do. Henry's manner is very much admired which you will naturally conform to, but I would have you careful in the use of capitals and have all your letters as distinct and fair as possible so as to excel Henry if you can.

Your mother has been ill for about ten days of the summer complaint but has fully recovered. My own health is as usual except I am afflicted with giddiness which has troubled me for a week or two. James writes that he is perfectly well at Newark, but has obtained no permanent employment. I doubt whether he will be willing to venture so far to the south as Pensacola, it would, as his friends think be too great a risk; nor can he easily give up the pursuit of the art.[15] George I suppose may be expected to return by way of Buffalo early in the fall, if his life

---

[15] James Catlin was torn between two desires: going to Florida or becoming a traveling painter. However, Clara's brother, Dudley Gregory, appointed him cashier of the Pensacola Bank, which he accepted, and soon after sailed to Florida.

and health be continued, on his way by Albany to New York—we shall remain anxious for his preservation.

I am very glad to learn that you are pleased with your occupation. I trust it will continue so if you are careful of your position in writing, to preserve your breast, your side and your lungs and take proper exercise daily, such as walking dancing keeping an erect attitude, good spirits, &c.

I will be easy now in regard to you believing you will take good care of yourself and form a good character and good habits and manners, and strictly and cheerfully attend to the duties of your station—which is the glory of a young man. You have learnt that parents have an indescribable solicitude about their children which will only terminate with life.

Your mother is planning a journey to get up to Lockport this fall by the way of Rome, which if convenient will be performed. I hope Henry & Mary will find you such a brother as they will not be ashamed of in Lockport, and I am sure they will be disposed to make the best of you they can. Have you not Francis now a good opportunity and a fair prospect of establishing a good name and good habits pleasing to yourself and all your friends? Why not then seize the present moment, & be what can and ought to be just such a young man as you yourself would approve of & such as our family and friends remember your brother Julius to have been?

If George lives a few years he will feel much interest in you and may have occasion to employ and assist you as well as some of his other brothers. Richard left us after a visit of ten days; his visit was a very pleasant one to us, & we think to him also. I do not recollect any news for you, Mr. McKinney has got well and in good spirits—It is with us haying and harvest time, but very rainy the crops pretty good. Little Putnam [Eliza's son] returned with Richard—we are somewhat lonesome in the absence of James.

Mr. Sutton & wife of Geneva are here on a visit and are going as far as Wilkesbarre, and perhaps as far as Washington, he has invented a model for an improvement of steam power by a rotary wheel on a simple plan, which, if he succeeds, will give some fame and fortune to him in this country & in Europe. He has high hopes, & intends securing a patent right.

Tell Henry I have not lately heard anything from Smith & Burfree or from Fuller or Hodgdon.

Give my love to him and all the family. Your mother and Abigail send love also.

Your affectionate parent
Putnam Catlin

. . . Keep in fine spirits, preserve your health and improve in good manners and morals as well as you can.

The story of John Catlin

WHAT ABOUT John Catlin, three years older than Francis? Putnam has but briefly mentioned him in his letters. He wrote about the other sons at great length; where they were, and how they got along, always ready to give them a pat on the back, but did not include John. Putnam wrote George that Henry, James, and Richard had accepted religion; John's name was omitted, and for a good reason. John started early to follow in his brother Charles' footsteps, and his parents' pleas fell on deaf ears.

John wrote several letters to Francis in 1833 from New Brenville, which must have been near Delta, New York, as he often spoke of both Asa Hartshorn and Anson Dart, his brothers-in-law. Richard was in that area, also. In his letters he mentioned his father occasionally, but never his mother. These were young, jolly letters, poorly spelled, but often including bits of family news; "Rich'd occasionally receives a letter from Miss Darwina Barstow [16] his dearly be-

---

[16] Richard Catlin and Darwina Barstow were married in May, 1834.

loved . . ." and "Mr. Hartshorn has a fine house, and will live like a king."

John wrote Francis on April 10, 1834, from Delta: "I rec'd yours from Mr. Hartshorn and I can assure you I was much pleased to hear that you had enlisted in so good a cause as that of religion. And oh! that I was one among those who enjoy religion. I hope and trust I may at no distant day—I have long been convinced that it is kneedfull, to live by, and more espetially to die by. When I was (as it were) upon the brink of Eternity last winter, and at a time when all supposed my case hopeless, I then thought that all I could wish would be religion—and oftimes before I got well I did solemnly promise that should I ever again be restored to health I would live a different life, and it is my opinion that most who are reduced so low, make the same promises . . ."

John died in August, 1834, just twenty-two years old. He was buried in Delta, New York, where his mother would one day lie beside him.

Putnam wrote to Francis in Pensacola on April 15, 1839: "It is painful for Parents and children to be separated so distant and so long; but we have had the privilege of corresponding, and ever since the death of dear John we have heard the echo, the distant echo, 'all's well.' "

In the land of the Comanches

PUTNAM CATLIN had always been a great reader of the classics. He enjoyed memorizing long passages to recite to himself when he couldn't sleep, or to his children when he wished to stress a thought in other words than his own.

In an old, spotted notebook there are fifty-seven carefully written pages in Putnam's handwriting. Page one is headed " 'Essay on Man,' by A. Pope." At the conclusion is this paragraph:

> G. Bend, Saturday April 12th, 1834
>
> The foregoing Essay was written by the undersigned on the 9th, 10th, 11th & 12th days of April 1834 entirely from recollection, the volume containing it being first sealed and placed in the hands of another person; and he declares solemnly that it is written without reference to any book, writing, notes or memorandum containing any line of the Essay. It is wholly from memory. The razures and interlineations appearing in the foregoing made by him at the time of writing it. He thinks no sentence or line is omitted, there will however, be of course some variation in the punctuation.
>
> (signed) Putnam Catlin.

It is very probable that in the spring of 1834 Putnam needed projects of this sort to keep himself from worrying over George, for the latter was embarking upon a new journey into the Comanche country.

That spring George was well rested, and ready to round out his collection of paintings and data on the North American Indians. He was impatient to complete his "gallery" and show it in the larger cities.

Not a great deal was known about the Indians of the great Southwest. For that matter, not much was known about that part of the country. Fort Gibson, in Arkansas Territory, was the extreme southwestern outpost on the United States frontier, and the vast country beyond was inhabited by Indians who had already shown hostility.

The savage Comanches roamed the plains from the Arkansas River to Mexico, and the equally predatory Pawnee Picts, together with two smaller tribes, the Kiowas and Wacos, occupied the territory from the head of the Red River to the Rocky Mountains. These four tribes were often good friends, and joined in constant attacks on the Mexicans, Texans, and other Indians of the north, as well as traders unfortunate enough to cross their path.

The United States Dragoons had been organized for frontier service. The regiment was under the command of Colonel Dodge. During the summer of 1834 they were to travel into the Southwest to meet with the Comanches and Pawnee Picts, and try to come to some understanding with them. George had to have paintings and information about these savages, and he obtained permission from his friend, Lewis Cass, then Secretary of War, for himself and a companion, Joe Chadwick, to accompany the dragoons.

Catlin met the regiment at Fort Gibson after a two months' wait. The expedition did not get under way until June, and the heat was already terrific. Several Comanche and Pawnee prisoners had been purchased from the Osages living in the vicinity of the fort to act as interpreters and hunters, and also to help in bringing about the interviews with the tribes. It was here, also, that George purchased "Charlie," a wild horse that had been beautifully trained by the Osages.

The mounted soldiers traveled several hundred miles to the mouth of the False Washita and Red rivers on the northern boundary of Texas, and stopped to rest a few days before continuing their journey. The heat was oppressive, and the only water was scooped from polluted buffalo wallows. Half the regiment became ill with bilious fever, and many died. Because of their late start Colonel Dodge had to push on. Those too ill to continue were left behind in the care of Colonel Kearny, and those able to mount their horses rode on into the Comanche country. Many more became ill on the way, carried along on litters. Certainly this bedraggled little band looked to be easy prey for hostile Indians, and they feared the worst.

They had been on the march four days when they began to see many fresh Indian trails, and smoke here and there in the distance. Finally they observed a large group of Indians sitting on their horses, evidently watching their approach. When the regiment came within half a mile of them Colonel Dodge rode forward with a few of his staff and an ensign carrying a white flag. This stirring meeting with the wild Comanches is best expressed in George Catlin's own colorful words:

"We then came to a halt, and the white flag was sent a little in advance and waved as a signal for them to approach; at which one of their party galloped out in advance of the war-party on a milk white horse, carrying a piece of white buffalo skin on the point of his long lance in reply to our flag.

"This was the commencement of one of the most thrilling and beautiful scenes I ever witnessed. . . . The distance between the two parties was perhaps half a mile, and that a beautiful and gently sloping prairie; over which he was for the space of a quarter of an hour, reining and spurring his maddened horse, and gradually approaching us by tacking to the right and left, like a vessl beating against the wind. He at length came prancing and leaping along till he met the flag of the regiment, when he leaned his spear for a moment against it, looking the bearer full in the face, when he wheeled his horse, and dashed up to Col. Dodge . . . with his extended hand, which was instantly grasped and shaken. We all had him by the hand in a moment, and the rest of the party seeing him received in this friendly manner, instead of being sacrificed, as they undoubtedly expected, started under 'full whip' in a direct line toward us, and in a moment gathered, like a black cloud around us! The regiment then moved up in regular order, and a general shake of the hand ensued, which was accomplished by each warrior riding along the ranks, and shaking the hand of every one as he passed . . . and during the whole operation, my eyes were fixed upon the gallant and wonderful appearance of the little fellow who bore us the white flag on the point of his lance. He rode a fine and spirited wild horse, which was as white as the drifted snow, with an exuberant mane, and its long and bushy tail sweeping the ground." [17]

Handshaking over, they all dismounted and the peace pipe was handed around. Colonel Dodge, with the aid of his interpreter,

---

[17] George Catlin, *Letters and Notes*, II, 55–56.

explained the friendly mission the dragoons were on. His speech was understood and appreciated, and in turn they invited him and his regiment to return with them to their great village a few days march away. They rode over the sloping hills by day and camped beside each other at night.

The Comanches were nomads who followed the buffalo over the plains. Their tipis, made of poles and buffalo skins, were easy to move from one place to another, for they simply attached the poles to a horse and dragged them along. Like the Missouri tribes, they were interested in games of all kinds, but their skill in ball-play did not equal that of the northerners. In horse racing and riding they excelled all others. The Comanches were short and stocky. When on their feet they were ugly and clumsy looking, but once on their flying horses they became gods. The southern plains abounded with wild horses, small and fleet, so many that the Indians used them for food when buffalos and other game were scarce.

Nothing but friendship and a natural curiosity were shown the regiment at their encampment. The natives were perfectly willing to pose for the artist who filled his portfolio and notebooks with Comanches and their way of life. When it came time to visit the Pawnee Picts, about ninety miles to the west, several Indians offered to lead the way. Half of the soldiers who had come this far were now too ill to travel, and so left behind. With them stayed Catlin, who had finally come down with the fever. His friend, Joe Chadwick, came to the rescue. He went along on the trip to the Pawnee Picts and made notes and sketches for the artist's use.

The Pawnee Picts were a semi-agricultural tribe, cultivating large fields of maize, pumpkins, beans, melons and squashes, but they resembled the Comanches in stature and mode of life. Again, the friendly council with the chiefs was successful, the head chief even consenting to ride back with Colonel Dodge to Fort Gibson for a visit. After a two weeks' stay, the regiment returned to the Comanche village to pick up their sick. Several Pawnee Picts, Kiowas and Wacos accompanied them, and George, regardless of his fever, picked up his brushes.

It was a long, hard trip back. Many men and horses died along the way. George became so ill he had to be carried in a wagon, and was forced to remain at the fort for several weeks. Finally he was able to climb upon the back of Charlie, and ride the many miles over the prairies to St. Louis and Clara, who waited for him there.

This expedition had been costly. Catlin said that of the four hundred and fifty-five men who had started from Fort Gibson four months earlier, about one-third had died, and that as many more would yet fall victims to the diseases contracted on the journey.

Letters from the Family

I T W A S necessary for George to have a good rest after his near-fatal expedition into the Southwest. He and Clara spent the winter of 1834–1835 in the South, and the balmy climate restored his health. It is amazing what he could stand, physically. Although George was considered frail, he was able to come through when others far stronger than he failed.

On the first day of January, 1835, Putnam wrote to his children in Delta, New York. Here lived Eliza and Anson Dart, Mary and Asa Hartshorn, and Francis, who was now working in Hartshorn's store.

> Great Bend Jany 1st 1835
> I have been putting off writing for several days not knowing to whom I should direct my letter. I feel a partiality, but I can truly say it is for each individual among you, and now address you all alike with the New years wish.[18]

---

[18] There are plenty of "Happy New Year" greetings in these old letters, but only one "Merry Christmas," and that was from one of the grandchildren many years later. The early Puritans did not believe in celebrating Christmas; its

75

I am happy to say the New year finds us all well here as usual, and we have abundance of snow which fell the day before yesterday at least two feet deep, the ground being well frozen at the time—we have not had so deep a snow in five years.

Those of our friends who intend visiting us by sleighing will find snow enough now and we shall now be looking toward Delta for a load. I have some journey to make which I shall put off till middle of January. I have not yet been to Bradford or Paterson. We are not to expect George and Clara till next summer; I presume they intend wintering at Pensacola, where the climate will better suit them than it would here in their present weak state of health—we received a letter from James yesterday dated 3 Dec'r, he writes that it is very healthy there. He had not heard from George; but I fancy George is with him by this time and they will have a very pleasant time, as Geo will be finishing his sketches and James will be looking on at every leisure moment. Our school has a vacation of 7 days, and will commence on Monday next—Little Putnam [Eliza's son] is very well & is looking out now for a visit from his parents.

I can think of nothing new to communicate—Miss Dubois is so recovered as to be riding out & will fully recover. We have a new Physician to commence this week a Mr Warner formerly from Montrose—but lately graduated in Massachusetts, he is, I believe, a very promising young man, has fine talents and irreproachable charater. He is to board with us at present, but has his office in J. DuBois' south west chamber, where the milliner kept formerly.

There is to be an interesting Rail road Meeting at Montrose next monday evening—the object is to get up a R road from the mouth of Lackawana to mouth of Tunkhannock, thence up that creek to mouth of Martin creek thence up that valley to Saltlick

---

feasting and pageants smacked too much of popery, and were therefore eliminated. True, the ban had been lifted before Putnam was born, but he and his family evidently held to the tenets of the past.

creek & Great Bend. Luzerne will join in this project and we have hopes it may succeed—you will see it is meant to keep off from the hills and along the waters edge the whole way opening to the coal region & head of the Penn'a canal.

I hope to hear a good account of the new store and of business generally at Delta. I shall now look daily for a visit from some of my children as the road will be good, we shall expect Eliza and Mary and both Anson & Asa—You can tell Mary that Doct Porter has commenced housekeeping in the S. West room, that Mrs. Fuller reserves the Parlour.

This is a parental letter without any moralizing, as I have not time, & think there may not be need of it at this time [Putnam was now speaking to Francis]. Your mother is about making up some linen for you to send by Eliza when she comes down.

Love to all

You wished me to mention the price of Salt here on acct of Mr. Elmer. I believe it has been selling for 20/ & 21/ per barrel. Flour is worth 5½ dolls per bbl.

Your affectionate father P Catlin

I shall expect a long letter from you when our folks come down.

On the 13th of January, 1835, Polly decided to take her pen in hand and give her youngest a few rules of behavior.

january the
13

Dear Francis

I have a few moments to write to you we are all well and have had a fine viset from our dear children we are pleased with the good account they give of you I hope you will indevour to please them in everything and strictly adhere to their good advise you will find your affectionate sisters like mothers to you, but you be ever carefull and on your guard how you treat them in one sence. I suppose you feel your self more under the care of Mr Dart as you live with him but I hope you will consider your self under the care of boath so you must strive to give satisfaction to all, they are all equally interested in your well doing.

I hope you will be ever carefull of your morals, ever carefull of the company you keep. let it be the best or none. now you are from your parents in your leisure hours you can reflect and think of all the good advise we have given you and strive to follow it. remember your Creator in the days of your youth dont go down the swift tide of life with the multitude that are thoughtless and careless, but remember you must die we all have a great duty laid upon us as to spiritual things, we must always ask if we expect to receive. I must leave the subject for you to think of and my constant prayers is with you. as to the news of the place there is nothing verry interesting. Miss D is walking all about. there is but too young men now at the school. John Dimmoe last week going to a ball at the widow troubridges froze his legs and feet I suppose verry bad I hope you will write me and tell me how you get along you must watch over your health I was surprised you should get your hair cut as you did and be so careless I hope it will learn you better nex time. I must leave you your affectionate Mother P. C.

Mother Polly wrote again:

Febuary the 18305
5

Dear Francis

this tells you that the family are all well your fathers health is more than usually good for him as for myself I am weak and full lonesome and mourn too mutch for my dear departed children but I thank God who has sustained me under my afflictions. we have received a letter from James last evening saying that George and Clarra has arrived at pensacola you will conceive that they are all verry happy. James gave them his

7 8

little comfortable room rather than to be in a publick house, whare he could take care of him, he was taken with the ague and fever on account of the fatigue of the Journey, but now is walking all over the town, he intends to return to the north in the summer by way of the lakes he is now going to new Orleans to exhibit his pictures. So I hope with the blessing of heaven we shall all meet again. I have some good news to tell you besides what has been related, in whitch I hope you will feel a deep interest, and feel to rejoice thare has been a protracted meeting at Montrose of too weeks by a Mr Spencer. George Bently and young Williston they say has experienced Religion Abigal saw George last Saturday she said he was verry happy and told her he should write to you and Mary soon. I hope my dear Francis this may excite you to your own souls wellfare and happiness strive to be one of that happy number that will lead a crossbearing life, and make sure the one thing needfull you are with your dearest friends who will always give you good advice. I hope you will be willing to be taught by those who are older than your self, you must be carefull to please all and at all times watch over your self doe justly with all speak evil of none you will see that your situation is quite a delicate one tharefore needs the greater care James says he is glad brother F has gone to delta he thinks it will be a good place for you if you manage right.

last evening we got a letter from Henry they are all well Henry is now building a three story store to rent I cannot think of mutch news in our place we have a fine young man that boards with us a son of Mr Warner of Montrose he is a doctor his shop and sighn is at Josephs store I think our drunken doctor now will give up I suppose some of your young correspondents has told you the story is that gustus ward and pamela troubridge is to be married and oliver to Mrs Tottles so is the saying Abby says she will write to you as soon as the mood comes over her we can hear of letters flying down here from above. I dont say from whare but I hope some will come to us soon.

79

give my love to Mary and Asa tell them as it is their turn to
come next I shall look for them in the spring tell Mary she must
set down and write me a long letter tell Eliza the same they
must not wait for me to write give my love to all the children

your Affectionate Mother
Polly Catlin

Francis returned to Great Bend the first of April. His father had
been ill, and he was needed at home. Eliza wrote to him on the 25th,
reminding him of his duty to his aged parents. Poor Francis—
everyone in the family seemed to feel that he needed his or her
advice, and no doubt he did. He was not a stable young man, and was
easily influenced by his companions.

Advice given, Eliza continued:

In several of our last papers we have had verry flattering
accounts of our enterprising brother George. you must let the
world have reason to speak as well of you. It must be a source of
comfort and gratification to our dear Parents to hear such good
accounts from George and James. as it respects their children at
Delta, they may not hear of their accomplishing anything
worthy of notice, *only that they have not* failed, nor are they
likely toe—a few weeks since there was a story circulated (that
Richard had *failed*) by that drunken vagabond John Treadway,
for which there was not the least foundation. Richard has not
been in the least crowded, this he will answer toe. This same
John Treadway was the one who first circulated the story about
our poor innocent brother John which set him crazy, and made
him leave us as he did. Richard would prossicute him but he
could recover nothing as he has no property.

At this time Anson is full of business, his boat has arrived at
Rome, loaded with wheat, his teams are unloading it, he expects
to start his boat this week to the city laden with corn, and bring
back goods for Mr. Breyton & Mr. Nesbot, he will then go west
again for wheat, after which he will go again to the city with a

load of corn. he has already made sale for 3000 bushels, for 76 cts pr bushel, he gave 50 cents. he thinks his boat will more than pay for itself this season . . .

adieu I am your truely affectionate sister
Eliza

Up the Mississippi

GEORGE CATLIN had been very willing to loll in the Florida sun until he had recuperated from his trip into the Southwest. But once that was accomplished, restlessness took over. June, 1835, came, and he decided to take Clara on a pleasure jaunt—what he called a "fashionable tour." They would go to St. Louis, and take a steamboat up the Mississippi to the Falls of St. Anthony, near St. Paul, Minnesota.[19]

Along the banks of the river were both large and small settlements; the Mississippi was no longer a barrier to the steady flow of migration to the West. Fort Snelling was about nine miles below the Falls, and a regiment had been placed there to protect the citizens on the frontier, and to keep peace between the Yankton Sioux and Ojibways who occupied the country about it. The former were a

---

[19] On this trip George met Charles Augustus Murray, grandson of Lord Dunmore, last English governor of Virginia. Murray had come to the United States in 1834 to make a tour of the country, and, like so many visitors from Europe, went home and wrote a book. British to the tips of his toes, he cared not for the "equality of station" in this country, much preferring the separation of the social classes as practiced at home. To speak of laborers as "gentlemen" was absurd, and to eat at the table with them on boats and steam-trains was much against his aristocratic taste. He found something to his liking here, however, for he later married an American girl.

Murray and Catlin became good friends, and it was Murray who later suggested that George take his exhibit to London. He considered the artist his social equal, for he introduced him to the elite of London.

branch of the great tribe on the upper Missouri, and although Catlin found their customs the same as those of their western brothers, their appearance was not. Here they were living on the fringe of civilization, and already showed the effects of whiskey and smallpox. They were poorly clad, as the game had vanished from this part of the country, and they no longer had the skins which furnished the tribes along the Missouri with such rich and beautiful garments.

While George and Clara were visiting the fort, a thousand or more of each tribe were camped near by. These two tribes were constantly at war with each other, and had now come to make long speeches, and air their difficulties before the Indian agent. It didn't take the artist long to get out his paint-box!

Fall came, and Clara, expecting her first baby, decided to take a steamboat back to St. Louis where she would stay with friends until George returned. Once again he obtained a birch-bark canoe, and with a traveling companion paddled down the Mississippi as he had done on the Missouri, stopping whenever he came upon something interesting to write about, or put on canvas.

The news that Clara was to have a child was probably the best news Putnam had received since George set out with his paint pots for the Indian country. His son would now stay home where he belonged! The following letter from Putnam to George and Clara has the most jubilant ending of any of his letters.

Great Bend Sunday Morn
Dec 26 1835

My dear Son & Daughter,

Your letter postmarked at St Louis Nov 16 has this moment arrived—a moment when we were in the most possible anxiety to hear directly from you, having not heard, since the pleasing letter from Clara the last of August, except through letters from Henry and Dart; the former had received yours of the 10th of Octo, the latter had met Gen'l Patterson at Green Bay.[20] It is

---

[20] Anson Dart was investing in pine lands for a group of eastern speculators.

now well—the present letter is truly consoling, you are both perfectly well, in good spirits and on the way home. This is the best possible intelligence we could receive; and I hasten to assure you your parents are both in good health, and have great joy in anticipating the happy moment of receiving you again, for which they are devoutly greatful to Divine Providence . . ."[21]

The winter has now arrived and we have had sleighing about two weeks, the Rivers and Canals are closed by ice, and I cannot help fearing the Ohio will be closed before you will get to Pittsburgh. I read that the Hudson is shut up as far down as Poughkeepsie.

I was in hopes you would have been up early enough to have availed yourself of the Canal for the passage of your Baggage to the city. I can now hardly imagine how you will manage with that or what your arrangement will be in that regard unless the Railroad will accomodate you. If you send on your heavy baggage to the City you must be careful to have it insured or safely placed—but this you will consider, and take care.

I thank God I may now expect to see you soon, and I will take care to keep in good spirits and stem another winter. I am proud of the invitation to meet you at Pittsburg. It would give me great pleasure indeed—but your mother thinks I might take cold on the way as my health is somewhat precarious and it would perhaps on the whole be best not to undertake it. Possibly I may venture, but you must not expect me. I will write immediately to Henry and he will be sure to meet you here. I will also write to

---

[21] Putnam wrote at length about Henry, whose wife, Mary, had recently died of apoplexy following the birth of a child. Henry wrote that George had suggested that he travel with him, and that he planned to accept the proposal as soon as he could make arrangements for his many children. Putnam wrote: "I think it will be the best course he can take to mitigate his grief, and he will be the best companion you can have. He has taste, talent, industry, enterprise, integrity, and uncommon perseverance." George was fond of Henry, and he would be a great help in staging his coming exhibitions. George decided to try Francis as a helper, also.

our friends at Delta, some of whom will come and I will write to Richard, but he will wait to see you in N.Y. You can hardly imagine how eagerly you are looked for—it will be a Jubilee with your connections, & the song will be "There is na luck about the house" and "are you sure the news is true?" and "I'll go tell the Bailie's wife that Collin has come hame." I can only add take care of each other. Tell dear Clara we send our double compliments to her on this occasion. Meet us as soon as you well can.

Your affectionate Parent
Putnam Catlin

PART THREE: HIGHLIGHTS AND SHADOW

1836–1840

1836: George and Clara lose their first child; George decides to take a trip; A disrupted exhibit in Buffalo; Where is George?; Where the red pipestone came from 1837: Land speculation and Anson Dart; Francis goes to Pensacola; A quick sketch of the Catlin family   1838: A Wild West show in New York; Francis decides to go to sea; George receives praise but no offers; Family letters 1839: Family correspondence; George says farewell to America.

George and Clara Lose Their First Child

GEORGE and Clara arrived in Great Bend the latter part of December, 1835, and one can readily visualize that happy reunion. Sleighbells announced the arrival of friends and relatives, the old house was full of bustle and confusion and the good smell of food cooking in the kitchen fireplace. The walls would long retain the echoes of the many voices and the sound of laughter. Putnam would look at his famous son with pride, and try to figure out what advice he could give him. He well knew he would have to choose his words with care; let George think that he, himself, had already thought of it. Putnam now held the parental reins in slack hands; only with Francis did he dare pull them tight. Sweet little Clara would be loved and coddled, and she and Polly would crochet small caps and jackets, and talk by the hour.

George was full of enthusiasm over his coming exhibitions, but because of the ice-bound rivers and canals he did not know how long his shipment of Indian portraits and artifacts would be delayed in reaching the east coast. The last of February he took Clara to her own family in Albany, New York, instructing both Henry and Francis to go to Pittsburg and wait for him. They were to help him with his exhibit in Buffalo.

The Henry house sighed and settled back into the old, monotonous groove, and Polly wrote to Francis in Pittsburgh:

March the 18 1836

My dear Francis

I now sit down in one of my lonesome hours to inform you of our health and tell you the news of the place. the family are as well as usual, we have had the pleasure to receive a letter from George & one from you I cannot tell you how lonesome and melancholy I was when all had left me and the long and tedious journey you had to perform in sutch cold weather caused me great uneasiness and concern likewise for G untill we got a letter from him whitch gave us great relief, to hear of your safe arrival although G was not well it seems but it was what I mutch feared after hearing of his first attack, but I hope you are now boath well. I hope you will take great care of your health and guard against colds we fear it will be verry sickly this spring.

We have received a letter from James they are all well Jame's salary is fiften hundred and Richard's 8 hundred and stays with James.[1] we have had a letter from Dart they are all well also from Clara. She is well and a letter from Darwina she is well and will visit us this spring with her sister Mrs. Land I cannot yet tell you what our arrangements may be if we should live this summer some times I feel as though I could not stay here but might as well spend the summer in visiting the children if we should, we shall want to meet you all I hope George will let us know whare.

Last week we was called to the house of mourning whitch is said is better than to go to the house of feasting, because it shows us our own fate. Mrs. Thompson is no more, old Mr. Burrel and his foolish girl are dead. I cannot tell you how things are to turn out here wheather better or worse the school I expect will not continue, some are going away and some may come in a verry respectable Doctor from the point is coming in here Mr. Jewel I expect will go. John Wiley has bought his fathers place and moves here in the summer, the old man is married to old granney Adams nearly ninety, Oh awful!

Nelson Baker is married to Miss Famor Charley White they say is to be married to Miss Leach your young Friends here I believe are all well they enquire after you when they see me. Taylour is fast coming to nothing we think all his property in doors and out is under execution mark the consequence of dissipation or wicked conduct through life, the end is misery and

---

[1] Richard Catlin had joined his brother James in Pensacola.

disgrace. I believe I have told you all the news I must soon close for your father a few lines.

Dear Francis you will not be surprised if we continue to warn you of the slippery paths of youth knowing you are but a stranger in the world and unacquainted with the snares and besetting sins of the world into which you may be drawn, the great safeguard will be to remember your Creator in the days of youth, be virtuous and good in all things then you will be happy dont fail to write give my love to George

your most affectionate Mother P Catlin

[Included in Polly's letter]

Dear Francis

Your mother has felt it her privilege to make you a long letter which you will kindly accept as you know she seldom writes. She of course has given you the village news and mentioned our intelligence from our friends at Delta and Pensacola, leaving me to tell about the snow, and how unkindly winter is lingering among us with all its chills & horrors. we have had no thaw of any consequence & the snow lies about as deep as ever. With you, I suppose, there must have been a movement of the water, & your rivers cleared of ice. It will however be a late spring, and retard the movements of George longer than he could wish, but will give him the more time for preparation. we have had a good long cheering letter from Clara which I think was mentioned in my last.

In regard to yourself Francis, in the first place, take care of your health, think often of your brothers Julius and John. Make this an important time for your improvement—fail not to do so. Take courage and resolution that you will achieve something to gain reputation; be active, industrious and persevering, now is your time to improve in manners, taste, & character; lose no time, not an hour of idleness or trifling; remember you are in the care and employment of a brother who is ambitious; be faithful and punctilious in everything you have to do, or can do, then he will have pride in you as well as comfort, & then you will have a good opinion of yourself—he will be more able to counsel you than myself, he will be to you in *loco parentis*, he will be delighted in advancing you, and will promote you, if you will take care to deserve it. May I rest assured that you will do your duty in that regard?

Your brother will soon have made up his mind which route he will take to the city, & let me know as soon as you can. Darwina wrote to me that she did not see Benj Case & therefore I have sent to her five dollars on your account. My love to George, tell him I have written to Clara a cheering letter.

Your affectionate Parent
Putnam Catlin

It was late spring before the baggage arrived in Buffalo. George rented a small church for his exhibit there, planning on opening on July first. Before he had a chance to arrange his collection, Clara became ill, and he rushed to Albany where she was staying with her family. George wrote to Francis in Buffalo:

Dear Brother,

Clara's sickness and the misfortune with her little babe have been the means of prolonging my delay here much longer than I expected.[2] It has been impossible for me to move from here before this, but I shall probably start about one week from the present time. If I can be patient, you certainly can. It is a hard struggle with me to make up my mind to the loss of time at this critical

---

[2] Biographers of George Catlin have mentioned that the births of his children were not recorded. Clara was known to be expecting a child in the summer of 1836, and since George never mentioned this infant who died at birth, it has been assumed that George's eldest daughter, Elizabeth, was the child born that year. Elizabeth was born in December, 1837. In later years George, himself, became confused over the ages of his children.

juncture, but I must bear it, for circumstances that I could not control have so ordered it.

Clara has suffered very much in her sickness, but is now doing pretty well. I shall bring her south with me, as far as Delta, and leave her with Eliza. The little child got to bleeding at the navel on the 5th day after it was born, and it not being possible to stop it, died the next morning.

Eliza is now with us, just leaving for Delta. Father & Mother, by last account, are well, & so with friends at Pensacola. James is speculating at a great rate in lands and making his thousands of dollars!

I suppose this will find you at Lockport and I address it there. Give my love to Henry and tell him I shall now be along soon.

In haste, your affectionate brother

Geo Catlin

George Decides to Take a Trip

THERE WAS but one week left in June when George returned to Buffalo, sad over the loss of his first child, and worried and upset by the responsibility ahead of him, with so little time to properly arrange his first large exhibit. Putnam packed his satchel and came to lend a hand. Handbills were ordered printed, and most of the paintings were on the walls when George heard that a boat was leaving shortly for Sault St. Marie, which was on the route to the pipestone quarries. That was all George needed. He announced to his astounded father and brothers that he was taking the boat, and told Henry and Francis to remove the paintings from the walls, pack up the exhibit, and store it all in Lockport; that he would be back soon and would put on another showing.

Putnam's pleadings were not heard. George had made up his

mind. He was going to the pipestone quarries, and he gave no thought to others.

George's abrupt departure on this extremely dangerous trip into the Indian country plainly showed one of his less happy traits of character: his complete unconcern for others if it interfered with his plans. His sick and grieving wife should have been enough to keep him home. He had incurred expenses in renting the church for the exhibit, which he left for his brothers to attend to. He left his valuable paintings in the hands of inexperienced persons, expecting them to pack, ship, and store them in Henry's house. He took it for granted that his aging father would see that everything was attended to. George had not planned to make this trip this year. It was a peculiarity that seemed to possess the artist at a time of great stress— the overpowering desire to throw off his worries in the solitude of the forests. Indian country was a "cure-all" for George. Many years later he would again seek health and peace of mind far from civilization.

He departed the first week of July, leaving an ailing wife and his father and brothers in a stew-pot of worry and indecision. While Henry and Francis were still packing up in Buffalo they received the following letter from George, dated Prairie Du Chien, Wis., Aug. 1, 1836:

Dear Brothers, Since I left you I have been rapidly traversing a part of the country which I never have before seen, and which it was of great importance for me to visit. My health, which was almost discouraging when I left you, is now good & I am just starting tomorrow morning for the Red Pipe Stone Quarry which will be a pretty hard traipse from here on horseback, if an unknown distance. as soon as it is in the power of man to perform it I shall accomplish it and be on my way back to Buffalo. If you watch the *Spectator* of Col. Stone you will soon see the importance of this trip, which the world cannot know the importance of—as well as myself, until they hear from me.

It seemed like pulling my eye teeth out to leave Father when I did, the very time when I felt as if I should have staid with him, but the only Boat for the summer was starting which would go to the Sault De St. Marys & I considered it the only time I could ever get off to accomplish the object which I have been for a long time impatient to do.

I was in hopes to have got a letter from you ere I left this place, but I now give it up, it is too late. No doubt you have written to Green Bay, and though I ordered letters forwarded on to this place they have not arrived. It is probable that ere this arrives you will have closed the Exhibition & moved with all to Lockport, where I shall want them on return.

I hope and trust & *know* too that you will take the greatest care of them for me, if my absence is protracted a little, never mind it. Francis need not fret, he must stay with you, and if he gets out of patience let him only reflect a moment on the difficulties & delays I have had alone in foreign land to go through to get them, & let him realize what I am yet enduring. And say never mind it will all be made up after awhile. I presume Father has gone home ere this—did I not conclude so I should have written to him.

I have written to St. Louis & ordered all Henry's minerals to be sent on by water to Buffalo, they will be there about as soon as I shall—

I have been writing 6 or 8 letters this evening & it is past 12 ock. So for the present adieu—your affectionate Brother

Geo. Catlin

Write to me at Detroit on rec't of this, that I may get it as I return.

A Disrupted Exhibit in Buffalo

PUTNAM went home to Great Bend as soon as the Indian portraits had been safely stored in Henry's house at Lockport, New York. Henry remained at home; and Francis, expecting George any day, stayed in Buffalo. Nothing more was heard from George until

November, and worry for his safety mounted by the hour. On September 11, 1836, Putnam wrote Francis:

Your letter of Sept 1 was duly received. We rejoice to learn that you were well at the time you wrote, though you had been indisposed for some time; we trust you will now be careful of your health, as the sickly season has arrived & Buffalo is somewhat unhealthy. As you could give no intelligence from your brother Geo, it is natural—it is unavoidable, that his affectionate relatives and his ardent friends should begin to entertain some fears about him—that he is sick & has no means of conveying a letter to his friends—or that some misfortune may have befallen him, by venturing too far in the Wilderness. We will hope for the best, and the more rejoice, when he does return to Buffalo. We have not heard from Clara but conclude she returned to N. Y. with her brother, and fear she will be distressed at the long absence of her husband—she could not bear the thought of his going so far as the Pipe-stone quarry & told your mother she should never see George again. By this time I hope and trust he is at Buffalo & that you will not delay a moment writing to us.

I wrote to Henry to see that the Boxes were all placed safe from fire. And hope nothing was left in the Church, but that you gave up the actual possession to Mr. Dibble—so that he will have no further claim for rent. Your brother will of course have paid out all his money. Henry writes to me Sept 3d that he had made an arrangement to receive a payment on his mortgage by allowing 20 per cent for the money advanced, and he intends accomodating his brother by advancing what he may need. As he has removed the box of portraits of the chiefs to his house (*ex majori cautela*) G will not be able to Lecture again at Buffalo as they wish. I may possibly dispose of one of my lots here within a few weeks, in that case, I could advance some money—the Gov'r of Penna was here on Thursday last, our prospects of a Rail-road are very fair & property will therefore rise.

Your mother is remarkably well, mine is better than when I left Buffalo—We go to Wyasox tomorrow to be absent about 6 days—Darwina and her sister intend spending two days with us about 1st Oct on their way to N. Y. She expects to take ship for Pensacola by middle of Octo under the care of Mr. Gregory so she writes. I shall write this day to dear Clara. I shall also write to Henry by this opportunity. *Our love to George*

P Catlin

Polly added a page:

September the 1836

11

Dear Francis

I could not let this oppertunity pass without writing you a few lines although your Father has wrote. I have wrote too letters to you when at Delta and have received one from you that come when we was gone, the letter you last wrote gives us uneasiness about George as well as your Self, I hope by this time G may be with you, but I am mutch concerned about him and was the moment I heard he was gone it seemes as though he was crazy but we must hope for the best Mr. Dart said he would not be home in too months when he left he says sometimes they are detained a month on account of the boats I am uneasy to have you stay so long at that place you say you have been so long with a headach and tremble you have had something else with it I am thankful to hear that you was better when you wrote. I hope you will take care not to take cold if you doe you will get sick again you are in a cold place you must be the more carefull, be sure to keep warm under cloaths and wholy avoid the evenin air. I hope dear Francis you will come home as soon as curcumstances will admit. I have been knitting cotten and wollen stockens this summer and now I am making shirts if George dont come soon I hope Henry will get his goods to Lockport so that you may come home. I have no great news to tell you only there seems to be something of action at the bend on account of the railrod we expect property now will rise. here all are well

> your most affectionate
> mother Polly Catlin

Where Is George?

ON OCTOBER 12, 1836, Putnam wrote to Francis in Buffalo:

. . . I received your letter of the 23d also one from Henry dated the 3d of October but not one word from George since his public letter from *Coteau du Praire* August 3d. I fear some misfortune has prevented his return, I am sure he does not willingly protract his return so long. we cannot expect letters for he can have no opportunity of writing from that wilderness. I fear he is sick and cannot let us know it. I shall be painfully anxious now till his return, everybody is enquiring about him and concerned; his wife I fear will grow distracted in his long absence and fear for the worst. I have written her today endeavouring to keep up her spirits—his mother has a thousand fears and sad dreams on the occasion. George must know the alarm his friends must feel, and be most unhappy, whatever may be the cause of his delay, particularly on the account of his dear Clara; but I will expect every day to hear of his return to Buffalo with favourable results, and full justification.

I have been thinking you might have neglected preserving the Cards opposite the portraits and the numbers marked on the respective portraits in taking them from the walls. I remember mentioning this to you when you commenced taking them down. I hope you have preserved them. . . . My great concern is [to] hear from George, I dont know what you can do if he does not return soon. I hope you have had consideration enough to have been in some employment enough at least to keep you out of bad company—I mean by reading and reflection. You must know that your character and fortune in life is now fast forming and requires your serious and constant attention. . . .

Poor Putnam—his letters were laced with anxiety over George and advice to Francis. The artist was long overdue, and Francis was alone in the wicked city of Buffalo. Another month went by without word from George, and evidently Putnam wrote Francis to go to Delta and stay with Eliza, for his next letter was addressed to him there.

Great Bend 25th of Nov 1836

Dear Francis

Your letter of 17th was received yesterday & was 7 days on the way. I had heard from Henry since you left Buffalo. George wrote to him from Tecumsuh 40 miles west of Detroit—the day before, he was overset in the stage, & his shoulder so bruised he would have to remain there a few days, not being able to ride in the stage—but thought he should be able in a very few days, & would press on with all possible speed. It is very well that his boxes are safe at Utica, to go in the cars, and not ice bound as I feared.

This last expedition of his, has been long, very tedious and hazardous; we all rejoice to learn he has a safe return to his friends. I hope you have taken all possible care that his boxes be placed so as to be safe in case of fire—the person in whose care they are left, should have been informed of their value.

The roads are so bad at this season, he has still to have a hard passage in the stage, & some peril in arriving at Utica, but you may now expect him daily. . . .

Polly added a note:

Dear Francis I am mutch pleased once more to hear from you and that you are again with your friends you have had a long and tedious summer out of business and alone I have worried day and nigt about you but I trust in that overruling hand that preserves us and keeps us you are now on the ocian of lif you will meet with disappointments but keep good courage and doe right in all things and with all and you will be sustained through life, all Georges friends has been opposed to his course this summer, but perhaps it is all for the best we are thankfull that his live is spared I hope a time will come this winter that you will come and see us. . . .

Putnam wrote to Francis on the third of December, having received a letter from George who was still in Tecumseh.

Geo is mending rapidly after having had much pain and discouragement—so now that he walks the room, and some out doors & thinks after 6 or 8 days he may ride to Detroit, and thence in steamboat to Buffalo. . . .[3] I shall still feel very anxious to hear of George's arrival at Utica; if he starts too soon from his lodgings it may protract his full recovery—if he shall have to remain much longer, the Erie will be frozen and the steamboats stopped; at any rate he will have to keep in the stages from Buffalo to Utica which he will probably dread—and it will not be long before the North River will be bound in ice— His return from the west has been extremely painful and discouraging to him. But I hope he will not despair, he will have lost none of his connexions or friends during his absence, and if he can but arrive in good health, he will not have to regret his last enterprise.

Amasa Troubridge returned from N Y yesterday, he delivered the letter to Clara & the bunch of shirts for you at Mr. Gregory's at Pocoles Hook, . . . Geo must have some baggage to bring from Buffalo; I hope there may be a passage for

---

[3] In this letter Putnam mentioned receiving a letter from Richard telling of his purchase of a great amount of land in Alabama for speculation. That portion of the letter is included in the next chapter.

him, by the Ontario and Oswego, but I am not certain—he will do the best he can to get through, & then all will be well. His expenses will have been accumulating, but in a few days, he will, if well, be able to meet them. . . .

Your affectionate father
P Catlin

Putnam wrote to Francis again on December 21. He had received a letter from George in Albany, N. Y. George had visited Lockport to talk with Henry, and was now enroute to Utica. "I wrote a long letter directed to him at Utica as he requested, in which I wrote a few lines to you, he has not mentioned the receipt of my letter, but writes that he shall be at Utica in a few days with Clara where he will have to wait, being winter bound from N. Y. as the Railroad by its charter bound not to carry freight of any kind. This is extremely unfortunate for him as he will have to remain in Utica and commence writing on his book of travels, & work on his portraits till some time in the winter when sleighing is good, then take his portraits and some part of the baggage to Albany and then Troy so as to exhibit a few weeks before the navigation opens. This I had feared, as it will cramp him as to his resources, and will leave you out of employment. He did not say he should exhibit at Utica—but I presume he will. . . ." [4]

---

[4] Putnam was no longer worried over George; he was alive and safe, but he enjoyed his "little frets"; small worries that he could bring out and mull over on cold winter days. Now he had two good ones that might last for some time: George was winter-bound and could not get to New York with his baggage (he must think of some advice to give him), and second, Francis wanted to go to Pensacola! In this last letter Putnam wrote several pages on the subject: "It is a subject of great importance to you and of great concern to your parents. . . . It is a great undertaking for a young man to go so far to the south on uncertainty, at this season of the year and without good company . . . your mother couldn't bear the thought of your going alone and so far"—on and on, regardless of the fact that Francis was twenty-one, and James had offered him a job. The old gentleman still clucked over his children, feeling it his prerogative to make all important decisions. Polly must have been a sweet, dependent little woman, perfectly willing to let her husband look after the mental chores. She was content if her children stayed alive.

Where the red pipestone came from

GEORGE had returned safely from his trip, putting his frantic family at ease once more. He had accomplished his mission, and if his family had worried, so had he! He knew he wasn't going on a picnic when he started.

During Catlin's travels among the different tribes of Indians in North America he had found the smoking of the peace pipe common to all. The smoking of the pipe was an ancient ritual with deep religious significance. George found that though the pipes were made in many different shapes, the bowls were fashioned from the same reddish stone, and that it all came from the same source: the sacred red pipestone quarry on the Coteau Des Prairies, west of Fort Snelling.

Many were the myths and fables connected with this quarry. Each tribe or portion of tribe, had its own variation of the belief that stemmed from the beginning of time, when the Great Spirit had spoken to the people at the site of the Red Pipestone, saying that it was a sacred meeting place for all tribes, where peace must be kept. (The tomahawks could start flying after they had left the place.)

Knowing all this, George was fairly certain that he would run into trouble, regardless of his friendship with the Indians in the past. They had told him that no white man could go to the quarry, that it would offend the Great Spirit who would punish them. It made no difference to the eager artist; the very thought of the danger involved quickened his pulse.

By way of the Great Lakes George reached Green Bay, Wisconsin, a name that became more familiar to the Catlin family later. From there he went to the Falls of St. Anthony, which he and Clara had visited the year before. There he was fortunate in meeting an Englishman, Robert Wood, who consented to make the trip to the quarry with the artist. The two paddled a canoe down to Fort Snelling, then set off on horseback for the quarries.

The trip was not as simple as it reads. This was Sioux country— Indians who spent their time looking for a fight, and who certainly didn't like having anyone in their back yard. When the two men were about 150 miles from their destination they stopped at a small trading post, and immediately a large party of angry Indians were swarming around them, telling them to go back, that they knew where the white men were planning to go—to find out how much the land at the pipestone quarry was worth, and take it from them. The red stone had been given them by the Great Spirit; the red men were a part of the red stone; and the red pipe was a part of their flesh. No white man could go near the sacred ground!

Catlin's flesh crawled as he saw the hatred in their eyes. To show fear might bring out the scalping knives, so he calmly asked them to listen to him for a moment. He had learned that they respected sincerity and understanding. In a quiet, pleasant tone of voice he told them that he meant no harm; that he knew many members of their tribe and that they were his friends, and that he had been doing all he could to help the red men who were his brothers, nor was he sent to spy on the land around the quarry. He had heard so much about the place that he wanted to see it for himself; that was all. He and his friend had traveled a long way, and they weren't going to turn back. With this, he and his companion mounted their horses and rode on. They were not molested but they knew they were followed.

After traveling miles over the velvety-green prairie the sacred ground of the pipestone was found on the summit of a high, broad ridge separating the Mississippi and Missouri rivers. The quarry was found with an almost unlimited amount of the pipestone. In color, it ranged from a beautiful pale greyish rose to the dark red, which was found by digging deeper into the strata. George collected many specimens for his collection, and when studied the pipestone was found to be a mineral not known elsewhere. It was named "Catlinite," and is still so called.

George wrote to Francis, in Delta, on December 29:

Utica, Thursday evening

Dear Brother,

I arrived here last evening with Clara, in good health &c. I should have written to you from Albany, but being almost every day on the start back I delayed it until I should get here.

After I left Delta, on my way to Albany, and while in Utica, I learned for the first time & some what to my astonishment, that the Great Rail Road, (which was to remove & carry mountains with perfect ease) could not carry a pound of *freight* for anybody! So of course my things must remain here until spring and, I, snug in a warm Room, must be as contented as possible—finishing up my numerous sketches & preparing my notes & letters for publication.

My greatest anxiety has been through the summer and still is, for *yourself* whom I have kept so long in suspense without yet having done anything of account for either of us. You know however, what to allow for the peculiar nature of my business and the disadvantages with which I have had to perform it. The time *will come* ere long when I can begin to make some money if I have my health, but I have got to spend yet some more before I begin.

I shall deem it best to remain here as silent as possible until I can move my things, and perhaps not exhibit them again until I have them more completed & open them in N. York. If I can meet all my expenses, that is the course I would rather adopt; for it would suit the N. Yorkers best, & might be of service to me. I think you had better bring your things and come immediately here, and we will consult together, like Brothers, about plans for the future. I hardly know what to do, and in fact, am at this time, most too *poor* to do *anything*. Clara has brought a package of some shirts for you from mother, and Clara thinks you have some for me brought from Buffalo.

The box of portraits must remain where they are until

sleighing is good—put them further from the fire than they were when I was there—as they may get too warm & stick together, lay the box flat down too, so that they may not get hurt. Before you start be good enough to tell all there that Clara & I will be up to see them as soon as the sleighing will permit.

George Dart staid one night with us in Albany & I saw him off at 9 next morning by stage for Poughkeepsie, & thence by steam boat. Clara is in good health & sends love to all.

In haste your affectionate Brother

Geo. Catlin

Land speculation and Anson Dart

JAMES and Richard Catlin were doing very well in Pensacola; Putnam had no worries there. James now was thirty-six, and cashier of the Pensacola bank, and Richard, twenty-five, was also connected with the bank. Both were happily married. James had several children, Richard none.

In Putnam's letter to Francis, dated December 3, 1836 (see p. 98) he mentioned having received a letter from Richard. "All are well in Pensacola; Darwina [Richard's wife] arrived there after a very pleasant voyage of 18 days from New York. Richard met her in the steamboat before landing at Mobile. He had just returned from a journey up in the state of Alabama of three weeks. He was sent up to take a view of the public lands for himself and others. He says James & the Gregorys (Clara's wealthy relatives) in Company, have bought 6000 acres of good, valuable lands, and he, himself, had bought 2600 acres of first rate land at 10 shillings per acre, and could sell some of it for ten dollars per acre, and had been offered 2500 dollars profit on 1500 acres of it. Mr. D. Gregory had loaned him two thousand dollars for that purpose, for two years. They seem in high spirits there. . . ."

With the endless migration to the West, and the thousands of hopeful Europeans pouring into this country, land-buying all over America was a business rapidly becoming a mania. Land sharks were buying up whole tracts of good land, advertising it, steering the new settlers in that direction, and making them pay through the nose to get it. At any time land speculation is normal, but not the kind then going on. New state banks were being chartered right and left, with "easy credit" their slogan. All a speculator had to do was borrow money from a bank (with little or no security) buy some land, sell it at a profit, pay off his note at the bank and borrow more, and continue on with the game, keeping his gains in his pocket. Government land offices all over the country were doing a terrific business; the expression "doing a land office business" was coined during this time. But these land offices were accepting bank notes of dubious worth in exchange for valuable property.

In the year 1836 land speculation really got out of hand. Land-sharks held on to their wild lands, expecting to make a fortune from the settlers, and exhorbitant prices were asked for acres under improvement. Something had to be done to stop this wildcat financing, and in July President Jackson issued the "Specie Circular," which required buyers of land, not settlers, to pay for it in "hard money" (gold or silver). No more state bank notes were to be accepted by land agents. This was a death blow to the speculators who had been doing a whale of a business on long-term credit; they could not meet the requirements of the Specie Circular. The panic of 1837 and the subsequent depression was the result. Hundreds of state banks suspended, thus making many millions of dollars in bank deposits inaccessible. Those who bought land wisely and paid for it in specie were safe; the plight of the rest led to the Bankruptcy Law of 1840.

Neither James nor Richard was affected by the "Circular." Henry, in Lockport, New York, with little money and many children, had jumped in over his head, and was now bankrupt. We shall speak of the effect on Anson Dart hereafter.

Let us jump ahead to a portion of Putnam's letter to Francis dated June 17, 1837: "It is well that the troubles of the times are not as severe at Pensacola as in most parts of the United States. The attitude your bank has taken and sustained is noble, but I cannot but think it would have been more safe to have also suspended, to save its specie, as it has been universally done in self defense. The internal improvements at the north are all suspended, and the prospects are gloomy. I hope your place may in some measure be exempted from the wide spread ruin. You will see in the papers that New York has to bear a great share of the calamity; it is hard times there, indeed. . . . I have not yet heard from Henry or Dart how far the times have taxed them. Eliza has written, but is silent on the subject."

Eliza's husband, Anson Dart, had been doing extremely well with his business of buying wheat in the West and selling in New York. He and Eliza had recently moved to Utica, where they now owned a beautiful home on three acres of land, opposite his farm of one hundred and fifty acres. They lived well, and Eliza's life was one of ease and happiness. There was no worry over the future.

Anson probably had been successful in speculating on a small scale in the past. In 1835 he went west as representative for a company of land speculators, and made huge investments in pine lands in Wisconsin Territory and other real estate in the Milwaukee area. His son Richard later wrote that Daniel Green, of Green Bay, once offered his father's company one hundred thousand dollars for their pine lands, and that his father laughed at the offer.[5] Dart was now in difficulty; Eliza's happy days would soon be over.

Francis goes to Pensacola

FRANCIS was now in Pensacola, but it had taken Putnam two months to make up his mind to let his youngest son go to Florida. He

[5] Richard Dart, *Settlement of Green Lake County*, Wisconsin State Historical Society, Proceedings, 1909. (Published by the Society, Madison, Wis.: published by the Society, 1910), p. 259, fn. 12.

no longer had big decisions to make for the others—they made their own. He wasn't going to let Francis slip from his hands until he ran out of words. This weighty issue was introduced in Putnam's letter to Francis, dated December 21, 1836 (see p. 99, note 4). It was finally resolved on February 23, 1837.

George, poor and winter-bound in Utica, could not help his youngest brother as he had planned. James had written Francis that a clerkship was open at his bank, and for Francis to come to Pensacola as soon as possible if he wanted the job. Francis was in Delta at the time, so his father was able to do a lot of oratory on paper. Putnam's true forte was pen-preaching. Four-syllable words flowed from his pen in ponderous rhythm, sounding so like music to his ears that he repeated them all over again. Here is another excerpt from his December letter: "You should have a profitable business to pursue and devote all your energies to succeed and acquire an interest, and become independent, such should be your purpose and you should pursue it with inflexible zeal and perseverance. It is very true that the patronage of your brothers and of Mr. Gregory would be of great advantage to you, but it will require energy, strong purpose, and untiring perseverance in yourself. You must get into reputable business somewhere to the best advantage you can with resolution to pursue it with perfect integrity, industry and perseverance. . . ."

After considering the situation from every possible angle Putnam decided to let another son seek his fortune in far away Florida. Joseph DuBois, a close friend of Francis and a fine and stable young man, was persuaded to go along, as James had written earlier that he could find him a position. They left Great Bend on the 22nd of February, to stay with Clara's brother in New York until their ship sailed.

That very evening Putnam received a letter from James saying that the opening in the bank had been filled. If Francis still wanted to come south James was sure he could find a position for him, but he could not promise to find two jobs!

Poor Putnam was in a tizzy—he would have to get a letter off to Francis on the early morning stage for New York. His letter was hastily written and his thoughts were jumbled. He told both boys to come home—no, Francis was to go on, and Joseph to come home—no, maybe they could find work in New York until he could hear again from James. Finally, he advised Francis to proceed on his journey, and Joseph to come home. Putnam promised to accompany him to Pensacola in the fall.

The letter was addressed to "Mr. Dudley Gregory, New York—to be delivered to Francis Catlin with Speed." Beneath this address, which had been scratched out, was written in another handwriting: "Care of James Catlin, Esq. Pensacola." The letter arrived too late; the two boys went merrily on to Florida.

Francis Catlin and Joseph DuBois were delighted with the warm and sunny South. To Francis this was high adventure; to Joseph it meant getting ahead and saving his money. James found a "reputable station" for his brother—a clerkship at the Pensacola Navy Yard, a few miles from town. He would now try to find a place for Joseph.

On April 11, 1837, Putnam wrote Francis:

My dear Son,

We are all well. Your letter of the 18th was recd 5 days since, and one from George and Clara by the same mail. Also one from James 4 days after, and now this morning I have received one from Richard [in Marianna, Florida] dated March 26—also one from George this morning—4 days since I recd one from Henry, all are well. All which letters will deserve my thanks and my answer. It is you know, my highest pride and favourable employment. Dart has removed to Utica and Eliza is well suited; they have a new beautiful house, three acres of land with a splendid garden on the Utica side of the river, opposite his farm of 150 acres all in the suburbs of the city. Geo is still waiting for the opening of the canal; the railroad, by a clause in its charter is forbid carrying freight. Dart & Eliza making us the yearly visit, took me with them in the stage to meet Geo and Clara in Utica where Hartshorn and Mary met us. I attended George's Lectures five evenings—he continued his lectures 10 evenings, & closed. I found him highly patronized and he might have continued it another week to advantage; but he intended getting to Albany by snow next week and was prevented by the badness of the road; and again commenced writing his travels and finishing his Landscapes. I had written him yesterday, among other things cautioning him of the danger of fire, as I had recently read of the destruction of valuable paintings in N. Y. by fire in the Acadimy of Design, though ensured to the amt of the pecuniary loss—his letter this morning informs me of a great & destructive fire in Utica at midnight. he was alarmed, looked from the window while dressing himself, he saw in the direction of his painting rooms a prodigous light which appeared to be the same building, but on arriving, found it the buildings in the block adjoining his rooms. The wind being favourable to him carried the flames in an opposite direction. He says that in the bustle, he and a couple of friends ran to his rooms, & locking the outside door packed up the principal part of his things in order &c. The flames spread before a strong wind to the westward until the whole block was in ruins, & crossing the beautiful Genesee street swept its way until about 40 or 50 houses were destroyed, and those some of the finest in the city. The day after the fire a parcel of little boys were picking up iron among the ashes and cinders, a Brick wall fell & crushed 4 of them to death & their mangled bodies were taken to their distracted mothers—This was a narrow escape for your brother G—there will always be danger of his collection.

Your letter and Joseph's have been read here with great interest and there will be great enquiry about you. James & Richard both mention that you have a good and reputable station for the first year at $600—your board at $20 pr. Month, which is perhaps as favourable as you could reasonably expect the first year, they both say you are to board at the best private house, where James has boarded 2 years. . . . No language can express the anxiety that parents feel for their children when they enter on the stage of action, to act for themselves and are to rise on their own merit. . . .

George Catlin in Brussels, 1868.

Putnam Catlin, from a portrait by George Catlin
made during the 1840's.

Polly Sutton Catlin, from a portrait by George Catlin
made during the 1840's.

Watercolor sketch by George Catlin, dated Ithaca, 1824.

Clara and George were very well and very happy when I saw them at Utica G. has been extremely busy through the winter in finishing his Landscapes &c and preparing for N York, and we shall hear from him shortly & how he succeeds there.

. . . God bless and preserve you all.

Your Parent,
Putnam Catlin

. . . Blind Jo is married—"and music is no more." *Apropos*, I hope on due consideration, you left back your Violin and your travelling knife as I advised, neither of them could be any advantage to you, but I fear of considerable disadvantage—the former degrading, the other as dangerous and disreputable. The fiddle always intrusive except at frolicks—the German flute, never or seldom so. The flute is parlour music and company for the Pianoforte, the fiddle not so, besides, the fiddle is vulgar & seldom plays any thing but jigs, and you can play the flute infinitely better than the Violin. *Reform* should be the order of the day with young men who change countries or climates.

You will perceive the difficulty with which I write by my erazures and interlineations & scratchings—the effects of old age —it is so with steps and my thoughts, "non sum qualis eram." I am failing; take care my dear son that you rise.

You Francis must remember the pride and the pleasure I have expressed in the advancement & respectibility [of] my sons and daughters, my sons-in-law, and daughters in law (they are alike sons and daughters indeed to me) they all seem to have combined to lay me under obligations that I can never fully discharge; it is the consummation of my fondest hopes and highest ambition to hear of their health, prosperity & respectability—their noted attachment and love to each other as well as their filial regard to their affectionate and admiring Parents.

Adieu.

May came, the waterways cleared, and the artist's freight was on its way to New York at last. George and Clara left Utica, stopped in

Albany to see Clara's ailing brother, and George promptly fell ill himself.

Putnam wrote Francis on June 17, 1837:

My dear son,

Your letter of June 1st was received the 16th. I also received two Pensacola N Papers of 23d of May and sent one of them to Mr. Dubois—we are all well at the Bend, & happy to hear that our friends at the South are all well. It is well that the trouble of the time is not as severe at P as in most parts of the U. States. The attitude your Bank has taken and sustained is noble, but I cannot but think it would have been more safe to have also suspended to save its specie, as it has been universally done in self defense.

The internal improvements at the North are all suspended and the prospects are gloomy. I hope your place may in some measure be exempted from the wide spread ruin. You will see in the papers that N York has to bear a great share of the calamity, it is hard time there indeed.

George remains at Albany, detained by a severe illness for a week, was bled twice, blistered &c, and is fast recovering. Mr. Gregory has also recovered. It is probable that G will go to the city about this time, the times will somewhat effect him but not ruin him. I have not yet heard from Henry or Dart how far the times have taxed them. Eliza has written but is silent on that subject. I have been expecting a letter from James, I ardently hope that he and Richard may not be disappointed in the result of their purchases, as the public works are going on with you—you and they will see in the papers the state of things at the North, so I need not undertake to inform you.

My health has been tollerably good through the winter & I think of making a journey to N York & Phila this summer where I have some business to attend to. I still have hopes I may sell one of my places, & have finished a handsome fence inclosing the Seminary & River Bank, & Lyon has raised his new house, which improvements make the corners at this place more pleasant. The season with us is very late & backward but the crops are quite promising—no news from this place to communicate—matters and things are going on as usual, and we are anxious as ever to hear from our children from the North and South. You mentioned only that Joseph your friend is now well but did not say whether he had obtained a station for business, tell Joseph we see his parents & family very often & he should know that they express the most kindly remembrance and anxiety about him, of which he should be proud. You did not mention that Darwina had received her Pianoforte—when you write you should give me particulars about your employment. I hope you are well suited with your station. You must be so. Your happiness will depend on the character you shall sustain and the good nature you shall display toward all around you. It is all important to you to regulate yourself at all points and prepare to be useful and respected.

Here I was going on to moralize as usual; but I check myself, thinking it might be intrusive. I know my dear son, you will remember your parents, their love and their care; I know you will remember your brothers and sisters and take pride in them. you will remember also a large circle of young friends who will always be enquiring about you—respect yourself advise with yourself, admonish yourself, and acquire and enjoy self approbation.

It may be I can sell one of my buildings here, in that case I shall be ambitious to make the voyage to Pensacola, nothing on earth would be so pleasant to me as to meet my three sons next fall on the shores which my dear Julius and George & Clara have traced and described. Your mother would in the meantime be made very comfortable stationed with your two sisters in the North & take pride in my adventure.

I think there is no doubt that your brother George will do well if he is blest with health. It has been suggested by some of his friends that he should locate himself in N York and remain

there, make sale of his work to a company or *Limited* Partnership (so called) having a fire proof building erected, a price
agreed on for his Cabinet say $50,000 (more or less) owned in
shares, himself taking a good proportion of the stock, agreeing
to superintend it himself, semi-annual dividends to be made, &c,
&c.[6] It is thought this could be done & that the stock would soon
be subscribed to be paid by instalments. This it is thought would
save him a good deal of trouble and make him at once
independent and as reputable as to travel and lecture. I have
written to him on the subject which I am inclined to approve, he
will think of it and best judge. He has been winter bound, &
hindered by accident & sickness so that he has not been able to
lay up money as yet, & the pressure of the present time such as to
depress his career, but I am assured by himself and Clara that he
has not in the mean time been idle, he has availed himself of the
opportunity of finishing and retouching his portraits, landscapes,
sketches, groups, &c to the best advantage, & which he thinks on
the whole, to have been absolutely necessary. Clara thinks so too,
—in one of her letters from Utica she says she wishes I could
take a peep at him in his painting some day to see his dexterity
with his brush & the effect of his re-touches, particularly of his
landscapes and unfinished groups, from morn till night—in the
evenings in his chamber with his pen preparing for the publication of his book of travels often until midnight—her task being
to copy his letters which have been published.

I have had the satisfaction of seeing his works at Utica as well
as at Buffalo, and the extent of his well earned popularity, and
proudly felt the *"orna moi."*

I wish when you write, you would generally write to me, and
your young friends will all hear of you, for they enquire often.
Oliver Trowbridge has been absent this 3 months with his
lumber & will not perhaps return this month to receive your
letter. It makes you considerable postage; when you write to me,
write fine and fill your sheet, but dont pay the postage. . . .

---

[6] This "idea" sounds like something hatched in Putnam's brain.

My love to James, Richard, Abigail, Darwina & the dear children and to your good friend Mr. Dubois.

Your affectionate father P Catlin

Your Mother joins in sending love to all she intends writing a long letter before long.

The following is a typical letter from Polly to Francis, dated August 7, 1837:

Dear Francis

I now seat myself to write to you and acknowledge the receipt of your letter whitch came to hand a few days since, whitch gave us gret pleasure to hear you were all so well but poor James we feel verry uneasy about him, but we must hope for the best.

our health is as good as usual at this season of the year we have great reason to be thankfull that we are spared to hear from our dear children once more

since I began this letter your Father received one from you whitch gives us good news I hope we shall all be thanful to that kind hand that supports us we give you great creadit for your attention to your business but you must take care of your own health and take time to rest I feel verry uneasy about you in that hot climate you have been so well, you must be carefull of your diet and of going in the water your friends will tell you what you must doe better than I can, we are all plesed to hear that our friend Joseph is now in business with you and that you all keep together you are a little band of brothers and sisters in a far country from those you love and you must not seperate but be happy every day. you cannot conceive my der Francis what pleasure it gives us all to hear you and Joseph are well and so pleasantly situated we saw a letter from Darwina to a friend speaking of you and your friend and your room we was mutch pleased.

you say your head is not well use the scotch snuff it is often recommended we heard Richard was feeble but I hope not we received a letter from George and Clara a few days since they

113

are in Albany and seem to be in good spirits but verry anxious about you all at pensacola he will be in New York the middl of September so advised by his friends in the city, all are well at Darts and Delta in Elizas last letter she said Burr was there and worked in the garden and on the farm and was verry steady he could not find work at his trade for the hard times. Theadosia is teaching a musick school in Montrose James is with Fullers at printing Eliza expected us to visit them in June but we could not leve home without some one to take care but now we are provided for we have rented the front room and bead room over the hall to Snuden so we can leve when we please they are verry kind and helpfull to us I am mutch pleased with the arrangement if we are sick we shall not be alone and it is more cheerfull and takes my mind off from lonesome and gloomy feelings we calculate to go in September if we are well I dont know but your Father will trye to meet G in the city if so I must get company to go with me and little Elizabeth who has been with us since last winter.[7] you must not expect to see your Father this fall. you mentioned in your letter a visit from me but I took it as a compliment for you know you could as well get me up to the moon as to pensacola we can not get to our dear children but they must come to us. we just received a letter from Eliza they are all well but Mary Hartshorn is sick coming home from meeting on the Sabbath she fell down in the road in a fit they thought for some time she was dead.

I hope we shall hear she is better if you should loos that affectionate sister you would remember her good advice to you we are all fast traveling to the grave dear Francis I hope you will spend your time in wisdoms ways dont let things of the greatest importance pass by neglected a virtuous good life is the sure road to happiness, I hope you and Joseph will improve your precious time in that way you will wish you had when you come to die. I hope you have the gospel preached with you and I hope

[7] Six-year-old daughter of Eliza.

you are regular in going to meeting, it is a strict command to keep the Sabbath day holy to enjoy is to obey.

I have no news that is interesting to give you from the Bend it seems to be a time of health, your friends are always enquiring after you, tell James and Richard they highly affronted Mr. Julius Catlin when he was in Pensacola, he has wrote a flaming letter to his friends in Montrose I denied the charge at once.[8] from what I have heard of him I think he is a conceited fop. tell D and Abigl I long to see them. I hope they will write to me and give me all the particulars, oh how I should delight to take you all upon surprise but that cannot be I hope if you all live untill another summer and we live that some of us will meet again if your health shuld seem to fail there you must come home.

tell Joseph he cannot immagine the deep feeling and interest there is in his fathers family as well as ours in receiving sutch good letters as soon as one gets a letter the other knows it. so you see how it goes here. I shall never forget Joseph for his kindness and brotherly feelings towards you you must continue like brothers and doe all the good you can for each other. Give my love to Richard and James tell them I hope I shall live to see them again, tell Antonett she must write me a letter and let me know how she likes the Southe tell the little boys I often think of them and want to see them, they must be good children my love to little Caroline, she must be a fine little lady.[9]

our family consists of four we keep no boy a girl of thirteen helps me doe the work and goes to school, in this there is a saving, it has been hard times in this Country, but we have had a plenty and helped some of our neighbours. we have too large gardens filld with vegitables and looks finely.

---

[8] Julius Catlin (Putnam's cousin).

[9] James had three children in 1837 (Antoinette, James, and Caroline). Polly had so many grandchildren that perhaps she was confused when she wrote of "the little boys."

Langly took the Great tavern Stand at the bend but has sold out to a man at the point he wanted to get the big house but your Father would not Consent to it. Mr. T. Saylour lives with Cottston ever since the Great Lawsuit with Lusk he has been confined to his room I think he will not live long.

tell Joseph Emroy is well the young ladies often come to see us I suppose to hear something from the boys as we say. I must come to a Close for I am sure you will be tired of reading sutch a scrall of imperfection dont let any one see this letter. love to all   your most affectionate Mother Polly Catlin

A quick sketch of the Catlin family

PUTNAM CATLIN often spoke of his "interesting family." Of the fourteen children born to himself and Polly, seven were living in 1837. Henry, the eldest, was forty-six, and Francis, the youngest, twenty-two.

Henry was a man of good intentions, but Lady Luck was constantly tripping him up. His flyer in land speculation took his last cent, and from then on he would be trying to reach the bottom rung of the ladder again. He was gentle, good-tempered and honest, but allergic to work and with a somewhat sluggish mentality. His later letters are most amusing, but they were not meant to be funny. Henry was a very serious man.

George, five years younger, possessed the qualities Henry lacked. He was keen, self-confident, and extremely ambitious. With complete assurance as to his capabilities he steamed ahead, certain of reaching his goal. His letters show deep affection for Eliza. It was Eliza he called when Clara lost her first child, and it was she with whom Clara so often stayed when he was traveling in Indian country. George showed his fondness for Henry by helping him financially whenever possible, but James seems to have been his favorite brother after Julius died. Whenever George was in Pensacola he stayed at his home; James was extremely fond of this brother with his sharp wit and endless tales of adventure.

James had always been a hustler. It had taken him some time to settle down, but he was now content. Perhaps there were times when he wished he could have had a little fling at painting, but with Abigail and three children to look after, he kept his mind on his business and was now a highly respected citizen. Besides being cashier in the Pensacola Bank, he was also half-owner of the Smith and Catlin Drug Store, which advertised everything from Dr. Jayn's Expectorant, Tonic Vermifuge and Hair Tonic to paints, perfumery, fish hooks, and Japanese lanterns.

Richard was a young Putnam except that he had the gift for making money, which his father certainly lacked. He was developing a keen financial mind, and a nose for smelling out values, both in land buying and in trading on the New York Stock Exchange. In another ten years he would be a wealthy man. Like his father, Richard conformed to the conventions and rules of genteel behavior, with no desire to change them. He was handsome, cultured, polite and proper, with a charming wife and a beautiful home, accepted by the best people. Richard was well aware that he was a successful young man, and enjoyed bragging about his assets to his brother Francis, who, although only five years younger, didn't have a penny to his name. One good thing can be said of Richard: he was very kind to Henry. He and Darwina helped to bring up many of Henry's numerous offspring. Still, all things considered, Richard was rather stuffy.

Francis was the family problem. Putnam wrote him: "I have, dear Francis, been lately told by several persons well acquainted with you: 'Indulge no fears about Francis, he will soon have sowed his wild oats; he has talents and a good nature & will be sure to take a proper, stern resolution, and not lag behind either of his brothers.' " Francis was like a recalcitrant puppy: he didn't want to stay in the back yard, or in any yard with a fence around it. He looked up to his brother George who had managed to climb over to freedom, but he did not have anything like George's paint brush to help him out. All he could do was pull off a few palings and peek at the greener grass on the other side.

Francis had many of George's characteristics. He had the same genial disposition; the same colorful personality that brought him friends. He loved fishing and hunting, anything connected with the great outdoors. Like his brother, he had a fine sense of humor, which no doubt came from their mother's side. But he had no special talents or abilities—he was just a likable young vagabond who had no thought of tomorrow, and cared less.

Judging by their letters, Eliza had far more character than her sister Mary, who seems to have had a mousey personality. Mary's letters are extremely boring; she chewed on one subject until it was in rags. She was forever quoting from the Bible—it's too bad she couldn't have applied some Biblical precepts to herself. Her attitude toward her only sister showed a distressing lack of Christian charity. Eliza later wrote that Mary's letters took all the joy out of living.

One feels that of all her brothers, George and Francis were Eliza's favorites. She had been a spirited girl, and had she been a boy, she too would have wished to break away from the straitlaced, uncompromising past. Her life had been mapped out in her youth by the dictates of an age in which a good woman could have but one career: the home. To attempt anything beyond this sphere would blacken her name. It was a stifling age for a woman with a good mind and ambition. If a girl couldn't catch a husband, the only one road open to her was to become a baby sitter and diswasher in the home of a relative. Eliza's strength of character was fully brought into play when financial disaster struck her family. She did not call for smelling salts. She met the trouble head on.

Altogether, Putnam did have an interesting family.

A Wild West show in New York

GEORGE CATLIN had the usual optimist's faith in himself and his undertakings. The years from 1830 to 1837 had been hard going; his ventures into Indian country were fraught with danger and extremely expensive, but he never gave up. Had he stayed with his portrait work he no doubt would have lived a life of ease and luxury, but fortunately for the coming generations the Fates steered him onto the thorny path.

George was the personification of two of his father's pet words, *perseverance* and *determination,* and they never left him, even when the sky was blackest. Adventurer, showman, egotist that he was, he knew his crusade for the red man was a worthy one, and he never abandoned it. Each year spent among them strengthened his early belief that the Indian in his natural habitat was of an honorable race.

Now he was prepared to tell the skeptical East the truth about these proud people who had been his friends, who had never lifted a hand against him. He had an enormous collection of their artifacts— from tipis and beautifully decorated tribal costumes to simple implements and utensils. He had hundreds of portraits from the forty-eight tribes he had visited; paintings of villages, buffalo hunting, tribal dances, and religious ceremonies. These he would exhibit throughout the East, and with his persuasive speaking show how these people had been misrepresented by those who, from greed for land and money, called all Indians ignorant, evil, filthy savages.

The Indians had been called savage and warlike because they dared to fight for the land that had been theirs for generations. They were called liars and thieves. Never in all his years of travel had Catlin found this true. They believed in retaliation, but never harmed a white man who had been honest with them. General Clark made a similar statement. The Indians had first welcomed the white men and trusted them, considering them wiser than they. Treaties were made—kept by the red men, ignored by the whites.

Catlin found tribes living near the frontiers and settlements, and thus in contact with the white men, degenerate in both morals and constitution. Not so with the strong, healthy and clear-eyed Indians west of the Missouri. These were the people for whom he was fighting, and would continue to do so all his life. Though some writers speak of his purely altruistic conception of the red men, they often forget his over-all goal: to picture them for future generations and to have fairer laws enacted for these children of the forests and prairies who still roamed in comparative freedom. Perhaps he omitted that which was detrimental to the Indian character. He saw more good in them than bad. Here is his Indian Creed, written in 1868 in answer to the critics who spoke of him as "Indian loving Catlin":

I love a people who have always made me welcome to the best they had.

I love a people who are honest without laws, who have no jails and no poorhouses.

I love a people who keep the commandments without ever having read them or heard them preached from the pulpit.

I love a people who never swear, who never take the name of God in vain.

I love a people who love their neighbors as they love themselves.

I love a people who worship God without a Bible, for I believe that God loves them also.

I love a people who have never raised a hand against me, or stolen my property, where there was no law to punish for either.

I love a people whose religion is all the same, and who are free from religious animosities.

I love the people who have never fought a battle with white men, except on their own ground.

I love and don't fear mankind where God has made and left them, for there they are children.

I love a people who live and keep what is their own without locks and keys.

I love all people who do the best they can. And oh, how I love a people who don't live for the love of money! [10]

Putnam spent the month of September, 1837, in the East, and wrote to Francis on October 16, shortly after his return to Great Bend:

My dear Son

Although I wrote to Richard a few days since (and writing to one is writing to all) your Mother is every day teasing me to write to Francis, which you will allow is a sufficient apology though I have nothing new to inform you. In my letter to Richard I spoke of my pleasant journey of 4 weeks. I can only say we are all well and preparing for another winter & I have got rid of the cold I took in New York.

George has been so engaged that he has not written me since I left him, nor has my newspaper said much of him, only that he has lectured 20 evenings successively at Clinton Hall, up to the 10th instant, and commences the next evening in the *Stuyvesant Institute* for a few evenings, after which he will spread his works in a Gallery for visitants. I have learnt by our neighbour MCIntosh, who attended his lecture on Friday evening the 6th instant when he had a full House about 400 and understood it was so the preceeding evening. The three first evenings did not average more than 60, and as he continues lecturing, I apprehend he is doing tollerably well in these hard times, he rented the Clinton Hall at 10 dollars per evening. The best of it is, that he has been able to lecture so many evenings without exausting

---

[10] *The George Catlin Indian Gallery*, Annual Report of . . . the Smithsonian Institution, 1885 (Washington: The Institution, 1886), p. 739.

himself, and is fond of it. I shall hear more particularly within a few days. . . .

Your affectionate Parent
Putnam Catlin

George Catlin opened his New York exhibit at Clinton Hall in September, 1837, and in October moved it to larger quarters, the Stuyvesant Institute, on Broadway. Admission was fifty cents, and nightly lectures accompanied the exhibit.

Crowds filled the room; nothing like this had ever been seen before. There was no photography until some years later, and the West was a fanciful country of each one's imagination, populated by savages living on land said to be unfit for white habitation. With his paintings and lectures George was able to change their way of thought. Bernard DeVoto wrote: "Among the 494 paintings which the gallery contained in 1837 were the first portraits of Plains Indians ever made in their own country and the first pictorial representation of the far West . . . his landscapes are the first pictures of the upper Missouri country, or any part of the far West. In his pictures Americans could see for the first time portions of the country which, by 1837, was exercising an exceedingly powerful influence on the national imagination." [11]

Catlin's portraits showed intelligent-looking Indians—not what the audience expected. They gazed with awe at the beautiful costumes of soft, white dressed skins, which George had brought home to show how the "savages" clothed themselves. His landscapes were mediocre, but they were pictures of the unknown West, and therefore sufficient. Here were softly sloping prairies, lush with foliage; great herds of buffalo, deer and antelope; wide rivers and winding streams, green fields and groves of trees. The landscapes were not well done technically, but good or bad they depicted a country the people had heard about but never seen. Regardless of later and better paintings

---

[11] Bernard DeVoto, *Across the Wide Missouri* (Boston: Houghton Mifflin Company, 1947), p. 393.

of the upper Missouri, these "firsts" became indelibly printed in the mind's eye, were the basis for songs, poems, and stories, copied over and over again. In his paintings of Indians and buffaloes, George Catlin showed the master's touch.

George's lectures describing his paintings and telling of the western Indians, brought both praise and skepticism. Those who had always felt a kindliness toward the red men were with him, and their former opinions were greatly strengthened by his vivid descriptions of Indian life on their home soil. Those against the natives doubted much of what Catlin had to say; all Indians were alike, none of them any good.

The religious ceremony of the Mandans, the O-Kee-pa, was questioned by many. They didn't believe such a rite was practiced by any tribe, and if it was, a lone artist would not have been allowed to witness it! George had an affidavit signed by J. Kipp, agent of the American Fur Company, L. Crawford, clerk, and Abraham Bogard, testifying that they had witnessed the ceremoney with the artist, and that his paintings faithfully represented the ritual, but die-hards declared that Catlin had made up the whole thing to draw attention to his exhibition, the Mandan tribe having been practically wiped out recently by the smallpox.

The exhibition continued to draw. At first the New York papers were noncommital, but soon they were speaking highly of the artist and his tremendous accomplishment. George now felt that his years of hardship had been well worthwhile; his big dream coming true. Congress would buy his paintings as the nucleus of a National Museum, there would be a fair and decent policy for the Indians, and he could further his idea for a large park in the great West, where the Indians and buffalo could live in freedom forever.

In the latter part of December, 1837, Putnam made a four-week "journey." Perhaps some business called him to Philadelphia, but no doubt the desire to see how George was getting along took him on to New York. He was gone over Christmas—evidently Puritan Putnam saw no reason to delay his trip to spend that day with his wife.

Polly did not date her letter to Francis, but as she had just received one from him in which he spoke of spending Christmas with Abigail and James, her letter was probably sent around the first of January, 1838.

Dear Francis

Once more I attempt to write to you last evening I received your long and interesting letter, your father received your last to him he was just about to start a journey I was affraid he would not write verry soon and thought I would write to you. . . . my health is as good as usual your Father left us too weeks since in good health and spirits for New York and Philadelphia, you see he does not take your advice, to keep warm by the fire he has got so old he will not take advice I tried to frighten him with all my fears but that did no good but I feel verry uneasy about him. . . .

George and Clarra is in good health and I suppose walking on their high heeld shoes they have a fine little daughter [12] he is going to Phila and washington I suppose he has gone by this time. . . . you mention spending Christmas with Abigal that must have been pleasant to meet so many dear friends in sutch a far Country and among strangers, you may think that those days ware lonesome to me not one Dear Child to come in and partake with us not a relation to viset me here alone none but my family whitch consists of three beside my self Oliver and his sister and Elizabeth who is with us yet. . . . I hope you will not look at the mistakes I write so imperfect and so awkward and dont mind my stops and marks and poor spelling and poor composition so it is all poor you must look over it and not look at it I am ever your most affectionate

Mother Polly Catlin

---

[12] This letter dates the birth of George's daughter Elizabeth as sometime in December, 1837. The date is verified by Clara's letter to James' wife, Abigail, dated Boston, September 29, 1838 (see p. 138), in which she said she was thinking of weaning "Libby, now 10 months old."

Putnam himself wrote later that month:

Great Bend Jany 21 1838

Dear Francis,

Your letter of Dec 11th was received while I was absent on my journey to New York and Phila. I have received one from James since which I have replied to in my general letter to all at the south. . . . Henry is in the most unpleasant situation at this time, being at the seat of the Canada war, on the Bank just below the falls—say ¼ mile, where he must see and hear everything. It is strange he has not written me a word. Our Government is now taking rigid measures to preserve a strict neutrality. Our people on the lines, will it is to be feared, make our Country serious trouble—we should have nothing to do with Canada.

George has gone to Charleston S. C. to take the portrait of Osceola & other chiefs, there in confinement, he left N Y the 13 in a steam-packet expecting to be absent two weeks, he has directions from the Sec'try at War to take five portraits for the war department.[13] It will be important to his Gallery as it will bring thousands of visitors. I believe I wrote to James that he had two Grisly Bears in keeping at Jersey city 18 months old male & female, for which he paid 500 to the fur comp'y. He will be prepared to cross the Atlantic—he took 21 portraits of the visiting indians[14] this winter with great dispatch—his collection now is immense, and his success as an artist and enthusiast complete everywhere. In which we will take pride. I am proud

[13] The first of January, 1838, George had cause to close his exhibit in New York. There had been a Seminole uprising in the South. Chief Osceola came to the American camp under a flag of truce, but was seized and imprisoned at Fort Moultrie. The chief was very ill at the fort, and died shortly after George returned to New York, but the artist was able to paint an exceptionally fine portrait of the great warrior whose flag of truce was not respected. George never forgot this gross injustice.

[14] Kee-o-Kuk, chief of the Sauks and Foxes, and several relatives.

and thankful to hear that you have full employment *prenes gardez vous, tout les temps.* You cannot expect a better situation I think.

The season with us continues to be very mild. Your mother is in good health and loves to hear me speak of you. Burr is with us now and has been with us 3 weeks, he is a noble looking fellow has a good disposition and is more than 6 feet high. . . .[15]

It will please all of you to learn that I have full confidence in the successful career of your brother George—you can hardly imagine the splendor of his Gallery as exhibited in N. York, it appears now to be double the extent it had at Buffalo & he is ambitious to enlarge it still. I have never been acquainted with a man more popular than he is among all classes—you should often visit James and Richard & their family, and think of the pride I have as a Parent. I shall take special care to preserve my life until I can meet my dear sons once more. I trust you will avail yourself of the favourable opportunity you now have of making friends among strangers and establishing a reputation among the worthy. . . .

I remain dear Francis your affectionate Parent

Putnam Catlin

At the 1837–1838 session of Congress, the purchase of Catlin's Indian collection came up for discussion, only to be set aside. George

---

[15] Although their children were far from home, Putnam and Polly were seldom without a grandchild or two. Burr, Charles' oldest son, was now with them. Putnam was concerned about him; he was too fond of parties and pretty girls. Burr was twenty-one, just two years younger than his uncle Francis, and he wrote the latter on March 7, 1838: "We had seven parties here week before last—such a gitting upstairs you never see (instead of Parties they are called Trains here)— Lucy McE. is almost blind with love eyes—good gals to train with here—Allen has started a new tavern over the river between the Thompson place and the Indian sign it is called Eagle Hall, we have a great quilting party there this week friday I expect by appearances it will be a tall one—Trowbridge's Bucks & Newmans Gals are all in fine order—Dimon's gals are hearty & rugged. . . ." Just a newsy letter to a pal, with no Puritan inhibitions.

was disappointed, but he had received too much praise for his exhibit to be downhearted as yet. From the above letter George was even then considering displaying his work in London if Congress showed no interest in it.

Putnam wrote Francis on March 18, 1838:

. . . It is snowing fast now, the snow is deep & the river not broken up, and some danger that our bridge will go down this spring. Matters and things are as usual in this place. Hartshorn had while here, the good fortune to sell his house in Montrose to Ward for $1500. I do not yet find a purchaser for the Bowes House. Your brother Henry has got tired of Niagara & is inclined to return to the waters of the Susq'h. The pressure of the times has much embarrassed him, has left his house at Niagara & returned to Lockport with his large family and out of business, he has been unfortunate. I dont know how Mr. Dart will get through his difficulties. The times have not yet become better at the North—Business is very dull we hope for better times, the foolish insurrection in Canada has not succeeded our men on the lines have been checked. The affairs at Washington are somewhat of better aspect but uncertain.

George wrote me 10 days ago he should move from N. York to Phila or Washington with his Gallery & his family. He was fortunate to get the portrait of Osceola just before his death, he has made a perfect Lithograph of him on stone at full length 26 by 20 inches which is well spoken of which are struck off and circulating which will be profitable to him. He mourns the dreadful destiny of the indian tribes by the small pox, which report is verified, but unquestionably that shocking calamity will greatly increase the value of his enterprize & his works, and I think he will be able to give his friends a good account of himself. James and Rich'd each have good stations and doing our family credit.

You my dear Son have been fortunate in regard to station and I will not entertain fears as to your success. . . . So long as you can enjoy health at the south it is far better to continue there two

or three years than to leave your employment and come back to
the Bend a place so unpromising to young men of enterprise.
. . . Love to all

I am dear Francis your affectionate Father

P Catlin

I write blunderingly & do not look over & correct mistakes which
you will excuse. We are satisfied you will not forget your parents
but bear for us the most regard.

Francis decides to go to sea

THE EXCITEMENT of being far from home soon wore off for
Francis. Being stuck at the Navy Yard seven miles from the bustling
little city of Pensacola wasn't exactly his cup of tea. He wasn't having
any fun, and Joseph wouldn't spend any money—just wanted to save
it. Discipline was strict, and Francis thought one of the officers
needled him unnecessarily. Francis evidently suggested to his parents
that he come home. Not finding them agreeable to the idea, he
decided that it might be exciting to go to sea, and wrote to his brother
in Pensacola.

James answered the letter on April 22, 1838: "I consider it a very
bad plan to keep changing one's business, for my own experience has
taught me the truth of the old adage about the 'rolling stone.' If you
can consistently remain at the Yard I think you ought to do so.
Richard thinks as I do, and so do your sisters here, and I am confident
that Father and Mother would greatly lament the change you
propose, and I think you should get their consent before you go on
shipboard. You perhaps know the dread that Mother feels about the
sea, and I should really be afraid that it would make her perfectly
unhappy were you to do such a thing without first appraising them of
it, and obtaining their consent. . . ."

So Francis wrote his parents, as James suggested. The following letter is their answer.

Great Bend May 4th 1838

My dear Francis,

Your letter post mark'd 19th April had a quick passage. It gave us great pleasure to learn of your health and your fond recollection of Home. And it found us well. I know that our health and comfort will be the great desideratum with you while so distant from Home. I therefore commence an answer to your letter without delay. It is the least I can do. Your mother urges me often to write, & she is every day speaking of you with tenderness and tears.

She is of course startled at the thoughts of your going to Sea on any account, it would make her unhappy, and I hope you will have no occasion to leave your present station which we think is quite a respectable one, and so far congenial with your constitution, which is of great importance. Aaron Catlin the brother of Lynde Catlin went to St Domingo on business of his bro—but died of the [fever] on his first Voyage, much lamented, he was an accomplished young man, and much lamented, he was about your age.

It would give us pain to have you leave your circle of friends and kindred at Pensacola and go among strangers and further from home, & perhaps expose yourself to unmerciful fever. You can easily get along with your Officer, pleasantly I am sure, if you will take a little pains, and that I think should be your policy. we have sometimes occasion to "stoop to conquer" never mind trifles,—Officers will feel and exercise Authority—it is a matter of course, be careful and precise & it will do you no harm.

George is at Washington, & has been there two weeks with his Collection, & will be leaving it about this time, or a week hence, for Phila & N York. I had a letter from him this week, I find he begins to be tired of Exh'n & Lecturing, it becomes painful &

129

slavish & keeps him in constant agitation, & takes up every moment of his time, and deprives him the use of his pen and brush; nor is he certain that his receipts will much more than meet the necessary expenses. He has been advised by his friends not to go to Europe but to sell his Gallery to our Government to be placed at the Capitol at a reasonable price. While at Washington, if there is a disposition in the Government to retain them, he will know it before he leaves the city. It will be for his credit & fame if the Government should take them off his hands, & let him return to his eazel and his brush & domestic comfort. It would certainly take off his shoulders an immense load, and make him at once independent enough. I think so, and have written to him advising not to reject a reasonable offer from the Government. He will probably know before he leaves Washington what course he is to take & will let me know.

Last winter while at Paterson I contracted to purchase the remaining *unsold land*s in Brooklyn [16] &c of Miss Mary M Wallace about 1800 acres, the payment of purchase money to be made in three equal annual instalments from the 1st of Octo next with interest from that time. I consider it a safe purchase at all events, and will occupy my mind and keep me for a while busy to the advantage of my health & spirits. I have it on moderate terms, about 5/ per acre, as lands here are going in large tracts. . . .

Dudley Gregory Esquire is elected Mayor of Jersey City, which is right, for he is very worthy. I had a letter from Clara last week she is now at her brother Walter's. Henry's son William came down this week in the stage to make his Grand Parents a visit he is I think a fine good looking and sprightly boy, Henry writes me that he has given up the thoughts of returning to live on the banks of the Susquehanna. The unfortunate change of the times last year has embarrassed Henry a good deal but I hope he will get through it and save a

---

[16] The new name for Hopbottom, Pennsylvania.

part of his property—with some aid from his brother George.
. . . Your Mother wishes me to leave a little space for her pen.
Love to all.

Your affectionate Father
P Catlin

My dear Francis

your letter has just come to hand we are pleased and thankful
to hear that you are well, but your letter gave us a great shock,
we cannot think for a moment of your leaving your friends at
Pensacola and going still father from your parents into unknown
lands doe my Dear Son think of all the inconveniences of it and
I am sure you will give it up. your officer may yet become your
best friend but you must bear and forbear and stoop some time
you may if you leave get into worse hands you must to doe well
keep a steady course and not to change often, if you cannot live
withe the man get some other place, but dont leave Joseph and
your brothers I am in low spirits this morning to hear sutch news
your sisters and all are informing us of your doing well, and all
are pleased I must close I hope when you remove it will be to
come home Dear Francis I shall not give up my hold on you
love to Joseph and youre self

your affectionate Mother P C

Francis remained at the Navy Yard—for the time being.

George receives praise but no offers

E L I Z A and Anson Dart now had six children. The eldest, George,
was seventeen. Eliza was a contented woman, happy with her family
and many friends. She still hoped that Anson would be able to

arrange his financial affairs so as to enable them to keep their lovely home in Utica. Her following letter to Francis was mainly written to give him information about a mutual friend.

Utica May 1838

Dear Brother Francis

After so long a time I have got snugly seated at my table to answer your letter, which gave me so much pleasure, it being the first long letter I ever received from you. I hope (if we must be separated) I shall have many such letters to lay up in my letter drawer. We are all well, and I trust very thankful, for such a blessing—Anson is very much hurried with his farming business —the season being so backward. George counts one man, Putnam and Richard one. we have one man to work in the garden and eight on the farm, if you were here you would think we drove business. We are hourly expecting Father and Mother to make us a visit. I shall try to keep them through the summer, Mother if not Father. I suppose it will be impossible to keep Father since he has entered so largely into speculation in his old age.

We see by the papers that there is a prospect of Brother George's selling his Indian galery at Washington for 100, or 150,000 dollars this sum will pay George well for all his toil and privations, and risk of life among the Indians. Should he be so fortunate as to sell for that amount it will be gratifying to his numerous circle of relatives and friends—but especially to his Parents.

Delta has become a desolate place since we left there, there are but five families there now, that were there when you were there. . . . Asa and Mary are anxious to get to Rome or Utica, great improvements are making at Rome, as well as at Utica— we could not find a more pleasant situation on the globe than where we now are, I hope we shall be able to keep it.

. . . When you write tell me how long you think of staying at the south, what your prospects are. I am very anxious about you, as well as the rest of the family at the south. . . . Brother

Henry has a great deal of trouble with his large family and being very much indebted. I believe George has bound himself to pay quite a large amount for him. I believe he is going to farming—I think by this time you must be tired of reading my letter, so good by—all send much love to you and all the Brothers and Sisters, from your ever affectionate sister Eliza—

George Catlin's exhibitions and lectures had been well attended in New York despite competing attractions. Plays were being staged at both the Park and Old Bowery theaters, and Chang and Eng, the Siamese twins, were back at Peale's Museum. That Congress had at least discussed buying his collection had give him cause for optimism, and he was anxious to show it in Washington, where he had so many influential friends. Both Daniel Webster and Henry Clay were great admirers of the artist, and in favor of Congress purchasing his Indian Gallery as a start for a national museum. So George took the show to Washington.

Putnam wrote Francis on July 12:

. . . I have not heard one word of your brother George since the 28th of May, of course I have not been able to direct a letter to him. I fear he finds his Gallery to be a continual and tremendous weight on his shoulders. He has had at Washington as much applause as he could expect or wish, but I fear his expenses are enormous, and possibly beyond his receipts, or nearly so. I suspect that his friends have detained him in Washington with expectation the Government would make a purchase of his works; he had been intending to exhibit at Phila 3 weeks ago. . . .[17] I am exceedingly anxious to see George settle down in independent circumstances & finish his books of travels and have a comfortable home. If he should have to go to

---

[17] George went to Baltimore from Washington, where he exhibited for a couple of weeks. In late August he moved his collection to Boston. He had now announced publicly that if Congress failed to purchase his Indian Gallery he would take it to Europe, and sell it to a foreign government.

England I should never see him again. I shall probably hear in particular from him within a few days & not fail to communicate to you the results. . . .

I am sorry to hear that expenses are so ruinously high at the South, I expect James & Richard will also complain, they will, having families, learn that economy is a great virtue always— particular in these times. You ask what I should think of your changing climate in the fall or next spring and what I should advise. It remains difficult and often impossible to get into good employment here. Burr has been in our family ever since last Christmas and still remains without employ although he is a first rate workman of Saddles & bridles— he worked for Haydens, in Binghamton last fall at 19 dolls per month & board, a month or two, until he had supplied their wants & used up their materials. He seems to have no bad habits, is very ingenious, and active & very influential among our young men, but will have to leave soon, & thinks of going to Dundaff for a while.

Henry's son William 15 years old is with us this summer and goes to McCreary's school in DuBois' store room. And last week I found it necessary to take Amanda's James from Fullers printing office on account of misconduct, having had a quarrel with an older apprentice (Ed McDonald) in which he used his knife and wounded Ed in the arm, not dangerously, indeed, but has given a bad character as to ungovernable passion—So that although I have not one of my children at home or within the state, I have three grandsons, under my care in our family. It is said by Mr Jessup and others that there is the worst set of Boys in Montrose of any place they know of—Although among the adults there seems more piety and morality then in most Villages & Boroughs. . . .

We have been pressed hard by your sisters to make them a visit this summer while Clara is there but we find it impossible to leave home at present—to leave our garden, our two cows, our two horses, and our three grandchildren, though we could have a Cabin passage in the Packet boat from Binghamton to Utica—

your mother would not venture again in my travelling carriage. . . .

Your two last letters are written in a new style—handsome and ingenious I admit, but with me guess work to read them it is somewhat like a goose-track in the snow—your letter preceding the two last, imitating James hand pleased me very much. I would have you settle down and adopt that style it is so plain— your last will not be approved in bookkeeping I should think.

Your affectionate Parent
P. Catlin

P. S. You will of course let our two families in Pensacola know of our welfare and present our love to all, including Joseph, his friends are all well. . . .

Family letters

P O L L Y wrote to Francis on August 21, 1838:

Dear Francis

We have just received your letter and are happy to hear you are all well, this leaves us in tolerable health. The hot weather is verry oppressive to us your Father for some weeks has been quite feeble but I hope when the weather becomes cool he will be better but we must expect so far as we are advanced in the Journey of life to feel many new complaints, but we have great reason to be thankfull to our kind benefactor for his long continued mercies and blessings to us. we have a family now of three Grand Children a young girl to doe the work it makes us a great deel of cares and work, quite too mutch for old people. Burr seems to linger here at the Bend dont seem anyway anxious to leave I cannot tell his motive he says nothing to us, but the word is through the place that he is going to be married to Sally

Clark, what think you of this he has had advice enough from us and if he will not take it I can only say as the old woman did when her husband froze to death, she said it was his own job. I saw a letter from Theodosia a few days since to him it seems he had mentioned something to her and she gave him a close rub, What, she sayd to marry and scarsely exist. Since I began this letter James has had a call to go to Towanda and has gone. I expect to go to Utica in September if my health will admit I can now go with all ease the Packets runs every day from the point again. your Father says he cannot go with me and stay as long as I shall want to stay but can come up and return with me. I can have William and I expect a girl for Eliza, and perhaps Mrs. Dubois Josephs mother

Clarra has spent too months with Eliza, she has returned to New York and they are now on their way to Boston, and he expects to go to Philadelphia in the fall he has been disappointed in his prospects this summer.

you say you have mutch to doe I hope you will not let it injure your health you must have time for exercise. Since you have been so blest with health I hope you will take the greatest care to preserve it I hope next spring we shall meet again, if it will be for the best. I think you can find business somewhere in this country. . . .

I finish my letter in a great hurry we expect to start our journey this week four of us your Father goes and returns in three or four days give my love to all the dear children when you see them, love to Joseph his friends are all well love to your self

your most affectionate
Mother P C

I hope you will excuse this miserable letter if you can with all your learning make out to read it I shall be glad

On September 8, Putnam wrote a note to Francis: "I received a letter from George & Clara who are now at Boston, he had exhibited two weeks and stopped to spread them for a few weeks if he could get a suitable room. They speak in high terms of Boston & of friendly treatment. The hot season has been impossible for lecturing evenings. He hopes to get Faneuil Hall to exhibit in which would be a compliment to him. He speaks of going immediately to Phila on leaving Boston, from thence, bring Clara up to make us a visit at the Bend. . . . I returned last Saturday from Utica & Delta leaving your Mother to complete the visit. She will return in about 10 days. Burr is here yet, William has returned to Lockport little James to a printing office in Towanda.

"I learn that the Bank at Pen'a is doing little or nothing, & that James contemplates returning to the North, the prospects being unfavourable at P'a Perhaps Richard will be disposed to hold on a year or two, if it should please Darwina. . . ."

Pensacola was now feeling "the pressure" of the times. James had written Anson Dart to find him a suitable farm near Utica. However, he stayed with the bank until it suspended in 1840. Putnam, being a Whig, laid the blame for the depression at the door of Jackson's high-handed administration, followed by that of his hand-picked successor, Van Buren.

On September 23 he wrote Francis:

It is unfortunate that the public improvements are so suspended at Pensacola. We will hope, however, there will be a favourable chance, resulting from the approaching Election. . . .

Your brother Geo. is now at Boston, & has the favour of spreading his gallery in the famous Faneuil Hall, after having lectured two weeks in another building. He will leave Boston about this time for Phila, where he will probably remain till the meeting of Congress. It will then be decided whether he will go to Europe, or dispose of his collection in our own country. It is with him, as well as with you at the South, expenses swallow up everything. I advise him to dispose of his Gallery for a reasonable sum, take his comfort—and go to painting again. . . .

There seems to be a prospect of a change in the administration, the result of the State Elections this fall, it is thought will decide the question, but it is uncertain, for we learn that *Maine* has gone for the Van Beuren party and led the way contrary to expectation. . . . The result will, we think be all important to our country. *Clay* is the man we want for President. . . .

Burr is here yet, and like to remain, for he has unadvisably engaged to marry Miss S. Clark, which has given me much pain; he might have done well, he is a proud young fellow & has no bad habits and is must esteemed by the young people here, . . . but has I fear foolishly enlisted. . . . Give my love to all at Pensacola. Your affectionate parent   P. Catlin

Clara wrote to James' wife, Abigail, in Pensacola: [18]

Boston, Sept. 29th 1838

Dear Sister Abigail,

I feel very guilty for neglecting you so long, but now in your affliction, I can be no longer silent. I sympathise with you in the loss of your little one. It brings before me so freshly, the death of my own sweet bud. . . . I am just thinking of weaning my "Libby" now ten months old, and it is a hard trial to make up my mind to it I assure you. We are peculiarly favored in having a very healthy and good natured child. I wish you could see George acting the parental part. I often think of Mr. Dart's description of James' and Porter's nursing Antoinette and Daniel.

"Libby" will be a painter beyond all doubt, if she lives, for she has a most remarkable perception of colours and pictures. Every body says she is the image of her father, and of course she is very pretty.

---

[18] By courtesy of the Missouri Historical Society.

A letter from Eliza today tells me you are going to locate near them. I am glad of it, for I shall see you once in a while. But if you stay south, I am afraid I never shall, though I long for the wings of a dove to be with you this winter.

You see we are in Boston, the Athens of America. George's reception here has been very gratifying. He lectured three weeks, to a good audience every night, although it was at a most unfavorable time, as most of the wealthy inhabitants are out of town. He was unable to find a room large enough for his collection, and from a suggestion of the Mayor, was induced to ask for Faneuill Hall, which is called the Cradle of Liberty and a most sacred edifice, with the inhabitants, and is never used for any thing but public meetings—he had little hope of getting it, but it was granted him free for a month, without a dissenting voice. His collection makes a fine show on the walls, and it elicits praise from all. He has had invitations from all the neighbouring towns, to visit them and I have no doubt he would do well for three months here. His portraits are becoming more valuable every day [page torn] number of the far western tribes, having become totally extinct, by the smallpox, during the past year. If the bill for its purchase is not passed this writer and George will probably go to Europe early in spring. That is if [he] gets ready. I am much pleased with Boston and its inhabitants. I have been treated with much kindness and friendship. The environs are beautiful, in every direction the roads are as smooth and hard as the floor and the numerous villages and country seats are perfectly beautiful.

The ladies here I find attend much to intellectual pursuits. There are lectures every day and night, upon something interesting. I have been attending lectures on Anatomy and Physiology given by a lady. She admits no gentlemen, and her manner is pleasing, and her lectures are very instructive.

I spent a very pleasant summer with Eliza, became acquainted with Mrs. Gregory and Mrs. Wise formerly of Deposite, but now of Whiteborough. I regretted that I never became acquainted with their amiable daughters whom they lost by consumption.

My paper is almost filled, and I must be brief—I hope you will write, as soon as you are able. Tell James he must not wait for George to write, for his time both night and day is so continually taken up, that I see him only at meals and late at night. He joins me in love to you all.

Very Affectionately your sister
Clara

On October 15, Putnam wrote Francis:

I ardently hope that the prospects at Pensacola will be more favourable by next spring and that the public works and the Bank will prosper. I have had occasion to think much of Pensacola—Julius was my first emigrant, then Geo & Clara, then James & Rich'd with their families then yourself and Joseph. . . .

"My children were once assembling at Delta but have scattered—next to Pensacola—where am I to meet them again? I find myself incapable of advising or directing them. I trust they will judiciously decide on the best course and take care to do well and make me a fair Report.

I have not heard a word from George this six weeks. I suppose he is still at Boston or in some other New England city & will shortly be at Phila—from thence make me a visit. I hope he has not gone to England as suddenly as he left us at Buffalo.

Love to all *prenez guardez vous*

Your affectionate father
P Catlin

Polly wrote to Francis on November 16, speaking of James' plan to buy a farm in the North, and Richard's saying that he would leave the South in a year or two, "so I think all my Dear Children will again come to their own native land."

Polly was in a good writing mood that day. After listing all the deaths in the town, and those about to die (which gave her a good opportunity to question her son on his morals, and inform him of his closeness to the pearly gates), she got down to the news:

> Burr left us last week for Philadelphia to find work for the winter I expect he calculates to return in the Spring and get married strang infatuation. . . . we received a letter from Theadocia She is in Germantown near Philadelphia . . . it will be so pleasing to her to meet her brother and her uncle George and Clarra who are now on the way to the City whare he will exhibit as soon as they pay us a visit I shall expect them next week George has got quite tired of traveling with his pictures he hopes to sell them this winter. . . . I paid my children a long and good visit Mr. D situation is beautifull mutch more pleasant than Delta I found them all well and left them so.
>
> Mr. McCreary was ordained last week Mr. Page has left for good and no one is sorry. . . . in your letter you wished me to let you know what kind of a lady your correspondent was I cannot give you any information untill I know who she is. I expect to know when you come home there was a tell for Burr this summer that is that all the catlins that married their wives had to work to maintain them So you must take care and lay up money But I presume you are not as far over the dam as Burr is I believe it gave Burr a start. . . .

For the reader's gratification, Burr did not marry Miss Sally Clark.

Family correspondence

JANUARY, 1839. The winter, as usual, was a bad one: George visited his parents for a couple of days, and wanted to bring Clara and the baby but the "extremity of the seasons" prevented. Putnam wrote to James on January 4:

> Geo had intended exhibiting in Phila, and going twice there, could not engage a suitable room, all having been engaged for the season, he has procured a room in N York, not for exhibition, but for the purpose of finishing some of his works that require it, and take some leisure to write what he has long promised the public; so that he will be fast spending money, instead of laying up. It is very doubtful as to his selling his works to the Government.
>
> Our prospect of having a rail-road here is not very fair, you will have heard of the shameful insurrection at our Capitol, it is like the Canadian Sympathizing, hardly over yet—the agrarian spirit spreading more or less through Penn'a, & it is feared our public works will not be happily sustained. I have partly contracted to sell the white house and 4 acres to a young Baptist Clergyman for 2000 dollars, and he is here preaching, but it is doubtful whether he will be able to succeed. I shall know by the first of March.
>
> We have had a protracted meeting in this district by the Presbyterians within these two weeks of considerable consequence. It was got up without much exertion and fully attended from day to day with strict attention, solemnity zeal and influence by all denominations, and free-thinkers amongst the rest; & those who were prone to scoff, remained to pray—the whole population pressd in from day to day. Throughout the ten days, the Meeting house was filled to overflowing; and never was seen such order, attention and solemnity on such an occasion. The Rev'd McGraves of Honesdale was the Orator, and with great regularity delivered three sermons every day. . . .
>
> We were anxious to hear of the safe arrival of the Ship Russel Baldwin and its Passengers. We now rejoice that our friends arrived safe and in good health and spirits notwithstanding the

risk, the suffering and wreck of that Vessel—and we strongly hope the results of that peculiar voyage may be favourable and blessed. . . .

I flatter myself that Francis will have improved his manners and formed good resolutions, that will govern him through life and will render him useful and happy. As an affectionate parent, I send love to all around you. . . .

Putnam Catlin

Should Francis be superceded at the Naval Yard, I will hope he may find employment near you. I cannot think of his going to N Orleans, the Grave of northern emigrants, 'sed nulli vestigia retorsunt.' [19]

Putnam wrote to Francis on April 15, 1839:

My dear Francis,

Your letter of March 25th was received with great pleasure last evening. Your parents have been anxious about you, and abundantly thankful that Divine Providence has blessed you with continued health for so long a time. . . . You have had an opportunity of forming good manners and habits in the station you now occupy, and I trust you have formed resolutions as to character and merit which will benefit you through life. It is painful for Parents and children to be separated so distant and so long; but we have had the privilege of corresponding, and ever

---

[19] Francis had stayed with his clerkship at the Navy Yard, but expected to be replaced in the spring. His restless mind skipped from one new venture to another. He wanted to go to New Orleans, but apparently his father's remark about "the grave of northern emigrants" helped dissuade him. Another idea was to erect a sawmill on the Perdito River, about fifteen miles away. Putnam said the very name of the river seemed adverse and uncomfortable. Francis then wrote James about growing Japanese mulberry trees. James told him it would be hard work and expensive. Francis remained at the Navy Yard until fall, and then went back to Great Bend.

since the death of dear John we have heard the echo, the distant echo, *'all's well.'*

I hope my life may be spared a few years to meet my children again, & see them in property, & for that purpose I shall study to preserve my health by cheerfulness and moderate exercise. I go often to Brooklyn and Montrose in my easy carriage, with careful Jack [the horse], attending to my unsold lands, then return home and arrange my papers and accounts, & write letters; for two years past I have come into the habit of using the flesh-brush from head to foot just before I go to bed, sometimes also in the morning. Of late I have another course that is walking in my long hall, walking briskly for an hour, whistling revolutionary tunes and keeping time with the music, & sometimes dancing partly, which I find to be good exercise. I have no relish for visiting & have few calls except on business. George writes to me often, Henry writes sometimes, stating to me his difficulties and embarrassments arising from the pressure of the time and difficulty of selling his costly building. George has paid about 1800 dolls to Henry's judg't creditors to save the building & taken a deed of the same for his security. Henry is honest and industrious, but unfortunate in his calculations and has a numerous family of children, that render him no help.

George is now in Phila exhibiting in a fine building and lecturing. The Editors give him great applause. I have sent you one of their papers—he calculates going to england in the Fall of the year. Burr is with him & very active, discovering a taste for painting all at once, so says Oliver Trowbridge who went down the Delaware on a raft and has returned—saw his paintings, &c. Every one advises George to go to England without hesitation saying he will make a fortune without fail. I had however wished he had sold to our Government for a moderate price.

. . . We have got through a hard winter comfortably, having a convenient wood house adjoining the kitchen, filled with all sorts of fuel, & a Franklin Stove in the middle room which your mother is pleased with, as it is placed several feet from the chimney with a very large pipe which warms the room. The spring has commenced, the ice gone out of the river, & the bridge saved. . . . Your affectionate father P Catlin.

George says farewell to America

FRANCIS received a letter from his father, dated June 7, 1839, with the information that Anson Dart had just received the commission of Construction Superintendent of the Lunatic Asylum being built near his home in Utica. It was to be the largest building in the United States. The letter continued:

Your brother George is still in Phil'a. The Philadelphians have given him great applause & seem determined to prevent his voyage to Europe. I hope they may succeed, and I think they will, he has offered his Collection to the Government for 60,000 dollars, which is considered a reasonable price. G and Clara are intending to make us a visit this summer & Clara is to continue with us a month or two. Your brother will within a year or less time become independent if his life is spared, he is now more popular than ever in all the country as well as in the cities. He certainly has done our family great honour, more than we could have expected. It will please James & Richard as well as yourself and all our family—he has truly laid us under great obligation to love & respect him, myself particularly. James & Richard are doing us honour. I am exceedingly thankful that my life has been spared to hear my dear children for their merit. I wish I could express to you my feelings on this subject; you will think of me and imagine what I would say, perhaps better than I can express. Your parents think & talk of you every day; you must not forget that you are our youngest.

You will have seen and learnt a good deal of the world since you left us, and we will imagine that you have improved in manners and habits and formed good resolutions to become useful and respectable in the course of your life, and now is the important time to lay your course for prosperity and happiness, and we will applaud you, continue to love you, and help you. If my life be spared another year I hope to render you some aid. In the mean time do the best you can, take great care of your health, *advise yourself*, do as you would advise a brother do that's the way—love yourself sincerely, as you would wish to be loved by a true friend—be wise, be cheerful, be true & faithful in all things, indulge pleasant hopes & be happy. . . .

I have written to George this week, but have not received his answer. I stated to him your inclination to commence business, and he will let me know what he thinks of it. He has several times offered to purchase of me the white house at the Bend and keep it in the family, rather than suffer a stranger to have it. He will not fail to visit us this summer when we shall converse about matters and things in the family line. . . .

I am your affectionate parent
P Catlin

George Catlin had dreamed a beautiful dream, but it remained no more than that. He had offered his six hundred paintings and entire collection of Indian artifacts to Congress for sixty thousand dollars, saying he would add to it, go further into the West beyond the Rocky Mountains, and paint members of every tribe on this continent before he was through, but Congress was not interested.

In his fervent efforts to get across to the people all that he felt about the Indians, George often spoke too hastily and too strongly for his own good, and thereby alienated important people. He knew he couldn't expect to get a decent government policy for the Indians unless he could convince the people that their government was treating them unfairly, and that the demoralizing influence of the fur traders would not only ruin a noble race, but would bring on Indian trouble all through the west.

However, military men who had fought Indians in the South were against any move to help the red men. The South was definitely anti-Indian, and there were too many Southerners in Congress. They wanted Western lands for slave states, and would have no glorifying of the Indians in speech or painting.

Fur traders had no intention of leaving the whiskey bottle hidden when they bartered with the Indians for their valuable furs; it was with their cheap, diluted liquor that they made their rich profits. There had been laws passed against selling liquor to the red men; in fact, since 1834 it had been illegal to take any liquor into the Indian country, but the American Fur Company, lord and master of the country, could afford to bribe any government officials who made inquiries. George spoke heatedly on this subject, for he was well posted on what was going on in the West, and in doing so made many political enemies. Votes were votes, and regardless of personal feelings, no one was going to lift his voice in favor of anything that would jeopardize his career in Washington. Catlin was called "Indian Lover," and Congress turned a deaf ear to his pleas.

When George finally announced in the summer of 1839 that since his own country didn't want it he was taking his collection to England, a storm of protest arose from the press. Congress was besieged with irate messages, and the newspapers printed angry editorials against a government which made no effort to keep such a valuable work here where it belonged. They spoke of the disgrace it would bring to this country if a foreign government purchased that which belonged to America, now and in the future. Great was their acclaim for Catlin and what he had done for the preservation of Indian culture.[20]

---

[20] *The United States Gazette:* "Mr. Catlin has accomplished a work which will forever associate his name in the highest rank of honour, with a subject that will interest the civilized world every year more and more through all coming

Regardless of the appeals from the press and many learned men in the country, Congress remained silent. No doubt there were members who were fully aware of the importance of the Indian collection to America, but they were more concerned over the next election. Politics and parsimony sent George away from his native land, not to return for thirty-two years.

Putnam was seventy-five years old in 1839, and no doubt grief-stricken at the thought of an ocean separating him from his beloved son who was so highly regarded, and whose paintings had received praise wherever shown. Putnam did not believe in quick decisions. Perhaps he had suggested to George that he go back to his portrait painting for a while—give Congress more time to think it over. He could continue exhibiting his collection in an inexpensive hall with Henry, perhaps, as overseer. Henry could explain the paintings to those who came to view them, and he would guard the place, as well. But George had made up his mind to exhibit in London.

Putnam wrote to George on November 12, addressing his letter to the Stuyvesant Institute, New York. No doubt this was the last letter George received from his father before he sailed. Putnam wrote the usual letter about members of the family, with only a paragraph in reference to his son's departure: "I trust you have fully recovered of the complaint that confined you for a week in your room. And I imagine you are constantly engaged in preparing for your voyage, but steadily and philosophically as you ought, not despairing in the least. The approaching winter will be important to you, more perhaps than any part of life. To hear of your safe arrival at London will give me

---

time. We have learned with great regret that he will certainly take his museum to England in the course of a few weeks. We know too well how it will be valued there, to imagine that it will ever be permitted to come back. . . ."

The American Sentinel: "This is the last exhibition that will be made of this wonderful collection in the United States, as it will be taken to England at once and there be disposed of. . . . We do not think that, all circumstances taken together, there has been produced in this age any work more wonderful or more valuable. . . ."

Other papers made similar statements.

great joy; I shall then not fail of entertaining the highest hopes of your final success and safe return."

On November 25, 1839, George left for London on the steam packet-boat *Roscius*. Clara, expecting another child soon, would join him later. He took along his nephew Burr, as well as Daniel, his helper for the past two years. Stored in the ship's hold were his entire Indian collection—eight tons of it—and two grizzly bears.

No doubt George watched the slowly fading shores of America with mingled excitement and sorrow—the former because he loved adventure, the latter because he had expected a last-minute call from Congress. What lay ahead of him were years of triumph and sorrow, interlaced throughout with uncertainty.

Only in later years could George Catlin's works be truly evaluated. He was not the *first* painter of the Plains Indians, but the few who had painted the red men before George steamed up the Missouri River left little of value. Harold McCracken says about our Western artists: "The first artist of real stature to go into the West for the express purpose of delineating a documentary record of the various Indian tribes was George Catlin. He covered more territory and pictured more different tribes, in greater detail, while they were still in their unspoiled primitive state than any other artist. . . . What shortcomings he may have had in artistic craftmanship are insignificant in the light of what he accomplished." [21]

Catlin's watercolor miniatures on ivory, executed during the first years of his art career, cannot be surpassed. A number of his Indian paintings show his lack of training in that his handling of anatomy and composition is somewhat childlike. However, his Indian dances disclosed a keen perception of design and rhythm. Being self-taught, his technique was his own, and he painted what he saw before him, with no "sweetening."

---

[21] Harold McCracken, *Portrait of the Old West, with a Biographical Check List of Western Artists* (New York: McGraw-Hill Book Company, 1952), pp. 47, 56.

Catlin was followed in Indian country by two artists fresh from the ateliers of Paris. Charles Bodmer, with Prince Maximilian of Wied-Neuwied, followed Catlin to the upper Missouri in 1833. Bodmer was a superb draftsman, and his landscapes far excel Catlin's, though his buffalo are no better. Another fine artist, Alfred Jacob Miller, made the land trip to the Rocky Mountains in 1837, as the guest of Captain William Drummond Stewart. Miller's watercolor sketches are lively and delightful. His paintings of the Indian country are beautiful, but being an admirer of Turner's style, he added sentimental touches. Miller's painings are less important from an ethnological standpoint than those done by Bodmer and Catlin.

Thomas Donaldson wrote in 1885: "Mr. Catlin's drawings and paintings have furnished illustrations and data for thousands of works on Indians in America. They have been modified, cut, altered, changed, but they remain Catlin's work. Authors in all lands have used them. Menageries, 'Wild West' exhibitions and theaters to this day use his 'war dance,' 'scalp dance,' and other views for advertisements, both in Europe and America. A new work is announced on the Indians, with illustrations; either Catlin pure and simple in illustrations, or modified, can be found within its covers. Thousands of stories have grown from his descriptions. It can be said with justice that no other painter or writer on the North American Indian has had so broad and wide an influence in the diffusion of knowledge of the North American Indian as he has." [22]

---

[22] Donaldson, *The George Catlin Indian Gallery*, pp. 745, 746.

PART FOUR: PALACES AND PIONEERS

1840–1842

1840: An artist in London-Town; Anson Dart is in difficulty; Clara arrives in London; Eliza prepares for the Wilderness West; News of the pioneers; London has its dull season; Eliza writes about Green Lake   1841: Francis is told what to bring to Wisconsin; Letters from London; George publishes his book on the North American Indians; News from the pioneers.

THE CLOSELY-KNIT Catlin family was scattering. The year 1840 began with George's arrival in London; it ended with Eliza, a sad Eliza, making a home for her family in the western wilderness.

London in 1840 was a city of extreme contrasts; a city of mansions and indescribable slums. The young Victoria had been Queen for three years now, and although the pattern of the Victorian age was beginning to show, much of the decadence and extravagance of the Regency years was still in evidence. It was a gay and colorful London that greeted the American artist.

To George Catlin, reared on a farm, the cities on the east coast of the United States had been the epitome of grandeur and wealth, regardless of pigs rooting for food in the streets. His first acquaintance with one of the greatest cities in the world was enough to shatter any country-boy's composure. George was completely bedazzled with London. He saw it with the eyes of an artist; the beautiful, centuries-old buildings of mellowed brick and stone. He loved the crowded streets with their hackney-coaches, gaily painted omnibuses, and private carriages. The shrill whistles of the river boats mingled with the raucous screech of the organ grinder. He watched the street cleaners with their clumsy brooms scurrying about like frightened mice to keep clear of the lunging hoofs of the horses. He admired the handsomely dressed men and women, and gave pennies to ragged beggars until he found himself nearly pulled apart by their clutching fingers. This was his first impression of London. He would get used to it, but never forget it.

George had been given many letters of introduction to people in London, but his greatest help came from the Honorable Charles Augustus Murray, recently made Master of the household to Queen Victoria, who had written George that he would give him all possible assistance when he came to London. It was he who suggested the Egyptian Hall for George's exhibitions, and he who introduced

George to the aristocracy, only too pleased to present as his good friend this cultured American artist. It was through him that the doors of London were so quickly opened to George, who was accepted thereafter for his own merits.

London was an exciting place. George's early letters home showed a boyish enthusiasm and pride. He had to "show off" a little; make the folks back home prick up their ears at what he was doing and seeing, and the "big" people whom he met.

London. 10th Jany 1840

My Dear Parents,

You will no doubt be pleased to hear from me at this period and at all other times when it may be possible for me to write to you. You will have rec'd ere this the little journal which I sent to Clara, instead of a letter, which was at that time all I could send.

I might have written you several times since that, by sailing packets, but the Steamer Liverpool being advertised to sail on the 14th of this month, I supposed her letters would reach you sooner, & therefore delayed. She is now just again advertised not to sail until the 30th & I write you this, & one to Clara also, by the Ship Roscius, the fine vessel that I came out in.

The Liverpool has been due here, from N. Y. for 10 or 15 days, & there is the greatest alarm for her safety. No packets have arrived either for some weeks, & I have not had a line from N. York since I left there—the suspense is painful to me at this critical time, beyond what I can possible describe. The news which I must get from Clara in a few days must be very cheering and gratifying or sad & heartrending to me & allmost destructive to my happiness & to the energies which I am now just making for our final welfare.[1] I will trust, however, that all is well, & that she is ere this, able to write me & encourage me.

I am now in the midst of strangers and in a few days to make my bow to the Lords & Ladies—and in the midst of confusion

---

[1] This "news" would be the birth of George's second daughter, Clara Gregory, born in late December, 1839.

and difficulties of arranging, and hanging, &c &c, you can well imagine something of my anxieties. I had great difficulty about Rooms, have got them at last, central, extravagant & fashionable —& only ones in the city that would do, for one year (could not get them for less time) Rent £550.! i.e. $2750. all other expenses heavy, but, if I get what they call a "run" these are nothing, so all tell me, if I do not, they *break* me.

It will be several days yet before I get all things arranged to invite my Lords & Ladies &c. And after I get a little agoing I shall have enough to write you and time enough, I hope too, to give you some more entertaining account. And, above all, I hope, (though I am not yet *certain*) some more flattering account of success than I have heretofore been in the habit of giving.

I shall prepare letters for the sailing of the Liverpool, which sails on the 30th—and will get to N. York nearly as soon as this will reach you.

I shall see the Queen open the Parliament in a few days, having been furnished a ticket by Lord Monteagle (formerly Spring Rice) to admit me.

May Heaven preserve the lives & secure the happiness of my Dear Parents, is my constant prayer, & will be till I again see them. adieu, Geo. Catlin.

My Rooms. "Egyptian Hall," Piccadilly, London.

Catlin's exhibit was opened to the public on the first of February, 1840. In the center of the large hall he had erected a Crow tipi made of buffalo skins and elaborately decorated. On the walls hung six hundred of his paintings depicting the North American Indians, and a great number of articles of their manufacture. His two grizzly bears were not allowed in the place, so were kept at the London zoo.

Three days before the public opening, there had been a private viewing to which the Honorable Mr. Murray had invited many members of the English aristocracy as well as representatives of the London press. Catlin had been dubious of his reception. He was not only a stranger in England, but had been told that national prejudices might hinder his success. England had not yet forgotten the Canadian border trouble in 1837. However, his pleasing personality and the excellence of his exhibit won him applause from the start.

The London press was unanimous in its praise.[2] The artist's ego and optimism were steadily climbing. He wanted to see his father; let him witness his son's success. George would be proud to introduce him to his friends, and Putnam, in turn, would have something to talk about for the rest of his days. George was expecting Clara soon—Putnam could come with her!

His next letter was a joyful one, in spite of his expenses:

London. 17th Feby 1840

My Dear Parents,

I assure you that nothing else in the world, while separated so far from you could afford me so much pleasure as sitting down to tell you how I am and how I am getting along; but of all the hurries & bustles of life that I ever was in, I assure you I never before have been in any which made it half so difficult as at present, to get the requisite time to address those whom I hold most dear to me.

You will all rejoice to hear that I am well, although almost half crazy with the bustle and excitement I have been continually under in this great & splendid City—amongst nobody but

---

[2] As quoted in Catlin's *Eight Years of Travel and Residence in Europe* (2 vols.; London, published by the author, 1848), I, 208:

The Art Union: "Mr. Catlin's collection is by no means to be classed among the ephemeral amusements of the day; it is a work of deep and permanent interest. . . . It is not a common mind that could have conceived so bold a project, nor is he a common man who has so thoroughly accomplished it."

The London Quarterly Review (I, 205): "Mr. Catlin's object in visiting England with his Indian Gallery, it would seem, is to sell his collection to our Government, and we most sincerely hope that his reliance on the magnanimity of the British people will not be disappointed . . . we submit . . . to all who are deservedly distinguished among us as the liberal patrons of the fine arts, that Mr. Catlin's Indian collection is worthy to be retained in this country as the record of a race of our fellow creatures whom we shall very shortly have swept from the face of the globe."

strangers, and those of the most difficult and particular kind to deal with. I have had the trembling excitements and fears to contend with which beset & besiege a green horn from the backwoods when making his *Debut* & his bow to the most polite & fastidious part of the whole world—I have kept as cool as possible—have pursued steadily & unflinchingly my course, and have at last succeeded in making what they call here, a *"decided hit."* i.e. I have produced, by my Ex'n & by my Lectures, which I have commenced, such an interest and excitement as has called forth from the press, of all politics, just the same general expressions of surprise and applause as I got in my own country, and all now tell me that you want but the weather to clear up and become fine to bring you what is called a "run" and that in London they say, when it begins, insures a man a snug little fortune, in spite of his teeth. I send to Clara a number of the London papers, which she will send to you after reading, & you will see what they say of me and my works here. I was invited to deliver a Lecture in the Royal Institution (the first in the world) on friday last, to commence at 9. in the evening. I did it gratuitously but with great success, and with a fuller house and with greater applause they all tell me than any man ever before received within its walls. over one thousand were in it, and at the end of every sentence, was "hear, hear," & loud & repeated cheers—which is not customary in their building. The papers as you will see give me great credit for "clearness—for emphasis, for self poss'n and all the requisites of a finished Lecturer and a popular speaker." I shall feel the benefits of it, no doubt in my second course of Lectures which commence tonight in my own Lecture Room.

My Ex'n Room is open every day, & in the same building I lecture 3 evenings in the week. The weather, since I opened has been the most unfavourable, raining every day. Yet I hope we shall have a change soon, and *I* confidently hope, that in a few days I shall be overrun with company—and my coffers filled, a little, with money. Expenses are very heavy—all hands—printing—Rent—&c—£8. per day i.e. $40.! Rent for 3 rooms £550.

i.e. 2750 dols.! But dont fear. Ill make it cheap, but I have got
to work hard for it. My expenses since I left N. York have been
already 2000. dols. Such is the way of going to work here.

I have written to Clara today—she will write to you. I have
proposed that she comes out on the B. Queen, and told her to
write at once to you to prepare. The B. Q. sails from here in 10
days from this—i.e. on the 1st of March—will be in N. York
from 14th to 31st. 15 or 16 days. She will bring you letters from
me 10 days later than this, and money to cover your expenses,
and you must not fail to come. by this arrangement you can have
25 days at the Bend after receiving this—If Francis is at home,
there is nothing to prevent you from coming—& it will be the
greatest feate & féte of my life—13 or 14 days only on the water
lands you at the wharf in London. Whether you come or not
you must write me by the Western, which will start 10 days
before the B. Queen.

By the papers you will see an account of some of the noble
Lords & Ladies who have attended my Rooms, and you will see
in them also a long account of the marriage of the Queen, & the
grand illumination. From the Hon. Mr. Murray, I got tickets to
the Palace for Burr & myself, where we had the grandest view
of the whole procession, of the Queen & all the whole magnificent retinue, passing so near to us that we could have touched
them with our finger! this grand spectacle was enough to have
crossed the ocean for alone, & I cannot describe it to you now as
you see.

I write again in a few days and give you further accounts. A
plan is concocting for getting her Majesty & Royal family to my
room in a few days. Burr is well and writes by the same vessel.

Love to dear mother & Francis.   Geo. Catlin
                                   London, 29th Feby, 1840
My Dear Father,

I wrote you by the Great Western, 10 days ago, which letter
you will have rec'd ere this. I am yet well, and making pretty
fair progress, though not getting as much *money* as I would

wish, nor as fast as I expect to in a short time, when the weather gets better & the season for such things comes on. I have just written to Clara and Mr. Gregory & enclosed $400 for hers & your passage out, & I shall positively look to the event of your arrival & to the pleasure I shall take in showing you some of this part of the world, as the pleasantest period of my life—Clara will write to you at once, as I have directed, and you will have abundance of time to get ready for the British Queen. Get no clothes, if you can avoid it till you arrive here, for they are here but just half the N. York price. to cross the Ocean is but to sit down in a fine hotel, and pass the time away in good company.

My expenses here in commencing have been very heavy, & I can yet send no money for anything but your passage out; when you return you shall take some home with you, & if you should not come I shall soon remit to you more or less as I may be able to do it—I am beginning *well* here & you need not fear the expense of your tour.

Dont fail to bring your Certificate of Revolutionary service which is in a frame in Clara's room.

Love to Dear Mother, who will certainly be proud to hear of your fashionable Tour & justify you in it. Love to Francis—tell him to keep cool—fear not—nor grieve at anything, he is young enough to do all he wants, he will take care of Mother & her flowers 'till you return.

Burr is well & writes to Theodosia [his sister].

In great haste
Your affectionate Son
Geo. Catlin

Putnam did not go to London; he did not feel that he was well enough to stand the trip. On April 23, 1840, he wrote to Clara, whose trip had been delayed because of her own father's illness:

Mrs. Clara Catlin
Dear Child,

I have been anxious for several weeks to hear from you, and should have written before this, but I was uncertain how to direct a letter, since which, Mr. Dart informs us by letter that he had the pleasure of meeting you at Albany & that the two children were well, and that you were to take passage in the British Queen the first of June. A number of occurencies have prevented you from sailing as early as your husband ardently expected—which may be all for the best on many accounts. You have had the privilege of meeting your father, so dear to you & his family, during his severe illness, and it turns out that the state of my health has not improved, & that if I had come to the city I should inevitably have been placed on the sick list. I find that my complaint is obstinate and if not immediately dangerous will be troublesome and hard to remove, it is the catarrh cough, which I have to meet with various syrups, etc—one of the misfortunes of age. Mr. Dart will be here in three or four days, we shall then hear more particularly of your Father's case, we will hope for his recovery. Abigail will we fear miss seeing you in New York, she will have taken passage about this time.

Mr. Dart will make us a short visit and start from this to Green Bay, Wisconsin, etc, to dispose of his lands in that quarter or fix a residence there with his family, & intends Francis shall be persuaded to accompany him, to be absent two or three months leaving his wife with us.[3]

There has been in Montrose within two or three weeks, a singular stir of Religion. Within four of five weeks, several young people in that vicinity have died, much lamented, & the result is that the remaining youth have principally sought religion, held meetings with great ardour & zeal, and preparing to join the Church—all the young Lawyers of that Place, merchants, clerks, students, and all the young women came forward to join the good Cause.

We shall have a great deal of anxiety about Abigail & her children, until we can hear of her arrival. Unfortunately, the

---

[3] Anson Dart made the journey to Wisconsin Territory in hopes of selling land which he owned in partnership with a Mr. Armstrong, of Rome, New York.

Vessel Escambia and its *Capt Dunham* with whom she came to the North last spring, has lately wreck'd, and all on board lost except the Mate. This she has heard, which will of course give her some uneasiness on her voyage.

Your brother writes it will be best that you go in the B. Queen and have all the comfort that can be wished in a chosen room and your voyage safe & short. You must remember that one, two, or three of your friends, & relations, could not be the means of your safety or control the winds and the waves—You will have the notice of distinguished ladies on board, who will take notice of you and keep you in good cheer & safety.

I presume you have heard from your husband within a week or two. I have not heard from him since 29th Feby, nor have I seen any notice in the papers. I trust he is well and doing well. I have some fears he will undertake to Lecture too much & weaken his lungs he ought to be careful. I need not counsel you to take care of the little girls and yourself, & meet your husband, your anxious husband as early as you can.

Mrs. Catlin, Eliza, Elizabeth and Francis send their best love. My best regards to your suffering Father.

I wish to be remembered to your Revolutionary Uncle.

I am dear Clara your affectionate father

Putnam Catlin

Anson Dart is in difficulty

WHILE GEORGE was exhibiting in the exciting city of London, life went on for the folks back home in the sleepy little village of Great Bend, Pennsylvania. Francis married Joseph DuBois' young sister, Elizabeth, early in 1840. Eliza wrote to him from Utica, New York, on February 22, 1840:

Dear Brother Francis,

Your letter came to hand when I was confined to a sick bed, where I had been for a week all of which time Anson was in Albany—immediately on his return, he was taken sick, with quinsey and disease of the lungs—he was confined to the bed and house for more than a week—he is getting better, but is much reduced in flesh, he says he can never live an other winter in this climate—he is casting about in his mind where he shall go, this summer.

If the roads had been ever so good, you see, I could not have made my anticipated visit. The snow has entirely left us, the roads are not even passable—you must not look for me untill the roads are settled or there is more snow, which is not impossible.

I am very anxious to see how you act at housekeeping—I presume by this time you have got reconciled to it, you say you have sowed all your wild *oats*. I hope the crop will yeald well, and be profitable to your through life—I highly approve of your choice of a companion—I hope your voyage through life will be a smoothe one, uninterrupted by waves of trouble. . . .

your ever affectionate sister Eliza

Following the Specie Circular in 1836, and the Panic of 1837, the company of speculators in western pine lands (which Anson Dart represented) tottered unsteadily until the spring of 1840, then collapsed. Anson Dart found himself penniless and in serious trouble. Either Dart had borrowed a large sum of money from his brother-in-law, Asa Hartshorn, or the latter had invested heavily in the venture on Anson's advice, for Asa was sadly reduced in circumstances. He blamed Anson for his loss. The friendship between the two men was shattered.

Eliza wrote that she would not mourn over their poverty if they alone were the losers; it was the thought of the good friends caught in the net that made her weep. And later Eliza wrote Clara that the subject was mentioned in every letter she received from Mary, which took the joy out of living.

Anson was now disgraced in his community; the family shunned. He would do all he could to make reparation—he could do no more. Perhaps Hartshorn was the principal loser, for Anson was not considered a criminal by the world at large, as Putnam indicated in his letter to George on May 11, 1840.

Putnam was now seventy-six years old, and his penmanship had become very shaky. He apologized for his erasures and blunders, but his mind was as keen as ever.

His letters to George are always interesting, despite occasional repetitions. He touched upon every item of interest to his son, and the two following letters from the old gentleman are worthy of being given in full.

Great Bend May 11th 1840

My dear Son

I have the pleasure to thank you for the receipt of your four interesting letters. I had certainly written to you twice and you had cause to reprove me as you had not received one from me. We have been long correspondents and affectionate ones. I am now indeed proud that you censure me on this occasion, as it assures me of your constant and filial regard, and I will not waste paper in making a longer apology. Clara writes me from Albany, that she and both her daughters were well, very well, and that she is to take passage in the B. Queen the first of June in good quarters carefully arranged by her affectionate brother, in company with one or more of her female acquaintances, of great respectability, as passengers. She could not have avoided going to see her father on his deathbed (as every one thought it to be), & to see him, as it were, "to take up his bed and walk" It was best that I did not conclude to hurry on with Clara as you proposed, as my complaint had not subsided, but followed me up, and probably will continue in some degree to the close of my pilgrimage.

I am thankful that you enjoy health, and so well received in the greatest & most civilized country on earth, I trust you will be careful of your health, but you will have to talk so continually, and I shall have fears. My continual hope is, that you will have an opportunity of disposing of your works for a reasonable sum and return to your country and friends as early as possible. In the meantime I will strive to patch up my constitution to receive you and converse with you again and with your dear family.

My family is now extremely scattered—Abigail with her five children took passage the 28th of April for Mobile. Mr. Dart with your brother Francis left this, the same day, for G. Bay & Wisconsin; Mr. Dart's object was to make sale of his lands in that Quarter, or make arrangement for moving his family there in the fall; his two eldest sons were to meet him at Buffalo on a fixed day, having the care of some furniture in boat, boxes &c. Mr. Dart had previously written to Francis to view that country and get into business there. Eliza, with little Charly, have been 6 weeks or more with us and Mr. Dart came down the 27th and remained with us only one day; he brought with him Mary, Elizabeth & Richard who will stay with us, & Francis' wife. Dart & Francis expect to return within two or three months, they will then judge whether to take their families to the west or not.

I gave Francis an 100 doll Horse, & my easy Waggon, with 100 dolls in money, and advised him to sell the horse, waggon, & harness at Buffalo for cash. In his letter from Buffalo Francis writes, all arrived there in time, & well, he had not sold his horse & waggon on account of the scarcity of money & has taken his horse & carriage on board for Green Bay, his freight paid $40 for self, horse &c. We had expected that Francis would be content to stay with us through the year, but he was anxious to get into sum business; he will never be content to live on a farm, we gave him house room & board in our family but he grew uneasy. He is certainly a good clerk & serviceman and surveyor. One time I advised him to stay with us a year & pursue his study in Mathematics, which he attended to for two or three weeks & made rapid progress; I had told him the result would be more useful to him than any of the professions. But you know he cannot bear dictation. It is uncertain at this time whether he can commence in business to advantage at the far west.

Mr. Dart has a letter from Gov'r Seward to Governor Dodge & other gentlemen in that quarter, highly commendable to Darts talent for office and usefulness in that part of the Country, and I am informed, that my early friend and acquaintance I. P. Arndt of Green Bay, is acquainted with Mr. Dart, & will remember us as his connexion, & I shall write him for his influence in their favour. I am not able to state the condition of Mr. Darts affairs; but fear it will deeply affect his and our dear friend and connection Mr. Hartshorn, in the result.

We received a letter from your sister Mary this morning on the subject fearing that all the steps taken by Mr. Dart to secure his bail Mr. H. will prove inefficient, and saying Mr. Hartshorn is anxious to see me on the subject if the state of my health will permit me to make the journey. This state of things is deeply afflictive to our family.

Eliza is in sound health and all her children are so. Mr. Dart will do the best he can to repair the misfortune, and you will probably live to see him again in prosperity, with his lovely family. I cannot express my feelings on this subject & will not dwell on it.

Francis & his wife are truly happy in their Connexion and I trust they ever be so. I received yesterday a letter from your brother Henry informing me he should start for New York the next morning for the purpose of disposing of his minerals to the best advantage he can, which will keep him employed through the summer.[4]

---

[4] Henry had always been interested in minerals. His collection apparently consisted of hundreds of beautifully colored rocks he had been gathering for years. George brought him a small collection he picked up during his travels in Indian country. They could be used as ornaments or in jewelry.

Doctor Barstow has sold his farm at Wysox for 8000 dollars and is going to remove his family to Pensacola in the fall. James & Richard are still in the Bank, which like other banks here are doing little or no business in these hard times. You will see in our papers the strong ground we have to hope there will be a Revolution in our Government and better times after our approaching Election.

You must not have too much concern about your parents. We are comfortable as usual and above the frowns and flattery of the world, & proud enough of our children and grandchildren, so dear to us. We cannot expect very long letters from you, knowing how continually engaged you must be. Clara has promised in one of her letters to be a faithful correspondent when she arrives at London & she will often send us a London paper noticing your Gallery and your prospects.

It is hard work for me to write long letters, as you will see by the interlineations and erazures. I shall write to you again within a few weeks on the subject of Darts affairs, it is certain his misfortune will amount to a complete wreck; his family is here and there. I shall hear from Pensacola and from Green Bay every two weeks, and shall write to you often; the greatest affliction with him is that his brother Hartshorn will unexpectedly be held to the amount of 8 or 10 thousand dolls, by a late decision in Law, since Dart left this, as he will learn by a letter forwarded by Asa H. We have ample room for Eliza and the children here, and admire every one of the family and must comfort them. I read last week a proud letter from our friend Burr to his sister Theadosia, it is well written & gives me high hopes of him; you will hear that his sister has become religious with all the youth in Montrose.

Your mother most affectionately joins me in sending best love

Your affectionate Parent
Putnam Catlin

Geo Catlin Esq

Great Bend May 20th 1840

My dear Son

I have this moment the inexpressible pleasure of reading your letter of 30th April. And was about setting down to write to you a long letter to go by the British Queen 1st of June. Clara will certainly go then, and be with you and study your health and happiness. I beg of you above all to take care of your health, and not expose it by lecturing; it is too labourous for you. I can not but hope you may succeed by honorable means and influence of friends to induce some Corporation or Nobleman to take the Gallery off your hands—in that case, it will require your attendance for several months to arrange & place everything in order, and to dispose of disposable other articles accompanying your Gallery; which would extend Clara's visit as long as she would wish. The British Museum would I think do well to secure your collection and let you return to us.

The weather has become very pleasant here, and crops look fine so that your favourite Bend is complimented as usual, a very large Hotel is erected in Turnpike street a few rods below the former Hotel on the opposite side, several other buildings have been erected in that quarter since you were here, also a two storied school house for an Academy, is erected on the school lot opposite your lot, the former school-house being burnt.

The State of N York has determined to go on with the N Y & Erie Rail road at all events, and have granted the present Session an appropriation adequate to the task. The Petition to our Legislature respecting this road was read & a favorable Committee appointed to Report &c, unfortunately, our Representative, Mr. Chandler, died a few weeks after at Harrisburg of the Small Pox.

The pressure of the times in regard the currency, over our whole country is very unpleasant but we get along as usual with all difficulties and feel assured we shall have a change of Administration at the fall election, Harrison will be President, and he will have the aid of Clay & Webster in his Cabinet, the two best characters in the Union.[5] Your expenditures are indeed enormous & cannot well be avoided, you will therefore find it your best policy and your duty to yourself to learn as early as possible what you are to expect; time rolls on and changes will take place. You will no doubt have sterling and noble friends who will aid you, and everyone here is anxious to hear that you obtain a competent remuneration for your labours. I saw in the papers yesterday that France is like to have another Revolution in their Government; also the nations of the far East have rumors of war. I am concerned only in the present movement in London, in Pensacola, at Delta, Green Bay and Great Bend, and the safe trip of the British Queen to London. Within a few days I shall have letters from James & Richard, also from Green Bay and in due time from London. As to my complaint (a settled cough) I will manage it as well as I can, and think of old Doct Chandler, who told me many years ago, he had lived 50 years in a fever and Ague clime and was contented, because that kept off other worse fevers.

I received your letter also, inclosing a draft on Prime, Ward and King of 300 dollars and inclosed the same to Mary M Wallace payable to her order with which she will be well pleased, because she loses about 6 percent on the Pennsylvania bills I send from this quarter.[6]

I fear you will be too anxious to assist me in making payment on the Bond she holds against me, the next pay't due to her is

---

[5] The staunch old Whig had suffered over every Presidential election for forty years, ever since Thomas Jefferson was elected in 1801. This time his wish would come true; William Henry Harrison would be elected President, and although he died shortly after his inauguration, there would still be a Whig in the White House—John Tyler.

[6] Putnam was never free from debt. He was still paying on his land speculation in the Hopbottom tract, interest on a four hundred dollar loan he had taken out seven years ago, and a mortgage on the "Bowes Mansion." In expectation of a whirlwind success in London, George had made an agreement with his father to pay off the loan on the house, securing it for his future use.

not payable till first of October next. I have collected & remitted to her since 2d Jany 1839 to May 8th 1840 2757 dolls on the bonds due to her, the check now sent makes $3057 which is doing well. The Scotch gentleman in N Y who lent me 400 dolls 7 years ago does not require me to pay more than the yearly interest which I send him punctually 1st June every year, so that I have always money enough to meet my engagements, & have fortunately sold the most of the lots I purchased of Mary M. W. and taken bonds & mortgage on interest at 3 dolls per acre of which I have received about 1200 dolls, the residue of lots will be sold this year.

Eliza and her four youngest children, Mary, Richard, Elizabeth and Charles are with us. George & Putnam are with their father at Green Bay, they took charge of the Baggage & furniture that he takes to the west, and went by the canal to meet their father at a certain day at Buffalo & met him there. the better part of furniture &c was sent down the Chenango Canal, to Binghamton, and brought here the day before yesterday. Yesterday with my permission they carefully had their furniture and goods (two waggon loads) moved into the white house to wait for Mr. Dart till the fall of the year, he then will have concluded whether to move his family to the west (which is his calculation). Eliza is in very fine health, also Mary, who is a charming girl, Richard active and helpful, even the little ones who will go to school are very attentive to their grandparents going to the post office &c. They have yesterday spread their carpets, beds & furniture and portraits to the best advantage and chose to move over there fearing they would give their G parents trouble here with us. Eliza is truly philosofick & judicious, loves her husband more than ever on account of his misfortunes. They will be near us and we can occasionally be useful to them. Mr. Hartshorn has not been down here, nor written to me. Mary writes that he wants to see me, but the journey would be too hard for me. We will hope that Mr. Dart & Francis will be able to step into some business at the west, &

not lose their journey. We all have loved Mr. Dart and Mr. Hartshorn, and will love them. I intended to write you a long & interesting letter, but have had trouble to get through it, you will excuse my blunders. I shall endeavour to write to Clara before she takes passage. This will go by the British Queen.

Your mother & Eliza & all send best love to you and dear Clara.

Your affectionate Father
Putnam Catlin

George Catlin Esquire

George knew that his seventy-six-year-old father was mainly interested in his son's health and progress. At present he could assure him only of his well-being.

During his painting period in Indian country he was relaxed and confident that his collection would be purchased in America, and he could spend the rest of his life adding to it. George had grown weary of exhibiting and lecturing before he left for England. He was an artist; he wanted to *paint*.

His five months in London had brought him much social prestige and praise for his Indian collection. Regardless of the excellence of an exhibit, public interest palls after a time. Had George announced that he planned to return to America in another month, it is possible that he would have received an offer for his collection. However, he still had hopes that Congress would call him home.

Clara and her two children were now on their way to London.

London, 3d. June 1840

My Dear Father & Mother,

The Great Western Steamer starts tomorrow for N. York and I am glad to be able to say to you that I am well, and also that I am pleased to have a conveyance by which I can so suddenly and so certainly convey this intelligence. In your present advanced age I am sure that nothing is more calculated to afford you pleasure than to hear of the health and success of your children who are abroad, & particularly one who has had to bristle up against every obstacle in pushing himself forward to the highest pitch of fashion & elegance in the world—Mine has been an experiment all the way, of trembling anxiety and solicitude, for myself, & no doubt equally so for those friends who have anxiously watched & prayed for my success. I wish really that I was making more *money* than I as yet am, that I might do more to gild your latter days, with comforts & luxuries which after all you might not thank me for, saying that you had already enough to make you happy and contented—Happiness consists not in wealth, however, my dear parents, of which you are as well aware as myself—& if you have good health, enough to eat & drink & your children around you & well you are happy & blessed.

We who are younger, are more eager & impatient for the goods of this world, and more uneasy if we do not acquire them. As for myself I see no great chance of making a fortune in London unless I sell my collection, of which there is some chance. My Rooms are what they call here "well attended" & fashionable, but expenses eat up most, but not *all* of the receipts.

How much I shall make in the event I cannot yet tell, but rely on it I shall do the best I can.

By Clara's last letter I suppose her to be at this time on the wide ocean in the B. Queen Steamer, with her two dear little babes. I shall pray for them all the way both night and day, & when they arrive, oh what feelings of joy and thankfulness I shall have! it will be the happiest moment of my life, certainly—

She wrote me that you had entirely abandoned the thought of coming out, & probably for the best, for when I think of the fatigue you would have met with in this endless bustle it seems as if it would wear you out.

By the British Queen I wrote you and also sent you a Draft

for 300. dols. by Baring & Brothers on Prime Ward & King in N. York, which I presume and hope you have rec'd. I shall soon send you more.—

Love to Francis & his Lady, to Eliza and all about you—in haste, your affectionate son

Geo. Catlin

Burr is well and sends love to all.

Clara arrives in London

O N T H E 29th of June George wrote his parents that Clara and the babies had arrived. It had been seven months since he had seen his wife and small Libby, and he now saw his six-month-old daughter, Clara, for the first time. His letter reflects the joy of their meeting.

My Dear Parents,

You will no doubt take unusual pleasure at the receipt of this letter wherein I am describing to you the happiest epoch in my whole life. The British Queen arrived a few days since with my Dear Clara and her two little babes, all well and in as good order as when they were shipped. I was prepared at the Dock at the time, and watched, with throbbing heart, the approach of the noble Steamer, until she came so near that I recognized amid the throng on her deck, the well known face of my fair & dear little Clara & Libby lifted in her arms, gazing amongst the crowd for some kindred friend to hail. I at length caught her eye & waved my hat, and in a moment was on board, with Burr at my side! I cannot possibly express to you the gush of pleasure of that moment. over the great ocean safe and sound—in the great city of London with her two little babes and her faithful servant girl Bridget, all as well and as sound as I left them!

Here we are then, at this time, in the great Metropolis of the world, seated down in our snug and comfortable quarters, where we have been living for some days, talking of home and friends behind, and on this day (Sunday) both leaning over our table writing back to our friends west of the Atlantic. The first wish we have to express, & the one to which we will daily pray for, is that these letters, and all others that we may write will find you all well and enjoying life, and so may Heaven grant it, until we can return, and again embrace you all.

I did not know certain until the moment of the arrival of the Steamer, that you was not on board, although I had learned from your letter & from Clara's also, that you would not probably come. Although I had long anticipated the pleasure of showing you this great city & other wonders of the Continent, and notwithstanding the unique pleasure I should have felt in so doing, I am at last decidedly of opinion that it is best on the whole, you did not come, for one of your age the voyage over and back would have been very tedious, and the endless jar and buzz of this everlasting, tiresome, *world* of *itself*, would soon become painful and fatiguing to you.

With my dear little family about me and my gallery, I will try to preserve the reputation I have gained, and struggle amongst this world of strangers for some of its *goods* if I can honestly get them. as yet, I have not been able to make a great deal, on account of my very heavy expenses, though I do not complain, as the prospect ahead of me is fair. There is a great deal of talk about its purchase here, but whether anything is done time alone will decide. I may go to France, to Edinburgh, or to St. Petersburg, before six months are out or I may not, all will depend on advice I may receive & on the success which I may meet with where I now am. Like the whole of my life, everything ahead rests on uncertainty, and, as I *have been*, I am ready to meet the chances, such as will come. I have no fears if my health is spared, but that my labours will eventually be turned to good account. I rec'd your two letters by the B. Queen, which afforded me great pleasure by informing me that you were all well, and that you and Mother were surrounded by so many of your children. The most cruel news you gave me of Mr. Darts misfortune in these unlucky times, has given me much pain and sorrow; that one so honourable, so industrious & so liberal & noble in his heart should be thrown down in these disastrous times, when he had so well earned a fair & competent living for his interesting family, is too hard, is too cruel—he is a philosipher however, & young enough to rally and long outlive his present, temporary adversity. Eliza has courage and philosophy enough I trust also to bear the adversity without being discouraged. I know nothing to say better than what her own good sense, and your advice has continually dictated to her, that is to be contented and happy even in poverty, while she has good health & enough to eat and drink & her little ones about her. In the country where Mr. Dart and Francis have gone I have little doubts of their success, and I wish it them I am sure, with all my heart.

As for myself, who have crossed the Atlantic with 7. in my family, and seven daily to feed & to clothe, I feel some considerable anxiety, yet I will harbour no fears until danger is very close at hand. I will struggle amongst strangers for respectability & a living, and wend my way as well as I can.

Clara has seen but little of London as yet, she has been so busy preparing her clothes & her apartments where we are commencing to live. on last sunday she and Burr & I went to St. James Park, where we all had a perfectly good view of the Queen & Prince Albert as they rode to the chapel to attend divine service, and we afterwards walked in Hyde Park where amidst thousands, we had another good look at them as they were taking their usual ride in the park in an open Barouche & four, with outriders.

On thursday last, again Clara had a much better view. My faithful friend the Hon. C. A. Murray, who had called on Clara the day after she arrived, and who is Master of the Queen's Household, politely presented us a couple of tickets admitting us to the Grand Hall in Buckingham Palace on the day of the Queen's Drawing Room or Levee so that Clara had a perfect view of Her Majesty & the Prince, as well as the rest of her household & attendants, as they descended the grand stairway from the Throne Room in full dress and took their carriages for St. James' Palace, where the Levee was held, & which is about a half a mile distant from Buckingham Palace. Then, through the politeness of another friend of mine, who has charge of St. James' Palace, (with his good Lady) seats were prepared for us in the grand avenue or hall to that, to which we instantly repaired, and there had a full view of the whole procession of Ladies & Lords, of Duchesses & Dukes, princesses & Princes, in full Court Dress—with laces & plumes & glittering diamonds as they were alighting from their splendid carriages & entering the drawing Room of the palace.

This scene to Clara was no less gratifying than it was for me, & thus had she the good fortune, in one day, to enter two Palaces & see the Queen & all her court & all the fashionables who flounced about and glittered in it!

I have been in hopes that her Majesty would have been predisposed before this, to visit my Collection, but I now despair of such an event. There are but very few Exhibitions in London, even those which are purely National. If she had condescended to pay me a visit some two months ago, I would have been sure of a rich harvest about this time, however, she may come and see me yet, and if she does not I will not groan about it.

I did intend to send you some money again by this Steamer but as my rent of 750 dols (one quarter) is due in a few days, and as I am sending a considerable amount today to Mr. Gregory, I will wait until the sailing of the Great Western by which I will remit to you.

With love to Dear *Dear* Mother & all the family around you, I must bid you adieu. Your affectionate & dutiful son, Geo. Catlin.

You mentioned in your last letter that Mr. Dart's family had taken poss'n of the Big House, that is certainly all right, and I hope my dear sister may be comfortable with her little ones in it until Mr. Darts prospects may brighten up somewhere in the West.

George was riding high. His life in London was a whirl of exhibiting and lecturing, and attending entertainments and soirees given by his aristocratic friends. He had become a social lion; the "distinguished American artist, Mr. Catlin," was well known and admired in the best circles, and of course he was enjoying it. The great honors shown him in London helped atone for the slap he had been given at home. His only worry was money. He couldn't appear among the handsomely garbed Londoners looking like a country cousin with a lean purse—which was too true. Traveling in high society took its toll, for he lived and dressed in style, giving the impression that he was a man of means. It was possibly good for his business and social standing, but hard on his pocketbook.

George was perfectly at ease socially, for he was among his own kind. But among strangers in the business world, many not friendly toward Americans, he felt insecure—this shows in his letters to his father. George knew he *had* to make good in London. English laws against debtors were stiff. Both he and Clara wrote of the "harpies of the law," and their fear of being caught in the net. Still, George had too much optimism about the future to think it necessary to economize—yet.

Eliza prepares for the Wilderness West

WHILE GEORGE was enjoying the bright life of London his sister Eliza and her husband Anson Dart were having experiences of an entirely different sort.

In the early 1800's the Wisconsin country was home to about 15,000 Indians; tribes of many names, but belonging to two main

176

peoples: Algonquins and Dakotas. As late as 1830 civilization was to be found only around Green Bay and Prairie Du Chien. The rest was unnamed wilderness.

After the Black Hawk War (1832) settlers began to pour into the country beyond the Great Lakes. In 1836 Congress established the Territory of Wisconsin, extending from Lake Michigan to the Missouri River, and General Henry Dodge was appointed Governor. The country south and east of the Wisconsin and Fox rivers was divided into counties. As soon as a treaty could be made with the tribes in a certain area, the land was surveyed and opened to settlement, and its former inhabitants eventually escorted beyond the Mississippi. In 1836 and 1837 the Menomonees and Winnebagoes ceded their lands to the government, and the Green Bay area was ready for market in 1840.[7]

Anson Dart went to Green Bay in the spring of that year hoping to sell some of his "wild" land, and so save his farm at Utica. Unable to dispose of any, he had no alternative but to make a home for his family on the western prairies. With Mr. Beall, land agent at Green Bay, Dart made a trip around Green Lake, about eighty miles from the Bay, and laid claim to an eighty acre tract on the south shore. There were no other settlers; just small groups of Winnebagoes here and there, their tipis dotting the lake shore.

Putnam wrote to George on June 23, saying that he had received a letter from Dart and Francis, and that Dart and his sons were erecting a log cabin for the family.

---

[7] Reverend Samuel T. Kidder, to whom Richard Dart told his story of pioneer days, said: "Mr. Dart says that the rank and file of the Winnebago knew nothing of this government purchase. It was effected by agency men who got the chiefs drunk and secured the cession papers. The government paid no principal, but ninety-nine years' interest with no entail to the Indian's family or children after his death. The rate of interest was small, and mostly eaten up in advance through the Indians getting trusted at Fort Winnebago for adulterated and poisonous whiskey. Mr. Dart considers that the Indians were badly treated by rascally traders and agents." *Settlement of Green Lake County*, Wisconsin State Historical Proceedings, 1909. (Madison, Wis.: published by the Society, 1910), p. 253, fn.3.

I cannot conceive how he will get along, poor fellow, nor how he can remove his family to such a distance and without money. Eliza is in good spirits & Francis' wife is willing to go. But I suspect that Francis will return soon and give up the enterprise. The Pensacola bank, it appears, is in a bad condition and James is tired of it as he writes me. I shall shortly hear from that quarter. . . . Mr. Hartshorn writes to me, that the Judgments entered in the Utica Bank or Banks, against Mr. D will at any rate more than cover the whole of his as well as D' property in that county,—that he himself is holden for more than 20,000 dollars as Bail, this is painful and shocking beyond expression. He wants me to come up if possible to advise him, hitherto I have not been able to make the journey. It seems to be a complete failure a distressing one indeed, a great shock in my family.

Your mother is active as ever being in full health, and I promise to nurse my complaint as well as possible on your account, and be prepared to meet you on your return as the happiest day of my life

Putnam Catlin

Your Mother & Eliza, Elizabeth and Mary send best love to all and wish to be remembered.

Letter-writing had now become quite a task for Putnam. The following letter was dated July 9, 1840, but not mailed until the 20th. He had probably set aside a certain time each morning of the intervening days to add something to the pages. Letters always were important to him. They were not to be written hastily. It was his duty to keep the recipient informed of what was going on.

Great Bend, July 9, 1840

Dear George and Clara,

I intended answering your letter of June 3d on return of the Great Western Steamer; but I have become slack in everything,

& had waited too long. I shall be in time to send this by the British Queen. The opportunity of communication between the two countries has become grand indeed, and certain & safe. Abigail was 40 days on her Voyage to Mobile with her five children, her friends in north and south not hearing a word from the ship in all that time; but arrived safe at last, having no passengers, except the six of my family.

Francis returned five days since from Wisconsin in good health. Mr D has fixed his station at Green Lake about 75 miles south westerly from Green Bay as being the first settler in Marquette County except a french-man halfblooded, within two miles of him having a large family, is rich, friendly & profligate (in some degree) came there two years ago. The Indians in that territory having been removed *secundam legis,* beyond the Mississippi. Dart, with the aid of the neighbor's team, has plowed & planted 3 acres of corn, two acres of potatoes and intends sowing about 20 acres of wheat this fall, will put up a log house & prepare for his family in September. he is 14 miles from any village. It is said to be the finest location, the best land, mildest climate, best water,— precisely on the great course of the contemplated public canals and railroads and waters to the Mississippi. Francis gives a favourable account of the country and thinks of settling there. Dart had not received your letter when Francis left.

Eliza is well and in good spirits, & seems not to dread the Expedition. Francis says that money is extremely scarce in the west, even at Buffalo and all the way to Green Bay, & that it will be impossible for Dart to sell his wild lands at this time, as he intended. I hope it will be in my power to help Eliza with some money on this occasion, if she must leave us in Sept.

The misfortune of our friend Dart, so unexpected, will give our family a shock, and it will fall heavy on Mr. Hartshorn, which seems most to be regretted. I have not been able to see him and learn the extent of his liability. It is a painful subject for me to dwell on, I will leave it & hope for a more favourable result, & that D will be able to remunerate Hartshorn in the arrangement he is now making in the west.

You will be anxious to hear of the state of my health. I am able to attend to my business in some measure, by riding in my waggon to Brooklyn & Montrose about once a month—at home with letters and arrange papers; at the same time use Balsoms and syrups in defence of the *old man's cough*, without much pain or fever, and in hopes of mitigating or curing the complaint. I am now using the second bottle of Doctor Taylor's advertised "Balsam of Liver-wort" a pleasant medicine, if not a successful one, you will probably hear the result in my next.

The arrival of your family in London I am sure will consummate your highest hopes and happiness, and I rejoice to hear that there is some chance of your selling your Collection in London as the happy result, which I presume is your object, that you may return with safety and success to your own Country. To continue exhibition, will be too tedious for you, & not without some risk, besides, the expenses you will find to increase, and your leisure taken up. If you sell, you will be required to arrange the Collection in its permanent place which will take some time, and some-time you will want to prepare for publishing your travels & perhaps in London, to advantage, as I have heard you say.

I can imagine that you will have formed some friendships in England that may incline, here and there one, to come to our Country on your return and be Neighbor to you in this Village perhaps,[8] or some, that would be suited in the Wisconsin Territory from which the Indians have recently removed beyond the Mississippi having sold their land to our Government

---

[8] When George wrote his father that there was a chance of selling his Gallery in London, the old gentleman probably relapsed into day-dreaming, seeing his famous son at home once more, with some of his fine London friends giving prestige to the little town on the Susquehanna. No doubt he contemplated selling the old Bowes Mansion to the Duchess of Whizzet, and taking her for a ride to Montrose in his "easy-wagon."

& which our Government are now selling to settlers for one dollar and 25 cents per acre, which has been surveyed into sections of 600 acres, and where Mr. Dart has settled prefering the quality of the land and the climate to any he has seen in the west.

In this village, there is some alteration since you left us, three houses erected on the Turnpike near the Hotel and finished and a very large Hotel adjoining the McKinny house, and a new store adjoining it. A handsome Academy erected and finished and painted where the school-house stood and the school to be opened there next week by an accomplished teacher, this is opposite your lot.

The work on the Erie Rail-Road is going on with spirit, the Legislature having at their last session granted a competent appropriation for the work as far as has been laid out; it is generally believed the River route will be used though no act therefore has yet been passed.

I think Francis will decide on going to the west in Sept, or next spring, and your mother fully consents to it, which was not expected; his vivid description of that part of the country, the soil, the timber the prairies, the waters the springs the early spring and the mild climate, would induce any one to go there. the timber principally oak (or all oak) and straight & have only to be girded to raise crops in the commencement, there being no underbrush, & the trees being at a convenient distance the plow may be used and not be impeded by the roots of the trees, the soil too is the best he has ever seen; such is the face of the Country and a sufficiency of prairie adjoining—there is easy traveling without a population, in waggons or on horseback. I have said too much of this, should have left it for Francis to describe.

Mr. Dart in his letter to me by Francis, asks the favour of me of a loan at this time on Eliza's account, of 200 dolls, which he thinks would help them over the present pinch, that is, carry them to next Fall harvest, which is but reasonable, and which I shall endeavor to send him by all means. He has placed his gold watch in the hands of Francis to sell and give the proceeds to Eliza to bear the expenses on the removal of the family this fall, the watch cost him 135 dolls. The 300 dolls you sent me is indorsed on the Agreement May 20 1840, the next payment in August next, say the middle of Sept 500 dollars, which I hope will be convenient for you to send me as I shall have occasion for money about that time, which is difficult to be raised here.

You may imagine that we are exceedingly anxious to hear that you are all in good health and good spirits and that Clara will not fail of giving a long letter to us.

Your mother & Francis, Eliza, Mary, and all send best love to all, including Mr. Burr Catlin, of whom we have a good account. His sister is doing well in her music school at Montrose which he will be glad to hear.

Your affectionate Parent
Putnam Catlin

The following is rather hard to believe, but it shows the transportation problems in those days: In Putnam's letter of May 11, he mentioned that James' wife, Abigail, who had been in the north with her five children, had "taken passage last month for Mobile." On June 23, Putnam wrote: "We have fears for Abigail and her children, who took passage for Mobile the 29th of April, but had not arrived the 30th of May. Richard sent a paper of that date, writing on it that she had not arrived, nor had he heard of such a vessel, and that James had gone that day to Mobile with fear. Her brother was at N. York at the time she sailed, and says there were no passengers on board but Abigail and her five children, and said he had fears at the time. I saw him 10 days since, and he expressed great fears on the occasion." On July 9, Putnam was happy to write: "Abigail was 40 days on her voyage to Mobile with her five children, her friends in the North and South not hearing a word from the ship in all that time."

Putnam did not bother to say what had caused the delay.

Evidently what had happened to the ship was too common an occurrence for anyone to waste ink on!

For the Catlin family in Great Bend, the summer of 1840 must have been one of tense, tearful, and swirling emotions. Putnam was seriously troubled with what he called "the old man's disease; the catarrh cough." Eliza, with a heavy heart, would be preparing for the faraway West, and being completely dependent on her father deeply hurt her proud spirit. She was in a shameful position, but one she was forced to accept.

On August 24, Eliza answered a letter she had just received from Clara, in London:

> I am sorry to say I have not enjoyed myself as well this summer in the society of my dear Parents as I have always thought I should, were it my good fortune to be placed near them, you know dear sister, circumstances alter cases. The ill health of my dear Father has cast a gloom on all around, he has been labouring under a most distressing and alarming cough, that with the constant anxiety he has for the welfare of his children, has made him for the most of the time in low spirits. I never knew till now that independence contributed so much to ones happiness. I have been wholly dependent upon Father this summer for the comeforts of life, with four children, Anson left me with the certainty of selling some of his land in the west, but found that like all his former expectations, that too failed—poor man, my trouble is nothing when compaired with the mortification he is made to feel. I cannot find it in my heart to sit down and groan over my situation and find fault with my husband by alluding to what we once were, neither can I fold my hands, in listlessness and inactivity—but by the constant exercise of all my powers, by kind and affectionate treatment, anticipating all his wants, and by ever wearing a cheerful countenance in his presence I may be instrumental in dispelling the gloom, which might otherwise pray upon his spirits—Through our united efforts we hope to gain all that we have lost—should I wring my

hands in despair, he too would give up. by my efficiency, mildness and fortitude, I may not only save him from a depression of spirits, but perhaps from proffligacy and vice—How many men have been driven by loss of property, and the reproaches of relatives and friends, or an imprudent wife, to degradation and ruin.

Dear Sister I never thought wealth could make me happy were I to be possessed of it. I have found more real pleasure in the society of my husband and in the cares of my family, than amid all the gay and fashionable acquaintances—I do think the pleasure arising from a conscious discharge of the duties of life is infinitely superior to the glittering of wealth or of fashion. Poor indeed must be the individual whose *mental resources* will afford no antidote for the loss of fortune, if we can have courage to appear poor, we disarm poverty of its sharpest sting. I shall now have an opportunity to test the sincerity of former friends—as adversity is the only true test of friendship. After all the good resolves I have made and all the fortitude I have summoned to stem the torrent of misfortune, I am almost driven to despair when I think that some of our best friends will feel the blow that prostrates us. could we be the only sufferers, heaven knows we would not complain.

A few days more, and I shall be winding my way to the far west, with 4 children and furniture enough to make us comfortable, we go alone. . . . we will not be without the hope of some day, not far distant, of seeing you and George with the dear little ones under our own roof, partaking of our humble but welcome, more than welcome fare. I trust your stay in London will not be protracted beyond the sale of the Indian Galery at least I think it would not, did you but know the great desire our Parents have to see you once more, we do rejoice to hear that George has been so highly complimented in England, we are pleased to see his name in so many of our country, as well as city papers. . . . I shall ever feel indebted to brother George, for the kind feelings he has expressed for my husband in this time of trouble, I am happy to find there is some one beside myself that knows how to appreciate his worth and talents. . . . I want very much to see little Debby, and have an introduction to Miss Clara, tell Bridgit she must take good care of them and bring them safe back to America [Our] Mary has been confined to a dark room for two weeks or more, with sore eyes, leaches were applied, she was cupped and blistered, and is now better. . . . There is one subject you will pardon me if I do not dwell long upon that of parting with my dear Parents, tis a painful subject —how I shall bear it is all unknown as yet. . . . . as a sister you will not forget that we shall be living this winter two miles from a neighbour depending upon letters from our friends, as our only company, you and George must write long letters, and direct Frankfort Post office, Fox Lake, Dodge Co, Wisconsin Territory, we are 18 miles from this office but shall think nothing of going that distance provided we can get letters, having filled my sheet I must say adieu Dear Brother and Sister, from your truely aff. sister

Eliza Dart.

Putnam added a note to Eliza's letter:

Dear Clara and George, I avail myself of this opportunity of adding a few lines to say your mother is quite [well] again and active in preparing Eliza, as much as we can for the dreadful movement with her dear family that we may not expect to meet again in life, it is thrilling and inexpressible indeed. She will have to leave her heavy and best furniture, nothing however will discourage her of the enterprise, she goes without a protector, may Heaven bless and protect her. . . . .

Eliza and her four younger children, Mary, Richard, Elizabeth, and Charley, left for the West the first week in September, 1840. For Putnam and Polly it was a last goodbye to the little family so close to their hearts. To Eliza, it was a complete and final break with the happy past; from now on she would take each day at it came, and as long as she could keep her family together she would be content.

The little band of travelers to the Wisconsin wilderness went to Buffalo by way of stage and the Erie Canal, from there to Mackinac, Michigan, on the steamer *Consolation*, and then by schooner to Green Bay, Wisconsin. Anson Dart was waiting with an ox team to take them to their new home on the prairie.

News of the pioneers

A L L W A S W E L L with the pioneers. Putnam wrote George on October 17, saying he had received a letter from Eliza.

[Eliza] had arrived at Green Bay with her dear children and found Mr. Dart and two sons well. She gives us a very interesting account of her voyage; we had been extremely anxious to hear of their safe arrival, they had indeed some dangers and difficulties on the way, but was befriended throughout. Dart was waiting at Green Bay with a team to take them to their *locus in quo*, Green Lake, about 60 or 70 miles south of Green Bay, though the house was but in part finished, they call their place the garden of the world. They remained a week at Green B where they received the utmost attention and respect. She says when the Vessel came along side of the Dock, they discovered Mr. D making his way through the crowd—Mr. Plumb at one elbow. Messrs. Beal, Whitney McCarty & others were introduced to me [Putnam was copying Eliza's letter, and occasionally slid into first person] before she could reach the Astor-House. Mr. Beal & Mr. Arndt insisted that she should go direct to their houses, but she insisted in going to the Astor-house where Anson had prepared rooms for them, where they could change their dress; Seven Gentlemen and their wives were announced, and waiting to pay respects to the family. It was something unexpected to me, we were invited to dine and take tea, but Anson was waiting with his team for Green Lake. . . . This morning four carriages stood at the door, each brought Ladies to pay their respects &c. Mr. D and Mary have gone to dine with Mr. Ellis where she will most likely remain through the winter and perhaps longer.[9] So much I have given you of Eliza's letter. The great difficulty will be the want of *L'argent* at Green L, nor can I imagine how he can get it, or do without it. Eliza says she had only 25 dollars left when she arrived at Green Bay. . . .

The day before yesterday we had the pleasure of an addition to our family, of a fine little grandson, that is already named *Geo the 2d,* all in good health and cheer.[10] I think I wrote you in my last, that James had removed to his plantation in Alabama in the village of Brooklyn, and has accepted the appointment of President to an Accademy within a short distance of his farm (say half a mile), which will be convenient for his exercise with a salary of 1600 dolls pr annum. . . .

While writing, I received a letter from your brother Henry. He has at length disposed of his collection of minerals in N York and returned to his family at Medina. He sold for a mere trifle. Had made an exchange of part of his, for east & west Indian shells to advantage, he has now about 3000 of such, which are now worth more than his former collection. Exchanged some of his minerals for Jewelry, received 100 dolls in cash enough to bear his expenses. . . .

Last week we voted in our district (4 Counties) for a seat in Congress; Lawyer Dimock I presume will be elected. It is said if you had been here you would, or might have had, a full vote;

---

[9] Fifteen-year-old Mary Dart remained at Green Bay for the winter. She had taken piano lessons in the east, and was invited to stay with friends of her father, and teach their children.

[10] First child born to Francis and Elizabeth.

your thorough knowledge of the United States, your patriotism and your popularity would ensure you a high station. Your patriotism and your connections here will call you back. I have been thinking for some time, that you may be called to spend the winters at Washington "pro publico," the summers at home indulging your taste and advancement in the fine arts, and above all, domestic happiness and ease & at Home. I would advise you to think of this, and in the meantime, be careful to exercise your best judgment in arranging and disposing of your works on hand to the best advantage you can, without risk or loss. It is difficult to raise money here at this time, and will remain so for some time hence, it is thought the Banks however will pay specie by first of Jany.

I must try to forward some money to Eliza at all events or they will suffer in the wilderness, and I feel bound to make a payment to Miss Wallace, and help Francis a little.

Your mother, Francis & Elizabeth cordially join me in sending our best love to dear Clara and yourself and the two dear little children.

Your affectionate Father
Putnam Catlin

You will excuse my erazures & interlineations, as the Lawyers say "they do not *vitiate*." I find that my pen as well as my mind, body, and memory is staggering with age.

Let us picture the Dart family as they climbed into the crudely-built ox cart at Green Bay and journeyed to their new home. The air was clear, with the crispness of early autumn. Families of quail scuttled across the narrow, rutted, and stump-filled wagon road, and speckled prairie chickens flew out of the clumps of grass as the clumsy cart creaked and groaned over the many miles to Green Lake. It would take several days to make the journey behind the slow-plodding oxen; every passing hour taking Eliza further away from the peace and security that had been hers in the east. But every day brought a fresh and delightful awareness of her surroundings. This was a wild and beautiful prairie country. There were no mountains; just low, rolling hills and seemingly endless miles of tall, waving grass, now autumn yellow. Anson told her that in the spring the prairie would be carpeted with wild flowers.

The Winnebago and Menomonee Indians had, until recently, called this portion of the country their home. There were many of the former tribe still here, their tipis scattered along the shores of Green Lake, but they were being slowly collected for transportation elsewhere. No Americans lived within thirty miles of Dart's property, but a few miles away lived the half-breed fur trader, now farmer, Pete LeRoy, who proved himself a friend indeed to the penniless family.

So the ox cart trundled along the shore of the emerald-tinted mirror called Green Lake, and finally the Darts were home—a little, unfinished box-like house sunning itself in a field of golden maize. It consisted of two rooms and an attic. The large fireplace (unfinished when Eliza arrived) had a stick chimney plastered with yellow clay, and rough boards made the floor.

No doubt a picture of her fine home in Utica flashed before Eliza's eyes, but she was a "philosophik" woman, as Putnam said, and for the sake of her husband and children she buried the past.

The scenery truly enchanted her, and Eliza's delight in her new surroundings made the future look brighter to Anson, who was painfully aware that he had brought shame to the Catlin family. He knew there was a fine future in this new country; if Eliza would stand by him, he was sure they could build a good life in the growing West. And at present, under any circumstances, it was the only road open to them.

Richard Dart was just twelve years old when he went to Wisconsin with his mother, small brother, and two sisters. When he was quite an old man he wrote an interesting account of his family in the pioneer days for the Wisconsin State Historical Society. Evidently he had heard his two elder brothers tell and re-tell the events of those months at Green Lake with their father before Eliza and the younger children arrived. In writing of that period, Richard put himself there, too, having forgotten that he was one of the children who came west with his mother. He even said that he went to Green Bay with his father to meet his mother! But that is a small matter, for he wrote of many incidents not mentioned in the old letters.

Richard spoke of his father and Mr. Beall, land agent at Green Bay, exploring the lake shore until Anson found the land he desired. He then returned to the Bay to get his "three" sons: "It took us two days to wind up through the marshes to Green Lake. The last night we camped opposite the present Dartford boat-landing, where the road-bridge crosses toward Sherwood Forest resort. It was then surrounded with alders and marshes, and we did not know, that beautiful June night that we were so near the lake. . . . There was at this time no heavy timber around the lake, except at the foot, in the marshes—only what were called 'clay openings,' burned over each autumn by the prairie fires. . . . We soon crossed the lake and reached our land . . . and went to work to build a plank house. . . . We had in stock two barrels of flour, one barrel of pork, four barrels of potatoes, a few groceries, and $4 in money. . . .

"There being no mill, we made a huge mortar by boring out a hard, white-oak log, and, with a heavy hickory pestle, we ground our corn. As the mortar held but two quarts, it was only by rising at four o'clock that we could get enough meal pounded for a breakfast Johnnie-cake. The coarser part we boiled as samp, for dinner, and had cornmeal fried for supper, with neither milk nor butter. . . .

"When mother came, only 2 sides of the house were up. One side was partly open the first winter, except for a carpet hung up. Wolves and other wild animals would come and peer through the cracks at the firelight. Sometimes the stick chimney caught fire, and to prevent this occurring too frequently we had to keep it well plastered over with clay. Even after the house was finished it was very cold, for the joints were not tight. . . . Sometimes we used old newspapers, so far as we had any, to paste over the cracks. . . . We nearly froze in our crudely-built house, for we had no stove; only a big fireplace, where in 24 hours we would sometimes burn 2 cords of four-foot wood. It took hard work for the boys just to keep the fires going. Nor did we always have enough food; again and again I have seen my mother sit down at the table and eat nothing, since there was not enough to go around. . . ."

This lack of food must have applied to their first winter in the wilderness, for Richard wrote: "In the early years of our coming to Green Lake, there was plenty of small game—ducks, pigeons, and prairie-chickens. Deer was plentiful, except when they went south in winter to escape the cold. There were likewise wild turkeys and plenty of geese. Elk and moose were found upon Willow River, and occasionally around Green Lake. We saw no buffalo, but their wallows and chips and horns were visible, and seemed recent. Le Roy said that he had seen these prairies black with buffalo."

Richard wrote of an interesting experience on the prairie. Their house was built entirely of green oak, but sawed pine lumber was needed for finishing. It wasn't until their second year at Green Lake that they had enough money to buy it. An old wagon and a yoke of oxen were borrowed from Pete Le Roy, and George started out for Green Bay. Quoting Richard: "He arrived safely, got a jag of lumber, and a few groceries, and started home by the military road, east of Lake Winnebago. On the return, the oxen gave out from exhaustion somewhere between Taychedah and Fond du Lac. George camped on the spot, among the prairie-wolves, until morning, but rest had not relieved the beasts. So reluctantly, he left the wagon and the load by the lake-shore, and got the animals home as best he could.

"After almost a week at home, they revived, and then George went back after his load. But when he reached the place where it had been abandoned, there was nothing left but the wagon-irons. The prairie fires had run through and burned out the country for 20 miles each way. What could be done? We had lost the lumber, and the wagon was borrowed. As customary in those days, my brother had brought an axe with him; so he cut a timber crotch, bound stakes across, with withes tied on the burned wagon irons, and set out for home. It took a day and a half to drag the crotch and the load to our home. Father being a mechanical genius and a millwright, went resolutely to work, and hewed out a rough wagon of green oak, seasoned in hot ashes. It took a month or two to finish this rude cart, but at last it was done, and dear old Le Roy was satisfied." [11]

London has its dull season

M E A N W H I L E , business in London depended upon the weather and the seasons. Bad weather kept the "carriage trade" home; a sunny spell brought them out, which meant a "run," as George was told. Now he was learning the meaning of English "seasons." There was a season for this, and a season for that—all caused by the movements of the Rich.

George was now experiencing the "dull season," and financially he was not prepared for it. Both he and Clara explained its meaning very well; the following letter from George reflects his mood.

London, 30th September 1840

My Dear Father,

I write you this by the Steamer President which sails tomorrow, and inform you that we are all well. I have great solicitude for your health and for mother's also from the information which we got from your last letters & from those of Francis & Eliza, all of which we rec'd in due season. I hope you will not suffer with the colds which are so severe and so dangerous at the setting in of winter; I need not caution you however, who are able and wise enough to prepare against the danger, *sans exposure*. Sister Eliza's long and well written letter to Clara does her great credit & gave us great satisfaction that she is able to bear her misfortunes with so much philosophy, that she resolves so courageously and even *heroically* to follow up her husband and to love and encourage him in his adversity. it is a

---

[11] *Settlement of Green Lake County*, pp. 252–260.

fair test (but a cruel one) of dear Eliza's fortitude and perseverance for which we have always admired her; and if she has lost everything else she has not lost her place in our affections and confidence. Her resolves to join her husband, and to brace him up by her counsel and to stimulate and encourage him by her presence is truly praiseworthy, and will ensure him a strong heart and a certain success, provided they are blessed with good health. If he is poor in purse he is yet strong in such an ally as he finds in Eliza, and also in such force as his sons add to his means as they are now grown up and ready to lay hold with him to some effect. Would to God that it were in my power to aid him now, at the time when aid would be more kind to him than it ever can be again, but alas, I *cannot*. in this strange land, with a family of seven, whom I have shipped across the ocean, and for whose daily food, and return also, I am responsible, with other enormous expenses continually accruing, and the liquidation of those that I incurred at the time of leaving, I find it difficult to lay bye anything as yet, to help a friend in time of need, or even in time of absolute distress.

I am now going through what is called the "dull season" in London, and my Gallery does not at this time pay a penny over its own expenses! All the fashion are off, on the Continent, at the watering places or gunning, and London is seemingly a tissue of Sundays. There is a *season* for everything here, and the season for Exhibitions has gone bye. I am holding on with as much patience as I can, hoping the fall season to give me a lift again. I am expending some money in the progress of my publication which I hope to have out in a few months, and I am also advancing considerable money to get my dresses & weapons all mounted on figures, with shield, spear bow & lance in hand, which will show them to great advantage and probably draw much better than heretofore.[12] With all of these difficulties in

---

[12] George spoke of mounting the Indian costumes and weapons on figures, so as to show them to greater advantage. This no doubt added enough impetus to his

this season, when nothing is doing, it is plain that I can do no more than take care of myself and my own concerns. The world may think that I am making a fortune, and I dont know but it is as well for them to think so; but when I *do* make it, or any part of it, *you* shall know it, I warrant you.

I enclose you an hundred Dollars, instead of the $500. which I thought I should be able to send you at this time. It is all that I can send at this moment, and while I regret to the very core of my heart, that I cannot gladden the hearts of my dear parents at this time of their lives with enough to gild their declining days, yet do I not despair of having that satisfaction before long. I will cherish the belief (and insist on it) that their lives will be spared to see me back again with them and more abundantly able than at present, to administer to their comforts & happiness. I will have this one consolation, my dear parents, under all the bad luck and adverse fortunes of your children, of knowing that you do not deem the poss'n of wealth the positive guaranty of true happiness, but that you will estimate the comforts of life which you have about you, and the love and affection of your children, added to good health and good appetites to be, at last, the Philosophers stone, for which all are looking and few can find. Such is happiness, and such we shall deem you both to be enjoying with true philosophy and with a far better relish and with more grateful hearts than many of the thousands who are wallowing in the worlds luxuries and crushed down with worlds goods.

My dear Clara unites with me in gratulations for the recovery of my dear mother, who it seems has been very sick. Clara will write to her by next mail. I shall in a few days endeavor to sit

---

lectures to encourage him to use live figures in place of dummies. He hired twenty English men and boys to illustrate his talks with "tableaux vivants," having taught them Indian songs and dances, and how to give a most convincing war-whoop. Dressed in the Indian costumes, with painted faces and wigs of horses' hair, they were indeed an added attraction, and the hall was filled again. Bernard DeVoto has called this the first Wild West show, long antedating Buffalo Bill.

down and give you some account of London &c. at present I
have no room or time. Love to Francis & all.

Your affectionate son
Geo. Catlin

The following long and newsy letter from Clara to Putman and
Polly gives a clear picture of George and his London experiences:

London, Oct. 29th. 1840

My dear Father and Mother,

George is so constantly engaged that I am determined to
begin a letter to you this time, and let him finish it. I have
intended writing before, but having many letters from my
friends to answer by every mail, I generally find myself
behindhand. My friends have been very kind in writing to me. I
have received one letter from Abigail, since the death of her
little one, and I have written her twice. I have also written to
Darwina and to sister Mary; I intend they shall see I have not
forgotten them. We are all enjoying good health, and happy to
hear that you are as well as you are, after the late trial of parting
with Eliza. It is with great anxiety we open our letters from
home, my dear father wrote me that he has been almost entirely
free from pain, for three months. He had the pleasure of seeing
an only sister, at his house, a few weeks ago, whome he has not
seen in 35 years. All my other relatives are well. I have been
called to sympathise with a brother and two sisters, on the loss of
their infants with disease of the brain, since my arrival here.

Our little daughters are uncommonly healthy. Libby is fat and
chubby, and little Clara is now ten months old, and Libby
considers her as a rival in the affections of her father. I have not
weaned her yet, for she is backward in teething. George looks
very well, although he feels his old weakness in his breast, on
speaking much. Business has been rather dull, during the last
three months, but is now beginning to revive again. The east end
of London is devoted to commerce and trade, and the same
crowds throng the streets throughout the year, unaffected by the

vicissitudes of fashion. But in the fashionable or "West End" there is the greatest difference during the months of Aug-Sep, and Oct. The streets and squares are inhabited by the nobility and gentry, and they are at their country seats, or traveling, and a stranger would think the inhabitants had fled from the pestilence. It is then that exhibitions, theatres, and tradespeople feel that there is no one in town. George has done as well during the dull season as most of the exhibitors; generally been able to clear expenses heavy as they are. He has leased his rooms for another year, and they have taken off 50£ from his rent, he has paid up so punctually, and the lecture room, which he has no use for, he is enabled to rent, so that his rent will be reduced to 250£. His works are highly appreciated here, and I think the coming year he will do better. He is now trying the experiment of lighting by gas. He was obliged to put up the fixtures at considerable expense, but there are many who cannot go in the day that would like to go at night. He gives a short lecture, with figures dressed up in the Indian costume, and all seem highly delighted. He receives the congratulations of friends in America, at his great success, and many of them think from the accounts given by correspondents to the papers there, that he has already made a fortune. But they little know of the heavy expenses, of rent, advertising, and expense of living, which keep a man poor, if he is successful. George undoubtedly *has* done remarkably well for the first year, for it takes anything of the kind, a year, to become well known, and appreciated. He has warm friends here, and they are extremely anxious to have his work come out, and he will receive assistance from them to further it. He desires having it filled with sketches, lithographed, from his gallery.

There is a rumor that the British Museum intend making an offer for it, but I have no idea that they will give the full value of it, and I have yet a hope that when our new President is elected, the government will think proper to buy it.

He has at length got rid of his bears, which I am very glad of, although he did not get what they had cost altogether. They have been in the Zoological Gardens, and were the only pair of the kind, in this country, yet they haggled greatly at the price, but by disposing of them to that society, he did not have to pay any thing for their keeping, since they came.

We are much distressed at hearing of the situation of Mr. Dart, and Hartshorn. Eliza nobly sustains herself under her misfortunes and I trust that her husband will also bear up, and in their new home yet enjoy competence. A better heart, man never possessed than Anson Dart, and the good he has done to others I hope will not go unrewarded. George grieves that he is not able to assist him in the hours of need, we both esteem him, and feel how much more acceptable it would be now, than at any other time. But we are here in a strange land struggling for a living, and if a man is unfortunate here, there is a set of harpies ready to pounce upon him, and take all he has.

I leave the rest of the sheet for Geo. My love to Francis, Elizabeth, Mr. McCreary & family & the Dubois family.

Affectionately your daughter, Clara

My dear parents, Clara has left me a small space which I will fill with great pleasure. She has told you that we are well, and enjoying ourselves tolerably well, and we hope and pray that this may find you all in as good a condition. By your last letter we were much encouraged about Fathers health, which is a subject of great solicitation with us. She has told you that the few past months have been very dull here for my business, and that expenses run on as heavy as in the best of times. We are steadily striving and looking forward for good luck and great success, which may possibly never come exactly within our grasp. If it could happen *just now*, when we could hold up some of our dear friends by extending to them an assisting hand we should deem ourselves doubly and trebly blessed. As Clara has told you, George has made many warm friends here, and as the fashionable season is again approaching he hopes to do something better than he has yet done; if he does not he will not be discouraged, but say what the world all say, that he has done well—done what no other man has done before him, and what in probability none other ever will do. he will be contented with less money and more fame—will love life and his wife & little children—will live for them and his friends, and cheer them and console them if he cannot aid them with his purse. Our greatest care at this time is for the health of our dear parents, and we have fearful apprehensions at the approach of every Steamer that we shall get the sad intelligence of the exit of some of our numerous and dear relatives. you will hear from us about once a fortnight hereafter, such is the frequency of Steamers now running, and you need scarcely imagine us further off than the City of New York.

I enclosed you a draft in my last letter (which you have got ere this) for 120 dols. on Prime, Ward & King, from Barings & Brothers, and I hope to be able in a little time to make you further remittances. I wish Brother Francis & his [wife] success in their approaching cares, and I wish with Clara, to be remembered to all enquiring friends about you. My love to Dear Mother, and believe me still your dutiful and affectionate son, Geo. Catlin.

My model of Niagara I have sent as a present to the Emperor of Russia to be delivered to him by our Minister there, Mr. Cambrelling, with whom I am well acquainted. I am now constructing another far superior & on a scale 4 times as large, for which I think I can find sale in this country. I sent a letter to His Imperial Majesty and also the catalogue of my collection. I shall soon hear from these, and shall report to you.

Eliza writes about Green Lake

FRANCIS CATLIN planned to move his little family to the West the following spring. On November 10, 1840, Eliza wrote her brother glowing accounts of Green Lake; the climate, the way vegetables grew—"The rutabagas are so large that I can get but one in a water pail, and turnips as large as a dinner plate." She spoke of the fat fish in the lake, and the abundance of prairie hens. Eliza wished that her parents could see the beautiful country; "Mother could ride in any direction through the openings, and on the prairie, without any fears, as there are no hills, no bad roads. The roads can never be any other than good. . . ."

Yes, a beautiful country, but lacking "L'argent," as Putnam said. Life was rugged for the family used to hired help on the farm and in the house. Eliza's letter continued: "Dear brother I hope when you come to this country you will not have to labour under such disadvantages as my husband and children have had to. I hope you will have money to help build your house, to buy horses, oxen, and cows and provisions. I hope that you may not be obliged to do without or get the same on credit, or pay by hard day's work, the only hard crying spell I have had was to see how hard Anson and the boys have had to work to make boards for a floor to a part of our house—I had to think of the money that would be sacrificed on our property at Utica, but what cannot be helped must be endured. Mr. Leroy wants Anson to take of him a very valuable yoke of oxen, and a cow, but he will not till he can see what way he can pay as we have to get our provisions on credit. . . ."

Francis answered his sister's letter at once. Eliza wrote his wife Elizabeth on December 28, saying that his letter was the first received from the Bend since she left home. Eliza now wrote: "I was rejoiced to hear that Father was gaining. I hope and trust that by this time he has got entirely well of his cough. Oh that I could step in and see you all once more, nothing but poverty would have induced me to have left my dear Parents so far behind, but I hope and trust I shall see them again if life and health permit. . . ."

Anson Dart had made many friends during earlier trips to Green Bay, and Eliza had become acquainted with some during the week spent there before coming to Green Lake. Not all lived in the town; some had farms as far away as the Darts', or further, but Green Bay was the "city"—the common meeting place for all who lived in that neck of the woods. The farms were far apart, but loneliness brings people together regardless of the miles, and friendship in the wilderness was sought for and cherished.

Mr. and Mrs. Simmons lived midway between Green Bay and the Dart farm, and Eliza wrote that they came to visit, staying two days. They were not poor like the Darts, and knowing of their past troubles, had come to see how they were getting along, bringing with them a huge sage cheese and a fat hog. It did not take them long to size up the situation, and after they returned home they sent the Darts three more hogs, a dozen live chickens, a couple of bushels of beans, and some honey and butter, telling Dart not to pay for the livestock until it was convenient for him to do so. This friendliness meant a great deal to lonely Eliza, who wrote that Mrs. S. was the first female she had seen in three months, and that nothing had made the place appear more like home than the crowing of a rooster the first morning after they received it.

Things were looking up a bit. Mr. Simmons wanted Anson to superintend the building of a mill near his place the following year, and was to get three dollars a day for building a grist mill for Mr. Beall! He was a land agent, and very wealthy. His home was in Green Bay, but he was planning to move to Green Lake in the spring. Eliza said he and his wife lived in great style. Young Putnam had seen his silver plate which had cost over two thousand dollars, and his splendid furniture.

A few miles "down the road" from Darts' lived the kind-hearted and illiterate Pete LeRoy, who took the whole family under his wing. He loaned Anson everything he needed, brought his ox-team over to break up the ground the boys had cleared, helped them sow the corn. Now Anson was buying a yoke of oxen from him, for which he would build LeRoy a house next summer.

There was no school closer than Green Bay. Evenings at the Darts' were spent in reading history, and teaching the younger children. There was no church or meeting house. Eliza wrote that Sunday was the time she thought most of home, and she would sit down and read and sing the hymns her mother had so often sung with her in the happy past. Besides all the work she had to do, she had been making clothes. "Tell mother I have cut and made George and Putnam each a pair of pantaloons, such a thing as I never did before, and I am now making George an overcoat of a Mackinaw blanket, all the fashion at the Bay. I have made three shirts for Mr. Beall's man. . . ."

Christmas day, 1840. Eliza was evidently the only one in the family who held to the Puritan tradition regarding this day. In this same letter, written December 28, she wrote: "On Christmas day Mr. Beal sent his sleigh for Anson and Putnam, to spend the day at his cabin—they dined on venison, patriges and a squeril, Beal has a man to cook for them, George was from home, I was all alone with the little children, I thought much of home and friends."

Anson was proving himself adept in more ways than one, no doubt putting many pennies into the cracked cup on the shelf. He could do anything he was asked to do except shoe a horse. Eliza was amazed at the furniture he turned out, not only for their own house, but for others. "They think in this country that he can do anything and everything. He sets clocks and watches running that have been still for years for want of cleaning. You would laugh to see how many things he has made for people around here, that he never made before, and succeeds well."

This December letter to Elizabeth was a long one, a visit with a dear friend. Eliza finally wrote: "I must bring my letter to a close. I think you must by this time be tired of reading such scribbling. My pen has the same failing that my tongue has, when it gets a-going it never knows when to stop. This you would have known without my telling you."

On January 4, 1841, Putnam wrote to George and Clara:

I rec'd a letter from our friend Dart last week dated the 8th of Dec, his situation is indeed pitiful, though they are well. He went too soon and too far into the Wilderness, winter has arrived on them, their house unfinished for the want of boards & money the floors above & below are but half-laid, he is destitute of neighbours, without a cow, without butter, cheese wheat or bread-stuff except 2 bushels of corn which they have to pound. Nevertheless they all are well and in good spirits. Gracious Heaven! what a change in that family, how can they get through this winter which has approached, however, they will not starve, he says.

I have written to him that I will forward to him a hundred and fifty dollars at least, which may save him through the winter, & he must somehow get credit till he receives my letter inclosing a draught on some bank, probably an Albany Bank. He wrote that he had made and forwarded his affidavit to Asa that his Attorney may defeat the process of the *Post Mortgage* & *Usury* on the mills at Delta, so as he may in a great measure relieve his brother Asa, and he is anxious to hear the result; but I doubt there is no favourable prospect in regard to that defence, which will soon be known. . . .

I have thought proper at this time of life to make my *Last Will and Testament*, giving your dear mother and each of my dear children some Legacy and I have appointed yourself and your brother Francis my Executors of this, my Last Will and Testament. . . . Your affectionate father   P. Catlin.

Francis is told what to bring to Wisconsin

OUT IN GREEN BAY it had not been easy going for the Darts, their first winter in the West, but they were making the best of it. On Anson's shoulders fell the heavy end of the load; he was to blame for the family's condition, and he worked like a horse to earn a dollar. His only chance for a comeback was to acquire a good reputation in this rapidly growing country. Eliza's greatest grief was the knowledge that she probably would never see her beloved parents again.

However, the family's drooping spirits were now buoyed up by the news that Francis and his wife and baby would be coming west in the spring. There would be no more lonely winter months in the isolated homestead on the prairie—kinfolk would be living "next door."

There were many, many things that Francis should bring with him, so Anson Dart sat down and wrote a long letter:

Green Lake 11th Jany 1841

F. P. Catlin
   My Dear Sir,
your favour of the 24th Nov, was recd about one month after it was written. I should hav answered it sooner but, not having any chance to send to the postoffice ear this. your letter gives us much pleasure as it speeks more positive than ever that you will remove to Green Lake in the spring. this is as it should be. I do hope & trust that you will let nothing divert you from this reasonable determination. before I proceed I will inform you that we are all well, cut foots & all are well, we are getting more & more comfortable every day especially so far as our house goes. the winter thus far has been very pleasant no very cold wether except three days the 2d, 3d, & 4th of this month they were like our coldest wether in York State but we have not had a bad storm this winter the snow has been about twelve inches deep on an average no drifting in the openings, in short the climate is decidedly better than that of york state. the sawmill I think I shall defur untill you come as it is a short job. besides I want your opinion as to the best place to set it. the inlett to G. Lake is a good streem with huge tracts of very heavy timber near at hand. the little streem that passes my hous is better calculated for a grist mill than a sawmill I think I shall let Mr. Beall place his mill near our house, he will positively hav erected a mill with our run of stone the coming season. this puts me in mind that he wants you to fetch a black Smith without fale, he will set him to work as soon as he arrives, in fact you must fetch as many with you as you can either mechanics or farmers, there will be very little good 10/ lands to be had after next summer I think. before I forget it must mention some things that you must fetch with you without fale vis. at least one

hundred appletrees, som plums and cherries do [ditto]. Two good plows, 1 cwt of drag teeth, two or three log chains, one nice lumber waggon, a set of cast irons the tire to be in six pieces for each wheel five foot wheels, a good heavy span of horses & new harness would be good property & I think would pay the transportation to fetch them from at least as far east as ohio, you can get in ohio as good horses for $150 a span as you can in P. for 200, but the horses & waggon you must use your own judgement about fetching. you can hardly fetch any thing but what will be usefull in this new country. fetch as good a stock of groceries as you can, as every thing of the kind is high here, tell your shoe makers to fetch a good stock of leather with him, one or two pieces of good heavy woolin cloth for everyday wear would be good property also two or three pieces of brown factory shirting, one or two pieces of calico & many other things of the kind that will suggest themselves to your attention. It gives us great pleasure to learn by your letter that Father Catlin in gaining his health. cannot you perswad him & mother Catlin to come with you in the spring. we hav not as yet received any letter from him (your father) since Eliza arrived but hope we shall soon. you did not mention any thing in your letter about our brother Geo. in London, we get no letters from the South. giv my best respects to Father & Mother also to your dear wife & the dearest & sweetest little one must be kissed once apiece for each of us. Putnam will add a postscrip, write me soon without fale.

yours in hast
Anson Dart

[Note from Putnam Dart]

Uncle Frank

Dear Sir,   Pa says I must say a few words to help fill up his letter. I have nothing particular to say, but that we are all delighted at the idea that you are certainly coming in the spring, as you directed, I have chalked down on the rafter, *"Francis says in his letter dated Dec. 2 that he is coming on in the spring."* But the deer, grouse &c suffer much for want of killing the worst way. we get no time to hunt but I occasionally take a walk sundays, and (all by accident) generally bring from four to a dozen Prairie hens home, therefore the sooner that 35. Rods piece gets along the better. I must here take the opportunity to say that among the things you bring on in the spring I want you to purchase for me at Rochester, a cheap Rifle for which I will repay you, one say worth not more than $20—plain but good, carry about ninety. now sir if this is convenient you will do me the greatest favor by so doing as I am so far from every thing and every body, back in the woods—the rifle I had when you was here is broken so as to be unfit for any use, and I have been in perfect agony ever since. George and myself have been for the last 3 or 4 days cutting rail timber and the way it falls is a caution, not on the 5th or our eighty but on government land. Green Lake is all the go now. Fox Lake "cant shine" you mention in your letter, "tend baby &c." I hope you understand it better than when Mrs. Catlin was at our house at Utica, "dont put that child in my lap or I will drop it on the floor." but enough of that, ma says she should like to see that sweet little Geo Put. & kiss him. we all wait your coming with a great deal of anxiety—

My best respects to all

yours P. C. Dart

P. S. Pa says he forgot to answer that part of your former letter speaking of a certificate of deposite, he says a certificate of deposite is as good here as Spanish dollars.

Letters from London

CHARLES CATLIN's eldest son Burr, twenty-three years old, was still in London on February 7, 1841, when he wrote his "Uncle Francis," who was but two years older than he:

I wish you could see a Royal procession in this country, such as the Queen's opening of Parliament. you would be astonished to see the contrast between Riches & Poverty, the state carriage has the appearance of solid gold, the harness and other trappings beautifully emblazoned, the other house-hold carriages are also of the most magnificent description which contain the Lord Chamberlain & others of the Royal Household, and after seeing this pass turn around and notice the crowd that has collected, and you will see the most miserable, the most poverty stricken looking set of human beings that you could imagine or paint hundreds without scarcely a rag upon them, and these are men women and children, and some of whom are able and willing to work for a living but are unable to get employ, and starve to death in the streets, while the Lords & Gentry are giving their Grand Balls & Soirees and spending thousands almost nightly. The working classes are very poor indeed and the rich are very rich 20,000 Dollars would be considered no fortune in this country.

The English people are I find prejudiced against Yankees, and I have not the least doubt in the world that if Uncle Geo Collection had been made by an Englishman, it would have been purchased by some society or individual before it had been in England 3 months. Uncle Geo has got his subscription book started, and through the influence of the Hon. C. A. Murray (master of the Queen's Household) has obtained Their Majesties the Queen, the Queen Dowager, Prince Albert, the Duchess of Kent (the Queens mother) and many of the nobility's subscriptions which has given it a good start.

I know not when I shall return, but I am quite homesick & I am tired of this country and people, & hope this Canada affair will drive the English root & branch from America if it causes war it will certainly have that effect.

I have been to several Balls in Indian dress, my favourite dress is the pawnee with the red crest, and head shaved. I have worn a wig for nearly 9 months, head all shaved except the scalplock, and I pass for Simon Pure, & speak no English without an interpreter, i.e. at the balls. we sometimes have 20 men in full dress, giving the Indian Dances, Songs War-Parades —Battle & scalping, yells, signals—war whoop &c. all of which takes well here, as it is something new and novel. I obtain tickets to fancy dress Balls, Theatres, and all amusements free of expense.

Please write soon & remember me to Aunt Elizabeth & Grand Parents & all acquaintances at the Bend and let me know the changes that have taken place lately

With the utmost esteem

I am Your Nephew   Theodore B. Catlin

[Notation on back of letter:] 32,500 visitors to the Exhibition About 9433 dollars taken in Year ending Jan. 31st. 1841. Spent *all.*

George Catlin was now working overtime to get his "Great Work" (as he termed it) published as soon as possible. In February, Clara wrote a long letter to his parents:

London February 28th 1841

Dear Father and Mother,

We were much gratified with the perusal of your letter dated Jan. 4th. It is marked by my brother as having been received on the 12 Jan. He sent it by the first Liverpool packet. By a letter from Theodosia to Burr we feared you were not as well, but from the firm hand, and good spirits, evinced in your letter we should imagine you in good health. Our little family and ourselves are in perfect health. This is the best of blessings, for if we have health and strength, we ought to feel contented, if we are not so rich as some.

George is more harassed with anxiety than I could wish, but I still hope a favourable offer may be made him for his gallery, and if so, I shall strongly advocate his selling it although he yet fondly anticipates a price offered for it in his own country. But he has nobly earned a good price for it, and it is time for him to rest on his oars.

It is now fairly ascertained, that he never can more than pay his expenses by it in this great metropolis; much as has been said, London is no place to make money by exhibition. Rent and provisions are just double what they are at home, and the English grudge a shilling more than an American does fifty cents. There are so many shows and exhibitions here, too, that there is no doubt he would do better in some of the large towns. But the expense of moving is so great, that there is a hindrance again, yet he does not think he will remain here another summer, for from the experience of last, he might as well close doors, for after the fashionables leave town, such places do very little.

There are some seven or eight Americans here that have come to seek their fortunes, and find things so much dearer than at home that they get out of pocket money, and their last resource is to come and borrow of George, and he cannot refuse, for I believe if it was his last shilling he would give it to help any one in distress. I say to him sometimes, "I am sure you ought to be rewarded for your kindness to others, for I am sure there are very few who, in your circumstances, would not say no, sometimes."

Your account of Mr. Dart and family is distressing indeed. And George is distressed that he has not been able to aid them. Two such generous souls should never want. The unbounded kindness they have ever shown to kindred and strangers, will never I feel assured, go unrequited. If they can only struggle through this winter, I trust they will live comfortably hereafter. I wrote a long letter to Eliza by the last steamer, explaining to her George's peculiar situation here, and how it distressed him that now when her husband most needed the assistance of friends, that he was unable to lend a helping hand. And though friends at home think he is accumulating wealth, it is far from the case. He is in a country where if any accident should occur, the harpies of the law should soon strip him of everything.

George received a long letter from Henry the other day, strongly urging him to exchange the property at Lockport for a farm at the west, with the payment of a thousand dollars besides. But George thinks Henry may be too sanguine as to the exchange, and feels unwilling, as he has received so many favours from my brother to ask him to give up the mortgage he holds for another, and thought it better not to risk anything and advised Henry to wait until spring, take a favourable offer for his property, pay off the mortgage, and with the remainder of the money buy a farm and settle on it.

I received letters from Abigail and Richard a few days ago. Poor Abigail feels lonely. James and Caroline [their daughter] had just recovered from a long fit of illness, and [he] was about to become the principal of a school at 1,500 dolls a yr. He was anxious to have Theodosia as a teacher, but she refused. She is doing well in Montrose, and I hope she will be wise enough to remain there. She has good friends there, and as long as she gets as good a salary, she had better remain.

Burr is very anxious to return. George has so little for him to do that his time hangs heavy on his hands. I am sorry to see him have so little inclination for study or reading. He has a fine talent for painting, and George thinks he would do well if he could pursue the profession at home. He has copied portraits of the Duke of Sussex and Van Buren, and they are much admired.

George is at present just concluding a bargain for publishing his book. He has been advised by his good friend Mr. Murray, one of the first publishers here, and by others, not to let it out of his hands, but to publish it himself if he wishes to realize anything from it. And is making arrangements to that effect. It will necessarily be expensive, but he has found several kind friends who are willing to aid him by advancing a sum necessary for the commencement. He will have upwards of four hundred illustrations on steel. And will be obliged to reduce every one of them himself from his paintings. He has two artists to assist him, but still he will have to do a great deal to the drawings himself.

The subscription list is filling very well. Yesterday he had an introduction to the Duke of Sussex for the first time. He is uncle to the Queen, and is now upwards of 70 years of age. He is very fond of everything appertaining to Indians, and kept George one hour and half in conversation, denying himself to numerous visitors, for the pleasure, as he expressed himself, of hearing about the Indians. He has never been to George's room on account of infirm health, but he has promised to come with a large party very soon. He told George to send him his subscription book, and he would add his name and get him a number of others. And begged George to visit him frequently.

. . . My dear father has been confined to his room all winter with that painful disease, Tic Doloreux. You cannot tell the intense anxiety we feel for the arrival of each Steamer, always fearing the dreaded tidings of some near and dear relative's decease. When we open our letters, and find all are in comparative health, the pleasure is unspeakable. When I was writing to George here I had a seal with the words "All's well," and he said if he received a letter from me, and he was conversing, he had only to look at the seal to relieve immediate anxiety.

I have promised to leave a space for G, but he is so much occupied that he postpones writing until the last day, and then writes so hurriedly. That I tell him gives you no satisfaction. And as women have longer tongues I said I would for once give you a good long letter with all the news, and if you can get through it, you will do well. . . . Our little daughters are fat and hearty, and George feels very happy when he comes home at night, and gets one on each knee. . . .

Your affectionate daughter
Clara B. Catlin

George added a note:

My Dear Father and Mother, Clara has offered me a very small space for a postscript, and I use it with great pleasure and solicitude for your health. She has more leisure to write than I have, and has said all that I could have said myself almost relative to our condition and prospects. The times are dull here, to be sure, and as I am publishing, my anxieties very great. There is at this time a most dreadful prejudice here against Americans on account of the Boundary and other frontier questions, which operates very much against me. However, I despair not, but will do the very best I can, and trust to the event. Love to Francis and wife, and all enquiring friends.

Your affectionate and dutiful son
Geo. Catlin

These were difficult times in America. The Pensacola Bank had failed, and James had bought a plantation in Alabama. Richard's money was tied up in land, which he planned to hold onto until he could get his price. He was now looking for a position in the North.

The following letter from George shows a lack of his former exuberance. He had many problems. His hopes were now centered on the coming publication of his book on the North American Indians, hoping it would yield a sufficient harvest for him to clear up his debts and affairs in London, and return to his own country.

London, June 19th, 1841

My Dear Father,

This letter leaves Clara and myself & little ones all well, & all join me in the prayer that it may find you and our dear mother in good health and spirits. I wrote by the last Steamer, and also sent a pamphlet to you to the care of D. L. Gregory in Jersey City. We learned by a letter just rec'd from Mr. Gregory that Richard & wife are with you which is good and cheering news to us, inasmuch as their society, with that of Francis & wife will save you from the lonesomeness of your condition which would be cruel and painful were you beyond the vicinity & society of all of your children. Those who are now around you will be a comfort to you, and suffice perhaps in the absence of one who is older and whose business at this time more peremptorily calls for his exclusive application. It does seem as if I never should be free, and that my business more imperatively calls for all my exertions at this time than it ever has on any former occasion. I am so completely engrossed with my Book that I am getting out and with my Exhibition that I have scarcely time to write my letters to my dearest friends. What success my Book will meet with is yet to be decided, like everything else of my life, by the experiment.

It gives me pain to see that the fair & golden prospects of all our friends at Pensacola should have fallen to the ground by the disastrous turn of the times; yet by their breaking up there, there will be one consolation to you and dear mother in your declining age, the satisfaction of having some of your children around you. And for myself, who have laboured and toiled so long, I would gladly retire from the bustle & bother of the business world, of which I am completely sick, and draw myself and little family close around my dear parents in the decline of their lives, seeking and enjoying that inestimable pleasure which is found only in simple life, in retirement with those whom we love and adore.

How soon I may get through with the arduous & perplexing sort of life that I am now necessarily leading, and be able to hover about my aged parents, I am unable to say, yet I hope to see the time not far distant & I will look for it in constant hope. As the Rail Road is about to go through, and its location such as to benefit you at the G. Bend I am in hopes that Richard & Francis may find a prospect of something to turn their hands to at that place, or that property may command such a price as to enable you to realize something from your property there. My outlays for my Book are very heavy, and I am bound in self defence to make the greatest sales of the work that I can in this country, which will require me to travel about the Kingdom a while, visiting some of the principal towns with my Gallery, selling my Book at the same time. And at what time I may be able to turn my course back to my own dear country I cannot yet say. In my *necessary* absence I trust that Richard & Francis will deem it their duty to give you as much of their immediate attention and company as possible.

As to Exhibitions in London at this time they are all *dead*. Nothing is doing scarcely in any business, and a general panic has spread over this great and rich country owing to a difficulty amongst the Ministers which results in a few days in a dissolution of Parliament. This will operate very much against the sale of my work when it first comes out, yet I dont despair of its selling well. I shall write by another Steamer which starts in a few days, & I hope *really* that I shall be able for *that* to sit down and write a more faithful & careful letter than this which is scribbled off at the last moment. Give our love to Brothers and their wives and also to other enquiring friends, and believe us, dear parents, your affectionate children—Geo. & Clara B. Catlin.

George's next letter shows his sincere interest and generosity toward his family back home. Evidently Henry's oldest son had worked his way across the ocean in hopes that his Uncle George could find him a job.

London, July 3rd 1841

Dear Father,

A Steamer starts tomorrow for New York, and as Clara and self are preparing letters to send off to a number of friends I shall begin with you first on the list. This leaves us both well, and also the dear little ones, who are now so playful and so much and so good company as to take up every moment of time that we can devote to them. Libby has grown to quite a lusty and fat girl & a real little, old fashioned lady, & would chat Grandma almost to death if she could be with her at this time. She has a perfect recollection of her Grandma & "berries some" which she inseparably couples together and probably will all her days. "Conny" (as I call her) Clara is now a year and half old and just begins to run alone and talk a little, is full of fun and wit and makes us happy & good company. The next one will be a boy we think, and of him we may perhaps give you some account in our next letter. Clara is in pretty good health and joins in love to all. We heard of you the other day by the letter of D. L. Gregory who saw Richard on his way to Washington, and says that he reported you all well at the Great Bend. Save this intelligence we have not heard a word from you in the last month or more. We can imagine you and dear mother now, so well attended by your children that you will be able to enjoy life very much instead of suffering from the gloom that would be hovering around you if all your children were absent. I feel anxious, and exceedingly so that Richard may get the appointment at Pensacola, and I think his letter from Mr. Gregory to Judge Southard may be of some avail to him. Both Clara and myself are familiarly acquainted with him, and that may aid also.

I am exceedingly anxious to hear what is the prospect about the Rail Road by the Bend, for I think if it goes through there it will open the way for some kind of business there for Francis and perhaps for Richard also. If there is any prospect of selling the "Big House" to any advantage & you think best, I wish you to do as you please about it, as I before told you. If my business here had been as productive as I had reason to expect, I should have paid the whole amount for it ere this, and I would by all means keep it. But anything *for your own benefit* I would wish you to do, without hesitation. If you can get a good offer for cash, and you want the money, dont keep it for me, but sell it at once. Francis wrote enquiring about the price &c. of a part of the lot adjoining the house and garden. I leave it all to you to do as you think best with him. I am laying out all the money I can raise at this time in publishing my Book which I trust may repay me well, but I dont know certain yet. The London & American Editions, both of which I am getting out here nearly at the same time, will both together, cost me little short of 10,000 dols. but I hope they will soon pay me back again the money I outlay for them, and a great deal more. My mind & body have both been almost entirely engrossed in it, and I never before was so completely a slave as I have been for several months past, having had to make all the drawings myself, and prepare my notes. The Parliament has just been adjourned, or in other words dissolved, which calls a new Election and almost revolutionizes the country—all business is suddenly at a stand and nothing doing scarcely, in any business.

Henry, the *Whaler*, I sent off the day before yesterday to Liverpool, where he sails for N. York on Monday the 4th July on the Cornelia, a fine ship. I could not set him at anything here, & his best place is in America where he can get something to do. The sort of life that Burr is in also is a very dangerous one, & I think he will start also in a few weeks. I am anxious to visit some of the interior towns with my collection where I am sure of doing more than I can now do in London, as the thing is so well advertised through the kingdom. My Book must come out before I can move, after which I shall soon be off.

I wish you would drop a line to Henry and tell him that Henry junior is on the way after staying with me two months. I have clothed him and given six guineas to start with in pocket when he gets to N. York. Love to all, your affectionate son

Geo Catlin

George's life now revolved around two impending events; the publication of his book, and the birth of another child, which he hoped would be a boy.

George never mentioned his purely social life in his letters to his father, although he was a popular and sought-after guest in London society. He well knew his parent's Puritan-based disapproval of any public display of frivolity, and that a letter of reproach would arrive shortly after.

In the following letter, which included a note to Richard, who was visiting his parents, George added a jovial postscript telling of his taking Clara through the famous Bank of England. This certainly can not be classed as a "social affair," but finding a light touch in his letters is pleasing. George was well known for his keen wit, but evidently it was not appreciated by his father.

London, July 18th 1841

Dear Father,

I received your letter of June fifth the day before yesterday and hasten to answer by the Boston Steamer of tomorrow. I pray to God that this may find you and dear Mother in good health, and good spirits. It leaves us all well; little ones fat and playful and my dear Clara expecting daily to be the mother of a *John Bull!* [13] I rec'd Richard's letter from New York too, in due season, and I hope he will have succeeded in getting his appointment. If he should not, I hope he may find it somehow convenient, and for his interest to stay with Darwina and cheer the fireside of my dear parents till I can again get home and greet them once more. It is quite lucky that Richard and Francis can both be with you, and I can but hope that my business will so turn that I can join also in the circle of the dear homestead and enjoy awhile, at all events, some retirement and some relief from my increasing labourious & mental excitement. Whether such a period is to be allotted to any part of my life or not, I cannot yet tell, but I shall constantly look forward for it while I live. If the Rail Road is to be made through by the Bend, I confidently hope there will be either some chance for business for Richard and Francis, to enable them to stay by your side, and some purchasers for your property so that you can sell to

---

[13] "Johnny" turned out to be Victoria Louise; born in July or August, 1841.

advantage in case you should follow them anywhere else. The trouble and expense of getting out my Book has far exceeded anything I calculated on, & yet I am nearly through it, and confidently hope it will yield me something handsome.

Richard said something of taking the agency of it at the South which you all know I could join him with such high confidence, and with such pleasure also, were it not that I have long since entrusted it to one sale agent for the U. States who would only take it on the condition of having the sole management of it for the whole country. Wiley & Putnam of N. York have the selling of the work in America, and I have no power of appointing other agents.

As we must be separated yet a while longer and it is so difficult for you to write, I hope that Francis and Richard and their wives will save you the trouble of more than dictating—amongst so many there should be some one to sit down and give us a detailed report of the health & success of all about you. I should have ans'd Richard's letter today, but that I am writing twenty letters at least, & it would be cruel for me to write more than one to a place. Wishing health to dear, *dear* Mother and all Brothers and Sisters about you, and a prolongation of your life till we can meet again, I bid you all farewell, having a little space for my dear Clara to say a few words. Your affectionate son Geo. Catlin.

Dear Richard,

Since writing the above, Clara has gone to bed, too feeble for the task of filling up the sheet as I had above mentioned, & she desires to be remembered to all and excused by all for not writing. I mentioned that I was indebted to you a letter, and Clara tells me I have rec'd two of yours without having answered either, which brings me more into your debt than I thought. The times of our lives have passed by however when we should stand upon forms with each other, and as my life has been one of such crazy excitement I hope you will accept this short appeal to you an answer for both. If I were a man of leisure I would write much more deliberately and say more than I now can, and more to the point.

My transcendent anxiety now is for the health and enjoyment of our dear parents, and I hope you and Francis will do all that is in your power to aid and comfort them. Stay by them if you in any way can consistently with your interests, and do all you can to gild their latter days. Write to me on the rec't of this, and make it a rule for some one to write about them and their health by every Steamer. In haste I subscribe myself your affectionate Brother—Geo. Catlin.

[on back of letter]

But a few days since Clara and I with some other Americans went by permission through the Bank of England, which was a great sight. The building covers five acres of ground and has 900. clerks employed in it. To see the tons of gold and silver lying on wheelbarrows in the vaults was enough to make ones eyes sore. And whilst in the Treasury office under ground, the officer took out of one of the iron safes a bundle of Bank notes and put them into my wifes hands saying to her You have now two millions of pound sterling in your hands, and laying another package on the top of it, "You have now three millions five hundred thousand pounds in your hands. (near 17,000,000 dols.) poor little thing looked around most wistfully for a place to fly off, but could see no chance, and has been very nervous ever since.

George publishes his book on the North American Indians

PUTNAM WROTE to George and Clara on the 24th of August. His penmanship was shaky, but his mind as clear as ever.

"I embrace this opportunity of answering your letter of Aug. 2d which informed us of your health, and kind remembrance of us. We are well, except my continued weakness. Richard and Darwina are still with us, and comfort us, they are indeed a worthy and happy couple, in about two or three weeks they will leave us, they will remain 3 weeks in N York, 2 or 3 weeks in Phila. Richard will then proceed to Pensacola and attend to his affairs and determine whether he will return to the North or fix down on his lands in the South, in the meantime [Darwina] return from Philadelphia to spend the winter with us. R has about two thousand acres of land in Apalachicola & Alabama which cost him one dollar & 25 cents per acre in cash which he paid some years ago, he has two dwelling houses, one in Pensacola, the other in Apalachicola each rented at about $300 per year, more than he is indebted for the purchase; he brought with him about [illegible] of southward bank notes payable next year, which will not pass now for more than 50 per cent at this time. I am exceedingly pleased with him and his Darwina. It is uncertain whether he will receive an appointment, nor does he much desire it. Our friends at Green Lake are all well and seem pleased with their location. Mr. Hartshorn and family are well, Mary & her oldest son made us a visit to meet Richard here, she is in good health. we have not heard from Henry lately. we shall be exceedingly anxious to hear from dear Clara's health and safety; also for your success in closing your business in London favourably. I cannot express the anxiety I have in regard to your great work and difficulty, but strongly hope soon to hear of a favourable result, and trust that you will not be discouraged. In regard to my health I can only say, that I have hopes of recovery of my cough which has in some degree abated & will not end in a consumtion. It is with difficulty I write, and must end my letter presenting my best love to you & Clara and the dear children. your mother, Richard, Francis & Darwina send love & perhaps some of them will probably write to you soon.

Your affectionate father P. Catlin

219

Again, on October 4, Putnam wrote to George:

I commence a letter which will be short and clumsey, but will assure you that I am some what better of my long illness since the fall has commenced. the rest of the family are quite well. Richard & his wife are in New York, on their way to the South but will wait a week or two in Phila he will not fail of writing to you. He forwarded a paper to me dated 22 Sept which I rec'd last evening in the Newark paper bearing a friendly letter from R. R. Gurley to F Marcoe Esq. corresponding Sec'ty, National Institution Washington—much in your favour. It is intended to bring the subject before our Congress by your friends at the Winter Session. I hope it will be in your power to meet them in season, provided you shall not have an offer in London.

In regard to the N Y & Erie Rail road—A prodigious & uncommon meeting has been held in the city of N York & proceeded to Goshen as far as the road has been finished. more than 500 persons went up in the Car from the North river; the Governor, the men in office, the principal merchants, the officers of the Comapny &c. the meeting was held for two days, speeches made &c. The great object was to prefer the southern tier instead of the northern or middle tier, it is settled and marked & established about 8 miles up the river from Binghamton, thence to the Delaware river passing round the little Penn'a Bend with the consent of Penn'a, which is obtained, so that we can be certain of our advantage. . . . I received your Draft of $300, and one of $120 which are indorsed on your Contract at the time, I shall charge you no interest until 1st of January next, if you think best to keep the house & lot & come yourself. I have paid M M Wallace about 600 dols on my bond & mortgage for the 18 acres of land, the Residue of it about $800, if you can conveniently send me a Draft of three or four hundred dollars it will help me in taking up the bond & mortgage some time in Nov. and oblige me, but not to crowd yourself in doing it.

Your Mother and Francis and wife send their best love to you and Clara and the three dear little children. I hope to see you here this fall with your dear children.

You see that I am broken down with pen . . . .

Your affectionate Father
Putnam Catlin

George's great work on the North American Indians was finally published.[14] His book received extravagant praise from the press—comparable to that given the artist at the opening of his gallery of Indian paintings.[15]

A letter to his father shows George's elation, but he was holding his usual optimism in check until he found out how the book would sell.[16] The past year had been difficult and full of anxiety, in spite of the applause and early success of his exhibition. He was now more humble; he did not intend to crow until he could see the joyous light of dawn.

London, Nov. 3d, 1841.

My Dear Father,

I received your last letter in due season, about a week ago, and it gave us great pleasure to hear that all were well at the Bend; and the Rail Road actually decided to go by your village.

Clara & little ones are well, but our dear little Libby has narrowly escaped with her life, from a violent fever. We had the most impatient anxiety for her fate, but, thank Heaven she has recovered and is to be spared to us for a while longer, at all events. Our deepest solicitude is now for our aged parents, and

---

[14] In October, 1841, George Catlin published his two large volumes, *Letters and Notes on the Manners, Customs, and Condition of the North American Indian*, at the Egyptian Hall, Piccadilly, London.

[15] See Appendix IV for excerpts from the British press.

[16] In speaking of Catlin's literary achievements, Thomas Donaldson said: "His works had an enormous circulation, probably more than double that of any other writer of the North American Indians. . . . It is safe to say that more than twenty thousand copies of the large work (the two volumes) were sold . . ." (*The George Catlin Indian Gallery, p. 734*).

our greatest pleasure is to hear of their health and comforts. To their health I cannot administer, but to their comfort and happiness I feel as if I should be adding something materially by this time, and if I fall short of it much longer it will be cause of the most poignant and lasting grief of my life. To the proposal in your letter, how gladly would I reply by enclosing a draft for a thousand or more Dollars if it were *at this time in my power*. I have for 8 months past, been struggling against every obstacle, to get out my work, which was contracted to have been out in 3 months, & at last have got it before the world, with an expense of £1100.00 (ie 5500. dols.) for English Edition & £600.00 (3000. dols.) for Am. Edition, one half of which I have already been obliged to pay—while my Gallery has been lying quite dead, & scarcely yielding me anything. I have just now began to circulate it and receive its avails, and a few weeks will decide how well I am to be paid. I sell the Book, since I have published, at £2.10, about 12. dollars per copy & the Am. Edition will be 8. dollars. The commissions for selling are heavy and still my profits will be fair & considerable if I can give it an extensive sale, for which I must try hard. It has been reviewed in the most complimentary manner by the first Literary papers in London & consequently in the world. No book of the present age, it is said, has had so frequent and undivided applause. You can see by this, how critical and exciting a condition I stand in at present, and how pressing my pecuniary calls have been, and are to be while applying the first receipts from its sale. A week or two will enable me to say what I am to do and what I can do to relieve you from embarrassments, which should not hover around you in this time of life. I shall write you by the next Steamer, and shall live in the hope that your health may be spared,—that no unpleasant embarrassments may come upon you —and that time and good luck, in reward of my arduous and slavish labours, may render it within my power to aid you out of any pecuniary difficulties.

I rec'd a letter from Richard on his way to Pensacola, who

told me how much he regretted to leave you, but that business &
duty called him imperatively back. Francis I suppose is with you
and is a comfort and company for you and dear mother. In
the absence of all the rest of us, if he is not buffetting with the
world, in the anxieties and uncertainties of "business" in the
thankless pursuit of money making, he has the consolation that
none of us have, that he is calmly, & without incurring heavy &
dangerous expenses in the most discouraging times, enjoying the
quiet and peaceful fireside of his aged and dear parents, and
drawing from their society that satisfaction which business and
money making (or rather money *seeking*) cannot give. I have
ordered a number of my Books to be delivered to Mr. D. L.
Gregory for friends, and I have directed one to you, which you
had better send to his house for if any one is going down to the
city.

In great haste, with love to dear Mother, to Francis & Lady &
to other enquiring friends, I remain your affectionate & dutiful
son

Geo. Catlin

From Clara:

My dear Father & Mother

I was extremely sorry to hear from Richard & Darwina that
they were obliged to leave you—oh how often do George and I
wish we were safely settled by you in the big house, but it is not
to be—poor George has to be the publics slave a while longer,
our lives are narrowing to a smaller space, and we must be
resigned. Richard made application for one of our daughters—
ah, he will know—when he has them—how hard it is to part with
any of them. Ours are thriving and well. Remember us to
enquiring friends. It makes me proud to hear my dear husbands
work so highly spoken of by all his friends, giving him as much
credit for his writing as for his painting.

Adieu—ever your affectionate
Clara

Putnam answered George on November 29, but made no comment on the triumphant publication of his book. He was a sick old man, wracked with financial worries. It seems that George was the only son to whom he could turn for consolation and help. One wonders why Richard did not dispose of some land—even at a loss—to help his father out of his difficulties. Putnam needed but eight hundred dollars. Richard was not penniless. In Eliza's letter to Francis' wife Elizabeth, dated November 21, 1841, Eliza wrote: "I hope Richard will conclude to return in the spring, and settle at the Bend or at Green Lake, he has written Anson to select for him three to six hundred acres of land of the best quality near us. Darwina says in her letter to me that it is the wish of her heart to move to Green Lake. . . ."

Great Bend Nov'r 29 1841

My dear Son,

I received your letter of Nov 3 and now set down to commence a letter to you, having waited several days to be more able to think and write. I rejoice to hear that you and your family are all well, but that your engagements have been too great and difficult for your comfort, as I fear, but hope you will shortly find relief. my family are all well except myself I am very weak and confined to the house, but your mother was never been in better health, and taking good care of me, my cough has in some measure subsided, but my weakness continues.

I believe I informed you that in June last the family of Wallace at Burlington & paterson, chiefly sisters, have had a meeting and separated, and placed Eliza B. Wallace one of the sisters in the Room of Mary M. W, who (Eliza B.) is to manage the property in future; being in possession of the whole property. Since which, she has written four letters of her station, particularly in respect to my bond of 1200 dolls given to M. M. Wallace for the conveyance to me of eighteen hundred and 44 acres of the unsold pieces & parcels of land in the Townships of Brooklyn, New Medford & Bridgewater in the county of Susq'h, which bond and mortgage was transferred by M. M. W, to the said Eliza B, payable the 1st day October 1841, on which bond, six hundred and twenty dollars indorsed at different times leaving about 800 due. She wrote immediately the payment of the Bond, & set the day that I must come down and bring par money, & has since written three letters in singular stile, calculating what day I could arrive, or she would employ an Atty, she wrote that she would wait no longer than 6 days—in her last letter, she has used most insulting language, but at length if I would enclose $300 currency that the residue be paid within a month, the *Gentlemen* are advised to withhold further proceedings—and closes thus, "Please not to delay even for one day, an answer to the letter."

If you can be suited to keep the white house, I shall be anxious that you keep it by all means. The opinion is that it would fetch three thousand dolls next spring and more after the work is finished. You have paid already paid one check 300 dolls. another check of one hundred & 20—120 dolls.

In my last Will and Testament

	300
	120
	300
allowed to each of my sons—	$720

Leaving $1350 only left.

I was anxious to know whether you would think of coming home this fall or next spring, or whether you had any offer for your Gallery. I think you would do better with it here than in England, there is danger of fire there as well as water. I think of you every hour that I may never live to see you again.

In regard to the $800 I know of no way to raise it, but to call on some friend to advance the money from some friend who will exchange the money and keep the bond and mortgage for security of the white house. In a short time, this I could do if I was well, the girl said she called on Mr. Gregory but he declined doing it. I have thought of sending your brother

Francis to Wyoming [County] to see if our friends Hollenback and Esquire Beach who are very able. Hollenback called on me a few weeks ago & Laird Beach intended to see me this winter as an old friend and fellow soldier of the Revolution. Hollenback said Beach was worth $100,000. Hollenback is worth 300 thousand. They are both friendly to you. You will see this writing how broken down I am.

Give my love to dear Clara & the dear children.

Your dear Parent
P. Catlin

This may have been the last letter Putman Catlin wrote to George.

News from the Pioneers

BECAUSE of his father's failing health Francis did not go to Wisconsin in the spring of 1841 as he had planned, but in the early fall Putnam showed so much improvement that Francis was sure he would be able to make the trip the following year. On November 21, Eliza wrote to Elizabeth, Francis' wife. It reflected her happy state of mind and apparent contentment with her new life:

Anson has been writing to Francis on business, and I have many things to say to you which I could not crowd into his letter, your long letter gave me much pleasure as it assured me of the health of yourself and family. I am rejoiced to hear that my dear Father is better, and that Mother's health continues good as usual. It must have been a great source of comfort to them to have such a good visit from Richard and Darwina this summer—I hope Darwina will conclude to spend the winter with them, she will help them from getting lonesome and gloomy. I hope Richard will conclude to return in the spring, and settle at the Bend or at Green Lake, he has written to Anson to select for him from three to six hundred acres of land of the best quality near us. Darwina says in her letter to me that it is the wish of her heart to move to Green Lake—she said she has persuaded Richard to wish the same. Richard said he should like to secure some of the best land, but that it was not probable that he should occupy them for several years. I am pleased to find you are still anxious to come to our place. I hope Francis will be able to come in the spring, Olivet Dart [Ansons's brother] came by land all the way with his family in their own waggon, a distance of nine hundred miles. They performed the journey in four weeks. Their horses did not give out, as I should have expected. They sent their furniture by the Lakes to Green Bay—they are waiting for sleighing to bring it to Green Lake. They have been at our house six weeks. Their house is nearly finished they will move in a few days. They are delighted with the country. Sally is (as might be expected) a little homesick, because we have no meetings, no schools, and no places to visit, she has always been a great hand to visit, she will soon have neighbours enough. They will do well here, they have no such hardships to encounter as we have had. They have money and teams to help them—we had none, tell Francis Mr. Plumb is helping Anson build Mr. Beall's house, we shall number seven families this winter, we shall have a school, I think—if Francis comes in the spring I hope he will persuade some good Physician to come with him, three ladies from this place have had to go to the Bay to be confined, tis too bad, do not think I am speaking in reason for myself—tis very necessary that we should have a Physician here, and one would do well. F. must persuade some good neighbours to come with him. you will perceive by my language that I expect you earley in the spring. Elizabeth says she will supply you with hens to begin with, and pigs too. we put 4 large hogs in the pen to fat for our winters pork, but soon found three of them were going to have pigs, this will make Frank laugh, never mind they will all come in play if we can keep them through the winter, tell F we have got a horse and if he wishes to see him he must come soon, for he will not live always. Judge Perse from the Bay, I expect will build in the spring adjoining Mr. Beall. Francis is acquainted with him, tell Father and Mother they need not give themselves any unnecessary trouble on our account, we are doing the best we can. . . . Mary says I must stop writing for she wants to say something now dear sister if you love me you will not let this letter be seen—

[Note from Mary Dart added]

Dear Elizabeth,

One year has elapsed since we have seen each other or our good friends at the East and I sensure myself severely for so long neglecting to write you. . . . You cannot imagine our anxiety to have your family for neighbours we are quite confident you would be contented here although the society is small we live in hopes if it were not for hope we should have dispared long back. I came from the Bay in February last since then I have been from home but once and that was a visite of three weeks. Ma nor myself have never had one lonely or dispairing moment, in the summer months we could pass our time pleasantly in rambling gathering flowers strawberrys &c.[17] I have spent much time on our beautifull lake we hope by the time you get here to have a fine sail boat we are making great calculations about your joining us, relying on your promise of the spring, the writing on the rafter we have been obliged to discard. . . . your sweet little one I have heard praised so

---

[17] Richard Dart later wrote that he wished he could adequately describe the prairie flowers. "Every month during spring and summer they grew in endless variety—such fields of changing beauty, I never saw before. It was a flower-garden everywhere. . . . There was also a tea-plant, whose leaves we dried for tea. When in blossom, the oak and clay openings, for miles around, were white with it, like buckwheat. We also had splendid wild honey from bee-trees." (*Settlement of Green Lake County, p.* 261.)

highly I long to see more than you can immagine. I wish you to kiss him for me once a day untill I can have the privalige tell him to remember couzin Molly. I must make excuses for Ma as well as myself about writing our pen is so poor we have no knife or boy to obviate the difficulty and further we are obliged to write in such haste you will please excuse us

in haste yours aff
Mary

George and Putnam Dart wrote to Francis on December 24, 1841. George began the letter:

Uncle Frank
Dear Sir

In the first place merry christmas to all hands big and little old young And then in the next place you will find out that this is doing with a led pensil in sted of ink and pen. Because we have not got any ink in the house and soft maple trees are as scarce, but you must not think of that. But enough of this and now to the point. It is snowing like blazes from the North cost this is the first snow that we have had this winter I suppose we shall get about three or six inches this lick We have had warm weather this fall and winter untill too or three days past it has been cold some not much. The way we make the old saying good about (lite stroaks falls Great Oaks) is a sin no one but Put Lenk and my self in the spring we shall have this 80 all under a good fense. it takes about 8,000 rails but 4000 we split last winter and spring Father is at work at Mister Bealls on his house Mr Plum is at work with him it will take untill February to finish it. Mr. B. is drawing his goods from the Bay at this time his family will come on next month they dont wait for the house to be entirely finished. I shant say much about the Digins [illegible] for Put will do that for if I tell all of the doings he will have nothing to say. I want you should if you come to Wisconsum in the spring to fetch me a rifle one worth $25 or 30 dolers Short and light caring big ball say 50 to the pound if you will do so I will pay you all costs of transportation and trouble if you will do so I wish you would write and let me now in your next if you think it would be to much trouble i must loock out some whare else fore when I go hunting I have to go to or three miles to borow a rifle and then it will snap six times before she goes. Put will tell you the rest, all are well and more contented give my respects to all of my relutry

yours G Dart

Uncle Francis, dear Sir,

Geo has left a great deal for me to say but to make out much I am afraid I shall be deficient. we are all driving along about as usual—(which is work every day) & when people pass here they invariably say—you get along very fast. I never saw any farm improve as fast, considering the help—& I can assure you we have got a smart chance of a settlement here—Mr. Beall is driving business in the large way. Pa & Mr. Plumb are the carpenters, they have got up a neat log house 20 by 26 for a kitchen & adjoining a frame, two stories 32 by 25 feet & altogether comfortable & neat (for the country) house. Mr. Bealles family will move in about 3 or 4 weeks probably. his teams are already hauling over his plunder. I suppose you have already heard the whole routine of Olivet's family's arrival & of his being snugly settled in his little log cabin. the family are all very well pleased & contented except aunt Sally (who, as you know such old women are never exactly contented) all her prejudices are no society—villages—roads—waggons—carriages &c &c everything else suits very well, beautiful country climate & soil. . . . I know of nothing else that is of importance to communicate at this time I think. Sometimes you must think very strange that the sum & substance of all the letters you get from here are continued praise of the country & the fact is that is all we can find to write about. . . . the family all join me in sending a great deal of love to you & family—

I am very Respectfully yours
Putnam C. Dart

PART FIVE: WAR-WHOOPS AND TRAGEDY

1842–1845

1842: Letters from George, Eliza and Richard; The death of a patriarch; the end of an era; "Poor Henry" and the Bankrupt Law; George goes to Liverpool; The Dart family writes to Clara 1843: War-whoops in London; The Darts urge George and Clara to come to Wisconsin; Letters from Henry and Mary; Eliza writes to her mother; George writes to his mother; Francis disappoints the Darts. 1844: Letters from Anson, George, and Polly; The death of Polly—Letters from Mary, Henry, and Eliza; More war-whoops in London.

CONFIDENT of reaping a fortune in London, George had agreed to pay off the mortgage on the Bowes house at Great Bend. His desire to help his father was sincere, but his expressions of remorse over his inability to do so become monotonous.

The following letter from the artist held one item of extreme interest, and could have filled a page or two. How Putnam would have enjoyed reading at length about his son's visit with the Queen of England! However, the "big names" were but briefly mentioned in George's adolescent account of his own success and popularity. Perhaps self-adulation was necessary to George at this period to cover up an unfamiliar sense of insecurity.

London, February 3d, 1842

My Dear Father,

Since the date of my last letter which you have received ere this, we have all enjoyed good health in our little family, and we have only to trust to kind Providence that yourself and dear Mother & all around you of kindred ties have been enjoying the same. We are at this time extending the most anxious feelings of our whole lives towards our beloved country & our dear friends whom we have left there. Clara, to her dear & kind Father, whose health by the last accounts threatened his annihilation in a few days—and I, to my dear Father, who is suffering in his advanced age, (when he should enjoy the quiet and stillness of peaceful life) harrassed & distracted with pecuniary troubles. This to me is mortifying beyond all my powers of description, inasmuch as I, with all my *wealth* and eclat, am as yet unable to lift him out of his present difficulties. I hope however to see him soon raised above want, and for that period am severely struggling with my affairs.

I cannot indulge the belief that Mary M. Wallace would

allow her termigant sister to distress you about the Bond, and I confidently hope that *some arrangement* will have been made ere this, resting it upon such a footing as may help you along until I can do something for you. The White House will be enhanced in value, and so your other property, by the location of the R. Road, & it would be a pity to sacrifice them now after you have held on to them in the worst of times.

You will see by the papers sent that I am still honoured in this country—that I have had the distinguished and envied honour of an interview with Her Majesty & the Prince Albert in the Palace for the purpose of exhibiting to them my model of Niagara (a copy, about 3 times as large and ten times as elaborately finished, as the one you have seen). I was introduced to them by my sincere friend, Mr. Murray, and had the opportunity of conversing with them both.

I often think, and as often tell Clara, that this will give our dear Parents great pleasure to think that, from a little *go-to-mill-boy* I have worked my way across the Atlantic, & at last into the Palace & presence of the Queen of England, and more than all that, received from her own lips her thanks for the interesting information which I had given her.

The King of Prussia is now in London and I expect Him and the Baron de Humboldt, who is with him, to visit my Rooms tomorrow. they may not, but I think they will. The whole expense of my book (the English and American Editions, 2,000 copies) has been £1860.00 (9000 dols.), which is nearly paid to itself, and I hope will soon be able to produce me a continued and handsome profit. It has been most honourably reviewed in the three greatest Reviews in the world, the Westminster—the Quarterly & the Edinburgh Reviews, and all alike speak in the highest terms, and recommend it to the reading of all, and it must sell. before this reaches you, you will undoubtedly have rec'd a copy of it from Mr. Gregory—if not you are to send for it by first chance. He has a copy for you. The first pay day of my Publishers in New York (who are to settle once a quarter) will be on the 1st of April, at which time I hope (at least) to be able to render you some assistance. I shall do it sooner if practicable which may be the case. You have encouraged me through life, and I must beg you to listen to me in your old age. when nothing better than counsel is at hand, receive that and grieve not at embarrassments, for if you have good health & enough to eat and friends who love you *be happy*, and we will depend on meeting again ere long and in better times and under *better* auspices.

Dont let Francis get out of patience or discouraged; life is long for him, and chances enough ahead of him for him to succeed—give our love to dear Mother, to Francis & wife & all others of kin around you.

Your affectionate son
Geo. Catlin

Clara sends a paper with an account of the landing of the King of Prussia in the Greenwich Hospital. She and I were in the hospital, and from a window overlooking had a perfect view of the whole scene. The King, Prince Albert, and Duke of Wellington were in full view and close before us.

George's usual egotism was absent from his next letter. He spoke of the monetary upheaval in the United States, and its effect on Americans abroad. It is possible that he was beginning to feel this cool wind of disfavor, but he was in no position to pack up and go home.

London, March 3d, 1842

My Dear Father,

I write you this letter which I consider as an answer to the very handsome and affectionate one just rec'd, and jointly written by Francis and his wife. By that letter we rec'd great consolation, inasmuch as it assured us of your tolerable health and enjoyment, and also of the excellent health and happiness of dear-*dear* and ever kind Mother. Heaven we trust will spare you both again to bless us when we shall return from our long

235

protracted and tedious absence, where business and interest have doomed me to stay much longer than I designed.

This letter leaves us all well, with our three dear little girls chirping around us, and we are all struggling to do the best we can to enable us to get home again to the land of our birth & the bosom of our dear friends. You will have rec'd and read ere this, the copy of my Book, and no doubt heard *some* of the many (and in fact unanimous) encomiums which have been passed upon it in the Literary papers & magazines of this country. £1965, (i.e. $9825) has been the cost of the whole, and nearly all is now paid for, so that the prospect is that of a pretty fair profit in the end. How it may sell in America is yet uncertain, but the present scarcity of money will operate, no doubt, very fatally against an $8. work. I have the whole work now steriotyped, so that the future Editions will be printed off much cheaper, and consequently will afford me much fairer profits.

It affords me great relief to hear by Francis' letter also, that Miss M. M. Wallace has proposed an arrangement with the Mortgage which is calculated to give you a little time by which means I trust we can somehow or other soon manage to pay her off and save the property for some good purchaser whom the location of the Rail Road may send along, or for an increased value in your own hands.

It seems by the letter of Francis that the location had not yet decidedly been fixed for the valley of the Bend, but I trust that it will soon be located there, and if so, nothing is more certain than the rise of property along your bank, and the interest of the Catlins, for once, in a small degree at least, advanced by a public improvement!

The awkward condition of the Government's finances & the currency of the country has brought on almost a national Bankrupcy, and brought down upon us that stigma abroad that makes an American feel unpleasant abroad—his country in disgrace & himself in bad odour wherever he walks or talks. So that individuals at home are suffering from actual hard times, and those who are abroad are suffering the mortification of hearing their country condemned and feeling their own credit impaired. I am heartily sick of hearing of the breaking of Banks, of the rascally repudiation of State debts, &c &c &c, & I am yet more, much more, sick of the insolence of wealth and the wretchedness of poverty which belongs to this great polished nation, with its boasted Institutions—its wealth, its refinements, its luxuries—with its vices, with its incongruous mass of loyalty & disloyalty, Republicanism and Despotism—mixed & patched up together, soon to fall & crumble to pieces into the levels of Agrarianism, or the hands of Nations which will stand ready to prey upon the riches of the ruined & falling edifice. Such a scene we may not live to see but I deem it not far distant, & every thing & system I look upon around me seem to convince me of the truth of the remark, and turn my mind back, and my admiration, to my own dear land, where I am anxious to return.

As strangers here we can roam about and look upon the wonders & follies of the old world and enjoy the sights we are seeing, but as Americans, we see no place yet where we would be willing to spend our days. We have as yet seen but little of England however, having been shut up all the time since we arrived here, confined to the limits of London & its environs, of which we are now pretty familiar, and of which, when we get home we will be able to give you a faithful description.

We were sorry to hear by the postscript of Elizabeth that she had lost her dear babe; we can correctly sympathize with them for the bereavement as we lost our first born, though we had not become so endeared to it by the familiar embraces and society of it, but with what we felt at the loss of our own, and the tender attachment and love that familiarity has spun over our souls for those dear little things that are now our society & our existence, we can nearly appreciate the pang that must agonize the bosom when they are taken from us. Francis & Elizabeth are young yet & have a long life before them and should not despair of the blessings that flow from the society of dear little children or be in the least discouraged about the prospect of a sufficient proportion of the world's goods for their enjoyment through life. There will be another Steamer in a few days when I shall write again, and in the mean time all will share at the Bend, the warmest assurance of our love & anxieties for you health & happiness. Clara and Libby join in love to dear Mother & all.

Your affectionate son
Geo. Catlin

Richard Catlin wrote to Francis from Brooklyn, Alabama, on the 16th of February, 1842. The first part of his letter was to sympathize with Francis and Elizabeth over the death of their little son, George. Everyone in the family wrote the grieving young parents. The letters were similar; probably quoted in part from the same book on "Letters of Condolence to the Bereaved." This letter shows Richard a happy, contented and prosperous young man:

Brooklyn Ala Feb 16, 1842

Dear Brother

Darwina desires me to acknowledge receipt of Elizabeth's letter to her of 29th Dec. conveying to us the melancholly intelligence of the death of your first born & very promising boy —the intelligence was as painful to us as unexpected—we can deeply sympathise with you in this bereavement, for we became as much attached to him as was possible for any one but its Parents—We can hardly realize that his once smiling face and his tender and once active limbs have been consigned to the cold earth, there to mingle with its mother Earth until the general resurrection—We can hardly be reconciled to the thought that we shall never again see his smiling face and hear his prattling tongue—but it must be so. The only consolation we can have in the loss of those we love is that they are to be transplanted & to bloom in a more congenial sphere where pain & sorrow shall never enter—You now have one less tie on earth but greater treasure in Heaven—Your departed child knew not sin, and we must believe he is now at rest in the abode of the 'just' & 'pure in heart,' let this be your consolation dear Brother & Sister and look constantly to him who perhaps in mercy has afflicted you, and seek earnestly to lay up your treasure in Heaven—We shall not soon forget the lost one, but shall cherish a fond remembrance—Darwina will write to Elizabeth in a few days in answer to her letter—We were happy to learn that our Parents & friends are as well as usual. We hope you will write to us often & inform us of our Parents health &c, also write to James occasionally—as Father is so feeble we can not expect him to write to his children as he has been accustomed—We received a few weeks since letters from Wisconsin from Sister Eliza & Mr. Dart, they were then well and apparently in fine spirits.

I believe I have written two letters to Father since we arrived at the south—You will perceive we are still at Brooklyn with James, & presuming it will not be altogether uninteresting. I must say something about ourselves—as we came out by land to Montgomery we then got conveyance to Brooklyn. We have concluded to return to Pensacola to live—Darwina could have had a large class of music scholars & female boarders if she had remained here—Since I arrived here I have been to Pensacola twice and once to Mobile—& have been twice in Pike County 70 miles North east of this looking after my lands &c. I have sold 480 acres at a profit of 100 perct, & that which was the least valuable—I still believe I can sell all of my lands in a few years for cash—as I could not now rent my house in Pen'a for more than $200 a year, we have concluded to occupy it ourselves as all our furniture &c is there—I have no doubt but we can pay expenses hard as the times are. I returned a few days since from Pensacola with a carriage to take Darwina down in. When in Pike County I received a splendid large Horse in payment of land He is admired by all that have seen him—I rode him to Mobile & Pen'a & must say I am proud of him—I drive & ride him without a whip & he is still gentle & stops at a word & will also go at a word—You know I always was fond of a good horse

—I think I never drove a larger or better traveller before a carriage or an easier horse under the saddle. Tell mother she must not have any fears on my account as "she knows I am a careful driver." Our trunks are packed are to go by teams—I forgot to say I brought new harnesses & saddles from New York which we are now enjoying—James & family are all very well & he is very much engaged with his Academy & is doing tolerably well—He has let out his Plantation on shares & will get his land well improved & this season will make 20 Bales of Cotton & 800 bushels of corn &c of which he will have half. They have a comfortable house & can have as many boarders as they can accomodate. Business is yet very dull at the South & the currency deranged—I still hold my [illegible] & Life & Trust Co money & think it will get better at least it is getting no worse—I shall sell it, or part in the spring so as to pay all my debts—Pensacola is still a dull place, yet one of the most desirable places to reside in—If I can sell out at Pen'a I think I may then return North— We have not heard from Geo & Clara lately—I saw Claras Brother in Mobile ten days since. Remember us kindly to all our friends at the Bend & particularly to Mr. & Mrs. McCreary, Joseph & wife &c. . . . Our best love to Father & Mother, Yourself & Elizabeth

Richard Catlin

It was March, 1842, and the Darts had weathered their second winter in the wilderness, still enjoying the beautiful country, but no doubt bone-weary from the dawn-to-dusk labor. The family was no longer without neighbors; seven families now lived in or near the infant settlement called Green Lake, and more would be coming soon, for the Territory of Wisconsin was being populated rapidly; not only from the eastern states, but from Europe, as well. In 1838 the population was 18,000; in 1840, 30,000; in 1842, 46,000!

The United States troops were steadily ushering the remaining Indians out of the Territory. It was a big job, and it would be 1849 before the former inhabitants of the Territory were all relocated west of the Mississippi. The Dart family had become friendly with the Winnebagoes and had learned to speak their language. One day they walked to Portage to see their Indian friends being gathered in to be sent off to Turkey River, Iowa. Richard Dart later wrote: "They were greatly distressed to know that they were to be deported. Some would lie down on the bank of the river, break down and cry like children, and would beg the soldiers to bayonet them rather than drive them from their homes. Bad whiskey had been their curse. We traded more or less with them and sometimes one would say he had nothing to sell, but finally would bring out from concealment a fine, big buckskin of three pounds weight, worth $3, and offer it for whiskey. We never let them have it, but they could always get it at the Portage." [1]

In this spring of 1842 the Darts were all at work, as usual. Anson was putting much-needed dollars into his pocket by building houses for those who could afford to pay for the labor. He had finished Mr. Beall's house, and now was building one for Mr. Stevens near Fox Lake. When that was finished, he would start on Mr. Beall's mill. The boys were busy splitting rails for the fence to enclose the eighty acres. Eliza wrote that they already had six thousand rails cut, and not one day's help, and that eight-year-old Charley was able to "cut down small trees with his little hatchet." Thirteen-year-old Elizabeth looked after the chickens, and Mary and "Ma" did everything else.

Francis had written Eliza of the death of his small son, George, and also, because of their father's poor health, that he and Elizabeth (who was expecting another child) would not be able to go west that year. Eliza knew that her father had not been well, but now she realized that he might never recover.

---

[1] *Settlement of Green Lake County*, Wisconsin State Historical Society Proceedings, 1909 (published by the Society, Madison, Wis.: published by the Society, 1910), p. 268.

On March 11, she wrote Francis:

I now sit down to answer your letter, and to condole with you and Elizabeth on the death of your darling, and only child. I wish I could say something that would lessen your grief, but I, too, am a parent, and have felt as you now feel. . . . I shed many tears over that part of your letter which spoke of my dear Father his feeble heart, his weakeness, his Cough & &,—Oh Francis how can I bring my-self to think I shall never see my Father again,—I who has loved him as never did a child before. —I know I am unlike most children, who marry and leave their parents,—my attachment for my Parents has encreased with my years, and absence from them has made them doubly dear to me. I love my Husband and my children, and I love my Parents as when I was looking to them for every thing I wished to make me happy—when I was a child—

I was very much in hopes that George and his family would return this spring—to cheer and gladden the hearts of their aged Parents,—I still hope and trust they may arrive this summer. James did not do right in my opinion, to promise his parents he would return and live at the Bend and then conclude not to do as he promised—we had made greate calculations upon seeing you with your little family here this spring. I know you will not leave our dear Parents, without one of our Brothers can be with them, you will see that they are gratifyd in all their wishes, and made as comfortable and happy as they can be in old age. . . . Since I commenced writing this letter little Charles has fell and hurt his head very bad—I am giving him a powerful physic—you will excuse me for ending my letter in such haste, love to all dear friends, write very often you and Elizabeth—I am as ever your aff—sister E D

It would be several weeks before Eliza would receive the news that her father died on March 12, the day after she wrote the letter above.

Far away in London Clara would be informed of the death of her own father before George learned of his loss.

The following letter shows that the death of Clara's father sobered George. It brought more forcibly to his mind his own parent's state of health, and the presentiment that he too had bid his beloved father a final farewell when he left for England.

The death of a patriarch—the end of an era

London, April 3d, 1842.

My dear Father,[2]

This brings you a good account of us all, that is, we are all well and still enjoying life as well as we can away from our dearest friends, and those for whose welfare we have the deepest concern. I ardently hope and trust that it may find you all well at the Bend, and with a fair prospect of a further indulgence in the possession of life and happiness.

My dear Clara received yesterday the afflicting intelligence of the death of her aged and affectionate Father, who you know has been long suffering with an excruciating disease which has finally brought him to the grave, the only place that could ensure him repose and quiet. She is broken-hearted and disconsolate in the extreme, but I trust that her religious & Christian faith will support her like a helping friend in her grief. The thought that

---

[2] Within a few days George would receive a letter informing him of the death of his father. Francis was the only child at home when he died. According to custom, Putnam was buried the following day. There was no way of summoning any of the other children in time to attend his funeral. Henry, in the adjoining state of New York, received the news on March 20. It would take close to a month for Francis' letter to reach Eliza in Wisconsin. It is understandable why the subject of health was given so much space in the family letters.

she is to return to America and yet never again to see his face is heartrending to her, but she has philosophy enough to reconcile eventually to the dispensation and say that it is for the best, that he has exchanged a world of peculiar pain and anguish to him, for one in which his innocent and unoffending spirit must be requited with happiness & repose. On his death bed he had his sons and his brother around him, and all that human hands and human sympathy could do, but all could not save him. It seems that he died perfectly calm and resigned, in the strongest Christian faith in the inheritance that he believed was awarded him—praying from day to day to be released from the pains and anguish that were allotted to him on Earth. He was truly one of the most exemplary and excellent men I ever knew, and was undoubtedly beloved by all who knew him. His Brother Matthew who is ten years older than yourself was with him when he died, shedding streams of tears over his veteran, wrinkled cheeks.

By a Letter from Theodosia we had the last news from you, and she spoke unfavourably of your health. She said she had been making you a visit, and that your health had been very bad, but that you was again on the mend. No one, my *dear, dear* parent, can tell what is my anxiety for your health and the prolongation of your life for a few years at least—that I can battle through the struggle I have undertaken amidst strangers and critics, and amidst the enormous expenses attending my exertions. I *will* work my way through in a little time, and I hope be along side of you.

That necessity should have driven me away from your society at this important & precarious time of your life, and that I should so long be held away without those pursuits having been yet able to have extended the helping hand to you, is a source of continual sighing grief to me that no one can justly appreciate. But I *will succeed,* & I only pray that you may rally and brace up against the creeping on infirmaties of age that your society may yet bless me and that I may be able to repay that debt (in a measure) which I owe to dear Mother & yourself, of which I become more and more sensitive every day that I feed and tend my little dependent flock that I am rearing around me.

We have lately moved about three miles out of London to a beautiful little cottage with an acre of ground laid out in grand walks & flowers, and green grass plats, where our little *"chubs"* can run and play, getting the pure fresh air of the country. our cottage is elegantly furnished, has six spacious Rooms, & every convenience we require, and all for two guineas (10 dols.) per week, much less than we have paid in the city. In June we go to Liverpool for an Ex'n of two months, then perhaps to Edinburgh for a short time, or to N. York. I dont know which.

I feel as if I should leave my affairs here and run home at this time, if it were but to visit you a few days, but I cannot do it without the great expense and disarrangement in my business & prospects. I will pray for the health of you all a while longer, & leave all to the Great Spirit to indulge us or not. Love to Francis & wife, and to our dear, dear, kind Mother.

Your affectionate son—
Geo. Catlin.

Putnam Catlin died March 12, 1842, at the age of seventy-eight.[3] His letters show the character of the man and what he might have been. He had a keen and analytical mind and a gift for oratory— qualities highly prized and sought for in the early days of our country. He could have gone far, but he left no mark in history except that of being father of George Catlin. An honest, but narrow-minded New Englander, he was content to use his fine talents in oratorial essays to his sons.

In spite of his shortcomings, Putnam must have been a very dear old gentleman. His children were his world, and their success in life his prayer. Worry over Eliza's predicament and George's inability to dispose of his collection saddened his last years.

All of George's letters showed the deep affection he had for his

---

[3] See Appendix V for Putnam Catlin's Last Will and Testament.

father; he sought his approbation, strove to please him by his accomplishments. Now that his father was gone, he would reproach himself bitterly for not giving more serious thought of his failing health and his desire to see his son again. It is a pity Putnam could not have lived out the year. The death of Clara's father would naturally have alerted George to his own parent's condition. He and Clara might have gone home as planned, and the final chapters of his life might have read differently.

Henry's reaction to his father's death was typically Victorian. In those days it was "fitting" to express one's grief with ponderous thoughts and florid rhetoric. No doubt Henry, as the eldest son, felt it his duty to write a proper eulogy for his father, and impart wisdom and advice to Francis, the youngest. The letter to Francis was long, and very wordy.

Henry was concerned over his mother's welfare and interests, which he said called for consultations and attention. However, he didn't write to Great Bend again until June. Apparently, his concern for his mother was not as great as his need for another loan.

Lockport, March 21st. 1842

My dear Brother,

I received your letter yesterday informing me of the death of our beloved and greatly endeared parent. I had been preparing my mind to hear of the heart-rending event ever since the recipt of your former letter, in which you stated the particulars of Father's illness. The natural & outward expressions of a heart overwhelmed with sorrow & grief bespeaks the present feelings & emotions of mine at the present time, & I have to give way to my feelings while writing to you. If I could have been with you & our dearly beloved & reverend Mother at that awfully solemn & afflicting time, to have mingled my tears of sorrow & grief with yours, it would have been a source of consolation to me seeing & knowing that by order of Providence such an event must take place. I am well aware that you could scarcely have been prepared in your mind to realize how great a shock such an event would produce.

I am also aware that you must also have realized many painful reflections in the idea of the absence of all your brothers and sisters at such a critical and afflicting moment. Whether such a painful separation be Providential or not, I am unable to determine.

I fear that our dear Mother will hardly be able to survive so great a shock. She must feel the bereavement more deeply than children can feel, and yet her children one and all will feel as sensibly this deep affliction as children can feel on such an occasion. We shall one and all of us cherish a dear remembrance of our departed parent and to the latest period of our lives delight to lisp his name. He has left his precepts and example for us, the richest legacy that a Parent can leave his children. And we should one and all of us endeavor through life to cherish a remembrance of his virtues, & to imitate them. His early solicitude & Parental care over his children in early life and his increased watchfulness care and solicitude for them in Manhood while entering into the busy bustle of business of life —entering upon the Stage of Action, his intense interest for their happiness & general welfare will ever be fresh in my memory—& cherished with the most grateful remembrance. . . .

I shall see you at the Great Bend sometime in May next if my life and health should be spared. I will then counsel with you in respect to many matters and things. Our dear Mother's interests, happiness and pleasures must be consulted and attended to. I shall not disappoint you in my visit in May if my life and health is spared. . . .

Your affectionate brother
Henry Catlin

In your letter you speak of a Certificate of deposit in the Binghamton Bank. That would answer my purpose. I can obtain the money on it at our Bank here. This amount I can hand you on my return from the East, when at the G. Bend.[4]

Eliza's grief over her father's death was intensified by two years of hardship and loneliness; years in which she clung to, and re-lived, every poignant memory of her former life. On August 14 she wrote to Clara: "I have made several attempts to write you since the death of my dear Father and yours, dear sister by your own feelings you know mine, dear Clara our kind and best of Fathers have bid farewell to all the transitory things of this life, and we hope they have entered into that rest prepaired for the just, although knew they were fast declining, yet we seemed unprepaired to hear of such an event—we can yet hardly realize they have gone to the grave. Yes dear sister we have now long to mourn for our dear Fathers, we shall see their natural faces no more, we shall no more be permitted to hear their voices—no more hear their advise and good counsil, though I trust we shall not soon forget—Oh Clara, can I ever forget the *last farewell*, the last affectionate embrace, the last words he spoke to me, *"Farewell, Farewell, my dear child, God bless you"*—as he hung upon my neck with clasped hands, oh how that moment, that embrace, that word, that look, I knew in all probability would be the last, you may imagine my feelings—his last letter to me was in September, since that time he was not able to write. Francis has given you all the particulars relative to his death. Our dear sainted Mother is now alone—Oh that I could be with her at this trying time—Yet she has a higher source of consolation—Francis says during his last illness he called for all of his absent children by name. Oh how trying it must have been to F's feelings being the only child present to close his dying eyes. It affords me some consolation to think of the pleasure it afforded my dear Parents to have a visit from Richard and Darwina last summer. I am pained when I think how our family is scattered probably never more to meet. I was in hopes and did think Brother

---

[4] Evidently Henry, in an earlier letter to Francis, had asked for a loan.

George and yourself would return from England in time to see Father once more. . . ." [5]

So ended an era for a family who had been advised, counseled, loved, and united by a patriarch who tried to bring out the best in each of his children.

"Poor Henry" and the Bankrupt Law

HENRY CATLIN was a good fellow. His trouble was that he spent his time looking around the corner for prosperity, and when he did not find it, he blamed the corner. To get the full impact of Henry's letters, they must be read in their entirety. Henry must have loved covering the paper with his beautiful, masculine penmanship, but he never wrote a sentence that he could not manage to stretch into a paragraph. Perhaps he was a "wordy" talker, wanting to hold the attention of his audience as long as he could. But Henry's reason for writing letters always seemed to be the same: either asking for a loan, or giving reasons why he hadn't paid back the last one.

Henry's first crop of children were now grown, but having re-married shortly after his first wife died, he was well started on the second. It appears that the rest of the Catlins did not keep in close touch with him (probably with good reason), but no doubt they all felt sorry for "poor Henry."

The following letters were written in the summer of 1842. To Francis he wrote:

Lockport, N. Y. June 21st, 1842

Dear Brother,

I ought to have written to you immediately on my return from the East, informing you of the reason why I did not come

---

[5] For the rest of this letter, see p. 256.

by way of Great Bend on my return, which I most confidently intended to do, & did not think that anything could prevent. I went to the City of Boston with a fine & valuable collection of minerals which I intended to dispose of for cash at some price or other. I had made up my mind to make a sacrifice on them to raise money, but to my disappointment & surprise, I found that money could not be raised upon them at any sale without making almost a total sacrifice upon them. This I could not stand, & the only thing I could do with them was to dispose of them to a large dealer in foreign shells. He purchased my entire collection, advanced me money enough to defray my expenses coming & going, & paying all the attendant expenses in getting the minerals to market—transportation included, & the residue I took in shells. My whole collection came to $430 dollars. having just money enough to get home I had to take the most economical method of returning. I am now trying to raise money on the shells. nothing but the extreme hard times, as it respects pecuniary matters, can prevent my selling my beautiful shells. William is now at Rochester with a case of shells, situated in the Arcade, trying to sell, & will stay there a month or two. If he does not succeed there I shall send him to Cincinnati, Ohio, with the whole of my shells, & let him remain there through the summer & fall. I have a very great collection of Shells & if money was plenty, I should realize money enough to buy me a farm to the West & to move on to it. I am anxious to raise some money on them as soon as possible so as to remit the 25 dollars to you, which I borrowed. I will send it along as soon as I can possibly obtain it.

If I can do anything with my shells, I shall try to come & see you during the summer or fall. I want to see you & dear Mother very much. I see by your letter that you are inclined to settle yourself eventually in the western country. I am not astonished at all at the conclusion you have come to in going to Wisconsin. I am extremely pleased with the Illinois country, & yet I did not see the best part of the State. I travelled through the middle part of the State & was told by the inhabitants that the Northern part of the State, & the Southern part of Wisconsin were much more desirable than that part of the country which I saw. If I were going there to locate, I would not go too far in the Northern part of Wisconsin, but would settle down within 30 or 35 miles of Milwaukie on Lake Michigan. I would go back from the lake about 35 miles, cross the Fox river, & there you would find the Cream of the Country, & near enough to market, & a fine climate. I have no objection to go to Wisconsin with you whenever I can make arrangements to go. If you should be able to go first I will follow on. If I go there I should not care to own more than 100 acres of land. I am convinced that that is enough for any man. If I go there it is for the purpose of living easy by farming & supporting my family. I will never in my life time make a slave of myself & family to lay up money, but my ambition & pride is to enjoy life in a reasonable way, & enjoy with my family the fruits of my labour as I go along. I am convinced that I can support my family in that country with one fourth part of the labour that I can here. In thinking of making such an exchange as this, we must consult our dear Mother, to see if she would feel able and willing to go with us. I feel it a duty & a pleasure to consult her interest & happiness in any movement that I should make of that kind. I want to be situated near her, & to have her with me a part or all of her time, if she should choose, as soon as I can get settled down firmly for life, which I shall do as soon as possible. She will now need our care and attention, & nothing can possibly give me more pleasure than to administer to her comfort & enjoyment the residue of her life. You and myself must be careful not to make any hasty or inconsiderate movement that would discompose her, but only to make any such movement as would seem to be for our family's interest, & at the same time meeting with her full approbation. I wish you & Mother would let me know fully as to any calculations you may enter into of the kind. I want to know Mother's views & calculations as to the future. I am ready to advise & concur in all reason & with propriety. Do not hesitate to let me know any arrangement & calculations that yourself & Mother may be making for the future—that is, whether to remain where you are permanently, or to sell & remove as soon as convenient. It will be much more of an effort for me & my family to remove West than for you with your small family. Yet I would undertake it as soon as I can bring it about.

I have not heard from George since last of April. I saw his Books in Rochester the other day. They have them for sale in a Book store there. I know not whether he has sold the Copyright to any publisher in New York, or whether he has furnished the Booksellers in N. Y. with a quantity of Books to dispose of for him.[6]

When you get leisure, and tired of fishing & hunting, set down & write me a letter, informing me of any thing that you can think of as interesting in these dull & uninteresting times.

Having nothing to attend to at this time by the way of past times & amusements, I am going to take the benefit of the Bankrupt Law which has become the fashion of the country here.[7]

Give love to our dear Mother, and accept the same to yourself & family. And believe me ever

your affectionate brother
Henry Catlin

Lockport August 20th, 1842

Dear Brother

I expected ere this time to have been able to send you the amount of the little draft of money what I had of you in the

---

[6] George's April letter to Henry was probably in regard to their father's death. From the above letter it is evident that George did not send copies of his books to this brother. And from a later letter from Henry to Francis, neither Francis nor his mother made any effort to inform Henry of their future plans.

[7] A Bankruptcy Law was enacted in the fall of 1841, whereby a debtor, on surrender of his property, was released from all his obligations. The law created so much financial irresponsibility that it was repealed in 1842.

Spring, but notwithstanding my very great exertions during the Summer I have not been able to retain so much in my hands for you, owing to the unprecedented money pressure throughout the country. I have been wholly disappointed in realizing money for my shells—William did not succeed well in Rochester. I sent him to the West with shells, he has been able to send me but little money from time to time, all wanting shells but no money —Yesterday I received a letter from him in which he says I have only been able to sell three dollars worth in Cincinnati & tomorrow I shall start for home. I find the times are against the sale of such articles. Upon the strength of being able to raise money out of shells I ventured to proceed in taking the benefit of the Bankrupt Law which my friends advised me to do & which I was entitled to do & ought to do. I have proceeded with it as far as I can well do with my limited means. I shall have to stop with it (which would be a difficult thing to do) unless I can procure some little assistance from some friend to enable me to go through with it. I have not called on George for one dollar since he left this country. George would feel bound to assist me at any time if I call on him as matters & things stand between us which at this time it would not be policy for me to explain, & were I to call on him now I could not obtain any money in time to help myself with in taking the benefit of the Bankrupt Law. I can not think of any one else so ready & willing to assist me a little at this critical time as yourself if it should be in your power —I want about $35 dollars to enable me to get through with. On account of the Chancery suit now pending I cannot receive the rents of the store again until after the arguing of the suit in November next. We expect to gain the suit as a matter of course & shall then be procuring the rents again. Under the circumstances I write you to see if you can assist me so far as to enable me to get along with this business & wait on me until I can get some funds of George—If you can assist me to that amount, I shall want to realize it as soon as it could be mailed to me as I do not want to stop with my Bankrupt proceedings if it can possibly be avoided. If I could realize a part of that amount immediately & the residue in 4 weeks after sending a part, it would answer. A Deposit check on the Bank at Chenango Point would be good here as the one before. I want to see you and Mother & your family very much but how can I travel at this time when it is so difficult to obtain money—Nothing but the want of it prevents me from coming to visit you. I keep up good spirits & hope to see more prosperous times for me & my family than at present I wish you would write me immediately on the receipt of this and let me know what you can do. I write in haste.

Give love to dear Mother & accept the same to yourself & family. Have you lately heard from James—Richard & Mr. Dart?

Henry Catlin

I have just spent my last farthing of my money in the Bankrupt business not having enough left to pay postage of my letter, I should pay it.

H. C.

George goes to Liverpool—the Dart Family writes to Clara

WHILE HENRY was struggling through his bankruptcy proceedings, George received an invitation from the Mechanics' Institute at Liverpool to show his Indian Gallery in connection with their own very fine exhibition. His lease on the Egyptian Hall was about to expire, so he accepted, and in May, 1842, sent his entire collection to Liverpool.

George mentioned, in his last letter to his father, that he had moved his little family to a cottage on the outskirts of London. On

May 4, he had occasion to write a note to a friend, Mrs. Hall: "In the last five weeks we have been living near neighbours to you, in a nice, retired little cottage at Walham Green (Rose Cottage) . . . . We are so comfortably and so quietly situated now that my wife almost regrets to leave our peaceable little home, as you will have seen by my advertisements, she will be obliged to do in a few weeks.

"Since we moved into it, we have both been afflicted by the news of the deaths of both of our dear fathers, who died within two days of each other in our native land. This most afflictive information has weaned us in a great measure from the noise and society of the world, but led us more closely to embrace our dear little children, and relish the quiet of our rural little domicile, where we should be most happy at all times to receive a visit from you . . . ." [8]

On July 14, Clara wrote to her uncle, Mathew Gregory, from Rose Cottage:

> . . . My husband has removed his things to Liverpool, and is doing very well there. I have staid behind in my country residence for I felt unwilling to leave it until he decided whether he would remain at Liverpool. I have a pretty little cottage, and my children are healthy. I have just weaned my youngest, now eleven months old [Victoria Louise].
>
> The Income tax is just going in force; a notice has been left today. What if our income is less than 150 pounds—we must give notice to the Assessor of the parish. It will make sad work. The people are nearly in a state of rebellion. The Queen was shot at for the third time on Sunday last. God grant our country may never see the extremes of wealth and beggary as they exist here.— [9]
>
> Ever your affectionate niece,
Clara B. Catlin

---

[8] From the Pennsylvania Historical Society.
[9] From the Missouri Historical Society.

For several months George exhibited his Indian collection in Liverpool, again seeing the crowds and receiving the applause of his early showing in London. He made both friends and money, and at the close of the fair decided to tour the smaller cities of England. This he did, ending up in Manchester, where he planned to close the tour and return to America.

A letter written to Clara in London gives a fine description of pioneer life in Green Lake, Wisconsin Territory. It was written by Eliza and three of her children: Mary, Putnam, and George. (For the first part of the letter, speaking of Putnam's death, see p. 248.)

To read young George's contribution is like opening a window and letting in the breeze; young Putnam wrote as if he were quoting from a fancy pamphlet put out by the Immigrant Society. But all in all, the letter tells of a contented family in a wilderness paradise. A bit of bravado? Possibly. This life in the West was a far cry from what they were accustomed to, and Eliza probably instructed her children: "Don't mention our bad times. We don't want them to be sorry for us. If you want them to come here to live, write about the beautiful country. By the time they come things will be much easier for us."

Green Lake, August 14, 1842

Dear Sister Clara,

. . . It was with untold pleasure I perused in your letter the account of yourself, your children, your situation, Georges success with his Book and his Galery. I flatter myself that you will feel interested in having a short and hasty sketch of our proceedings in Wisconsin—

After parting with my dear Parents and friends, I proceeded to Buffalo, with my 4 children that had remained with me. I would really like to relate all the particulars of our journey to the Bay by stage, Railroad, canal, crossing the Lakes, &c, but my allowance of paper will not permit. I found my husband at the Bay waiting my arrival. he conducted us to Green Lake a distance of 90 miles, where I met George and Putnam. Without money, without a team, without any other help, they had got a house under way—no floors, no chimney—six weeks I done all my cooking on a fire out doors, we had to buy all our provisions for the first year, but had no money to by with, as Anson gave up every thing in the shape of property to his creditors. his friends have blamed him for so doing, but we are not sorry now, since we have lived through a hard beginning. I left Mary at the Bay to teach Music, our nearest neighbour was 2 miles, I will leave you to judge of the hardships we had to encounter, once I did not dream of hardship and fatigue such as I have gone through. . . . I left my furniture at the Bend for Francis to bring with him, as he expected to follow in the spring. Anson was obliged to make chairs, tables, bedsteads, wash tubs, pails, barrels, &c. . . . he has many, very many friends here, they have given him the office of Justice of the Piece, and have his name up for a representative to the Legislature—he has been from home most of the time since we came to Wisconsin, building and repairing mills, his labour has furnished us with means to live while the boys were tilling the land and preparing the crops, there never was a family so industrious and so determined to regain what we have lost, a good living, we all work too hard for our own good, as it regards our health. George's clever good heartedness increases with his years he loves his friends to excess, you in particular, Putnam is larger than George, but not as healthy he thinks as he always did he can do things a little better than any one else, has the same independence about him, he looks much like brother George, he will tell you all about himself and what he is doing—Mary is taller than I am, she is a greate help to me especially about my sewing, I seldom take a needle in my hands, she feels quite lost without her piano—Elizabeth takes charge of the Poultry, she has had 150 chickens this season, Charley feels quite above having anything to do with pigs or chickens, he goes with Richard to the woods, and with his hatchet cuts down very large trees, that is his delight—The children all seem delighted with

this beautiful country—dare I once hope to see George and yourself and the dear little children at Green Lake oh how happy
would I be, I was never more happy than when you were setting
by my side and at my table, dear little *berry-some*—how I do
want to see her, though hard I must say adieu Mary wishes to
write, Eliza ever yours.—

My Dear Aunt Clara

This is the first time I have ever attempted to write you a line I
hope however it will be acceptable from your niece who loves
you so dearly and from whome you have been so long seperated
you cannot immagine our delight when reading your long and
very interesting letter it had been a long time since we had heard
a word of your transactions in London But hearing of your
success and good health we feel amply repaid for the delay. I
think Ma has given you a long letter but she says she has not
written half she would like, she has told you all the hardships
and privations we were obliged to encounter in comeing into this
wilderness and making a beginning we think them very hard but
I suppose they are trifeling when compared to many our
forefathers have gone through. Pa says if we had no dark days
now we should have nothing to tell when the country becomes
settled. You must know that we have been very lonely since we
came to Wisconsin no society whatever neighbours of no
kind, no Church to attend no schools nor anything that could
delight us except the beautiful country Lake &c but we are now
quite different we have a very good society for so small a place as
Green Lake and we occasionally have preaching here by Ministers of all denominations. The society here are mostly young
people and more gentlemen than ladys. . . . I think dear Aunt
this of all other places would fasinate you I think it would please
your romantic taste more than any place in the world you would
delight to ramble through the beautifull Oak Openings and walk
on the pebly beach of our lovely lake or with your rod and line

try angling that I believe youre passionately fond of there is scarcely a day passes but we wish yourself and dear Uncle George were with us. whenever I think of strawberryes it reminds me of your dear little Libby how she used to love them when you were with us at Utica. . . . Please give my love to Uncle George and tell him his niece loves him as she ever did your affectionate niece

Mary

Der Aunt Clara

By the time you get as far as where I am trying to say something I think that you will be tired of reading so long a letter so it is not best for me to say much this time. But if you will excuse all my mistakes in bad spelling and bad penmanship I will go on. I believe Ma and Mary hav not told much a bout this country but I must refer you to Uncle George now and then. We are in a prairie country finely located but plenty of timber and fine water for all farming purpose, our location is one mile from the Prairie in the Oak openings we are on a fine little brook that runs all through our farm we have got 180 acres under improvement, fensing and so forth done, but we have had a hard time of it I can assure you we have past the rubicon as the saing is. . . . Uncle Geo. is right in his remark conserning his cabin and gun I think he would take more comfort here than where he is. But if I could believe that I should see Aunt Clara and her family in this far off country I could stand it a great deel better than now. you have all ways been my Aunt and friend if I am afar off in this western world I dont forget you and uncle George you are all most the only one that writes us out of real friend ship some of our letters that we have received from our friends or that was our friends in prosperity have been pretty cold ones. we are poor now, but we are the last ones to dispond for better days will come and no mistake I must stop for Putnam clames a chance ask little Elizabeth if she can remember when she use to ride on my sholder in Utica, and her little waggon. I want you to give my best respects to Uncle George tell him I shall loock for him before long love to all of your daughters and to Burr

yours   G Dart

My dear Aunt,

Nearly or quite all the news have I believe been told although I may find a few lines that may be interesting to you . . . Uncle George we well know has travelled all over this western world but I am sure here is one little spot of say thirty or forty miles square he did not see or he could not have left it. it is admitted by all to be the paradise of Wisconsin if not the U. S. . . . We have people here frequently who have come five hundred & a thousand miles to see the much talked of Green Lake country, & never in an instance has a person gone away but expressed their highest opinion of it and have gone back, sold out their farms and removed to this country. The Prince De Joinville passed here, and expressed a very high opinion of it said he never saw any new country & wild land to be compared with it. . . . Oh how I do wish you could live beside us as Uncle George says, in the cabin & with his gun he would have plenty to do with it, the deer are very plenty & Grouse are so numerous as to be troublesome to crops & game of all description are uncommon plenty, consequently we have plenty of venison. will you not excuse me now, as my paper is full. . . .

Your Affectionate nephew
Putnum

Richard Dart later wrote: "The first election in Marquette County was held in the autumn of 1842 at our plank house south of Green Lake. There were present Anson Dart, his sons George and Putnam, Pete LeRoy and his son, and William Basely, tenant on Beall's place.

These constituted the entire polling list." [10] Evidently his father's name was not on the ballot in this election or Richard would have mentioned it.

War-whoops in London

IN THE EARLY spring of 1843, near the end of George Catlin's two-month exhibition in Manchester, he received a letter from a Mr. Arthur Rankin. Rankin had arrived in England with a party of nine Ojibway Indians which he planned to exhibit, but had been told that he would nave no success unless the Indians were under Catlin's management.

George had planned to leave for New York with his family and collection within two weeks. He was decidedly against exploiting the Indians abroad, but since they were here, he felt it his duty to protect them and their interests. He also thought that to exhibit real Indians in connection with his Gallery and lectures would verify the truth of his paintings and descriptions, and thereby increase the value of his Indian collection in England.

Clara must have pleaded with her husband to take her back to America; that he was in no way responsible for the Indians. But George, having seen the fine-looking Ojibways, also saw a chance to fill his purse before going home.

The impulsive artist made a verbal agreement with Rankin. He would manage the exhibition of the Indians, But Rankin, having brought them to England, would be completely responsible for them when not in the exhibition hall. He took a six-month lease on rooms in the Egyptian Hall, and the live Indians, with their bloodcurdling war-whoops, brought crowds there daily.

---

[10] *Settlement of Green Lake County,* p. 270.

Although the colorful Ojibways added to the excitement and interest of the exhibition and lectures, there were many Londoners who resented the Wild West atmosphere that resulted. Also, Rankin did not keep close watch on them, and they created several disturbances in the city. George was condemned by the press for exploiting the Indians for his own gain, although he made repeated denials.

When the lease on the Hall still had three months to run, Rankin, having nothing but a verbal agreement with Catlin, decided to sever connections and go it alone, and make more money for himself. He told George to advertise that the Ojibways would be leaving in ten days on a tour of England. The artist did this, but when the ten days were up, Rankin advertised that he had taken rooms in the Hall himself, and would exhibit the Indians for two months more. Worse, one of the Ojibways had just married an English girl, who was to appear on the platform with the Indians.

All this was bad for George's reputation. He was a showman, to be sure, but not a mountebank or huckster! He had used good taste in his exhibition of the Indians, but conservative England now looked at him differently. Catlin had accepted Rankin, so Catlin must be the same type of man. His good name took a fast swoop downward.

George had been working on another book, a large portfolio of lithographic reproductions of many of his paintings. With three months before the lease would expire, and with practically no visitors since the Indians had left him, he decided to stay and work on his coming publication, and then leave for New York. His social status was not what it had been in the past, but he still had many friends in London. One very happy event occurred in November, 1843—Clara gave birth to a son, named George. This date is verified by Clara's note to Polly in George's letter to Francis, dated London, May 18, 1844: "Our boy George is a fine specimen of an English baby, healthy & rosy, just six months old."

The Darts urge George and Clara to come
to Wisconsin

I T W A S S P R I N G , 1843, on the prairies of Wisconsin Territory. The once-reluctant pioneers were now fully at home, and from the tone of their letters had no desire to live again in the "civilized" East. Life was still a steady round of chores on the farm, but they were able to buy the necessities which made their work lighter. Anson's many talents kept him in constant employment. He was now building a grist mill for Mr. Beall, the land agent, and would run it for the next two years.

There were settlers all around, and Eliza had plenty of neighbor women to chat with. The boys ran the farm, which was flourishing beyond all expectations. They just couldn't get over the way things grew! Francis and his family were expected in the fall, and now they decided to lure George and Clara away from London. Evidently George had written that he and Clara would like to settle in the West.

George was opening his exhibit in Liverpool, England, on the day the Dart family composed another letter to be sent snail-like to Clara's brother in Jersey City, and forwarded by him to London. Anson started the family chronicle:

Green Lake, 14th May, 1843

Friend George
Dear Sir,
It is unnecessary for me to say that four long years has passed since I have had the pleasure of seeing you or my good friend your wife. your long and very kind letter (being mostly written by Clara) was duly received, and I assure you it gave us great pleasure to learn so much of your location, prospects, and condition. in regard to ourselves, I cannot say much myself, but the family will join me in this letter, so that what you do not get

from one, you may learn from another. The most important thing that I can mention is that we are all in good health, good health however is a blessing more generally enjoyed in Wisconsin I think, than in any other part of the Union our winters are cold generally, but the last was unusually so, it was about as hard as the York State winters, there has been much suffering mostly among the cattle as many hav died for the want of hay. we however hav had enough both for ourselves and stock, and our futer prospects are as flattering as we could expect, in short we hav no good reason to regrett having left the State of N. Y. it will however take us about two years more to get all the comforts around us. Now Sir, what do you say to the propposition that you leave Europe without delay and come to Wisconsin I know the change would be to the advantage of yourself and family, besides Sir, we have got precisely the spot, or such a spot, as you once marked out to me in Newyork as a place that would some and no very distant day be your residence, the sooner you leave the giddy seans of crowded cities, and densely populated towns the better you will enjoy yourself. I know what detains you, you want to put a few more dollars into your pocket. this is all a mistake, the facts are, that if you hav much money you will not come at all, five hundred or a thousand dollars is better for you to commence with in this country than five or ten thousand would be, the first would make you comfortable and happy the last sum would add many cares and enemies. consult on this matter with Clara and make up your mind with as little delay as possible.

I am Dear Sir as ever
yours
Anson Dart

From George:

Dear Aunt Clara

You must excuse our not wrighting to you before but it is not my fault for I have erged for some tome but you now how it is in the country where we have every thing to do, but the main reason is that we have been wating for a postoffice and Father is to be Post Master at Green Lake. all we are wating for is returns from Washington. I do not know what Uncle George will think of what Father has writen to him. But I hope he will think as he does for he often tells how uncle George and he use to talk how they use to think and tell about fine places in the country Mary says that I dont want fun enough but that is hard work for me you speak of my finding some one for a companion. But do you remember when you were at Utica you promised me when I wanted a wife you would find some one and I have not forgotten it and I shall wate until you do so for I will trust to you to find me one rather than trust to my own judgment I am now 23 years old and past and you can decide whether I am of suitable age or not and I shall leave all to you and you may commence on your duty as soon as you choose if you could onley be with us this summer and enjoy with us all of the luxeris of the west you cannot immagin how much pleasure it would give us tell little Lib or large Lib that we have more strawberries here than in Utica and such quantities of game and fish you cannot form any idea. you must excuse this short postcrip for Put and Mary want to say something you will find all manner of mistakes but you will excuse them & now Put will tell you what we have done Give my best respects to uncle George and all of my little cousins in England I am your old friend and nefew G. Dart.

Next came "Put" with an excellent treatise on "Why everyone who doesn't live in Wisconsin should." One wonders why George, the elder, misspelled so many words, and Putnam wrote as if he had had a college education. Richard Dart later wrote that Putnam had but a few years' schooling, but wanted an education badly enough to get books and teach himself.

Putnam wrote:

My dear Aunt Clara, At a late period from the receipt of your most welcome letter we commence this joint one hoping at the same time it will be quite as acceptable by the time it arrives, it gave us indeed the utmost pleasure to peruse your long and very interesting letter informing us of your Situation & prospects for I assure you we individually feel a deep interest in your welfare, and do heartily wish you may have success in all your undertakings either in England, on the Continent or in your native country would that Uncle George will dispose of his galery and return and to Wisconsin and live beside us in this beautiful country almost paradise and here spend your days, this would please us and in my humble opinion you would live more contented and happy, and you know this is the first aim contentment consequently happiness. I could fill volumes in describing the beauties of this country it is I believe unparrillelled in beauty & variety of scenery. The Lakes, rivers springs cascades, the rolling prairies & openings covered with wild flowers, the varieties of game of every description which abound on the western prairie the fish which comprise every variety almost, the delightful summers, comparative mild winters, the healthy climate and last or first the fertility of the soil, and even the new beginner finds a pleasant happy home here. we have some excellent neighbors near us, and have in all quite a settlement of enterprising people. Richard wishes me to tell uncle G. our hunting story if I am obliged ever to brag. he killed a great Buck last fall weighing 300 lbs. he shot him at arms's length, 35 rods, and wounded him and then fell to work with his gun and broke the stock over his head, run one mile home after mor ammunition and another hand finally killing him he says uncle G. must not think it is the only one he ever killed but the largest one. G. and myself have killed a great many (in hunting time September) it would please me to give you a description of my apiary and my success as an apiarian commencing with wild bees from the woods I last fall took 400 lbs. of beautiful honey from my hives, and now rapidly progressing in the business. I wish I could send you some honey. I have left but small space for mother and Mary accept for yourself my most sincere wishes for your prosperity—tell uncle George that I do not forget him, and wish him to remember me.

from your affectionate nephew, Putnam Dart.

From Mary Dart:

My dear Aunt Clara

Putnam has taken a larger share of room in this letter than was allotted to him but as he is extreemly fond of writing to the ladies he is excuseable my allowance is so small I must be briefe you have by this time learned that your double letter was received with the great pleasure and I return my sincere thanks for the part written by yourself to me. you spoke in your letter of my being lonely in wisconsin I can assure you I have never been in the least when we first came here every thing was new and strange and necessity compeled me to learn to work which in a great measure has occupied my time with rambling in the woods I could not be lonely and now as our settlement increases we again find many very pleasant friends, we have one excellent neighbour but a few rods from our house a young couple very gay and lively we have fine times here riding on horseback on the praries how we wish you were here to ride with us and little Lib to pick strawberrys, if she is as fond of them as she was at Utica nothing could delight her more than to see the immence quantities here we have a good boat on Green Lake in which we find it very pleasant to sail occasionaly this I am sure would please you. Our Piano is at Aunt Marys and Theodosia is teaching music on it she does not write to us and the reason we do not know it must be because we are poor. If so I am very sorry Prosperity is the time to gain friends and adversity to try them Pa has done much for her but now she forgets it, I hope Burr will succeed in his love matters for it is time he were married and Theodosia also. I hope uncle George will give us some encouragement in your next letter about what Pa advised I think you could have no objection. It would give us more pleasure than you can immagine, you say you shall soon expect to heare that I have changed my name I hope it will not be very soon. I intend to have you and uncle George at my wedding this day is my eighteenth birthday so you see there is time enough yet from my present age to twenty two that is the most fashionable age here, you undoubtedly know that Uncle Francis has not moved to Green Lake as yet nor is there much prospects at present our dear Grandmother cannot be persuaded to leave the homestead, for this she cannot be blamed it has so long been the home of our departed Grandparent it is not to be expected she can enjoy herself elsewhere. we have pressed her very hard to live with us the remainder of her days and we would do all in our power to conduce to her comfort and hapiness but she prefers remaining at the Bend. We are constantly receiving letters from all our friends and it gives us pleasure to think they do not forget us. Pa and the boys enjoy themselves perfectly in the woods although they work very hard they know that by industry economy and perseverence they can in a few years be more comfortable. In this place there are no lines to be drawn between the rich and poor for all have more or less tasted poverty they are nevertheless well informed intelligent and fashionable people that makes a good society. Will you please tell cousin Burr to write cousin Molly a long letter with all the news and particulars respecting himself. I see my paper is full and I have much more to say but cannot we have never received Uncle G's Book. we wrote to Mr A. Miller my old teacher from Delta who now resides in Ills. concerning the gentleman you sent it by he says Daniel Mersmore has not returned home but stopped in new Jersy. In due time we shall expect another long letter remember me to my dear Uncle George and little Lib Clara and the baby accept a share for yourself I remain your affectionate niece Mary.

P. S. I have a small space to appologize for Ma not joining us in this letter she has for a week past been troubled with a severe inflamation in the head which confined her to the bed most of the time it has left now but she finds her eyes so weak she cannot see to write, she says tell Aunt Clara in a short time as soon as her eyes will permit, she will write her a long letter, also that Grandmother has written for her to come home and spend the summer. she has not yet concluded to go she thinks the journey would be quite an undertaking. Lib says tell Aunt Clara she has got 50 hens and a quantity of chickings. Aunt Clara do you remember when you were a visiting us at Utica the jug of sweetening that Mr. Peck sent you, the boys made us a barrel of beautiful molases this spring I suppose you do not have it where you are we have peaches that are large enough to [illegible] that we raised from the pitts. Ma sends her love to Uncle George yourself Burr and the children.

Molly

Letters from Henry and Mary

In the little village of Great Bend more than a year had gone by since Putnam's death. Another winter of deep snow and worry of whether the bridge would be sustained had passed, and the run-down old homestead was now shaded by the green foliage of another spring.

Francis and Elizabeth had moved in to care for Polly. Perhaps they hoped the prattle of their year-old son would keep her from mournful thoughts. The gentle little lady of seventy-three had willingly lived her life in her husband's shadow. Now that he was gone, she would find solace in the worn Bible that had brought her peace so many times in the past. It would comfort her to know that Putnam had as many of their children with him now as she had. Polly's faith was strong; the family would be together again—some day.

Francis, as one of the executors of his father's will, was a busy young man. Putnam had left his affairs in a deplorable state, and Francis and Charles Dimon (evidently George wrote his father to appoint Dimon in his stead) had been trying to straighten things out. Francis may have been a problem in his youth, but he was twenty-eight now, and a more dependable person. He would never lack friends or an empty purse, and the latter didn't bother him a great deal. He envied his brother George, not Richard.

The Darts were expecting him and his family in Green Lake that fall. Polly wanted him to go, for she planned to live with Mary in Delta, New York. But Francis was trying to sell the two houses in Great Bend to help clear Putnam's debts. He was having a hard time because the houses were in bad condition. No doubt he had plenty of advice from Richard and James, but no financial help. He could not leave for the West until matters were settled one way or another.

On June 1, 1843, Francis received a letter from Henry, the first written to his youngest brother in a year. No doubt Francis thought on opening it, "I wonder how much he wants this time!"

Lockport, June 1st, 1843

Dear Brother,

It is a long time since I have heard from you. I should have written you before this, but thinking that you were more at leisure to write than myself, I have deferred it. I have had so many cares resting upon me, of a family as well as of a worldly nature, that I have hardly been able to set down coolly and calmly and collect & manage my thoughts & ideas together so as to write an intelligent & edifying letter.

I have for the last year past been engaged in arranging my business so as to enable me once more to commence the world anew. I got through with my Bankrupt business without any trouble or opposition of creditors. Consequently, I am for the present, level with the world again & can commence a small business with safety as soon as I can obtain a little sum of money to start with.

It has cost me a good deal to clear myself from debt by the Bankrupt Law, and in order to get through with this, I am now in debt to my friends here for the amount of about 25 dollars. This sum I want to raise as soon as I possibly can, to repay them. I am then clear of debt & mean to remain so.

You mentioned to me a year ago that there would be a little sum coming to me from our Father's estate. If so, that amount would be worth more to me now than a thousand would at a future time. You did not mention to me how it was situated, whether there were any debts to be paid out of the estate, and whether any property would have to be sold in order to settle the estate. Consequently, I am perfectly ignorant of the situation of his affairs. I suppose you have the care & business of settling the same.

I hope and trust you may not be under the necessity of having to dispose of property to settle the business, should there be any foreign or domestic debts to pay. Not knowing but that all things are right and easy in that matter, and also as to your own private curcumstances, I have ventured to ask you if you could let me have $25 dollars at this time to pay where I have borrowed of a friend to enable me to get along with my Bankrupsy, & let the same be applied to the little amount coming to me as above mentioned.

I am now living in the store. It is finely finished throughout for a private family and I have taken possession of it in order to take care of it, as the times are such that it cannot be rented. I have opened in the store part a large and valuable collection of shells and minerals, uniting with it the fruit business. I hope to do enough business to support my family, on the principle of economy, but can not do that and raise any particular sum to pay a debt.

The Bankrupt law was calculated to suit my case, and I have availed myself of its benefit of it, as also many of our best citizens have done so. I have occasion to feel rich that I am legally exonerated from the payment of all my debts, although it leaves me pennyless at present. I can get along again very well if I can only realize the little sum above mentioned, for that especial purpose. If you can see it in your way to send that amount to me, it would benefit me more than ten times that amount has ever heretofor benefitted me. I shall then be out of debt & ever remain so.

I want to hear from you & your family, and dear Mother. I suppose however you are all well, and I hope doing reasonably well. If it were not so you would have written me. Have you given up the idea of moving to the West? I should like very much to visit you with my wife if I could conveniently.

Have you heard from George lately? How is he getting along? I hear he is in Edinborough, Scotland. My family at present are well. All the children are with me except Henry, Samuel and Peter.

I must close. My family join in sending love to you & Mother & to your family.

Your affectionate brother
Henry Catlin

Postage was so high in those days that many people took advantage of the lower rate for newspapers when they wished to send but a short note, writing it on the margin of the paper. Of course this practice was frowned upon by the postal authorities and Mary Hartshorn. She wrote a long letter to Francis on September 21, 1843, apologizing for her son who had done such a thing, causing Francis to pay extra postage on the newspaper! However, she had to admit that she had done it herself a couple of times in emergency, and she was ashamed of herself for two pages.

Mary wrote of their financial troubles resulting from Anson's failure. "Asa manifests the greatest anxiety to hold onto his farm but he thinks he cannot, unless he has help from some quarter. I believe he is going to try some of his brothers. I have no idea they will be able to assist him much. Asa says if he could depend on a few hundred dollars he might struggle through and secure it from being sacrificed.

But I have said enough. Asa felt anxious that I should say something to you about it. We know you must have a load of care and difficulty upon your shoulders, in settling the affairs of our dear father. I assure you, my dear brother, you have our sympathy and confidence, and yet you know it would be unnatural if we did not feel somewhat interested, also, oweing to our *trying* circumstance. . . ."

Poor Francis!

Eliza writes to her mother

THE SULTRY DAYS of August came to the prairies, with the Darts expecting a letter from Francis any day announcing that he was leaving with his family for the West. He was to bring Eliza's good furniture with him, and no doubt she and Mary spent much time planning where they would put each piece, replacing the crude but serviceable things Anson had made.

Eliza wrote her mother on August 16, 1843: "Putnam starts for the Bay in the morning and it is now after ten in the evening all are sleeping but me, and I cannot let so good an opportunity pass without writing to you, as you are constantly in my thoughts, Oh if you could only know how much I wish to see and convers with you, when that time will be—is continually in my mind—I still flatter my-self you will come to Wisconsin with Francis, if he comes this fall—perhaps I am unreasonable in even thinking so. I presume sister Mary can make you more comfortable than I can, but your company could not make her more happy than it would me. I have heard that George and Clara were to return this fall, the first wish of my heart is that they may return to make you happy in your declining years.—George would be to you a Father—a Husband and a son. I will still hope he will be with you before Francis leaves you. Francis seems determined to come to Green Lake. I think he will do well to come now but he ought to have selected his lands before this. Anson has some in reserve for him—our house has been filled with people locating—for many weeks past. 14 families have located all around us within a week or two—last week we had a company visiting our young people from the *Bay* and *Fond Du Lac* they took Mary away with them, she will return with Putnam in a few days—two Gentlemen left here this morning for Utica and New York after their families, we wrote to Delta by them—"

With young Putnam around with his gilt-edged sales talk, no wonder there was a big rush for the land office. But this was really the way the West was growing. Curiosity brought many men from the East "to find out what all the excitement was about." The wooded prairies, the prosperous-looking farms, the healthy and enthusiastic settlers, the grand and natural beauty of this Western wilderness made many a man realize that the Great West was the future of America. So the parade continued; by foot, on horseback, in creaky carts and Conestoga wagons they rolled along the roads to the great Wisconsin Territory or—by now—even to Oregon.

Returning to Eliza's letter:

Tell Francis and Elizabeth we shall give them a hearty welcome, but they must not expect to know me, I have altered so much—tell Elizabeth she must bring Lydia Jean [her sister] with her, she will make her market at once, there are several young gentlemen just commencing for themselves whose prospects are highly flattering. we want her society very much, she must come if she does not stay more than one year. we have Meetings every Sabbath and sunday school—tell Francis he must bring a drove of horses when he comes for we are tired of riding after *horned horses*—[The oxen, evidently, were made to do double duty and used for both business and pleasure.] A Mr. Clark from Utica—an old acquaintance of Ansons is now building near us, his family are now at the Portage distance 30 miles—his wife and daughters all play the Piano to perfection

we shall then number 2 pianos at Green Lake [11]—and quite a
society of young people.

Anson says Francis must turn all his attention to sheep, as that
is a money making business, and not so labourious—he has
reserved a farm for him where he can cut several thousand tons
of hay for his sheep. a few miles from us is building a fulling
mill, carding and cloth dressing will be carried on in the same
building—our openings are the finest in the world for sheep—
and wool will allways bring money—if Francis comes, we shall
render him all the aid in our power. Anson will advise him at all
times for the best, he must not put his hand to the plough and
look back, perseverance, with industry will do wonders—a few
days since the first death accured at G Lake. Our friend and
neighbour *Butler G Plum* he was engaged in building a saw mill
and exposed his health by working in the water, there being no
Physician nearer than 30 miles he neglected him-self, till a fever
set in which could not be removed only by death, the Physician
was sent for when it was too late, his wife and two children are
left quite destitute, you will tell this to Mrs. Plums friends at
Montrose when you see them, our section of the country is very
healthy, 30 miles south of us there is some few cases of the ague
and fever, the water is bad there.

A few lines to Francis and Elizabeth—on the subject of
moving to Green Lake—Get all the money you can, for what
you do not want, I shall,—get all the friends to come with you,
that you can.—bring every thing with you that you have got, and
all that you can get,—for all that you do not want I shall want—
you should let us know what time you will be at the Bay or
Millwakie, that we may be there to help you on to Green Lake—
when you get to Buffalo, I want you to get me a B silk
fashionable Bonnet, as I have had none since I left Utica,

---

[11] To Eliza, possession of a piano in the wilderness was a mark of distinction.
She always mentioned the settlers who were rich enough to bring one with them,
and no doubt yearned for the one she had to leave behind.

Eizabeth will select one that will suit me I also want a dark mouselin delane dress, with a set flower, something pritty, a dress cap, and a pair of dark coloured corsetts, price from 10 to 12 shillings, if you can get the above named articles without discomoding your selves, it will do me a greate favour, as I have no way to get any such things. I will pay you for them here—I could think of many other things I would like very much to send for, but dare not dip too deep, till we are fairly out of the fire. I have been too ecinomical for my own good since I came into this country. I have been planning and looking out for my children and neglected my-self—I expect one of the boys will be going to millwackie after a loade of fruit trees, about the time you will be there, perhaps you will prefer landing at the Bay—as there is ague and fever between here and Millwakie,—we shall expect to hear from you again soon, I fear you cannot reade half that I have written for I cannot.—it is very late, Putnam is going to the Bay to see his Dulcinia he is in a bad way poor fellow, I fear nothing but a Parson or a justice will be able to cure him— George is not troubled in that way—yet. I shall expect a long letter from dear Mother. I want to know what she intends to do, and what her wishes are, Oh how much I wish to see her and all of you, accept the best wishes of all the family—I remain as ever affectionately Eliza.

On the 5th of September, 1843, Anson Dart wrote Francis:

Your favour to Eliza of the 8th Aug. is at hand. It finds us all in good health except George has been confined to his bed four days having eaten too much green corn & worked too hard at pitching hay. we trust he will be about again in a few days at most. It gives us great pleasure to see that you and yours begin to talk about right on the subject of Wisconsin. you had better come this fall if possible, at any rate if you await coming untill spring you will lose about one year by so doing. we will verry cheerfully take you into our family untill spring, or untill you can build, you will, I trust, escape the dispepsy or gout if you board with us. Still we have enough of the substantials but you will find a few of the nic-knacs of the east missing . . . fetch all the furniture you can. Be shure & fetch or send ours. you cannot buy furniture in Wisconsin as good as you would have, nor short of three times the price that you would get for yours at the Bend. fetch *lots* of such things as follows: shoes & boots, factory cloth, flannel, wollen cloth, calico, bed clothing, sugar, tea, coffee, stocking yarn as much as you can carry on your backs, a few hats & caps, powder, *not shot*, axes. the following are not very high in this country, but if you can get them there without money you had better fetch them all—all sizes of nails, window glass, white lead, linsead oil, a few gallons two log chains, drag teeth, hoes, shovels, spades, crockery wear as much as you can pack up, you cannot stuff in any thing that will come amiss. . . . I must leave room for Mary to write to that dear wife of yours, so I must close.

I am dear sir, with much respect,
Anson Dart

Mary Dart added some interesting information in a note to Elizabeth: "You wanted to know what we do about a doctor when we are sick. I will tell you. The *Married Ladys* when they are *sick* generally give the doctor an invitation to spend a week or so in the family, do you understand? Our nearest doctor is fifteen miles, or rather there is several but none nearer than that distance. We expect one to settle here this winter and one in the spring but it is not positive enough to place dependence upon."

George writes to his mother

A MUCH CLOSER relationship had existed between George and his father than with his mother. He was devoted to her, but there was no common ground upon which their minds could meet to exchange thoughts and ideas. In the following letter, George wrote what he knew would interest his mother; the health of his family and news of the children. He made no mention of his affair with Rankin, although it must have been reported to some extent in the American papers, and nothing about his coming publication. George obviously had not written to her for many months.

Manchester, 16th Sept. 1843

Dear Mother,

I am ashamed when I reflect back and see how illy I have kept my promise with you about writing, and as I used to do to my dear Father, I will hope to be excused, and will promise to do better in future.

I received your postcript to Brother Francis' letter, which I read with great pleasure as it informed me, as well as his own assertions, that your health continued good. So much have we been jostled about, and such the multiplicity of my avocations and anxieties and vexations here in this strange and expensive land that it is exceedingly difficult to get much time for correspondence. Yet I do not plead this as excuse for not writing oftener to so dear and aged a parent. it would be sinful to attribute my neglect to anything else than the most shameful carelessness. I should have answered the letter of Francis sooner also, which related to the unsettled affairs of my dear Father's estate, and which I fear is left in a bad condition. I shall write to him today and to Charles Dimon Esq. also, who is Executor of the Estate with Francis.

Clara and the three little girls are all well, and all send love to Grandma & to all the family. We have been near loosing our dear Libby, the oldest, with whooping cough which resulted in inflammation of the lungs. They have all had it, and Libby has been for 3 weeks with violent fever, & reduced very low, her life for some time despaired of. She is now fast recovering. We have moved 10 miles into the country to a very pleasant & healthy place to work off this loathsome disease, and what is most remarkable *I have had it* myself and suffered most dreadfully with it. I do not recollect to have ever had it in my youth, and the Doctor decides my case to be the whooping cough.

I shall go tomorrow to London for a few days, and Clara promises to write you by this steamer, for which she will have time enough. We scarcely know yet how to decide about coming home; probably wait till next spring, and may go to France the coming winter. This is yet uncertain, however.

I must here close my letter to you, my dear Mother, praying that God may spare your precious life till we can meet again.

Your affectionate son,
Geo. Catlin

Regardless of the fact that Putnam's estate was probably the sum of his "paper profits," George's unselfish attitude is evident in his postcript to Francis. It is doubtful that any other member of the family would have shown comparable generosity:

My dear Brother, I reserve this page to say a few words to you relative to the embarrassed estate of our dear Father, and I scarcely know what to say or what you can do with it in these hard times. Still I trust that things are getting better, and that perhaps some parts of the property may be now sold without much sacrifice. Father gave me an article of agreement for the big house, and I was to pay $2,100 in 3 years, the difficulty of doing this was seen by him and me before I left N. York, and even when the agreement was made, it was put upon that condition expressly that I could pay in that time. I paid on that agreement $300, and since that, $125. And since that, authorized Father to sell it at the best rate that he could, if the times would permit, and keep for his own use the $425, which I had advanced. Now it is my wish that the Executors should sell the property to the best advantage they can, paying off the mortgage to Miss Wallace of 800 dols, converting the balance to the benefit of the estate or to the Legatees, as prescribed in the will, and I will give up to them the $425, which I have advanced on it.

Miss Wallace wrote to me some time since desiring me to pay up the interest $140 dols. or so, to save it from foreclosure, which I told her I would do, but if the Estate can be sold as I have above named, it would be useless for me to advance more money on it, and I hope you and Mr. Dimon can effect the sale in an advantageous way. I have written to him this day, giving a power of attorney to sell, relinquishing at the same time my claim to the $425, and also any other claims that I might have by any clause in the will. If by settlement of the estate there should, by the tenor of the will, be anything coming to me, as included amongst the legatees, I wish to relinquish any such claims, and the amount of such share divided amongst the other legatees.

Let me know what you are likely to do by the first chance, and tell me what are the prospects of selling the estate. I see by the papers that the prospects of business are somewhat brighter in U. States, and I cannot but believe that a purchaser may be got for the Big house ere long.

Love to your good lady & all enquiring friends. Write by return of packet.

Your affectionate brother
Geo. Catlin

Francis disappoints the Darts

THE WORD "family" meant a great deal to Eliza. During the happy years in Utica she had her sister Mary for a neighbor, and other members of the family were always welcomed at her home. Clara had spent much of her time there before going to England. In the summer time Polly and Putnam "journeyed" to Utica, and the Darts returned the visit in sleighing-time.

Eliza now had neighbors on the western prairie, but they weren't "kin-folk." For the past two years the Darts had expected to have Francis and Elizabeth in Green Lake, but Putnam's illness and death had kept them in Great Bend. Evidently Francis wrote Eliza in the early fall of 1843 that he and his little family would be with them the last of October. The following letter was written by a very lonely and homesick Eliza.

Green Lake Nov. the 4th 1843

My dear Brother Francis

Your letter dated Oct 18 is at hand—I will attempt to answer it, but expect to fail in the attempt. our family, one and all are disappointed at not seeing yourself and family instead of the gloomy letter, for such it is to me.—from what you and Elizabeth said (in your letter before the last)—I was so positive you would be with us this winter, that I had made great calculations, and promised my-self so much enjoyment this winter, we have been expecting you for 10 days, we have been making our house ready for your reception, we have made a point of walking to the Prairie every night before sunset in hopes to meet you, we have talked of nothing else, for weeks past, only what we would do when Francis comes. Elizabeth had 40 hens set aside, to be fed double, the rest to be killed when Francis and family comes. on monday of this week we had a few inches of snow, fell,—in the morning Richard was missing—we were but just setting down to our breakfast, when in he came out of breath, saying I have killed two deer, left my gun standing by a tree, and want Putnam to go with me to fetch them in, & said now if Frank was only here, but he will help us eate one or both of them—Poor boy he looks quite sober, this evening, since your letter came to hand.—we are a sorry looking company, and I know not what to say to you, I believe I am doomed never to see a relative or friend—I expect I shall cry my-self sick, more than once. Mary says, I should not have filled so large a tub with eggs, had I known Francis would have disappointed us, she would not have taken so much pains to make her hair curl so pretty if she had not been certain of seeing F and E,—and—the boys had mustered all the guns they could, and had them in readiness to fire and welcome you to Green Lake. the children kept a bright look-out to see who would see you first—the letter which I call a gloomy one, puts an end to all our expectations and anticipations, and we all set around our *kitchen parlour* fire, with faces long, I can assure you, but none feels the disappointment as my-self. I have had the promis of a letter from Mother three months since, but have not as yet seen it. your letter gives me nothing respecting her or Elizabeth, you know I feel so much anxiety about my Mother's health, and happiness, that I am anxious to hear every particular. I know not whether she is with you, or with Mary H, you will have to write again to satisfy me. how long did Richard stay with you was he in good spirits did he speak of his sister Eliza, or has he forgotten me. I feel tonight as if I was neglected and forgotten by those whom I love and remember. you speake of coming to Wisconsin in the spring—do you think I can ever make any calculations upon it again—no never. you cannot blame me for being so faithless. There has been a greate rush to this part of Wisconsin this fall, imigrants are crowding us on all sides. The mill is doing a good business, making the best of flower. Anson gets much credit for building so good a mill. Putnam and Richard have been the farmers this fall, they have got in 14 acres of wheat, on the Prairie, and some in the openings George has not done a days work in three months,—he was first taken with a fever, which ended in the Liver complaint, such as he had while we were living at Utica, he has worked much too hard since we came to Green Lake. he is now able to walk about the farm and helps a little, stands in the door and kills Prairie Hens which he calls *keeping us in Pot-Pie timber*. Richard says, tell Francis he picked his too deer out of a drove of more than twenty. our winter has not yet commenced—he has spoken for several more besides those which George and Putnam may get.—

I am under obligations to you for the trouble you have had in sending my chairs, &c. Anson thinks they will have to lay in a store-house in Utica through the winter, being sent so late in the season, but I hope not, do you hear any thing from George—will he ever return to America—I have never been so home sick since I came to Wisconsin as I am this evening—owing to the great disappointment I feel at not seeing you and family here this fall. How long did Richard stay with you—it must have been a greate feast to my dear Mother to meet with him once more in this world of sorrow and disappointment. did Richard go to Delta, does Sister Mary visit you often—tis a long time since I have had a letter from her—tell dear Mother, if I ever receive the things she has sent me, they will be valued more than she can conceive of by me, a coming from an only surviving, and long long absent parent. I approve of leaving the Portraits and chairs till spring to come with some one that will take charge of them—not Francis Catlin, I will not expect to see him in the spring, no I will not. Anson and the children tried to persuade me not to write this evening but waite till I got pretty over my disappointment, but I had so good an opportunity of sending my letter to the office that I would write in spite of all their entreaties, they have been teasing me all the time and trying to laugh me into good spirits, but without effect. Lydia Jean wrote to Mary that Nicolas would start the first of September for the west, and that he would visit Green Lake, we did expect to see him,—what shall we think of promises after this,—tell Mother, if it is not too much of a hardship for her to write, I should be happy to have a long letter from her. I shall require several letters from you and Elizabeth to make up in part for disappointing us. in all of your letters be sure and not tell us you are coming west, for we shall not believe you if you do.

by the time you get through with this letter you will make up your mind that I cannot bear disappointments,—George says tell Francis I cannot hold on to his land much longer, for there are so many trying to get it—if I had money I would enter it for him and secure it—people coming in are culling out all the best sections—it grieves us to think you could not have raised money to enter land at Green Lake before this, as land is getting very valuable, without improving it. I shall expect to hear from you again soon, give my love to Mother and Elizabeth. The children wish to be remembered to all, your sister Eliza Dart

Letters from Anson, George, and Polly

F R A N C I S ' F A I L U R E to move to Green Lake the previous fall cast gloom over the whole Dart family. They had looked forward to their company during the shut-in winter months. Francis and Elizabeth were a fun-loving couple; with their small son Charlie to cuddle and pet, the house would have been full of laughter and family chatter. Anson finally decided to write his wavering brother-in-law to make up his mind, one way or the other, about moving to Wisconsin.

Green Lake 12th Jany. 1844

F. P. Catlin My dear Sir,

This letter is in answer to yours of the 18th of Oct last, you will undoubtedly say why did you not answer it sooner. I will tell you. they say a man & his wife is both one, and Eliza answered your letter the very day it was read, but I do not know what she wrote, but I think she probabilly scolded you some for not coming with your family to Wisconsin this fall pasd, we all had fixed our lips for a kiss, and a close hug, but now mind you will only ketch it the harder when you do come in the spring. The dutchman said when he spoke he always had something to say, now Sir in the first place I have to say that we are all well. we have had no winter as yet, we had our first snow last week about six inches. Green Lake was as open as in June, untill last week. our crops were all good the pasd season except that of potatoes which was little more than half a crop, wheat is worth 6/ corn 6/ potatoes 4/ pork 40 cwt, beefe $4.00 butter 16 to 20 cts, cheese 8, sugar 9, coffee 11, tea 3/ to 8/ dried apples 12/ the prices above named are for a cwt or more at Milwaukee, dry goods are as low here as at Binghamton or Utica. Now Sir I want to talk a little about your coming to Wisconsin, the 10/ lands are not all entered as yet I think we can locate you entirely to your satisfaction on 10/ lands unless you would prefer a place with some improvements. this you can get near us. in as much as my advice does not cost much, I have a mind to give you a little, which is this, if you have made up your mind like the laws of the Meads & Persians (that is not to be altered) to move to Wisconsin in the *spring next* in that case I will be proud to advise you to buy you a good span of horses & a waggon & start as soon as possible yourself. hav your family to come by the boats in the spring with your brother N. Dubois. by doing this you will gain one year. if you start in march you will get here in time to get your house built and some crops in the ground by the time your family arrives, in that case you could meet your family with your team at Milwaukee. Then as to your team & waggon if you should not want to keep it, we will buy it at once. now Sir I want you to look to this propposition attentivly. I think if you can get ready to leave in May, you can get ready to leave yourself in march. come all the way by land you can fetch some things with you, if the snow should be deep take your waggon to pieces & load it onto a sled, or sleigh. you could probabilly sell your house and take in part pay a good team, and if you were to take all the balance in merchandise it could soon be turned into money here. if you ever intend to come to Wisconsin you must not defer it longer than spring. all wish to be remembered to your self & family.

Truly yours
Anson Dart

N. B. You know I had deeded to you a half interest in some lands here for the use & benefit of Asa. Now Asa will not write me on the subject nor pay any attention to said lands. Now Sir I want you (without delay) to write to Gen. Armstrong of Rome and ask him in what way he will divide your, & his, interest in said lands your half must be separated from his before they can be sold. tell him to write you without delay.

A D.

A note from George Dart was added:

Uncle Frank Sir

As Father cannot fill up this monstrous sheet I have come to the conclusion to help him not that my supply of news is any better but onley for the name that is all. Winter has come at last and it is a great cry and little wool for we have but little snow not sufficient for [illegible] There is a few things that I can tell you that Father has not that is what we are doing Father is at work at his trade I am at work at fencing making rails Put and Richard are at work at thrashing wheat Our wheat is first rate. Game is scarce this winter and it is not good hunting on account of there being now snow Richard has kild four this winter, Put has not kild any this winter neither have I I have not even been hunting yet on account of my being sick in the best hunting time. Some of our folks think that you will yet come to Wiskonsum but I do not think you will ever come so take that but if you do come now is your time you may depend on that and if you bring a span of horses I make a traid with you I have got one of the finest proven lots in Wiskonson and there is 10 acres broke up or ploughed and 10 acres fenced you cannot find so fine a lot in northern Wiskonson as mine and then I will go to teaming for a living you cannot imagine how fast the county is filing up we have recd a letter from Uncle Henry he is coming to wisconsin in the spring positively you must get the start of him if you can for we cannot locate but one of you near us uppon Government land.

we have lernt that the things you sent are at Chicago we shall take the first opportunity of getting them

yours Respectfully G. Dart

Father says you must answer immediately for if you come we can be doing something for you   G Dart

When Francis received this letter from Anson, he knew the time for decision had arrived. The West, with its unequaled facilities for hunting and fishing, appealed to him, but farming did not. However, with a family to support, he decided it was the best thing to do—there was nothing for him in Great Bend. He had asked his brother if there were any opportunities in the South, and the answer was "No."

From Polly's letter to Francis at Green Bay, July 2, 1844, one can assume that Francis, with some friends who wished to see the West, made the trip by wagon sometime that spring.[12] Elizabeth's third child, Clara, was born the first of May, and as soon as she was able to travel, her brother, Nicholas DuBois, accompanied her and the two children to Wisconsin by way of the Great Lakes. Before they left, Asa Hartshorn brought his wagon to Great Bend and took Polly and her belongings back to Delta, New York. Putnam's unsold property was left in the capable hands of Joseph DuBois.

The following letter from George was addressed to Francis at Great Bend. George did not know that his brother had left for the West, and that his mother was now in Delta. The little village of Great Bend was no longer the home of any of the Catlins. George's letter was forwarded to Green Lake, so Polly did not receive her note from Clara.

---

[12] Richard Dart later wrote that it took his uncle Francis from spring till autumn to make the trip to Green Lake with his wagon. But Eliza wrote in her August 5 letter to Clara that Francis and his family had been with them for two months. Richard must have meant his uncle Henry, who had finally managed to get his family to Wisconsin. The way Henry did things it could easily have taken him that long to make the trip.

London, May 18th, 1844

Dear Brother,

I received your last letter with great pleasure, and should have answered by the last mail. We are overjoyed to learn by that and by Mr. Dart's letter from New York, that all remain in good health at Great Bend, and particularly that the health of our dear, *dear* parent continues so good.

The letter of Dart surprised us very much, as we did not expect him to journey so far to the East in some time yet to come. I believe however, that he will go to Congress yet, and he will well deserve the honour of it as the pioneer of the far and wilderness West.[13]

He says you are determined to turn your face that way also, and from the tenor of your letter I am convinced that such is the case. I never had a doubt but such would be the most prudent step you could take, except for the convenience and comfort of our dear Mother for whom it would be too great a distance to perform, and for the sake of the homestead property and affairs necessary for you to settle, in some way.

It constantly pains me to think that the inauspicious and cruel times have operated so disastrously to most all of our family. And I have felt double pain from the fact also that with all my long absence and constant slavery in this awfully expensive country, I have not been able to lend a helping hand to any of my worthy brothers and sisters at home.

This is one of the hardest countries on earth to *make* money in, and one of the most easy & necessary to *spend* it in. I have a family of 9 to ferry over the ocean and 8 tons of freight, and

---

[13] Anson Dart had no intention of making farming his life work. He was politically interested in the development of the West, and this trip East was probably for the purpose of obtaining some government position while the Whig President, John Tyler, was still in office. This is indicated in Eliza's letter of August 5, to George and Clara.

when we shall all be ready to start, I do not yet know. I trust that all will come right yet—that there *will* be a time and a *way*, when we shall all meet again, and prosper.

If Clay is next President, I shall sell my Collection for money, or for (perhaps 100,000 acres of) wild land (ha?), and then we may make a swell in Wisconsin.

It grieves me to hear of the dilapidated state of the houses at the Bend, and of the difficulty of selling them. I hope however, that you will see some better chance of selling than you anticipated; if I were able, I would advance the money to save them, but as I am situated it is impossible at present to do it.

I can scarcely venture to advise what to do, as you are on the spot, and more familiar with the affairs of our dear Father's estate than I can be at this distance. you are much more able than I am, to decide what is for the best. If the Railway is to be made by the Bend, I do not see why the value of the property will not be materially improved, and the chances for a good purchase much greater.

It is impossible for me to leave my business at present or I would run home, were it but to see and talk with my dear, dear Mother for whom we now feel the deepest solicitude—about whom we are daily talking, and whom we feel it our duty to be with in this precious part of her life. We will trust, however, in that Providence which has so long indulged us, that the time will yet come when we shall all meet somewhere in this world and feel less the steepings of poverty than we have heretofore.

I am writing this in great haste, as the number of letters today have thrown me almost behind the mailing hour. I will try to write by the next steamer (fortnight from this) and say more, and say it more at leisure. Clara and all four little ones are all in good health and spirits, and my health is also good. Give our united and affectionate love to Dear Mother, to your wife, and compliments to all enquiring friends.

Your affectionate Brother
Geo. Catlin.

The note from Clara:

Dear Mother, George has left but little space for me to address you. We were very happy to hear from Mr. Dart, and to hear him speak so cheerfully. I trust he will yet prosper. It makes us sad to think that a separation must take place between Francis & yourself, but the same kind Providence that wills this has also led us all through mercy, and tempered the winds & waves of trouble to each of us. We must think all is for some good, and all will be right. If we but reach that haven of rest where parting is known no more for ever, then we may rejoice, that through much tribulation we have earned that rest.

I look forward in anticipation to seeing you comfortably situated with sister Mary. I do not know whether she lives in the same place. I hope she will write to me when you get there. My children are in good health. Our boy George is a fine specimen of an English baby, healthy and rosy, just six months old. We saw Mr. Turner of Silver Lake often while we were in Manchester. Mrs. Turner is dead.

I think it very possible we may be home in autumn. Adieu, dear Mother, may God bless and spare you till we meet again. Libby, Clara, Louise, George send best love to Grandma.

Ever your affectionate daughter

Clara

Polly had not wanted to leave Great Bend, her friends, and her memories, but she knew it was "for the best" that Francis move his family to Wisconsin. The following letter sent to Green Lake is from a lonely old lady mourning for the past.

Delta Julye the   1844

2

Dear Francis
I now sit down to answer your long expected letter whitch came to hand the twenty fifth of June we heard by way of a letter

from Mr Davis that you got safe over the water but still was affraid some of you was sick but we are thankfull that you and all your friends met in good health, my health is as good as usual in warm weather but I have not yet got over the hard Journey we was four days on the way with all my fears and verry bad roads parting with my dear children and the little babes and old friends and home was a great trial to one of my age, but through the mercy and goodness of kind heaven I was brought safe but in great weakness but I have been constantly taking things to strengthen me to answer your question I am as contented as I should be anywhere I feel like one a lone in the world and lonesome. I hardly dare to think whare I am or to look back on things that are past but to hope all is for the best and be resigned to Gods will in all things we have a quiet place here almost too still I want to hear a little noise some times we only number three in family Horace is tending store from home. Thomas is at school at Hammalton. Dear Francis I am happy to hear you are so well pleased with the country it will give you new ambition and new spirits that you have never felt before it is a great change and will prove a happy one through life I hope but mutch will be required of you from the great good giver of all your blessings, things of the greatest importane and of the most solem interest I hope you will not neglect always take good care of your health whitch is a duty I received a letter a few weeks since from Theodosia all were well a few lines was from Richard he said he could not find a place for you but you are better provided for he had visited James found him in poor health and sick of that place I wish he was only with you I got a letter from Andrew and have answered it according to your directions Mr. Hartshorn wrote to Mr. Bentley but no answer yet not a word from George have heard from the Bend bye a letter from Mr. Mac saying all friends were well and he has another son. the old place would be sold in a short time Dear Elizabeth since we parted you have passed through many new scenes you have been kindly carried safe through waves and stormes and dangers for whitch you have reason to be thankfull. I hope you will be pleased with your situation you must be happy with your little family and friends who is so happy to meet you. it is far different with you to what it was with Eliza, you can think a little how she has felt there a lone you must not feel homesick for a moment but feel that every dispensation is right we set here and enjoy it with you tell Eliza so tell her I shall write to her before long Mary will write the last of the weak Mary hardly gets time to write her milk and butter keeps her busy tell Eliza I am made verry comfortable here tell her the butry is turned into a bedroom for me so I sleep near them the back chamber she has given me for my things so I have room and a bed for my children when they come to see me but when will that ever be I want you to write all particulars wheather E has got the box I had sent did you take the things I left wheather Francis got the pay for what was sold I left the green cushen and all my cushens and rode on a leather one this was a great mistake and the bolster to my bead I mention this because it will be a satisfaction to think that you have got them I want to know whare our friends all are that went on with you tell little Charley Grandma sends her love to him tell him he is a good boy not to forget G tell him I crye when I think of him and when I go into the garden I talk to him and say his hym oh how I long to see that little lamme boy he is a delicate tender plant great care must be used over him dear little sister as Charley says I just began to love her I must close I can write but a little while at a time M and Asa sens love to all give my love to Mr. Dart tell him when he comes this way again I hope he will give us that call he promised me love to Eliza and all the children I shall want letters as often as I can get them

your ever affectionate mother
Polly Catlin

I hope you will excuse this miserable letter I never made quite so bad work before

[Note on edge of paper] I know Sister Eliza thinks hard of me

—but I certainly will write by next mail if possible, and before long to you, dear Sister E. love to all, Mary.

Francis wrote on the back of the letter: "From my Mother July 2, 1844. The last letter I ever rec'd from her and probably the last she wrote. Peace to thee Dear Mother."

The death of Polly—letters from Mary, Henry, and Eliza

POLLY CATLIN, mother of fourteen children, died July 15, 1844. She was seventy-four years old.

Mary Hartshorn wrote to Francis on July 24. It was a long letter, splotched with tear stains, giving every little detail of Polly's illness, death, and last words. The following is sufficient: "I have not yet felt composed enough, nor do I now feel as though I could pen a letter to you. you have before this received the paper and my letter to Eliza, bearing the unexpected intelligence of our dear Mother's departure. Oh, my brother, I wish I could find words to express what I have suffered for the last two weeks, but it never can be expressed. So sudden, and unexpected was her sickness and death, that I feel like one smitten into the duste by a blow, from which I cannot soon recover. I go about our lonely house from one room to another, calling on her dear name, but all is silent. . . .

"She told me she had thought for a great while, she should not be here long. She seemed not the least surprised or agitated when her symptoms were more unfavorable. I believe I have written to Eliza many of her last words, which were full of joy and peace. . . . We feel that the Lord has come very near us, and laid His hand upon one

293

of our dearest comforts. He has called and she has answered Him, and I pray I may not rise against His will. . . . Oh, that you may be happy & prosperous in that new country, & be faithful in all your religious duties, remembering the example we have had & ever praising the Lord that we have had such a Mother. . . ."

Brother Henry was notified of his mother's death in July, but it was November before he wrote to Francis, needing money, as usual. He did not know that Francis had been in Wisconsin since June—the family did not write to Henry unless it was necessary.

Niagara Falls, Nov 11th. 1844

Dear Brother

I write to you and direct my letter to you at the Great Bend hardly knowing whether you reside there or whether you may have moved to the West, as you said to me in your last letter that you intended moving there as soon as you could arrange your business so as to leave. I received a letter from Mary Hartshorn in the last summer informing me of the death of our Dear Mother I was much shocked at hearing of such a sad & afflicting stroke of Providence although we could not reasonably expect to have her with us many more years, according to the course of Nature—such events as these occurring one after another solemnizes my mind and at times makes me feel gloomy and tired of life. Mary informed me that she had written to all the children except George. I wrote to George immediately on the receipt of Mary's letter. I feel anxious as a Brother to know what calculation you are making for the future as to your movement etc. Have you heard from George lately? what is he about? I have not heard from him by letter in a long time. I see by the papers he is gaining great notoriety throughout Europe and that he is publishing a Portfolio, which promises to be lucrative to him as he has secured all the necessary patronage to authorize him to publish and that he publishes by subscription only.

I left Lockport the first of May last. I had nothing to do there—and finding myself unable to go West for want of funds I have concluded to rest here. I have been engaged the last summer in the Mineral and Shell business & have done tolerably well. My staying in Lockport last winter out of business with my large family involved me in debt and has taken my earnings for the last summer to clear myself from debt—

I shall do better another season if my life & health is spared— I am making up this winter about one thousand canes, which are a great article here to sell in the summer. This connected with my other business will ensure me a living & something more. I want about twenty dollars at this time or between now and first of January to assist me in purchasing my family provisions for the winter. I could get along with that amount and not be a dollar in debt in the spring—perhaps it may be in your power to let me have that amount sometime between this & first of January if you are not intending to move West this fall—I could let you have it again in the spring soon after my business commences here.

I do not wish to go in debt here for one dollar if I can avoid it. My family are well & join in sending love to you & yours. Sarah is at Norwalk, Ohio with her Grandmother—William is also in Ohio near the same place teaching school—a first rate teacher & highly qualified to teach—Samuel is farming, and Henry is whaling, & Peter is at the Tailoring business.

In haste your affectionate brother
Henry Catlin

The summer of 1844 had started out to be a wonderfully happy one for the Wisconsin pioneers. Francis and his family had arrived at Green Lake the first of June, and one can picture the excitement at the Dart farm. George and Clara, with their four children, were planning to return to America in the fall, and Eliza was in high spirits when she commenced the following letter to them.

Green Lake, August 5 1844

Dear Brother and Sister,

I need not tell you how delighted we all were at the receipt of your last letter, to hear of the health of your dear little family whom we hope ere long to see. we are all daily and hourly talking of the many—many pleasant meetings we shall have with our friends if our lives are spared—I expect to see you changed a little—George grown quite grey, and many rincles in his face—but oh! when you see her, who was once Eliza Catlin—what will be your surprise. tis astonishing to see what a change can be wrought by misfortune, afflictions, loss of dear friends, hardships, deprivations &c. my heart is still the same, filled with love for all dear relatives and friends—you will have heard before this, that Francis is an inhabitant of Green Lake, his family have lived with us 2 months while he Francis, was building his house. he is quite engenious, he and Nicolas DuBois have done all the work, he has a very neate Wisconsin Cabin—I will not describe it to you, as I expect you will see it not long first. F is very industrious he works early and late, he is determined to do something—Anson and the boys help him and advise him when necessary—he finds him-self among friends, he will move tomorrow, his house is but a few rods from mine, we can call each other to tea. Oh that dear Mother was with us to go frome house to house—she writes she is pleasantly situated with sister Mary—she thinks much of seeing your dear family this coming fall. we are making our little home in the west, a paradise every month something is added to its beauty. Putnam has injured his health by exceptive hard labour, he is able to oversee and work some—he is an amiable young man, beloved by all, he is correct (if possible) to a fault, we are extremely anxious to get him a situation where he will not be obliged to labour excessively. George is delighted with farming and is too clever to live with people in general—you must remember his disposition. he is a dutiful son thinks as much of his mother as ever. Mary does not think of ever getting married but our Lib—

thinks she is just the right age to flirt with the gentlemen—I wish you could see her *nip* and *prink*, and *fix* and *fuss*—she is very hombly, but thinks she is extremely beautiful. Mary looks well, and is not proud of her looks. She is a good girl, so is Libby they are all the help I have. Oh how much they talk of you and your little ones. They have almost spoiled Elizabeth's children since they have been here, with kindness, nursing &c. it has been a feast to us to have Fs family with us. you must not consider us living alone in a wilderness. hundreds of families have come to this Territory since we have. we are surrounded with inhabitants —every 4 or 5 miles there is a village, with Grist Mills, saw Mills Meetinghouses, &c. Francis has been so much engaged in building, he has no time to hunt, fish or ride on our beautiful Lake. the Indians bring us venison and little Charles supplies us with fish from a little stream near our house, on which stand a Grist Mill. Anson has a situation in reserve for George on the Lake. you speak of my meeting you in Washington, that would be delightful—Anson is determined to get a situation there for George. he thinks of going to Washington again on the same business. he has many friends in this country. The Whigs of this county have nominated him for the council—the same as Senitor in the states, if elected he will spend the winter in Madison, the Capital, we are extremely anxious to get something ahead, that we may relieve Asa Hartshorn, as we fear he has been put to much trouble and some expens on account of our misfortunes— this has been the greatest trouble of my life Mary speaks of it in every letter to me, which breaks my heart, and prevents me from enjoying any thing in life.

Anson intends leaving the farming with the boys and embark in some business, where he can pay off all hones debts, then and not till then, can we be happy—Richard is a farmer, as tall as his Father not a scollar, but a successful hunter, when he can get time to go out with his gun—talk to your little children of their aunt Eliza tell them I love them and hope to see them (may I say) within a year, yes dear Brother and sister it must be so. Oh that we could meet at Delta, with dear Mother, and Mary—I will hope and it may be so. you will write again soon we are so anxious about you and your return to your country and friends. Francis and Elizabeth will write soon—

[Mary continued the letter] Dear Aunt Clara, Ma's letter is unfinished and the mail leaves this evening she would have finished it herself but a few days since she recieved the heart breaking intelligence of her dear Mother's death and it has rendered her unfit for writting or business of any kind you must by this time have recieved a letter giving all of the particulars of her death it must have given you as severe a shock as it did us we cannot as yet realize that our dear dear Grandmother Catlin is no more, so short a time was she sick and but a few days before we had a very long and interesting letter from her little could have Uncle George thought when he bid adieu to his parents that he should never see them more, poor Grandmother how she wished you to return that she could see you all once more but she has gone and mourning friends can not recall her. Ma is in an agony of grief if F and E were not here as sympathiseing friends I know not what would become of her, she is if possibl more anxious than ever to see all of her brothers and sisters and is so sanguine in believing you will return this fall we tell her she will be disappointed still we all as furvently wish it as herself. I will close this by saying we are all well and doing well and hope our friends in London are the same. I would write more but it is very late and the mail leaves at day break in the morning and the musquitoes you cannot immagine any thing about them first on one hand and then on the other and one of the warmest nights we have had this summer our farmers are at their harvesting and very busy Uncle F and family are well and send much love to all. Now do not consider this a letter for it is written in such haste Ma will write in full when she is more composed.

Dear Aunt give our love to Uncle G and the dear baby and young ladys and write soon your affectionate niece, Mary Dart

More war-whoops in London

EXCEPT FOR his mother's death in July, the year 1844 was kinder to George Catlin than the one preceding it. His connection with Rankin had left him with debts and a smeared reputation, but the unstinted praise that followed the publication of his portfolio in the early spring put him back in London's good graces.[14]

George now felt that his work in England was completed, and that it was time to take his family back to America, but once again he delayed. Several ships had been sunk recently with all lost on board, and inventive minds were at work to find a way to save lives at a time of disaster at sea. Always eager to put extra money in his pocket, George set his mind to the subject and came up with an invention he was certain was the perfect answer. It had something to do with disengaging, and floating, the vessel's quarterdeck, but after spending much time and money he found that someone else had had the same idea, and that it was already patented. Catlin kept his model, which he called the "slipper," and later asked his brother Francis to patent for him in the United States.

With no more projects on his mind, George set the day for their voyage home. For more than a year Clara had been writing that they were coming back to America, only to write again to say their return would have to be postponed. Now she would have to unpack her trunks once more; fourteen Iowa Indians arrived from America to tour England under the management and care of Mr. G. H. C. Melody, and with the permission of J. M. Porter, Secretary of War.

Catlin knew this tribe well. They were from the plains between the Missouri River and the Rocky Mountains. Several times he had been

---

[14] *Catlin's North American Indian Portfolio. Hunting Scenes and Amusements of the Rocky Mountains and Prairies of America.... ,* published by subscription, at the Egyptian Hall, London, 1844. Printed by the Lithographic Press of Day & Hague.

given hospitality in their villages. When the Indians saw the artist they greeted him with joy, calling him by his Indian name, "Chip-pe-ho-la." They said they had come to dance with his exhibition. Catlin had known Melody in the United States, knew of his fine character and his sincere affection for the Indians; and he could not disappoint them after they had come so far. He took another lease on the Egyptian Hall, and the show was on again! Both the public and the press spoke well of these Indians, and soon they were receiving calls and invitations from distinguished people, among them Mr. Disraeli, who invited them all to his home.

In late fall Catlin and Melody took the Indians on a tour of the provinces, but finally the strenuous life and the damp English climate brought illness among the Iowas, and two died. Winter passed. Some of the Iowas were ready to go home, but others wanted to go to Paris and see the King, as they had not been able to see England's Queen.

Clara wrote Eliza on December 26, 1844, that they would leave for America before long. Perhaps she said "after a short trip to the continent," but Eliza did not mention that in her answer to Clara on February 23, 1845. George probably felt that he might as well complete a European tour before returning to the country from which his beloved parents had departed forever, and where his Indian collection was not wanted. At any rate, in the spring of 1845 he packed his belongings, gathered together his family, and with Melody and the excited Iowas left for Paris.

PART SIX: THE SKY FALLS DOWN

1845–1864

1845–1853: The Darts expect a visit from George and Clara; Tragedy in Paris; A change in the life of the pioneers; More tragedy in Paris; The axe falls; The "Harpies" gather for the kill   1850–1861: Oregon Territory; Anson Dart and a census Report; A vagabond artist; Letters from Wisconsin; 1861–1864: The tale of the pioneers comes to a close.

The Darts expect a visit from George and Clara

HOW MANY TIMES Clara had written that she and George would soon return to America—how fervent her desire must have been to go home! One feels great compassion for this young woman who so wanted to live among her own people; to be where her children could put down healthy roots in her native land.

The following letter from Eliza was written in happy anticipation of the early arrival of George and his family. Her remark regarding George's response to Clara's wishes shows that his wilful disregard for others if they interfered with his plans was well recognized by the family.

Green Lake Feby 23, 1845

My dear Sister Clara

Your letter of 26th Dec came to hand this evening it was handed to Putnam to read aloud. Oh dear Sister could you have been in some secreted place where you could have seen the cheerful and smiling countenances of our little family group, you would have seen the big tear falling from the eyes of her who now addresses you—yes dear Sister, I wept for joy that you and your dear family are yet among the living, since the death of our dear Mother, tears have been my only relief—you do not mention the receipt of my two last letters I fear you have not got them, if not, you must think we are very negligent. we could not neglect such a dear kind Sister as you are, one in whom we have ever felt so deep an interest.—

We were all much disappointed at hearing you would not return early in the coming spring we had already made great calculations to that effect, but disappointments seem to be the common lot of all mankind I am pleased to hear you say you are tired of living in England thinking it may expedite your return —knowing that *George is all acquiescente to your wishes or at least he ought to be*—what an anxious creature I am. I am already building upon a few words contained in your truely welcome letter, (*so you George Dart may be preparing for us*) Could I have a positive promise from George that he would be at Green Lake at a time specified with his dear little family, with what a light step could I go to my daily tasks—nothing would be a burden to me. my heart is bound up in my remaining relatives. I have this day received a long and excellent letter from Richard and Darwina bearing the painful intelligence of the death of our dear orphan niece Theodosia Amanda Catlin she went to the south with Richard for her health—poor dear girl she has gone the way of all the earth, yes that dear girl is no more. . . . The dear girl lived to mourn the death of our excellent Mother, to whom she was devotedly attached—At the name of *Mother* a *thousand* fond endearing recollections are called forth—the heart is ever sensible at the word *Mother* however hard and callous to other things. We can have but one Mother and when she is taken from us, our hearts must be hard indeed if we can be unmoved. . . . As those we love fall one by one, our affections cling the closer to those who are left, and as dear Brother George said respecting our dear Mother, strive to imitate her virtues—love our children as she loved hers. . . . I am extremely anxious to have an introduction to your dear little family—my *Baby* is now 9 years old, a smart lad I can assure you—his big head was a good one as Doct McCall of Utica said when George brought him to our house to lecture upon his Phrenological bumps. he reads writes and spells well, syphers some and has never been to school one day—my love to dear Brother George tell him to write my love to all the little ones. adieu for this time dear Sister adieu Eliza. . . .

Tragedy in Paris

IN EARLY APRIL, 1845, George Catlin and his family arrived in Paris. They were followed by Melody and his Iowa Indians and Daniel with the eight tons of Indian paintings and artifacts. Catlin had engaged the Salle Valentino in Rue St. Honore for his exhibition, and application had been made for an audience with King Louis Philippe.

The Indians were delighted with Paris; everywhere they went they were greeted with friendliness and hospitality. They loved the beautiful wide streets with their trees and flowers, and the splendor of the rooms they visited. The Iowas liked this bright city far better than London, and said they were glad that they saw nobody in rags or begging, which meant that the French people had enough to eat.

The King received Catlin and the Indians at the Palace of the Tuileries. The artist was not a stranger to him. He had been one of the earliest subscribers for the recently published *Portfolio*, and had read his books on the North American Indians with great interest, having traveled in America in 1792 when in exile during the French revolution. He was eager to talk to the American whose works brought back memories of those days long past.

Catlin's Indian collection and the Iowas with their songs, dances, and war-whoops drew great crowds. Fashionable Paris came, as well as those from the scientific and literary world. Victor Hugo paid a call, so did George Sand. The noted German scientist, Baron de Humboldt, was a frequent visitor. The press gave Catlin exceptional praise.

Everything was running smoothly until the wife of one of the Indians died. Having buried his little son in England, the husband wanted to go home. Others in the group were homesick, and after holding council together, they informed Mr. Melody that they were leaving in a few days. Melody had pledged his word to return with them whenever they desired, and so it had to be. This abrupt change in his exhibit was hard on George. The attendance was increasing daily, but the expense in starting had been so great that several more months were needed to realize any profit.

In the midst of his financial worry a tragic event occurred—his beloved Clara became ill, and died of pneumonia on July 28, 1845. Her body was sent back to be buried in her native land. Clara, at last, had gone home.

George was completely bewildered in his grief. He didn't have money enough to clear his debts and pay for the passage of his family and Indian collection across the Atlantic. Just when he was at his wit's end, a group of Canadian Ojibways appeared in Paris. They were under the management of an Englishman who had heard of the departure of the Iowas, and hoped his group could take their place. To Catlin, here was a way out of his dilemma; he had an unexpired lease on the hall and his paintings were still hanging there. He signed up the Ojibways and advertised that a new company of Indians would join him. A nurse was put in charge of his motherless children, and George went on with the show.

Louis Philippe had formed a great liking for this personable artist from America, and invited him to bring his Indian collection to the Louvre for a private viewing by the Royal family. This Catlin did on the expiration of his lease at the hall. The paintings brought back many memories to the King, and he commissioned the artist to copy fifteen of them to be hung permanently in the Louvre.

The exhibit closed, George left his collection at the Louvre, planning on returning the Ojibways to London by way of Belgium, exhibiting them in Brussels and Antwerp in hopes of earning enough to pay their expenses home. His purse was lean; he had gained nothing by taking on this last group of Indians. Paris had heard enough war-whoops.

At Brussels, where Catlin had made all preparations for the exhibit, one of the Indians fell ill with smallpox, and soon seven more were prostrate. The exhibit was cancelled, and George was detained in Brussels for two months before the surviving Indians were able to travel. With aid from friends in Paris, George sent the Ojibways back to London.

This experience ended Catlin's "Wild Indian" exhibitions forever. He returned to Paris the first of February, 1846.

A change in the life of the pioneers

ALL OF ELIZA'S letters show her affection for Clara. What must have been her reaction to the news of her death! In her loneliness so far from home, after the loss of both parents, Eliza had been building her dreams around the hope that George and Clara would soon be living near them. They had written that they were coming! The whole Dart family was making plans for that happy event. The death of Clara brought a shocking end to all her dreams, and this may well have played a large part in Anson selling the farm, for Eliza had made no mention of such a possibility in her February letter to Clara.

Quoting from a short biography of Anson Dart: "In 1845 he sold his farm which now comprised about 200 acres of land, and settled at the outlet of Green Lake; here a village (now Green Lake), named Dartford in his honor, grew up. . . ." [1]

Richard Dart later wrote that his father sold his farm in 1846, but he made several errors in dates in his article. It was Francis who sold his farm in 1846, for seven hundred dollars.

Anson Dart had become very active in politics. In 1847 he ran for the state assembly on the Whig ticket, but lost to the Democratic candidate, M. C. Darling. In 1848 he campaigned vigorously for Zachary Taylor, Whig candidate for president, and was evidently told, following the Whig victory, that he would be rewarded for his services. The summer of 1849 found him in Washington.

[1] A letter from the Wisconsin State Historical Society, to author.

It is very probable that Francis Catlin joined Dart in the campaigning for Taylor, for he went to Washington in the spring, and his appointment as Register of the Land Office for the District of Lands at Willow River, Wisconsin, was signed by Zachary Taylor, on April 12, 1849. Nicolas DuBois wrote Francis on May 3 that he had seen a notice of his appointment in the newspaper. "We were all much pleased that you had been successful, and that it would prevent any further ravages of the California gold fever as far as you were concerned."

Eliza wrote Francis in August, directing the letter to Stillwater, Minnesota Territory:

Dartford Aug 26 1849

Dear Brother & Sister,

I shall offer no other excuse for writing at this time than this —I am confined to my chair with a lame ancle, and have nothing to do but think of absent friends and write to them often. I have been troubled with lameness since Charley's birth. Anson has been absent three weeks at Washington, it is very doutful about the appointment—the Charge at Peru is not to be removed, but a gentleman at Washington wrote to Mr. Dart to come down and try for one of five Charges that were soon to be appointed—he repaired there as soon as was practicable—the President is now absent, and no appointments will be made till late in Sept. after the President's return. All is uncertain. . . .[2] I hope and trust the cholery has not reached your section of the country, there has been much of it at Milwaukee and Watertown. . . . We would like much to get a long letter from you as you must have commenced business ere this, write and tell us all about the country the society the prospects and all about the dear little children. . . . we have not heard one word from Henry since

---

[2] The following year Anson Dart was appointed to the first office of Superintendent of Indian Affairs in Oregon, created by Act of Congress, June 5, 1850.

he left us, this is about the time he was to be here with his family. Richard says Darwina is teasing him to build her a house at Dartford and to move here in the spring it may be so [3]. . . . Putnam says he wishes Elizabeth would condescend to write to him as it would give him very great pleasure to answer the first letter from her—he thinks if she would commence one to him, when it was finished it would be to George.

> adieu dear Brother and Sister, and believe
> as ever your affectionate sister Eliza Dart.

More tragedy in Paris

GEORGE CATLIN returned to Paris from Brussels early in February, 1846. With his four little children and their nurse he settled down in an apartment to paint the fifteen pictures for Louis Philippe, having stored his Indian collection in a building nearby. He devoted all his spare time to his motherless brood, and his namesake, George, not yet three years old (he was born in the late fall of 1843), was his constant companion. The little fellow was always happy; laughing and chattering, and beating so furiously on his little drum that his doting father dubbed him "Tambour Major."

George found a certain peace in returning to his easel after his years of anxiety and sorrow. He was a tired man of fifty now, and his grief over the loss of his beloved Clara was ever with him. No doubt he blamed himself for Clara's death; he could have taken his family home instead of to Paris. George had never intended to be a "showman." It was a serious-minded artist who went into Indian country. He had painted the American Indians for posterity, not for

---

[3] James Catlin died in 1847; Mary Catlin Hartshorn in 1848. So many deaths in her beloved family since she came to Wisconsin seem to have left Eliza unconcerned over the movements of the remaining members.

the idle amusement-hunters in foreign countries. His collection belonged in America, and he had brought it to England in hopes that such a drastic move would bring Congress to its senses. But once in England he was stuck. He had no business acumen whatsoever, and his expenses grew to such an enormous amount that he was willing to do whatever he could to entice people into his hall.

Before George left London for Paris he had declined an offer of 7,000 pounds ($35,000) for his gallery.[4] He said he didn't want it stuck away in a duke's castle where it never would be seen by the public and would be soon forgotten (as well as the name of George Catlin). During all these years Catlin had never ceased hoping that Congress would purchase the collection. He had written countless letters to influential friends and members of Congress to intercede for him. At one time he had been certain the English government would make an offer—the press had so strongly advocated it—but they made no move; possibly, as Burr said, because the artist was an American.

In the spring of 1846, George made another attempt to win Congress, sending a memorial and offering his entire collection for $65,000. His plea was supported by memorials from American artists in England and France. On July 9, Senator J. M. Clayton from Delaware presented Catlin's memorials, as well as one signed by leading artists in New York.

Mr. Clayton stated before the Senate that possession of such a valuable collection was a matter of high national importance; that it would be discreditable to Congress to allow it to be purchased by a foreign government. The memorial was referred to the Committee on the Library.[5] On July 24, the Joint Committee on the Library reported to the Senate: "The bill which has recently passed the House for the establishment of the Smithsonian Institution provided that there shall belong to it a 'gallery of art'; . . . No productions, your committee believe, at present exist, more appropriate to this Gallery than those of Mr. Catlin, or of equal importance. . . . The

---

[4] Alan N. L. Munby, *Phillipps Studies No. 4* (Cambridge: Cambridge University Press, 1956), p. 55.

[5] *Congressional Globe,* July 9, 1846, p. 1072.

Committee therefore, recommend that the bill for the establishment of the Smithsonian Institution be so amended as that provision shall be made therein for the purchase of Mr. Catlin's gallery at the price mentioned by him—namely, sixty-five thousand dollars—payable in annual instalments of ten thousand dollars." [6] No decision was made; evidently the subject was left for later consideration.

So the artist stayed in Paris and finished the fifteen paintings for Louis Philippe, who expressed great satisfaction with them. Again the two men sat and talked on the subject with which they both were so familiar; the Indian country and trips down the Missouri and Mississippi. This led to the mention of La Salle and Hennepin, and their expedition in 1678. The King commissioned Catlin to do a series of paintings of their travels, using for backgrounds the country which the artist could paint from memory.

George's personal life was now built around his children. He wrote: "The society which fascinated me the most, and called for all my idle hours, was that of my four dear little children, whose arms, having been forever torn from the embrace of an affectionate mother, were ready to cling to my neck whenever I quitted the toils of my painting room . . . and weeks and months of my life were passing on whilst my house rang with the constant notes of my little girls and my dear little Tambour Major, producing a glow of happiness in my life." [7]

But this happiness was not destined to continue. In the late summer of 1846 the dreaded typhoid fever struck them all, and George's beloved little son died. His body was sent to New York "as a lovely flower, to be planted by the grave of his mother. . . . Two idols of my heart had thus vanished . . . leaving my breast with a healing and a fresh wound, to be opened and bleeding together." [8]

In the fall of that year Catlin went back to London for the purpose

---

[6] *Memorial of R. R. Gurley*, U. S. Senate, 30th Congress, 1st Session, Misc. Papers No. 152 (July 24, 1846), p. 8.

[7] George Catlin, *Eight Years' Travel and Residence in Europe* (2 vols.; London: published by the author, 1848), II, 323.

[8] *Ibid.*, II, 324.

of raising some money, if possible. He was now willing to sell his collection for the sum he had refused earlier (see p. 310), but found no market for his works. While there he met the ethnologist, Henry Rowe Schoolcraft, who had gone to Europe to get Catlin's permission to use his Indian paintings for illustrations in a statistical work on the North American Indians, which Schoolcraft hoped to edit for the government of the United States. He told Catlin that his paintings would help to insure its publication, and make a fortune for the artist. He also added that with his political influence he could then easily secure the passage of the bill to purchase Catlin's collection. George refused. He replied that he had gone to a great expense to publish his own works on the Indians, illustrated with his paintings.

The wily Schoolcraft had counted on Catlin's paintings for his works, and from that time on was Catlin's enemy. Considered the official ethnologist in those days, Schoolcraft had many political friends who were willing to oblige him. So, in 1847, Congress passed an act creating the office "Indian Historiographer to the Congress of the United States," and authorized Schoolcraft to collect statistical material relative to all the Indian tribes of the United States.

After his fruitless trip to London, George returned to Paris and started working on the La Salle commission for Louis Philippe. The series consisted of twenty-nine paintings which took seven months to complete. They were finally delivered to the King's minister just before the French revolution got into full swing.

France had been in a political turmoil for years. The people wanted a more liberal government, which Louis Philippe (though democratic in his personal tastes) opposed. This simmering rebellion came to a full boil on February 22, 1848, with the streets of Paris swarming with angry, destructive mobs. The King and Queen were hastily spirited out of the country. Because Catlin was known to be his friend, he was advised to leave Paris at once, before the rioters could damage his works. George managed to get his three girls and his entire Indian gallery back to London. Francis Catlin later wrote that George returned to Paris six weeks later and retrieved his La Salle paintings, which had been preserved. Evidently (and fortunately)

George left the collection in storage in Paris. Neither the deposed king nor the French government was now interested in the purchase of the La Salle paintings, so Catlin was never paid a cent for his seven months of weary toil.

The axe falls

1848. GEORGE CATLIN and his three little girls were living at No. 6, Waterloo Place, Pall Mall—cheap rooms, just large enough for living quarters and to show some of his collection to the few interested enough to pay a shilling to see it. George had become quite deaf, and was no longer the voluble, spirited person whose wit made him such good company in the past. London acquaintances who had once clamored for his society were not interested in a deaf has-been. The Honorable Charles A. Murray, who had been George's greatest friend and benefactor, was now Minister to Persia. He visited London with his American bride in 1858, but no record shows that he met his former protegé. George's life had run parallel to Eliza's in the sense that prosperity gave each many friends; poverty lost them.

George had planned to write a book on his experiences abroad, and had filled many notebooks with data against the time when he could leisurely write of this colorful period in his life. This certainly was not the time, but his financial distress made him pick up his pen, and late in the year he published *Notes on Eight Years' Travel and Residence in Europe*,[9] in two volumes. This work cannot be compared with his publication on the North American Indians. The latter showed a scholarly approach to the subject, and had been several years in the making. Catlin had the ability to make this last work a very interesting and worthwhile report of his years in Europe. Instead, it was a somewhat rambling account of his London and Paris

---

[9] Catlin, *Eight Years' Travel and Residence in Europe.*

313

successes and his connection with the Iowas and Ojibways. Some parts were well written and informative; but many pages were filled with boring conversation. It was natural that he emphasized his friendship with European nobility. After all, the book would be read in America, and he needed to expand his deflated ego as much as possible. George was a sad, disillusioned man. Under happier circumstances, the book might have been worthy of its author. As it was, it was written only to put money into his empty purse. Fortunately, it sold very well.

The lonely artist stayed close to his rooms, dividing his time between the care of his little daughters and copying his paintings to sell to the few friends who remained faithful. In this way, Sir Thomas Phillipps acquired replicas of many of Catlin's original paintings. In May, 1849, Sir Thomas loaned the needy artist 100 pounds, George leaving with him twenty original paintings from his gallery as security. In 1851, unable to return the sum, George made an agreement with the baronet to copy fifty of his Indian paintings (reduced to 15 × 16 inches in size) for 2 pounds ($10) apiece, plus 2 shillings each for canvas and stretchers! [10]

On February 27, 1849, the bill for the purchase of Catlin's collection came up for discussion in the United States Senate.[11] The move was made to "insert an item of $5,000 for the purchase of Catlin's gallery of paintings and curiosities, being one year's installment of $50,000 to be paid in 10 years." [12]

Daniel Webster, Senator from Massachusetts, gave a stirring and

---

[10] Munby, *Phillipps Studies No. 4*, p. 56.

[11] Biographers of George Catlin have erred in placing the 1849–1850 Senate debate, including quotes from the speeches of Webster and Davis, as occurring during the 1852–1853 Congressional Session. Neither Webster nor Jefferson Davis was in the Senate at the later date. Daniel Webster was Secretary of State from July 22, 1850, until his death in 1853. Jefferson Davis (Senator from Mississippi, not Kentucky) resigned in 1851 to run for Governor of Mississippi. Also, as seen in the *Congressional Record*, Davis did *not* kill the bill singlehandedly.

[12] *Congressional Globe*, February 27, 1849, p. 604.

powerful speech in favor of purchase.[13] Jefferson Davis, from Mississippi, a friend of the artist in earlier days, praised Catlin and his excellent portrayal of the American Indians.[14] However, at the end of his lengthy oration, he said he would have to vote against the bill for political reasons. (The South wished no favors shown the Indians; they wanted their lands for more slave states.)

After the debate, the yeas and nays were called for. The result was *yeas 23, nays 25.*[15]

The following day (February 28) the bill was brought up again in the Senate. The question was decided in the negative—*yeas 15, nays 21.*[16]

The Harpies gather for the kill

GEORGE was still living in his small quarters at No. 6 Waterloo Place, copying his Indian paintings for a pittance, and caring for his three little girls as well as he could. He was full of fear, and it was but a feeble glow of optimism that kept him going.

The year 1852 found George in desperate straits, clutching at straws to keep afloat. He had written to Congressmen; he had received letters from friends at home who were certain that the next Session would bring action in his favor. George was so sure that his Indian collection would be purchased by his government that he went berserk in borrowing money, giving his gallery as security. He was far over his head in debt.

He wrote to his good friend, Daniel Webster, now Secretary of State, on April 4, 1852.[17] He thanked him for the wonderful speech

---

[13] See Appendix VI.

[14] See Appendix VII.

[15] *Congressional Globe*, February 27, 1849, p. 604.

[16] *Congressional Globe*, February 28, 1849, p. 613.

[17] See Appendix VIII.

he had made in the Senate three years earlier, and with great humility spoke of his alarm over the fate of his collection, and his fervent prayer for a favorable decision.

Much was to happen to George before purchase of his collection was brought before the Senate in July. Poor Clara was right when she wrote of the perils of getting into debt in England, and of the harpies who descended upon anyone unable to cancel them. They now fell upon the helpless artist. George was arrested, and sent to prison. His collection was to be sold at auction to satisfy his creditors.

On July 20, 1852, the purchase of Catlin's gallery was again debated on the floor of the Senate. William Henry Seward championed the bill. He said that letters had been received from the artist while in a London jail, in which he informed them that he had been arrested for debt, and that his collection had been advertised to be sold in satisfaction of his debts.

Quoting Seward: "If, then, this question is ever to be decided at all, (and it has been before Congress many years,) a state of circumstances has arisen which renders it essential, and due to him, and due to the country, that it should be disposed of now. . . ."[18]

Seward then read a recent letter from George, addressed "to the Hon. Mr. Pearce, Chairman of the Committee on the Library, United States Senate, and gentlemen of the Library Committee." It was dated Paris, June 24th, 1852. Mr. Seward remarked that, by this letter, it appeared that Catlin had in some way obtained his liberty and he was in Paris at the time it was written. George wrote:

"Some weeks since I addressed a letter to your honorable body on the subject of my Indian collection, having been informed that my memorial to the Congress had been referred to your consideration. I now take the liberty of addressing you again, and of inclosing to you the auctioneer's advertisement, which will show you the reason I have for alarm for the safety of my collection, and the cause of this, my second prayer, that some step may be taken, if it has not yet been done, by your honorable body for the rescue of the works of my life,

---

[18] *Congressional Globe*, July 20, 1852, p. 1845.

which you discover I have not the power myself of doing. By the inclosed circular, it will be seen that the collection was to have been sold on the 22d of this month, but by a hard struggle, aided by some American friends, the sale has been postponed until the 19th of July, on the grounds that there was a prospect of the Congress voting the appropriation to enable me to pay my debts, and to return the collection as the property of the Government of the United States. . . .

"I am ashamed that my speculations have not been better managed than these results prove, and that I should be under the necessity of asking for help to preserve my works; but my desire to see these memorials preserved and treasured up by our country is above all delicate and selfish feelings, and I again pray, gentlemen, if it be not too late, that you may lose no time in recommending to the Government, *not to appropriate money for my relief*, but to purchase the works of my toilsome life, which I have gathered for my country, and which I offer as justly worth the price I ask for them. . . ." [19] George offered the collection for $50,000, $15,000 less than his former price.

Seward read to the Senate the auctioneer's advertisement; a stupendous list of Indian paintings and material.

The Senate debate was long, and hotly contested. George's work was compared with that of other Indian painters; he was spoken of in words of great praise—and denounced with bitter sarcasm. Finally a member announced that there was too much public business that required the Senate's attention to spend any more time on the merits of portrait painters. The motion to table the resolution was carried by a vote of 26 to 20. [20]

It is natural that George preferred not to dwell upon his detainment in prison. We do not know how long he was kept there, but since Seward mentioned that letters had been received from Catlin while he was in a London jail, it can be assumed that he was not

[19] *Ibid.*, p. 1845.
[20] *Ibid.*, p. 1846.

released immediately. It is possible, because of his three little girls, that George notified Clara's brother Dudley Gregory after his arrest, and the latter caught the next ship to London. Also, because of the children, Gregory could have been one of the "American friends" George mentioned, for with his wealth and influence, Gregory would have had no difficulty in obtaining George's release from prison, and postponing the date of the sale. For Gregory, George's release was imperative; there must be no stigma attached to the name of Clara's daughters!

Gregory took the three girls home with him. That George was friendly toward him in later years belies the suggestion that the children were snatched from their father's arms. George was no fool. He knew he was destitute, and that his growing girls had not been getting proper care. They needed a home, and a woman's love and attention. Nevertheless, the separation was a blow to the father who so loved his children.

No doubt Gregory told George it would be best for him to get out of London as soon as possible. He, or brother Richard, may have offered to pay his fare back to America, but George, having had visions of returning in triumph, refused the offer, not wishing to slink home like a whipped dog. If Congress passed the bill before the date of the auction he would go home. In the meantime he would go to Paris.

The creditors, in their haste to demolish his quarters, overlooked the artist's small painting room not connected with the others, and George was able to save some of his work—a collection of watercolors, and a large number of "cartoon" copies of his originals. They were done on a white cardboard manufactured for this purpose, on which the oil dried much more rapidly than on canvas, and which he used for his paintings from this time. He called them cartoons to distinguish them from those done on canvas.

So George gathered together what was left of his life and crept back to Paris. The Senate's rejection left him in darkness and despair. Had it not been for the humane behavior of Joseph Harrison, from Philadelphia, the Indian collection would have been heard of no more. Mr. Harrison was one of Catlin's largest creditors, but he was also from the artist's home state, and a patron of the arts. He quickly and quietly paid off Catlin's main debts, and had the collection shipped to Philadelphia. On his return home he stored it way in his boiler factory. Catlin later wrote: "my collection was saved to my country by an American gentleman—an act so noble and patriotic that I cannot believe my country will forget it." [21]

Colorful Paris was a city George loved. The memories of his first months here would be cherished forever. He had been so happy with Clara and the children, success, and many friends. Alone in a shabby room, with only memories for company, George must have spent lonely hours, reviewing the past and flicking over the possible future. He had been too optimistic—too sure of success—and he had lost everything; his wife, his children, his gallery.

He wandered through the familiar streets with bowed head, not wishing to greet former acquaintances. It did not occur to him that they would not have recognized the shabbily dressed little man shuffling along with his coat pulled up over his ears. He spent much time in a reading room where scholars gathered. Here he met a man who had done much research on old Spanish legends, and who told George the tale of the lost gold mines in the Crystal Mountains of Brazil, sought for, but never found again. The legend stayed in his mind.

George Catlin had been under terrific tension for many years. His old lung weakness had returned. He was sick, deaf, and destitute. Physically and emotionally he was at low tide, and what had happened in 1836 repeated itself now, though on a greater scale: George sought escape in the wilderness. One day he was in Paris; the next day he was gone. He told no one.

---

[21] George Catlin, *Last Rambles Amongst the Indians of the Rocky Mountains and the Andes* (New York: D. Appleton and Company, 1867), p. 56.

WISCONSIN became a State in 1848. Francis Catlin, as first Register of the Willow River (Hudson) Land Office, was well acquainted with the early settlers of the northwestern section. He dealt with the men whose purchases laid the foundations for the future fortunes made from pine lands, but Francis had neither foresight nor pocket money to gamble on the future.

Francis was a contented man in 1850. He was noted for his skill with the rod and rifle; completely happy in this wild country with its virgin forests, rivers and streams, seemingly designed for his pleasure. This was the life he truly loved. He worked at his job because he had a family to support. He and Elizabeth now had three boys, Charles, Frank, and Fred. Their little girl, Clara, drowned in Green Lake at the age of one year.

In 1851 Elizabeth became ill, and Francis took her and the children back to her family at Great Bend. In August of that year she died of consumption. She was just thirty-four.

Shortly before her death she wrote to Francis—a sad, sweet letter from one who had been full of laughter: "You wish to know about your boys. I have no care of them whatever, but I believe they get along very well. Frank and Charley go to school and Fred manages to spend most of his time with some of his little cousins. Frank is a noble hearted, kind little soul, always bringing me candies and nuts to share. When strawberries first came he picked a little cup full for me, and said he had not eaten one. . . . You must write me and tell me all about the Willow River folks. Are my things that I left at the house there, or has some one else taken possession of them—have you sold the cow or stove? Did you see pay for the horse? . . . May God bless and protect you from all harm."

On the back of this letter Francis wrote: "This is the last letter written by my dear wife, and did not reach me till about the middle of September after my return from the Bend, some 3 or 4 weeks after her death. I often look over these pages, and think of her who was the only true friend I had on earth, and one who had shared the trials of life with me, who was ever ready to forgive my faults, and whose prayer was always that I might be happy on earth and join her in Heaven after the closing of this earthly pilgrimage. May God grant her prayer."

Anson Dart had been appointed Superintendent of Indian Affairs in Oregon Territory in June, 1850. It is said that at the time of his appointment to Oregon that his appointment already had been made out as charge d'affaires to one of the South American Republics. Owing to his relationship and association with George Catlin, the great Indian traveler and painter, he was urgently solicited by the Secretary of the Interior to go as Superintendent of Indian Affairs to Oregon. Dart was supposed to be intimate with the habits, character, and language of the Indians in that territory.[22] He accepted the position and arrived in Oregon City the first of October, 1850.

Indian affairs in Oregon Territory had not been running smoothly. The migration to that part of the country was heavy, and because Congress had just passed a law giving every settler in the new Territory a section of land, the purchase of Indian land was imperative. Settlement was heaviest in the fertile valley of the Willamette River, south of the Columbia River, and agents had been sent there to buy out and remove all Indians to sections east of the Cascade Mountains. It had not been done. A look at this portion of Oregon Territory (which attained statehood in 1859) will show the problem Anson Dart was up against.

The part of the Territory that was settled most rapidly was the Willamette Valley, west of the Cascades. The Indians there were few

---

[22] It is doubtful that Dart had ever before been west of the Rockies. However, he was very familiar with the country and its Indian inhabitants east of these mountains. Dart had been a miller in New York State, and had done much traveling in the west for wheat, since the Great Lakes was a natural highway for freighting purposes. He had also speculated in western pine lands, and other real estate.

and had long been accustomed to white people. They wished to stay on. In the coastal valleys of the Rogue and Umpqua rivers, the Indians were definitely hostile. They refused to move east of the mountains where they would be expected to farm for a living instead of subsisting on the salmon to which they were accustomed.

Dart and the agents under him well understood the attitude of the natives, and adopted the plan of allowing them to remain on small reservations on a part of their tribal lands. Nineteen treaties with different tribes were made in 1851, thirteen by Dart, but not one of them was ratified. In November of that year Dart went back to Washington to give his superiors a clearer picture of the situation.

Anson's mode of travel to the east coast was to take a steamer to San Francisco, embark again to Panama, go overland across the Isthmus of Panama, and again by steamer to New York. He was ill the entire trip, and landed in New York a very sick man. His son Putnam was in the city at that time, on his way to join his father in Oregon. Eliza told the story of their meeting to Francis, recounting what Putnam had written her.

Milwaukee, Feb. 6, 1852

Dear Brother Francis

. . . It was altogether providential his [Dart's] meeting Putnam in N. Y. P. was staying at Newark, was to start monday afternoon of the 22nd in the *Dan Webster* by *Nicaragua*, he dined at James Keenes, started for N. Y. with bag and baggage steering direct for the boat, the little boys were crying *buy a penny paper sir*—he said he thought he would buy one to get the latest news before leaving, the first thing that met his eye was the arrival of the *Georgia* on Sunday the day before he was to leave. among the names of passengers he saw *Anson Dart Superintendent of Indian affairs in Oregon* he started for the Hotells went to twelve before he found him he was at the Aster House, what a happy meeting, he said he hardly knew his own Father he was so thin and his skin so yellow, he had been sea sick all the way and completely worn out, hardly able to set up or walk about. Put said he flew around got him shaved, and clean clothes and a standing collar, sent for a Physician, had him doctored up, so that in a few days they were able to procede to Washington, Putnam got his ticket transfered to the boat two weeks ahead, which gave him time to assist Pa in his world of business at W. They arrived at Washington at the commencement of the Holidays, one week passed before any buisness with the Government could be done, during which time Pa was very sick from the effects of his long and tedious journey. A Physician was sent for, Putnam had his hands full, waiting upon Pa, writing his reports, gentlemen calling continually, to see Pa on buisness. It was three weeks before Pa was well enough to leave Washington Putnam got his tickets transfered two weeks longer, which enabled him to stick to his Father till he was well enough to start for Milwaukee. Pa could not have got his business done without Putnam and he was able to give him instructions what to do when he arrived in Oregon Putnam said he could never be thankful enough for his meeting Pa as he did. Putnam sailed on the Dan Webster 22'd of January. Pa brought a bag of dust to the mint at Philadelphia to be coined, from which he took some large lumps of solid gold, to show his friends as specimens of Oregon gold some pieces are as large as a butternut some as large as a thimble the largest weighing from forty to sixty dollars, they are as pure as the dollar pieces they set the Milwaukee people crazy—they are now at D[dartford] setting them all crazy there. I expect Mr. Johnson and Libby will return to Oregon with Pa, if so, they will go into the splendidly furnished Superintendents House, and board Pa and Putnam. Pa has a good job for Johnson, building government Store Houses.[23]

Pa brought a splendid assortment of specimens found in different parts of Oregon, he will not part with them altho he has been offered great prices for them. They are truely valuable and splendid. When Pa returns if there is a moment that he is not busy with people calling on him, I will have him write you a

---

[23] Mr. Johnson was Elizabeth Dart's husband. Mary Dart was married to Augustus Keene.

long letter of particulars. Nicolas [24] was well and doing well, is contented likes the country much. . . .

your affectionate sister E D"

Richard Catlin and his wife Darwina were now living in Ripon, a town near Dartford. Henry and his family had a small farm in the Dartford area. With the exception of George, the surviving members of Putnam's family were now inhabitants of Wisconsin.

Eliza wrote to Francis on December 19(th), 1852: "Since you were here I have seen nothing of my *dear good brother* Richard. He got offended at R Dart and has been to dartford twelve times without coming to see me, when he gets over his pett I think he must feel very much ashamed of him-self. . . . we have letters from Pa and Putnam by every mail Stemer, they will return in the spring unless they should conclude to stop awhile at San Francisco—that seems to be *the place* to make money George is digging gold in the Rogue River mines, we do not hear as often from him as from the rest. Pa says he is doing well, Johnson has gone to San Francisco to work at his trade, he will do well at that. You speak of going to Oregon. I think the chance for making money is better in San Francisco than Oregon. . . ." Eliza's youngest son, Charles, added a note: "It is currantly reported here, that a man by the name of Franklin Pierce has been elected President, have you heard of it?"

Anson's long, hard trip to the East had accomplished nothing. He was finally told that his treaties would be sent to the Senate for consideration. Back in Oregon again, he found that the delay in ratification was making trouble; the Indians had signed in good faith and wanted pay for their land, and Anson was unable to make them understand the situation. In October, 1852, he was informed by the Commissioner of Indian Affairs in Washington that the treaties had been rejected by the Senate, and not to make any more until the general policy of the government was determined. Anson Dart promptly resigned.

Richard Dart later wrote: "Mother, my two sisters and one

---

[24] Nicholas DuBois was Anson Dart's secretary in Oregon.

brother and I lived on at Dartford, but father never came back there to live. He had various political appointments, and after coming back from Oregon he was in Europe for two years." [25]

What had happened between Eliza and Anson Dart? Why did he only visit Dartford now and then, no longer making his home with his wife? Later letters showed that her children were supporting her except for an occasional ten or twenty dollar bill from Anson or her brother Richard. Perhaps a small item in the 1850 United States Census for Clackamas County, Oregon Territory, tells the story. The Census lists "Anson Dart, age 50, Superintendent of Indian Affairs, born Vermont." It also lists "Elizabeth A Dart, age 10, born Illinois." They were not living at the same address. It appears that Elizabeth and two other small children were being cared for by the Millard family. There is no further mention of the child. [26]

For its bearing on this odd situation we quote from a later remark made on the floor of the Senate in 1860, during the debate over Dart's "claim," by Senator Lane of Oregon:

"[Dart] has no honesty, no integrity, and I know it. I know that his claims ought not to be allowed. It was an insult—an injury to the country. He was loathed in Oregon. He was loathed by every honest man and every decent family in the country; and I can give the reasons, if any gentleman wants them, why he was loathed by all respectable men. . . ." [27]

Eliza went her way; Anson went his. Eliza had her home in Dartford, but spent much of her time with her daughter Mary in the east. In her letters to Francis she referred to "Pa" (or "Mr. Dart") in a friendly manner, but no longer as a member of the family.

One notices a change in her letters, also. They have a staccato quality; you can almost hear the scratch of her pen, and see the straight line of her mouth. Eliza had wanted members of her family near her. Both Richard and Henry now lived in her vicinity, but she

[25] Richard Dart, *Settlement of Green Lake County*, Wisconsin State Historical Society Proceedings, 1909 (Madison, Wis.: published by the Society, 1910), p. 272.

[26] See Appendix IX.

[27] *Congressional Globe*, June 13, 1860, p. 2911.

seemed to enjoy giving occasional "digs" about both families. Good-natured Eliza had developed a sharp tongue.

Anson Dart went to Europe in the spring of 1853, probably on one of the government appointments his son mentioned. It is said that he was one of the official family of the American minister to Italy at one time; this may have been the time. Eliza was in Washington visiting her married daughter Mary, when Anson returned on July 9, 1854. She wrote Francis the next day: "Your letter directed to me at Dartford was forwarded to me, and received while I was on a sick bed, tis now two weeks since we arrived at W. Augustus, Charles and self have been under the Doct. care most of the time since, all are now convalescent. Pa arrived last evening in a Bremen Steamer, we have been long expecting him, his health is good. . . . Pa took unwearied pains to find some clue to our brother George's whereabouts, all he could learn was that he left Paris a year ago, in miserable health, not expected to live many months, his children have not heard from him the past year. Pa thinks he is not living—he was in the last stages of consumption—discouraged and disheartened—poor dear brother George. I have had a very hard cough for the last three months, which has stripped me of some of my flesh . . . excuse this short note, more next time all join in love to you, write on receipt of this to your ever affectionate sister E D."

As Eliza was penning these words, poor dear brother George was possibly boarding the *Sally Anne* at San Francisco, brown from the South American sun, hale and hearty, and on his way to paint Indians in the Pacific Northwest.

A Vagabond artist

FROM 1853 TO 1858 George Catlin was a vagabond artist. With health regained he spent most of these years tramping through the tangled wilderness of a land undisturbed by the broom and

embroidery of Progress—South America, with its jungles, its tower-
ing peaks, its softly rolling miles of pampas, and the mighty Amazon,
king of waters.

The search for the lost gold mines proved futile. Later, writing of
this pilgrimage, the artist said: "Moral: in this wise Dame Fortune's
kind favors were solicited; and if she bestowed not upon me the
visioned mines of gold, should I complain? She has given me what is
better—life, and health, and wisdom, and greatly added to my only
wealth, my portfolios, to which she has long been a liberal and kind
contributor." [28]

On foot, horseback or by canoe, the artist traveled the length and
breadth of the continent, his portfolio bulging with paintings of
primitive Indians and scenes of unforgetable beauty. Until the
summer of 1855 Catlin's traveling companion and helper was Caesar
Bolla, a huge, friendly ex-slave from Havana.

Catlin's coverage of South America was done in two trips, separated by a journey up the entire west coast of North America and
across the Bering Sea to Siberia, with Caesar Bolla stowing away
painting after painting of the Indians who lived along the shore. The
captain of the small craft they had boarded at San Francisco
obligingly stopped several times to accommodate the artist. On her
return trip from the north, Catlin and Caesar left the boat at
Portland, Oregon, for the artist wished to paint portraits of the
Indians who lived west of the Rockies.

The two vagabonds then traveled south and east to the Rio
Grande, and in a canoe paddled the eight hundred miles to Mata-
moros. From there they sailed to Sisal, in Yucatan. Here Caesar and
Catlin parted, for the latter was on his way to London.

George did not linger in London. He went on to Germany to see
the Baron von Humboldt, and tell him of geological discoveries he
had made in the mountains during his travels. This was a subject of
much interest to both men, and made Catlin decide on a second trip to
South America and the West Indies.

---

[28] Catlin's *Last Rambles Amongst the Indians*, p. 80.

So in the late fall of 1855 Catlin sailed to Cuba, and after visiting most of the Lesser Antilles, went to South America. He was anxious to paint the primitive tribes who lived along the Uruguay and Paraguay rivers, and after employing Jose Alzar in Buenos Aires to take the place of Caesar Bolla, set off on his quest.

On the right bank of the Paraguay were the Payaguas: tall (all over six feet) and chiefly naked. They lived principally on fish and turtles, and had broad, muscular chests and shoulders, but their legs were slight in proportion, from spending most of their lives squatting in a canoe. On the opposite bank of the river lived the Chacos, horsemen who had great plains on which to hunt, and therefore in physical proportions were exactly the opposite of the Payaguas. The Botocudos, near the mouth of the Uruguay, were nearer civilization, and wore a semblance of clothing. Both they and the Payaguas wore decorated blocks of wood in the lower lip, just as did the Nayas tribe in British Columbia. "How surprising this fact!" Catlin wrote, "that on the northwest coast of North America, almost the exact antipodes of each other, the same peculiar and unaccountable custom should be practiced by Indian tribes in whose language there are not two words resembling, and who have no knowledge of each other. Such striking facts should be preserved and not lost, as they may yet have a deserved influence in determining ultimately the migration and distribution of races." [29]

By barge, by foot, and by canoe, the artist and Alzar reached the headwaters of the Uruguay River, and then slowly descended the river to Buenos Aires, stopping at many Indian villages on the way. Catlin painted chiefs with silver disks sticking to their cheeks; long thorns and feathers run through the nose and chin, and beads and feathers hanging from the lower lip. In the colder climate of North America beauty was obtained by the richness of costumes. Here, where clothes were unnecessary, the body itself was ornamented.

Back in Buenos Aires Catlin met an interesting family; a Portu-guese gentleman, his Auca wife, and their beautiful daughter, "Til-

---

[29] *Ibid.*, pp. 207–208.

tee" (the Firefly). The artist was invited to visit their home on the Rio Salado. George brought her beautiful pendants and fastened them in her tiny ears. He went on an Ostrich chase, and the finest wings were given to Til-tee. At the Grand Saline, where the flamingoes gathered to make their nests, the aging Romeo shot down a gorgeous bird and carefully cut off its wings—blazing scarlet, black, and white—to take back to Til-tee. He wrote of Til-tee on the back of the horse "Yudolph," racing with the wind: "her floating black hair and narrow shoulders of demi-red were alternately rising and sinking above and in the waving grass, and I thought, 'O lucky, envied horse! Were I in Yudolph's place with such a prize, I would gallop to the golden coast!!'" [30]

A second springtime was stirring in the artist's heart. In a later letter to his brother Francis, commenting on the troubled years, George wrote: "But I mustered courage yet to live—yet to love."

News that the Patagons were about to stage a war with Buenos Aires nipped the budding romance; the artist had to leave the country immediately. He traveled around the southern tip of South America and up the west coast to Panama; and now wishing to study rock formations, went again to Venezuela and Colombia. In 1858 he went to Paris; and two years later he moved to Brussels.

Letters from Wisconsin

MEANWHILE, Eliza had moved from Dartford to the nearby village of Ripon. Richard Catlin and his wife Darwina lived there, and brother Henry owned a few acres of land in Dartford.

Eliza spent a great deal of her time with her daughter Mary in the east. Her youngest son Charles, the once happy little lad who "cut down trees with his little hatchet," was now twenty-two, and

---

[30] *Ibid.*, pp. 266–267.

consumptive. Evidently Putnam Dart, too, had a tendency toward the disease, as Eliza had mentioned that the California climate agreed with his health.

The following letter Eliza wrote to Francis at Hudson, Wisconsin:

Ripon July 26th 1857

Dear Brother Francis

Tis a very long time since I have heard from you by way of a letter, do you think that because I have been sick for the last year or two I should be neglected or forgotten by my brother who is well and able to write? the year I lived in Washington my health was miserable which prevented me from enjoying the society of so many of my children as I had with me. Putnam and Charles were in poor health. I left W and came to Ripon for my health, while they dear children went to California. after remaining there a month, Charles left for Los Angeles, seven hundred miles down the coast in Southern California for his health, I have many fears that he will never return, while I was living in W—George returned from Oregon with a dear little wife, and is now living in Dartford, one of the happiest men in the world.[31] . . . I hear nothing from you only by way of a letter from Carrie to Anna and all she said was that she was going to Hudson in a week with your two little boys, now my dear Brother I trust she will find a pleasant home with you—she will no doubt, look to your comfort and that of the little children. I hope she may make valuable acquaintances, and in time find a mate, that she may have a home of her own.[32]

Anna is getting to be a very good girl, and is a help and

---

[31] George Dart married Anna C. Tichenor, daughter of Captain William Tichenor (Oregon Statesman) on September 2, 1855.

[32] Carrie (Caroline) and Anna were daughters of James and Abigail Catlin. James died in 1847, Abigail in 1852. As was the custom, the girls would have to live with relatives until they married. Francis' two younger sons, Frank and Fred, had been left with the DuBois family after Elizabeth's death. Carrie would now bring them to Hudson, and keep house for Francis.

comfort to me, she is improving in music and in many things, she
will make a splendid woman if she can have her health—she is
consumptive I have to be very careful of her. . . . After
Caroline has arrived with her little charge and you are nicely
organized, write and tell me how you are progressing . . . all
are well at your Brother R Catlin's it would seem that some one
was sick all the time the Doct is there so often, with much love I
leave you

as ever your affectionate Sister Eliza Dart.

Perhaps Caroline was not a good housekeeper; at any rate, Francis
married Mary Weed Tolbert in October, 1857. He was now Register
of Deeds for the county of St. Croix. It is possible that being a Whig,
he lost his position as Register of the Land Office when Franklin
Pierce became President in 1853.

The following letter from Eliza gave some interesting news of her
family, but her happiness over the safe return of her youngest son
was short-lived.

Ripon City, Sept 12th, 1858

My dear brother Francis,

I should have answered your most welcome letter ere this, but
my mind has been so excited, and filled with doubts and fears
about my absent children that I have not been in a right mood to
write to a dear brother, and I hoped by waiting a few weeks I
should have more of interest to communicate to you. a few days
since I was greatly relieved from my anxieties, by hearing of the
safe arrival of my Charley baby boy, in New York, after being
four months on a Clipper Ship round the Horn, for the benefit
of his health. I have received two letters from him since he
arrived. his health is so much improved that he has gone on to
Washington expecting to get his old place in the Gas office he is
yet feeble, and I fear not able to stand the labours of office life,
my great fears were that he would not live to make the
trip. . . .

331

Putnam is at Victoria on Vancouver Island, three hundred miles from the Frazer River gold mines, of which you have heard much of—when he wrote last he had only been there one month and said he had lived a year in that time, so great had been the excitement there, from his own account he was doing well, he wished George and Richard were there Mr Johnson was there getting eight dollars pr day, at his trade, a great town is building up. Putnam is trading in miners goods, Mary and family (four boys) are living at Patterson [New Jersey]. E. A. Keene is Superintendent of the Patterson Gas Works. George is living on his place at Dartford enjoying the married life hugely, has a dear little wife and daughter. be assured dear Francis that your only sister is living as hapily and as comfortably as four noble sons, and two loving daughters can make her, what more of this worlds treasures could I have. I thank you for the earnest enquiries you made concerning my wants, &c. Your brother Richard and family are well . . . . your brother Henry still has fits every time he works too hard, he has a lazy family of grown up children all of them are supported by your good brother Richard. Henry's wife calls herself 30 and lives by visiting, her girls do all her work I am sixty and do all my work myself washing scrubbing cooking &c. and feel the better for it. Charley writes me from Washington that he is homesick to go back to California—this is what I anticipated, there is something captivating in the climate of Cal'a. . . . I am as ever your anxious and loving sister Eliza

Ripon April 17 1859

My dear Brother Francis,

Tis with a broken bleeding heart, and mind and body completely prostrated that I attempt a reply to your kind letter received some weeks since.

My dear darling Charley came many thousand miles to see his Mother Brothers and Sisters, and was only permitted to stay three short weeks with us, he was with his sister Mary at

Francis Catlin during the 1870's.

Eliza Catlin Dart, about 1845,
after five years of pioneering.

Patterson several months under the care and treatment of a celebrated Physicion fearing to come to this climate, I was not able to go to him, as soon as it was ascertained by all there that he was beyond all human help, he was permitted to accompany his Uncle Richard to Ripon, to gratify his desire to see us all— still hoping the climate might prolong his days, when first I saw him my heart sank within me, his poor wasted form, and heaving chest told me I must prepare to part with my idol child my dear invilid boy, my baby boy, my dear good child. . . .

George never left Charles night or day during the eight days he was confined to the bed, he breathed his life away leaning his head on Georges arm, like a little infant was his sleep of death— Your Uncle and Aunt D. were friends indeed, they were untiring in their efforts to relieve and do kindnesses—which can never be forgotten. . . .

as ever your loving yet afflicted sister Eliza.

Eliza addressed Francis from Patterson, New Jersey, on February 21, 1860. This was the home of her older daughter, Mary. (The younger, Elizabeth, lived in California.) Eliza wrote: "If I do not go to housekeeping when I return I am bound to make you a visit, if it is but a short one. I find I can travel like any body. Mr. Dart is in Washington luging away at his claim. Frank, what do you think of old John Brown and the Harpers Ferry tragedy. If you are a *black republican* I pity you my brother, for their fate is sealed. They are a doomed race. when you get time write me and it will give me pleasure to answer. . . ."

Eliza mentioned Dart's "claim" again in her next letter to Francis, dated April 25, 1860: "Mr. Dart is still in Washington, his bill passed the House a week or more since, and is now in the Senate, they have a recess of ten days to attend the Convention at Charleston therefore Mr D has to wait till they assemble again for business. I think it very doubtful whether the bill passes, Lane is bound to defeat it. . . ."

Dart had stood high in the favor of the Taylor administration, and been promised a government mission to one of the South American republics. He had not sought the Oregon appointment, for the salary was low ($2500). But at the urgent request of the Secretary of the Interior Dart had accepted the Oregon post on the assurance that the salary would be equal to that about to be established for the same position in California ($4,000). The bill establishing an Indian Office in California was passed while Dart was in Oregon, but no change in the Oregon pay was included.

Dart now wanted the difference between $2500 and $4000 for the period of three years; also a certain amount to cover additional expenses which had accrued during that time, and which he had paid from his own pocket. The bill was hotly contested, but finally passed and became law on June 18, 1860. However, the amount to be paid Dart was debated for some time; Eliza was still mentioning it in 1862.

To return to Eliza's letter of April 25th: "Putnam is expected the middle or last of May, if he does return, and Mr. Dart gets his bill passed, I expect they will toat me off with them to Missouri or some other good place, if so, Richard will go with us, but as I told you in my last letter if these things do not transpire, I shall try hard to make you the promised visit which I have doated upon so long, you know how it is with me, I am dependent upon my children and they are not rich. Poor George has had the misfortune to loose his whole stock of goods [he had a small store in Dartford] by fire, he went to his Uncle Richard to borrow one hundred and fifty dollars to pay what he owed in Milwaukee so that they would let him have more goods on credit to commence again, do you think he got it? not one cent. Richard's [Dart] wifes sister a Miss Kinley let him have the amount he wanted . . . his Father will help him if he gets his due from the Government.

"I received a long letter from Darwina Catlin wishing me to make a home for Anna Catlin as Carrie's husband Keeler has left [illegible] and was going east with his wife and baby for their health, that they were worth little or nothing, not able to keep hous any longer or to make a home for Anna. Your Aunt D [Darwina was Francis' sister-in-law] said they have to support Henry's family, Antoinett Catlin, and she had Lizzie and Minna Catlin and she could not nor would not have Anna. If she had my cares, and griefs, and sorrows, with poverty, she would think it strange and ungreatful to be called upon to do that which she requests of me. I wrote to her if I went to housekeeping with my Husband or Putnam in Dartford or Ripon I would take Anna with me, but that it was all uncertain, and so it is. . . ."

The tale of the pioneers comes to a close

ELIZA WROTE to Francis in Hudson on October 9, 1861. The long smoldering dissension between the North and South had finally erupted with the firing upon Fort Sumter. The Civil War had begun.

Brother Richard and Darwina had been living in the East for some time, putting Richard closer to the money markets, but now they were back in the more peaceful West. Evidently Burr was now a resident of Wisconsin; Eliza wrote that he was Captain of a company from Beaver Dam. Francis had joined the State militia several years before, and was now appointed "Aid to the Brigadier General of the 2nd Brigade 11th Division W. S. M."

Dartford Oct 9th 1861

Dear brother Francis,

Do I owe you a letter? if so, will you forgive me for such unheard of neglect, I have been long wondering why you did not write me, and have now come to the conclusion that I am the one in fault, I have looked for your name among the Captains in the army—you must know our family is represented—Burr

Catlin is Captain of a company from Beaver Dam, the fifth Regiment.

I am very anxious to hear how you and wife and children are. That little baby boy,[33]—I wish you would pull Charley's ears for not letting know of his whereabouts he may yet be in Madison, for all I know—has your wife been to see her friends without coming to see me? if so, she must not let me know it. Your Brother Richard has moved his family to Ripon again and is building a splendid stone house there, the War drove them back, he says he is making money out of pocket—many can say the same, do let me know what you think of the War, and the state of our country in general, how you all are, and what you are all doing—I have been with George most of the time since I left Hudson I have not seen Mr Dart since he left your house, I only hear from him every three or four weeks, he is yet in Washington trying and hoping to get his claim—he did not succede in getting an office as he anticipated—[34]

Gussy Keene is Captain of the Home Guards and he may be called out to fight for his country, Putnam did not stay long with us, his health would not allow him to stay, he is now in Sanfrancisco, We are now getting Telegraph dispatches from California is it not wonderful? . . .

now I guess you are indebted to your only Sister for a letter, Your brother Henry is failing, he is not long for this world, I trust he is prepaired for a better world, than this, where the "wicked cease from troubling, and the weary are at rest," with love to all, I am as ever your loving, but deeply afflicted Sister Eliza.

A letter to Francis from seventy year old Henry, in Dartford, shows that the former had not kept in touch with his elder brother.

---

[33] William Weed Catlin, born 1860.

[34] In 1860 Anson Dart asked for an appointment as Joint Comissioner or Agent, Indian Affairs, in Indian Territory, stating that he had been connected with Indian Affairs eight years before 1853.

There probably was a good reason; this is the only letter from Henry in which he did not ask for a loan.

December 29th, 1861.

My Dear Brother,

I write you a letter at this time, directing it to you as usual at Hudson, not knowing whether you may be living or dead. I have always answered your former letters soon after receiving them. I find it to be more a task for me to write than it used to be. Therefore you must not be surprised if you do not get my letters by mail in the future quite as quick as you used to do.

My family at the present time those who are with us are well and enjoying themselves as well as might be expected. Sister Eliza is yet keeping house with George Dart in George's house. I run in often to see her. How delighted *Mrs. Catlin* & myself would be to see you and to wait upon you and any of the children at our house if all things should be consenting. Not one of my boys who have enlisted and gone into the wars have written to me to let me know whether they are dead or alive. If I ever get a letter from any one of them I will write you again & let you hear all about them. . . .

William is with us now he has a good school over the Green Lake, returns tomorrow. Martha and Theodosia are very industrious girls and I am proud enough of them you will not be ashamed of them. We keep Augusta & Harriet steadily at school this winter.

I suppose you are thrown into a great commotion & excitement & those around you in consequence of our foolish War. I fear that it will end in the ruin of our country. Brother Richard is very busy this winter in building his new house—it will cost him at least twenty five thousand dollars. This is pretty extravagant for the times. Augusta and Harriet are very fond of Musick and we are giving them an opportunity of learning it having a pretty good chance.

I hope you will write to me soon and let me know how you

337

are getting along and how the War affects you. I have never received a word from either of my boys who went into the War. I fear they are not living. George Dart and family are well at this time, and your Aunt Eliza Dart is living with George Dart, she is also pretty well at this time [35] . . . Write as soon as possible—Yours to serve—

Henry Catlin

The following letter from Eliza shows that she held no ill will toward Anson, and was willing to forget the past and make a home for her husband. Evidently Anson was content to leave matters as they stood.

Dartford July 1 1862

Dear Brother Francis,

George received a paper from you last evening. I thought sure you had gone to the War, as you did not write me, so I write hoping my letter will find you still at Hudson with your little family all well. I verily believe your wife has forgotten all her friends since that little Willie boy came to hand. In my last letter I believe I told you I was housekeeping on my own hook, in three rooms attached to George's house. last Nov Mr Dart sent me fifty, and Putnam sent me twenty dollars from San Francisco, with which I furnished a kitchen and bedroom, and went to living by my-self, to see if it would seem anything like old times, I have enjoyed it very much, thus far.

George furnishes me with my vegitables, apples and a great variety of fruit—saws my wood and brings it to my room and helps me in many ways, Richard [son] furnishes me with honey, and every three or four months my brother Richard gives me ten or twenty dollars, which he says he is more able to do, than I am able to do without it, my children all seem to be willing to gratify me in such a childish freak, as they call it, I call it keeping *baby house*. Mary is urging me to break up and come

---

[35] Henry and Eliza often forgot that Francis was their brother, not nephew.

and live with her in Paterson, thinking it may be easier for me. I have not seen Mr Dart since he left me at your house, he says they intend to cheat him out of his claim at W. I have urged him many times to come and make my home his own, but he seems wedded to Washington, altho he says when he leaves it he hopes never to see it again. I hope so too. . . . How I did scold when I heard you had let that frail Charley of yours go into the army.[36] There is no honour in fighting in such an uncalled for war as this, my brother, I hope dear Charley's life will be spared but I tremble when I think how his morals will be tried I trust he has a father's prayers constantly, for his safety.

Burr Catlin must be in the fight that is now going on at Richmond—he had better be with his wife and five little children, he advocated the War so he must take the consequences as they come.

If your wife has been to visit her friends at Madison without coming to see me she must be careful and not let me hear of it, I hope the little boys are well, and a great help to you and wife. George and Anna join me in much love to your self and wife and children, believe me as ever

your affectionate sister Eliza Dart

write soon

With the following letter the tale of the pioneering Catlins comes to a close.

Dartford Feb 9th 1863

Dear brother Francis

Ere this you must have received a letter from your brother Richard telling you of the death of our dear brother Henry. Richard and I were at his bed-side from Monday till Saturday evening, the first days he spent in prayer and advice to his children and friends, so loud and earnest that he could be heard in every part of the house, he told me he was happy and longed to

---

[36] Francis' younger son, Frank, enlisted as drummer boy.

go, what a consolation. Dear brother, I hope it may be so with you and with me, his sufferings are over, and yesterday (Sunday) we had a solemn funeral. Your brother Richard spared no expense, he had a Hearse come over with a splendid coffin, and there was nothing wanted that he did not furnish. Now dear Francis, there are but three left of the once large family of Catlin.[37] Love to wife and children.

sister Eliza

The above is the last letter in the family collection written by Eliza. According to Richard Dart, she died in Williamsport, Pennsylvania, in 1866, at the age of sixty-eight.

Eliza was a remarkable woman. Her life for nearly thirty years was one of extreme poverty, toil, and heartbreak, which she met with her father's fortitude and perseverance and accepted with her mother's "If God wills it, it must be for the best."

Anson Dart died in Washington D. C. in 1879, at the age of eighty-two.

---

[37] By this remark, Eliza meant Richard, Francis, and herself. George later wrote Francis that he had corresponded with Henry before the latter's death. Evidently there had been no recent letter from George, so Eliza assumed that he was dead.

PART SEVEN: THE WANDERER RETURNS

1860–1869

1860–1868: George the optimist picks up his pen again   1868: George tells Francis to come to Bruxelles; Francis Catlin's diary on his trip to Belgium.

IN 1860 George Catlin returned to Brussels. He was now sixty-four years old, extremely deaf, but in fine health and spirits. Housed in a couple of rooms in a quiet neighborhood, he started to write and paint again.

In 1857 he published *Life Amongst the Indians*,[1] and in 1867 *Last Rambles Amongst the Indians of the Rocky Mountains and the Andes*.[2] After so many turbulent years, George's self-imposed exile from civilization, and his return to nature's open road with knapsack and portfolio, added a happy chapter in the artist's life. George could paint with his pen. These two books have an exuberance of color which makes the printed page glow, and there is a touch of the poet in his beautiful descriptions of the Amazon and the Andes. Both books were published, and highly praised, in England. In 1865 he published a small book, *The Breath of Life*, advocating sleeping as he said Indians do, on the back, with closed lips.[3]

George had brought back from his rambles a load of paintings, and many quick sketches upon which he could now enlarge. He was still making "cartoon" copies of his old collection, stored in a Philadelphia boiler factory. It was his plan to return to the United States with a cartoon collection as large as his first gallery.

In 1856, while visiting a friend of Baron von Humboldt in Uruguay, he received a letter from the Baron, dated Potsdam, June 9, 1856, saying that he had been sent an immense three volume

---

[1] *Life Amongst the Indians: A Book for Youths* (New York: D. Appleton & Company, 1857). Published in London by Sampson Low, Son & Company, 1861.

[2] *Last Rambles Amongst the Indians of the Rocky Mountains and the Andes* (New York: D. Appleton & Company, 1867). Published in London by Sampson Low, Son and Marston, 1868.

[3] *The Breath of Life, or Mal-respiration* (New York: J. Wiley, 1861). Published in London by N. Trubner & Company, 1870, under the title *Shut Your Mouth And Save Your Life*.

Scrap-Book on the North American Indians, written by Henry Schoolcraft for the Government of the United States. "And I find," wrote Humboldt, "that he denies the truth of your descriptions of the Mandan religious ceremonies, distinctly saying that they are contrary to facts, and that they are the works of your imagination, &c.

"Now, my dear and esteemed friend, this charge, made by such a man as Schoolcraft, and *'under the authority of the Government of the United States,'* to stand in the libraries of the scientific institutions of the whole civilised world, to which they are being sent as presents from your Government, is calculated not only to injure your hard-earned good name, but to destroy the value of your precious works through the ages, unless you take immediate steps with the Government of your country to counteract its effects. . . ." [4]

Because George would not permit Schoolcraft to use his Indian paintings to illustrate his work, this petty politician was intent on killing the artist's former publications and the sale of his gallery. George later wrote that the French government had planned to purchase his Indian collection, and that he had learned from a reliable source that the negotiation was stopped from information received that the United States government had condemned his works as deficient in truth.[5]

Trying to refute the false charges, Catlin published a small book, "O-Kee-pa," in 1867, giving a detailed account of the Mandan torture ceremony, with engravings of the four paintings he had made at their village.[6] It did not sell. No institution wanted it because "by the authority of the Government of the United States" it was fiction.

In spite of Schoolcraft's fraudulent charge, George was determined to save his name and life-long work in behalf of the Indians from sinking into oblivion. Old as he was, he would not give up! He planned to make one last appeal to Congress.

---

[4] George Catlin, *Rocks of America* . . . . (London: Trubner & Company, 1870), p. 221.

[5] *Ibid.*, pp. 226–227.

[6] *O-Kee-pa: A Religious Ceremony; and other Customs of the Mandans* (London: Trubner & Company, 1867).

With this in view, George prepared a lengthy memorial, heavy with denunciation of Schoolcraft's baseness, for the man had seen the paintings of the ceremony with certificates of authenticity attached to them. George added additional proof of his honesty: letters from the eminent Baron Alexander von Humboldt and Prince Maximilian of Wied-Neuwied. In his fervent appeal, he asked that justice be done by Congress purchasing enough copies of his little book, "O-Kee-pa," to send wherever Schoolcraft's books had been sent. He told what *he* had done for the history of the American Indian without ever asking or receiving any help from the government.

George was certain his country would right the wrong it had done to a loyal American. He planned to go to Washington in the fall of 1868, and wrote to his youngest brother:

Hotel Duc de Brabant, Bruxelles
7th June, 1868

Francis P. Catlin
Dear Brother,

I have recently rec'd letters from Brother Richard and from our nephew, Burr, both of whom have reminded me that I ought to write to you. For this I am ashamed, for it was suggested just at the time when I was about to write to you and ask forgiveness for that neglect, which for the last quarter of a century has *seemingly* estrayed me from the natural love and attachment which exists between Brothers. Long as we have been separated no time and no circumstances have diminished that love I always bore to you amongst my other dear Brothers —but circumstances, too numerous to relate in this place, have crossed the winding path of my life, and disappointing, (and at times almost distracting) my brain with disappointments and with shame, have prevented me from corresponding with my dearest friends, amongst them, my own dear children.

The loss of my dear Clara—my little Boy George, and from unfortunate speculations which I was decoyed into in London, my Indian Collection—drove me almost to despair, but I mustered courage yet to live—yet to love—and again to trust my luck in the wilderness, some account of which, my friends and relatives who have lacked letters, will find in the two little books which I have recently published for them. If I have lacked the prompt correspondence of most men, in my long absence, it will be made up in a measure in these two little books of my Rambles, which other men dont write, and which I address to all who have any interest in me.

In the unsuccessful and wandering state in which I have been, it would have been but disappointment for my dearest friends to have heard from me, and continually in hopes to have better prospects to open to them I have delayed and delayed until I became ashamed to write. For all this, those who love me must forgive me, and by reading my little books, and others I am preparing, put up with me for the little time that is left me, the best way that they can.

Richard has written me of your family, of your sons, who I am glad to learn are doing you much honour. Burr write me that he is already a *grandfather*, which seems like an impossibility, and reminds me of *my* old age—now in my 72d year! I had sent to Burr my two last juvenile Books and instructed him when he has read them to send them to you; they will afford you amusement & information.

How our dear friends have fallen off since we parted! and how soon we must be joined to the list! it is the fate of man & the will of God. Brother Henry communicated to me the mournful list whilst he lived, and Richard has continued it since his death. I have rec'd these sad announcements in my solitudes and amongst strangers, where there was no one to understand my tears, and where I could do no good. dear friends—dear father and dear mother—dear Brothers and dear sisters—dear wife and dear little George! I believe I shall see them all in some form in the world to come.

I intended to have been in Washington during this Session, but Mr. Sanford, our Minister here, has constantly told me it would be time & money lost to try anything there during this Session, troubled with impeachment, &c, & I have postponed my application there, until the opening of next Session.

Richard wrote me that you have been engaged with a patent invention, and I was intending to bring you a curious invention & getting it patented for you; its simplicity & immense utility, I feel sure will give it a value, in case it has not been thought of. I have the model made & specifications ready. I have kept it in that state and entirely secret for several years, confidently believing that if well managed, a fortune may be realized from it. I shall bring it with me in the fall.

Richard has been saying something of taking the Tour of Europe this summer or fall, and I am still in hopes of seeing him here. Write to me on rec't of this, and I will tell you more of my condition and my views.

Your affectionate and ever loving
Brother Geo. Catlin.

George writes Francis to come to Brussels

THE HEALING YEARS of exile had enabled George to push the unpleasantries of the past into the attic of his mind. He was now ready to get back to his main purpose in life: his name honored in America, and his original paintings rescued from the boiler factory and given a proper and permanent home.

He had planned to present his memorial to Congress in person, but his deafness caused him a great deal of embarrassment among strangers. It now occurred to him that Francis and Burr could handle the situation as well as he, and once an idea was hatched in his brain, George's optimism bypassed all possible obstacles. It was *fait accompli!*

Beside presenting the memorial, he wanted his outline drawings (made from the original collection and from those later done of the Indians west of the Rockies) shown in a hall of the Capitol where the members might wander around, admiring them and speaking well of the absent artist. He also wanted subscriptions taken for the new Portfolio he was planning to publish, which would contain the outlines being shown, "to be executed in lines, in the best style of modern art." He remembered his old invention for saving lives at sea, brought out the little model, and dusted it off.

The following letters show his increasing excitement, and the working of George's imagination. The artist's fancy was so full of castles he could not see the clouds forming behind them.

> Hotel Duc de Brabant,
> Bruxelles, 9th Sept. 1868

Dear Burr,

I am writing today to Brother Richard and Brother Francis. And my programme for you and Francis I shall explain alike to both of you. I rec'd a long and interesting letter from Francis a short time since, and I had proposed in my letter to him, to give him the patent taken out in my name, of an invention which I have made, & which, (they having seen a working model) both Mr. Sanford out Minister here & Mr. Goodrich Secretary of Legation have told me is not patented in the U. States, and which they both believe will be of vast utility in the U. States, and of great value. Frank told me he was out of business and that he would take hold with you in the exhibition I had proposed to you, if he could be of service.

I have resolved on the following "platform." Instead of giving *you* leave to use the collection of drawings for one or two years exhibition and making Frank a present of the patent invention, I will, in consideration of love & affection, & of former services rendered in both cases, in my exhibitions, and never yet sufficiently requited, *present* to you *both, jointly*, the collection of drawings and the patent Invention, to be yours & his forever,

348

and to be Exhibited and worked for your mutual benefit, on the conditions that Frank will come to Bruxelles on or before the middle of November and receive them from me with the proper deed of assignments acknowledged before the American Consul, and receive from me so that he will perfectly understand them, my instructions as to the mode of making the Exhibitions, of working the invention, and presenting my memorial to Congress in the beginning of the coming session (first of Jany) all of which are to be conditions of the bequests. I shall not go to Washington myself—my deafness prevents it, and the coldness of the weather under the exasperating fatigue of trying to hear would knock me up at once.

You and Frank, whose ears & throats are clear to talk, can just as well attend to my application there—the Library Committee will give you leave to place the screens with my whole N. Am. Collection on them, in the library of the Capitol, for a short time, where all the members of both houses will see them.

In the meantime my application to Congress must be pushed, and that done, you can open the exhibition in some room in the city and begin to put money in your pockets—and one going a few days ahead to procure a Room & advertise, you may run them through the principal cities & watering places &c. And with the plan of publishing, a prospectus of my large work on the table, be taking subscribers, for every good one of which you shall have ten percent when the work is delivered, the price to be £20. When you have "done the U. States," there is nothing to prevent your going through England & Scotland, a rapid tour, for with my collection I shall not go there again.

The drawings I send, and give you, are all of one size, on cartoons, about 2 feet by 2½—have cost me more than two years hard labour, in the old age of my life, when time is precious. they make an exhibition, covering a screen 8 feet high & 75 feet long on both sides of a room.

I write for Frank to come, instead of you, because I want to see him, after 25 years, & he never has seen Europe or England

& you have. It need not cost much—join him in the expense—he can come very comfortably in second cabin, at half price—I have taken great pains with the drawings, for with me it is all honour and the publishing of my great work—they will make my name popular in the U. States, and for you & Frank, if you run them Barnum fashion, you may make a fortune with them.

Write me as soon as you can possibly have an understanding with Frank. I hope you are all well.

Your affectionate uncle George.

I need not write this letter over again—this will answer for both, and as soon as you can understand it enclose it to Frank.

Let nothing prevent Frank from coming—for I know I am greatly promoting the interest & welfare of both of you.

I have this day written to Brother Richard & given him some idea of the enterprise, and if money is too scarce with Frank & you—Richard will advance you for the purpose—I have told him to do it in case you want it.

Answer me without delay, both of you, & there will be time for me to write you again before he starts.

G.C.

hotel Duc de Brabant
Bruxelles, Sept 9, [1868].

Dear Brother Francis,

I rec'd your interesting and affectionate letter in due time, which gave me great satisfaction. And I shall answer it today more briefly than I expected, owing to a long letter which I have written to Burr, and which I have directed him to send to you as soon as he has read it.

By it you will learn that I have resolved to give the collection of drawings and the patent of Invention to you jointly, and forever. I have spent full two years in making the drawings, which has been hard work in my old age, & I am sure you & he can make money with them, for yourselves & get fame and subscribers for me & my great work. You must come for them, as

350

I have described in my letter to Burr, and then you will see something of the old world and see *me*, also, which may never be, otherwise. I need not explain the patent until you come, which will be in a little time—

Mr. Sanford, our Minister here, says it is *new*, not patented in Washington, and he and the Secretary of Legation, Mr. Goodrich (who says he knows you & has caught trout with you) both say it is of vast utility in U. States, & of great value, having seen my model & specification.

My collection of drawings which contains my whole north Am'n Collection of former days, and one hundred & 20 full length portraits made in and west of the Rocky Mountains, you can have little idea of until you come & see them.

You must come, without fail, as I have suggested in my letter to Burr, and take my whole instructions, which you cant understand otherwise.

Write without losing a poste. hoping you are all well,

Your affectionate Brother
George

Bruxelles, 18th Sept. 1868

Dear Brother Francis,

I write you again so soon, to acquaint you more fully of my views, & to ensure your visit to the Continent, as I suggested in my last letter. I enclose a model of the screens on which I propose the cartoons to be arranged, and by it you can easily understand the sort of Exhibition that you and Burr can make, and the facility of transporting it, and the little loss of time and the trifling expense of making your Exhibitions—the Collection will cover 20 screens like the one enclosed, 8 feet high, and both sides of a room 80 feet long—I ruined myself by the enormous expenses of my large exhibition—the loss of time in arranging—taking down—transporting &c. For this Ex'n rooms will be granted generally in Town Halls &c for a few days, without charge—& a running exhibition, with a good deal of noise, giving free tickets to the Press & to Big Bugs, will put money in your pockets & give me subscribers to my great work, a prospectus of which & subscription list you will have on your table, engaging to publish in the work every picture on the screens, and of which the subscribers will hold a catalogue. I give you a complete *Catalogue Raisonne'* which you will have printed & stereotyped, and sell at a profit in the Room.

The approaching awful war against the poor Indians never to be ended until they are all exterminated, is going to produce exactly the excitement in the public mind for the success of your Exhibition.

I will have a model of the screen, full size, prepared before your arrival here, and be able to explain to you everything I propose so that you will perfectly understand me. I shall have ready a number of large chromo lithographs for you always to sell in the room and other things, on which you will have a commission, and of the two little books lately published, you can get them of Appleton at the *trade* price (one third off) and make 33 per cent for selling them.

I am hard at work on the drawings yet, not having quite finished them—and as you can imagine, am working for a *name* —for the name of *Catlin,* in which you and cousin Burr cannot help but be willing to lend a hand—*you* will make a *noise* with it, and *I* must not leave undone a line or a touch that will detract from it.

I am old, and have but a little time to work, and the moment I am done with your cartoons my hand must be turned to my own Collection, not yet done, and which, for no consideration on earth, not even to see my dear children, can I leave it until it is finished.

You must come and see it—see what labour I have done in my life for the history of the poor Indians, & of which the world, as yet know but little. Nothing must stop you from coming, and as my drawings for you are not yet finished, there will be no need of your being here before the middle or last of November. I spoke of your coming in Second Cabin in the Steamer, to save expense—that is, if you have any difficulty about the money for expense of your voyage. The voyage is only of 10 days, & to put up with a little inconvenience for that time is nothing, I have travelled thus again & again across the ocean.

I want to see you, dear Brother again in this world, and all with me is now so uncertain, that it may be the only chance. Burr will join you in the expense, & if necessary, Richard will do so, too, and I have written to him to do so. You will see London & Bruxelles, & I will go with you for a few days to Paris, and you will then be willing to let the rest of the Continent take care of itself. As to the patent, Mr. Sanford says I must give you a power of attorney acknowledged before Mr. Goodrich, to take it out in my name, and then by a deed of assignment convey it to you. Send this to Burr, and write me on receipt of it.

Your affectionate Brother [torn]

George had a generous nature, and he was sincere in his desire to help his two younger kinsmen. According to his myopic reasoning everything was going to work out just as he had planned it. To Francis, idle at present, George's proposition was a gift from the gods; a chance to see Europe and make a lot of money as well!

In high spirits Francis Catlin set forth on his adventure in a fifteen-year-old overcoat and a clean but well-worn suit. He stuck a little three-by-six inch notebook into his pocket, in which he could write down items of interest to tell the folks back home.

Francis gave a very clear picture of George's life in Brussels, with his cage of mice for company. Evidently the high spot in Francis' trip was Thanksgiving dinner at the Embassy. All through the little book Francis scribbled notes, sometimes just a few words jotted down to remind him of the subject.

In reading Francis' account of this big event in his life, one can not help but feel a touch of pity for this jolly, friendly, happy-go-lucky fellow. He yearned for the good things in life that an empty purse put beyond his reach. But his desire had never been great enough to exert himself in reaching for the plums on a higher branch of the tree; he waited for the wind to drop a few to the ground.

Francis Catlin's diary on his trip to Belgium

LEFT HOME Oct. 22nd. Arrived at Great Bend 24th. Spent Friday, Sat, & Sunday, then on Monday went to N. Y. accompanied by Nicholas DuBois. Found Charley and all well at the Bend—Left my watch with Charley—He advanced me $100.

We arrived at N. Y. Found Fred well, and as far as I could judge and learn, all right. He has not yet learned to lay up his money—made me a promise that he would do so in future—time will tell. Spent Tuesday, Wednesday, Thursday, Friday & Saturday till noon in N. Y. Engaged passage on Packet Ship *City of Boston* of the Inman Line for Liverpool—steerage, $40 currency. Bought blankets, pillow & case, tin plate, coffee cup, knife & fork for passage. Embarked at 12 M, Saturday Oct. 31, 1868, for Liverpool. Shook Fred by the hand & bid goodbye to America for a season. Am feeling well & in good spirits.

Nov. 12th. Land Ho! *Mizzen-Head Rocks*—South extremity of Ould Ireland. Stormy and awful rough. 11 A.M. Fastout light—60 miles from Queenstown—250 from Liverpool.

Arrived at Liverpool in 12 hours. Went ashore at 11 P.M. Took room ate supper & went to bed. In morning at 7 went on board ship & got my duds. Returned, & to breakfast at 10. Got shaved, &c. At 11 took cars for London, arrived at 6½ P.M. In one hour's time was on board cars for Dover.

Went immediately on board boat, crossed Channel to arrive at Ostend at 3 in the morning. At station I laid down on a bench & took nap till 5. At 6 took train for Bruxelles. Arrived at 6½ A.M. Found my Brother—happy meeting after separation of 29 years.

Took dinner at 4 in his room—talked all the time. Looked at pictures, &c. At 7 went to Cafe—took coffee & brandy. Read papers and looked around. At 9 returned to room & retired about 10. Good bed & slept sound. Arose at 7 to coffee & rolls & boiled eggs at 9.

Sunday—Staid in doors all day talking & looking at Geo's works. Dinner at 4. Talked & laughed at his constant jokes & wit. At 7 went to Cafe as before. During the day drums rattling, soldiers thronged the streets, and in evening illuminations. Some sights. Baked apples & chestnuts at 9. Talked till 10 & retired. So far dark and rainy.

Monday 16th. Pleasant morning—Breakfast at 7—talked & looked over paintings till 1 P.M. Called at Secretary of Legation, then took a stroll—Cold & raw wind—Saw the King's Palace—Duc de B—Fountains—Statuary &c, &c—Boulevards—trees, fountains, concert places. Botanical Garden—pools of water—Houses uniformly 3 story and white—Monument to King Leopold. Big Lions. Returned ½ frozen. Mailed four letters home, written Sunday (yesterday). Haven't seen any wonderful thing yet—nothing to make my hair rise.

Spent most forenoon looking over pictures & listening to the explorations by Brother—no end to them. South Americans entirely naked —male and female.

NOTE: "South America on the Amazon" views of the forest with hanging boquets that root into others making the most beautiful landscape imaginable. *The beautiful dance*—of South America. Innumerable views and so pretty.

Dinner at 4. Delicious steak, bread, potatoes & tea. Brother makes no change in his diet from one end of the year to the other, nor misses his Cafe once a year.

NOTE: Geo. writes his works, letters &c. at Cafe for 2 or 3 years past. Good light, and being deaf has no annoyance.

355

One night in my room, cafe & brandy—chestnuts roasted. Geo feeds the mice, all the company he has.

17th. Bad cold—coughed all night. Business to-day. Some how I have but little inclination to look out doors. It seems odd to see & pass so many persons and not be able to talk with them. I find they know less of American language than I do of theirs. Dont think I would like to spend my days here—give me old America "The land of the free & Home of the brave."

Bro. showed me an agate yesterday for which he was offered in London twenty pounds. He has hundreds of them buried on the coast of Brazil, and contemplates another trip there to secure a large number. It was about the size of my head—a beauty. He says he has over 7 tons of minerals—some in N. Y. Phila, Paris & London—in storage. Will post me about them, in case he should drop off sudden I can find them. He is publishing a Work of mineralogy, geology, and accounting for the *Gulf Stream*—the latter has always been a great mystery and he says he has settled the matter. His work is in the hands of the publisher now.

NOTE: Agates—Brazil—10 or 12 miles along the cost from mouth of Rio Grande, on a little prairie near mouth of a small stream—or Rio Grande, I forget which.

Called on Goodrich, saw lady who has sister Mrs. Callahan in Eau Claire Wis—and very much of a lady she was, too. On return visited a very great curiosity—it is a remnant of an extension wall, part of a rampart built by Julius Caesar at the time the Romans invaded and subdued France, Belgium, England, &c. A stairway inside the Wall led up to the top about 40 feet high—So I have trodden on the same stones once pressed by the feet of the Roman Caesar, *well that will do to tell*. A magnificent Cafe is in front. The most gorgeous I have yet seen—Called for coffee—fee 3 cents a cup—cheap enough. Mirrors 25 by 20 feet, so arranged that every way you look you see yourself, and reflection from one to another gives you to

think you are looking at least a mile around. Ladies & Gents setting at coffee—a splendid concert room, chandeliers as big as wheat
stack. Glasses hung from windows so as to see all going on outside by
ladies within. The pissing places have a dozen or more pointed at
them.

Took a look in the show windows &c. Catholic Cathedral a mammoth
construction—gas lights reflect in windows evenings—beautiful effect. Got home at 1, but a slippery walking—tired. Shall take a stroll
this evening.

NOTE: Principal streets here swept every morning. Walk as much in street
as on sidewalks—sides very narrow—Streets covered with glass roofs
filled with shops. Carts run by hand—big dog under—Most outlandish
vehicles—horses bobtail, ahead of waggon. Some spendid equipment,
cabs in abundance and very nice. Ladies dressed mostly in dark. Splendid mink setts, and velvet. Sacks & bonnets same style as N. Y.

As usual went to Cafe. Returned at 9 & retired. Read me a long article on Cradles, with drawings—*The Man—The Idiot.*

18th. Smoky and misty every day thus far since I landed in Europe.
Coughing lingers on. Went out to see about cartoons—nothing
strange seen. Came back and copied for the Catalogue the descriptions of the Mandan ceremonies.

NOTE: Three years ago the French Government sent an envoy to get from
George the terms upon which his whole Collection could be obtained.
Afterward they declined buying it, having seen a large work sent
them by Schoolcraft, in which the religious ceremony as delineated &
described by Geo. was only in imagination, and that no such scenes
occurred. Schoolcraft never was within 1000 miles of Mandans. This
has worried Geo. more than anything else. Geo. cant ask Gov't to buy
his Collection since it has suffered the publishing of him as a liar.

NOTE: Find some members who were opposed to Schoolcraft. Why did
Government sanction the work of Schoolcraft knowing what G. C. had

published relative to Mandan Ceremonies, & knowing also that they had been exhibited in America and Europe. Why did they not call on Mr. C. to prove his representations before allowing and sanctioning the libel of Schoolcraft. What better evidence of the truthfulness can be demanded than the letters of Humboldt and Maximilian.

NOTE: Mr. Gurley can ascertain from Indian Bureau how many of Schoolcraft's Indian work has been circulated to the different Societies and Institutions. Trubner says 4 to 6 thousand.

NOTE: Schoolcraft's work published under authority of the Gov't on every page. Look at book.

Went to Cafe at 6. Dominoes and Backgammon—crowded, full of smoke. Stick sugar in brandy, little square pieces, one inch square. 4 to each cup coffee. Bow Wow—Oui, Yah, Bien, Oui? damned gabbing—all hurley-burley. Brandy in small glass, & saucer. Run glass over & fill saucer.

Saturday 21. Spent the whole day indoors writing and numbering the Cartoons—going this evening to call on Goodrich. I take no pleasure in the streets—so many things attract my attention—Still I cant say they afford me one particle of pleasure. My clothes are out of style —and I am out of style here myself. Have no desire to go to Paris even—the City of all the world for pleasure, show and pastimes. London is not to be mentioned—What do I care for all this show— No one to enjoy it with me and not a dollar to spend in that way. I have about made up my mind to return home without going to Paris or to London. When asked why I did not visit those cities, all I could say would be that I did not go to Europe to look at it—I had accomplished my mission, and it was not convenient financially for me to see them. Would like to have Richard ask me something about the country, cities, &c. I could tell all I know in 5 minutes.

Bro. G. has to-day been showing me the paintings in oil (beautiful) of all the Cartoons I have. He intends when he gets them all done to exhibit through the Continent—will also have his South American pictures in Exhibition. Mine were copied from them—He values them at $50,000.

Doubling Cartoons—finishing up Catalogues &c. Geo says he saw in South America one quartz rock—if crushed would yield all the gold he and I would want in the balance of our days. He travelled hundreds & hundreds of miles tracing up the roads made 300 years ago to the gold mines in Brazil—Did not succeed however in finding the mines. He is full of his anecdotes and fun making the whole time—Works from early light till dark every day.

At our coffee now—will go up to Goodrich about 7—his dinner hour is 6.—begins to crowd in, am writing at the Cafe—

Found Goodrich just dressing to attend a *Masonic Lodge*—Spent the evening with the Ladies—very pleasantly. One of the Ladies, Mrs. Fuirney from Meadville Pa. sister in Eau Claire Wis.—Lost her husband three months since. He was a member of Congress & visited Europe for his health. A very fine and social Lady—leaves to-morrow for N. Y. Returned to Hotel at 7 o'clock, until this evening have not been from the company of my Bro. 10 minutes.—

Sunday 22nd. Got up this morning and commenced writing immediatly after Breakfast, wrote till 4 without even as much as looking outside the house—at 5½ went to Cafe where I am now writing—Crowded indoors & out. Velocipedes with 3 wheels and some with but 2 one ahead of the other—go like fury. Rains mildly–old cloak, 15 years old. Same faces every evening playing at dominoes for 3 hours steady. Occasionally feel a little awkward with Watertown wardrobe, when I take a look around me and see the genteel dressed gentry—dont care a d– –n, no one knows me, what's the difference. Geo. in reaching over the table for a chair broke a goblet, cost him 8 cents, about 10 inches high, would be worth ½ doll at least in N. Y.

Poor business talking French. Say *one word* and you are be-fogged with a string of 100 words in rapid succession—they supposing you understand of course, all they say, and after a time you cant get a chance to say "Je pas parlez Francais" for 5 minutes. D— —m bother. I have dropped all my French and go on in the pure "American"— go by signs &. Damn them as much as you like in English, and it seems to please them. I have some fun in that way—"where ignorance is bliss."

Monday—Called at one o'clock on Consul, at his request & hour named—he was not in, Mile & ½ walk and back, for nothing. Rained all the route back—got completely drenched—got to sit around the rest of the day and *dry up*. An American is stared at here as much as a Japanise would be in Milwaukee or Seville even.

Asked Bro. today—Why not pack up all your paintings, finished & unfinished—and all his traps and go over to America, and told him he would there find enough that would be ready to give him any assistance he might need, & he could paint there as well as here. His answer was—"My great object is to finish my paintings, get out my great work and exhibit my paintings in the countries of Belgium, Italy, Prussia, Persia, and Russia. I want them to be seen there, and at the same time get subscribers for my work, and if I can sell at a good price I shall do so. Then I shall return to America. If my life is spared I shall do all this—if not, why my bones will be carried home to rest in my *native land*." He spoke feelingly, and has so before, but he cannot leave this country, or will not, until he finishes his work and gives the world a chance to see what he has done for the noblest race (he says) that ever trod the earth. If the Indian has a friend, it is *G. Catlin*.

At Cafe—Geo. says his evenings are always spent here, rain or shine. Here he sits and writes—The noise does not disturb him—has a good gas light & is perfectly at ease. He has not for several years spent an evening in company. It is very unpleasant to have women hallowing in his ear, and he says he knows he is a nuisance. He still can entertain—the ladies at the Consul's remarked to me that they could sit all night and listen to Mr. Catlin—he always had something to tell that was new and interesting.

Same old fellows here this evening playing dominoes. How the d– – –l they can be so engrossed in the game is more than I can see —Such a gabbling—I think the point is to see who can make most noise. It may be the coffee that is at work on them. It dont affect me in that way for I have the least desire to utter a loud noise. Smoke —Smoke. Every one smokes.—These old baldheaded *mullets* have a drink made of port wine and coffee—very sweet, & the way they go for it. Some stick in a glass of brandy, hot—I have not tried it yet, guess I wont for I aint ready to die yet.

Have not smoked a cigar yet in Belgium—Got acquainted last evening at Cafe with a young Hollander. He could talk just about as much English as I could Dutch or French—He came this morning to our rooms—showed him Indians. Bet he will dream tonight.

24th. Called on Judge G. He took me to see an old acquaintance, Mr. Autenson, with whom I got acquainted at Hudson—Had a fine time—took Brandy with him. He has 3 children—lives in style —Him and wife to call at room—Goodrich showed me the pissing statue and sundry fine edifices. Small towns in country, not on maps, have taller spires than Trinity N. Y. Returned at 3½ to room— Got my draft cashed.

At Cafe. 6 O'clock. Just beginning to come in—Coffee elegant, delicious—make it very sweet here. The sugar in square pieces made from beets, and as nice as any loaf sugar I have ever seen. Now I think of it, I will record I have never seen farming equal to Belgium in any country. Every square foot is cultivated and to the utmost—immense fields of turnips—am told that many country people subsist about entirely on them, their cattle also. Saw man and woman dragging in a crop with a harrow, pulling side by side like a pair of oxen. Dont know which was the driver—seemed to work quite even though I think the woman had a little advantage on the evens.— This is a dull season of the year—Raining, not cold, but on the whole disagreeable. Tomorrow I shall enjoy as I will have lots to do at the room in putting names of Tribes on the plates.

Goodrich has been here 8 years and says there never in that time has been a fire in Brussels, and so in Paris. The contents of a room burn but not further—all buildings constructed fire proof & under inspection during the building.

25th. Working on Cartoons—Great military doings outside. Artificial flowers made of iron and painted resembling beautiful flowers & shrubbery, bouqets &c.—Amputated the mouse's tail—Geo. can hear music when passing in the street, and can hear you when you talk to him walking out doors—inside house very different.

Cafe—nothing to note—Came home. Geo found a letter from Sanford inviting us to join him to-morrow at his house to partake at a thanksgiving dinner at 6½. Roast Turkey & Cincinnati ham—of course we go—Geo declines invitations altogether and has for 2 or 3 years on account of his deafness—But on this occasion will go—says he cant refuse. I dont care about it one way or the other—I think I can cut my way through at some rate. I shall have my whiskers greased & hair curled, and "go for Eau." Getting my bashfulness and awkwardness rubbed off some. Damn the French (the talking I mean)—that bothers me most. If I could pitch in and talk with them I would be all right.

Invitation to dinner—"My dear Mr. Catlin, I have your note and shall be glad to see you and your brother. Tomorrow is Thanksgiving day, will you not bring your brother with you, to join us over our Roast Turkey and Cincinnati Ham at six thirty. It will afford us great pleasure to receive you then, en famille.

Truly yours
H. S. Sanford"

26th. Finished doubling cartoons and numbers, names of Tribes, &c. Looks clear this morning, it has rained every day since my arrival with the exception of one or 2 days. About 3 o'clock this morning I was awakened by a terrible racket outside. I went to my window and directly underneath were assembled I should think a dozen women & about the same number males, and the way they were going on, with their umbrellas over one another's heads to the distruction of bonnets. And such a muss of French, Sacra Maitro, and loud talking—all drunk—Finally one woman retreated on a run, hurling back volumes of French—after she left the matter seemed to die out some. Had a notion to drop my chamber pot on their heads, contents and all. During the day and till very late in the evening all is quiet. Learn to have a regular round from 12 to 4. Brussels has the name of being one of the most quiet cities on the Continent. [next paragraph illegible.]

Last night at 9 I thought I would change the Programme—so I bought of an old woman who sits by the door 6 sardines, 6 boiled hot potatoes and 4 hard boiled & cold eggs for lunch. Eat the eggs & potatoes—but the sardines (as they call them) I could not go—So pitched them out the window—3 small fish guts &c all in and ½ dried & ½ smoked—would puke the d— —l one would think—well these French will eat 3 with their glass of beer—the worst I have ever tasted. They would set about ½ hour, and repeat, & how long it continues I dont know—till it kills, I guess—

Getting ready to go out to dinner. Geo. sewing on buttons on shirt and pants. Out of handkerchiefs. Barber cut my old carbuncle off. Bled me profusely. Geo. has got lots of linen collars, all old style, & any quantity of ties—but is sans handkerchiefs. Got to buy some. Geo has good wardrobe—everyone has in this country—everything is so cheap. We have fasted since morning and I fear we will hurt ourselves on the turkey, & ham, &c, &c. Well, I will report on the morrow.

Here we are. Called on the Minister—found Goodrich there with his white vest and plated harness. Misty eve. Mr. Sanford says, "My dear Mr. Catlin, am happy to see you. Come up. And so this is your brother from Wisconsin." Shook me strongly by the hand, and told me I was welcome. In a few moments Mr. and Mrs. Rush of Phil'a came in, then a lady, daughter of a gentleman of Pensacola, T. H. Blount, as I found in the course of conversation. She is staying here educating her children. The other has a sick husband she has been toting all over Europe, and he cant find the place he is looking for. That is when they never die. She also has 3 or 4 daughters at school here—The finest schools on the Continent are here—Eh Bien—At about 7 we sat down to our regular work 1st. Dark wine—wine medium. 2nd. Dark wine and pale wine—almost white. 3rd. Old Bourbon—smelled good, did not try it. 4th. Cogniac—tried that & am still of the opinion that I have drank poorer in America. 5th. Old Port, 63, this Geo & Mr. Rush went for—I told Mr. Sanford that it was so much older than me that I did not feel like making free with it. He laughed heartily, said it was a little different with him, the older his friend the more free he was, &c. Geo said it was not quite as old as he, but much richer. Mr. Rush took two glasses, said nothing & seemed to be pleased. Next was Sherry, two or 3 other somethings— I did not try them. Goodrich said he would send in his opinion after he had tested it. Then Cincinnati ham (veritable)—excellent—thin —various trimmings—8 changes of plates &c. Roast Turkey delicious. We had a good time. I noticed the ladies talking very easy after dinner. Generally turkey sits heavy and makes one dull guests. The wines settled that. We returned to the drawing room—coffee was passed—then [illegible]. Talked till 10 & went home. Mr. Sanford a very pleasant man—talked about hunting, has been at Hudson (the upper Hudson was thought)—recollects the spot well—asked me to call again & whenever I had a desire—would like me to do so. Did not see his wife, she was unwell and could not come down. I managed to get through tip-top. I noticed Goodrich could not keep up with me in amusing the company. Mr. Sanford said to one of them So I heard that if the young Mr. Catlin could be so entertaining, what might we not look for from the elder, if he was not deaf. He complimented my Bro. and so did we all—So we had us all a good time. Next time he will show me his house. It is magnificent—The rooms I saw were about 30 feet high—covered with pictures by 1st artists. Geo. knew many of their names—no end to statuary and beautiful vases and things from all parts of the world. Talk of Richard's treasures!

27th. Misty, smoky, foggy &c. Mean miserable day. Dont like the weather at all. At Sanford's dinner 3 valets—all richly dressed—short pants, white stockings, with shoes & big buckles, and big buckles at knees—very genteel—Sanford knows how to live, but how he gets money is a mystery, for he lives in the most expensive style. So dark I can scarcely see to read or write. At Cafe raining and foggy —Best coffee I ever drank. Great secret. I think it is in using large amount of sugar. I notice that little square cakes soaked in the Cogniac taste pretty good—

Amsterdam Dutchmen dress well, I guess. Getting tired of Brussels, guess will pull out in a few days. Just read of telegraphing without wires—are now sending messages across Lake Ontario in 3 seconds. I must learn and see about this. I have just found a complete match for "Old Phinney"—never saw two so near alike. Bro G has written a letter to Richard this evening that wont suit him any too well, I guess. Shall copy in morning. He has great confidence in "Charley & me"—

28th. Nothing to-day to record. been in doors till 6, then went to the Cafe.

29th. Have not had my boots on to-day. Have been talking and writing—Its dark & gloomy. as every day has been thus far. Geo made me a present to-day of a large knife which he has carried for 30,000 miles or more. I treasure it much, I assure you. I am tired of this kind of life and want to get off. Geo has a vast deal to do yet to the outlines, and I shall not wait for their completion—he will send them to me.

NOTE: Geo. extremely anxious to have the screens all right. Smithsonian to place screens in—to be examined by members. Mr. Henry, Sec'y.

NOTE: Report to Committee to be handed to the members of each House directly after the Memorial has been read. Memorial to be sent to each member immediately after reading.

At Cafe, same old crowd. Sugar & water—lots drink nothing else. I have never tried any fancy cafe—every time & every other night a *drop* of cogniac.

There is an old woman directly under our window who sells hard boiled eggs & hot boiled potatoes. Geo sends a handkerchief down on [illegible] line with 2 cents & hauls up 1 doz. potatoes & salt.— Eats them almost every night—when he cant get *Baked Apple Pistolets.*

Geo has been talking for an hour about affairs in America. He is perfectly posted in Politics—can teach Richard his letters. He sees the London papers every day and Paris papers, and every one contains American news by Telegraph. He rejoices at Grant's election, and we have good times talking—that is, I enjoy it, but dont do as much talking as he—He is the friend of the Indians. Knows more of their character and the abuse practiced by the whites than all Washington & Congress together. Must go to bed.

30th. Dark & smoky—not cold, but disagreeable. Nothing to do this morning, Geo is writing out *Prospectus*—getting it ready for binding. Some amusing remarks about the Prospectus under head of Donations—*Only a Suggestion*—if not room enough why just take the change & *give rec't,*—or very easy to put in ½ doz extra sheets if required—and let the writing & figures be small—&c, &c.—and if I dont get any let them go to the d– – –l, can do without.

At new Cafe. Geo talks too loud sometimes, without knowing it. This is the only pleasant evening since my arrival. After cafe we took a stroll and looked in the shop windows, so admirably lighted by gas, and such beautiful, beautiful display of nice goods—everything thought of. Such *Laces, Crinoline, Silks, dress goods—Fancy Toilets, Clothing, Ladies furnishings,*—Corsets—and oh Lordy the Milliner Shops—&c. I'll quit right here—more Jewelry, Glass Ware, Vases—oh what beautiful clocks—and in fact, I got completely tired out & out.

NOTE: Paintings in show windows are worth more than 100 of Richard's. Oh! how beautiful. Best artists in the world here, my Bro. says. I notice things dont show as well in day as evening—however a man dare not sell any article unless it is as good as represented. If he sells you a gold article and it proves to be not up to the standard you can make him smart for it.

No paper collars in this country—got my last one on & must buy some linen ones tomorrow—Never heard of such a thing here and cant hardly give credit to the fact until I showed one. Oh how I wish I had one or two hundred to expend for clothing. I'd go in sure—for clothes & shoes—

Just discovered how the mice tails grow shorter every day—Geo has an hour's amusement every day with his d– – – nasty little mice. An Outsider gets at their tails sticking through the wires of the cage and bites them off.

Dec. 1st. Pleasant day—been out taking a short walk. Streets full—Boulevard thronged—bought a box of collars. Paid my bill, 2 weeks $11.40, cheap enough—If I only had some money I would get some things you bet. Room is rather dark and gloomy but light is just right for Geo. He is digging into the cartoons poor fellow—I wish I could help him, but no use. I cant make Indians.

The tumbler is set for the mouse that bites at the tails of those in the cage. [Written at top of page: "did not catch him."]

At Cafe. These old Dominoes have their dogs all over the table. Ill-looking curs walking around amongst the coffee cups. I am wishing every moment that one would lift his leg. Every woman has a dog under her pettycoats or on the table. Geo burning brandy.

Saturday 5th. Cloudy & misty. Bad day for Geo to work. Took a little tramp this morning—got enough in short time. As we were go-ing to Cafe it commenced to rain, and in between showers made out to get home pretty dry. 3 traps set to catch the deserters—did not succeed. Here we sit in our dungeon, raining, fearfully dark. Oh what a night to be on the ocean—At such a time as this I go right into my bunk & make up my mind to abide consequences—we had two fearful days coming over, I laid in bed all the time, in fact could not be on deck—I shudder now at the thought of such a night at sea. Others almost as trying is in the fog. So dense that a vessel can-not be seen twice its length scarcely. Whistles blow every 5 minutes during a heavy fog day or night—well I have got to try it soon so I will keep my heart and nerves strong for the trial—I have not been able from any maps yet to find any conveyance home by land —So I give that up. Tomorrow is Sunday, and I think I will write some letters though nothing to write about—I am going to bed now to try and dream about home—which I have not done since I left home—so good night all—

6th. Raining this morning, but streets crowded with country people. Same every Sunday—after *Santa Claus*. Concluded not to write till the day or two before I leave. Am anxious to get away.

After a hard days work today, scarcely looking off his drawing, Geo says—"Ah me, It is hard work Frank and if by chance I shall live to finish my Works, and should then realize money from them, what good would it do me—I cant travel around & enjoy sights—I'll be too old. Still I would like to have money so I could go again in the Andes—a most wonderful country—charming scenery, but I may never see it again—I might as well wind up there and leave my bones to bleach in the sun as any other place." If his Works were finished he would be off at once, no doubt. He says he often wishes they were done, but if they were he would be still going at something else. He must work as long as he has life—cant be idle a moment. Some dark stormy days—too dark to see his work—then he is unhappy.

Hurricane last night. I never knew such an awful windy night— shook the building—Pleasant to-day. Sat for my Photo—not good I think. One cant feel otherwise than awkward here if not dressed in pretty good style. There are but few foreigners here and 99 out of 100 are travelling, and of course are able to put on good styles. My clothes of course are not stylish, and I really believe they dont know what to make of me—If I were genteely equipped—I would attract more attention than others—It must go so, I am limited in means and must look out.

Christmas 1868. Geo finished the Outlines—the last mark was the *dot* at the end of his name, and he said he never in his life was so glad to get a job off his hands—2½ years spent on them altogether. How glad he appeared to be—in less than 5 minutes after, he had some paint mixed & his brushes before him—Now, he says, I feel natural for the first time since I commenced the outlines, 2½ years ago.

NOTE: "Now I am G. Catlin again, look out for the paint."

[More notes from the diary:]

With Harrison in Philadelphia is a box, black & nearly square, with 2 locks he thinks. This box contains an immense correspondence from boyhood up—his father's discharge (original) from the Revolutionary army signed by George Washington, notes and memorandums of value to no one else, and of great value to him. All his wife's letters and correspondence, and private papers of 20 or 30 years accumulation. Black, square, leather covered trunk or box.

Designs sent by different artists for Gov't for a painting to fill last niche in Rotunda—Boone's entrance into Kentucky the subject. Catlin was in Paris. His design was delayed in London one month—consequently tardy in reaching Washington *one day* too late. One had been adopted at $10,000. All delegates from Kentucky, upon examination, decided Catlin's were the best by far, but *too late*. Artist finally substituted De Soto landing on Mississippi. Gurley of Washington has painting of Boone going into Kentucky by Geo. Catlin.

7 months Geo. worked constantly on the La Salle paintings. Fled from Paris to London with family when Revolution broke out. Returned in about 6 weeks to look after La Salle paintings—and was surprised in finding them all right. His other collection, 9 tons, he removed to London by waggons (rail roads torn up) at an immense cost. LaSalle paintings finished and to have been delivered to Louis Philippe in 2 or 3 days, when the Revolution broke out. Soldiers running through the town, destroying everything. By some means his paintings were preserved. One copy LaSalle finished—(5,000 figures) Has a copy of LaSalle designs partially finished.

345 Portraits in old Collection—154 added since Committee reported in favor—34 same size as original—and 120 full length though small as seen on the screens.

Mr. C. being an American artist, Congress might pass an act allowing him to bring his work in free of duty.

What number have been circulated by Gov't & by Schoolcraft—

25 paintings in oil descriptive of LaSalle & Father Hennepin's Explorations in America in the years 1650 to 1658, of their perils by

sea & land from Quebec to N. O. by way of the Lakes to Chicago (now) then by Illinois River to Miss.—up to St. Anthony back again.

Copies of Schoolcraft's work sent by Gov't to the heads of every Gov't on earth &c.

Wears peculiar style cap. has them made to order—

Models of Niagara Falls Summer & Winter are at Phil'a.

Have the Monument to the Fur company photographed immediately after memorial decided upon—6 paintings.—Halcyon Days, Last Buffalo monument, Weighing furs, Return after the Hunt. Whether Congress pays any attention to the memorial he intends to have the above lithographed and will furnish any number at a few cents each. Gives me the whole & entire right to sell liths &c in America—gilt frames & glass with print under & coloured will sell.

No display at funerals—5 or 6 carriages no one in them. About a dozen on foot following hearse—have seen but one here.

"Now I am George Catlin again"—Very independent.

Lowell to Chicago	5.15	Charley	10.00
Supper	.50	Fare on ship	40.00
Chicago to N. Y.	20.00	Shirt & drawers	3.50
Breakfast, Toledo	.75	Board on ship (gold)	5.00
Apples	.05	Boots (do.)	2.50
Shave	.15	Bill at Liverpool (do)	1.50
Breakfast, Chicago	.50	Fare Liv. to Dover (do)	3.75
N. Y. Room 4 days	4.00	Fare Dover to Ostend (do)	3.90
Outfit (for ship)	7.00	Ostend to Brussels (do)	4.90

PART EIGHT: THE LONG ROAD HOME

1869–1900

1869: "Push it Francis, Push it!"; The outlines and Mr. Steele   1870: The glitter of illusion; A clutch at straws   1871: The end of the road.

"Push it Francis—Push it!"

FRANCIS CATLIN'S diary shows a gradual shrinkage of his first excitement over a trip to Europe. George's life was humdrum—unvaried. He was a deaf old man, content to live on a meager income, with a cage of white mice for company. Poor Francis, from the wilds of Wisconsin, had no doubt looked forward to a bit of gaiety while abroad. George's promised trips to Paris and London evidently depended upon the amount of money his brother could bring with him, and according to the diary, Francis had little more in his pocket than boat fare home. To George, his younger brother was in Brussels for a purpose; if he carried out the artist's plans he would make a fortune for himself, and could later visit the old world cities at his leisure.

Evidently, Burr Catlin declined his uncle's offer to join Francis in gathering up the fortune awaiting them. Perhaps he could not take time from his business. It is also possible that his months with George in London had acquainted him with the artist's flights of fancy which had produced nothing but numbers on the debit side of the ledger. So it was up to Francis to do the job alone. No doubt he had qualms. From the following bombardment of letters, George must have told him he would keep him advised as to when and how to accomplish the mission.

The artist gave Francis a very well-written prospectus for his coming publication.[1] He instructed him to keep the book always on his table for the perusal of members of Congress and visiting celebrities, who, upon reading the artist's description of his planned Portfolio, would be very anxious to sign their names for a copy to insure its publication.

There never was a more visionary man than George Catlin. In his

---

[1] See Appendix X.

present state of mind any failure of his project was impossible. He was already basking in the warmth of its success.

Bruxelles, Monday
Jany 4th 1869.

Dear Brother Francis,

Not having heard from you since your note written at Ostende, I suppose you got off, by a hard scratch, by the Steamer of the 30th for which you was aiming.

I went up this morning to Sanford with the Power of Attorney and the Deed of Assignment,[2] and had them duly attested, and enclose them in this. Mr. Sanford told me to send them to him this afternoon, with this letter, and that he would send them tomorrow morning in his mail bag, and save me postage, and that he would enclose in them two letters for you which would be of service to you in Washington, so you will have all these in due time.

I hope you will have had a good voyage over the Ocean, and that you will be on your way to Washington in the shortest time possible.

I wrote to Brother Richard on New Years day, telling him that you would be in N. York about the 10th or 12th Jany. I explained to him distinctly the importance to both you and myself, of your being able to reach Washington with your collection during the present Congress, and that as he was a Brother, and with ample means, it was his duty to lend you a helping hand in the present emergency, and I have no doubt but he will do so. I told him that you was honourable, and would soon be able to return him his money with interest—and that for any sum he might loan you, all that I possess in the world shall be responsible. He will write to you I believe, and if so—if he offers to aid you, accept it & say nothing of the past—Brothers

---

[2] These pertained to the "slipper" and the subscriptions for proposed Portfolio.

(at all events in old age) should agree—and Brothers who have such ample means, should help brothers, & if he refuses to do it, I never will call him "dear brother" again. (this however, is strictly between ourselves) You are charged with all the ideas about screen & catalogue, which are the first things to get up—and as I shall write you again before you get to Washington, I need say no more now. You carried letters to Mr. Gregory and to my children, and they will receive you with kindness. I shall write again to Gregory in a day or two—he can give you letters of great importance.

My health remains good, and you can imagine me going ahead with my work.

The little pets are all well, and apparently very happy. "Bobtail" was ingenious enough for another trick—he turned the latch of the door and let all out of the cage. I placed the cage on the floor the next night, with the door open, and in the morning found "Dolly" and her mate, grinding away as usual. And the trap took up "Bobtail" and another beautiful creature, with head and tail as white as snow!

All grinding as usual. Your affectionate Brother

Geo.

Bruxelles, 9th Jany 1869.

Dear Brother Francis,

I wrote you on monday last, and sent you letters of Sanford which you will have rec'd ere you get this.

This will find you covering your screen perhaps. The face side of the screen, at all events, should be planed down and smooth, to make the paper lay flat. And in pasting on, the paper need not be sponged before the paste—in such narrow strips, pass a broad brush of paste over the slips of paper and let them lay a few minutes to expand, and then lay them on, passing a wet sponge over the back, which will lay them flat down, where they will hold fast, and dry without rising. The screens, in fact, should be planed on the backs as well as in front, for their backs will sometimes be seen, and in travelling, if rough, will be apt to chafe the cartoons. The red tape, about the sort you saw in my room will be the best contrast to the cartoons.

I have had no letter from Richard since you left; but, as I said in my last, I wrote him a long letter, and told him it was his duty, as a loving Brother, to assist you in starting, and I have little doubt but he will do so.

In Washington your first step will be to deliver the letter which Sanford gives, to the chairman of the Library Committee of Congress, with the view to getting your screen in the Library. You will state to him clearly the objects in view, and put in his hands a copy of the *Memorial*. When he has read that, call on him a second time for his answer. He is a member of the House of Representatives, and perhaps will offer the Memorial, or get some influential member to do it. Dont circulate the memorials to any but members, and to them, not generally, until it has been presented and read.

First thing—enquire if Mr. Grenley has returned—if so he will make your task easy, if not, *dont flinch,* for you can do it alone.

The little slip, translation of the French letter in the Memorial, dont fail to have printed and gummed on all of them—this should be done in N. York so as not to lose time in Washington.

The memorials of artists in London & Paris, with Report of Committee on my old collection—as well as the package of correspondence with Maximilian, are to be kept on your table, and handed to members of Congress when in your Room, and the memorials to be sent to each member after it has been read in the Congress, to be distributed (with permission) in the House, or sent to their lodgings, as the Chairman of the Library Committee will advise.

I have written to Trubner, requesting him to write to Lippincott of Phila—and order him to send you such copies of the Okeepa as you may write for, and I will account to Trubner for them, at "*Trade price*," ie, at 33 percent discount. They are sold by Lippencott at 5 dols. per copy, and if you have orders for them you will sell them at the same price, accounting to me (when you have money) at 33 percent less.

My two vols. of drawings have been returned to me by the Librarian of British Museum, with answer that "they are works of great interest, but not *antique* enough for our Institution!"

Dont let the memorial get into the hands of the Editors until after it has been presented in Congress. There should be no announcement of it until that has been done.

You will have seen in the Deed of Assignment I have named 15 per ct. for obtaining subscriptions, instead of 20 per ct, as I suggested when we were together; this on mature consideration of the heavy expenses of binding,—25 per ct. duties &c, &c, which will reduce me to small profits, if any. And I believe that a run to Canada & to London, would pay, and furnish a larger subscription.

I do not think of any more to say at present, and stop here wishing you success, and believing, (unlike another brother) that your energy and good address will ensure it.

Your affectionate Brother
Geo. Catlin.

Richard had not yet replied to George's letter telling him to give Francis financial aid while in Washington. Richard did not like to be *told* what he must do. He no doubt gave Francis some money, but saw no reason to tell George about it.

The following letters from George show that he missed Francis' company, and that writing to him helped make up for his absence. And, judging by the detailed instructions, he felt it necessary to jog his brother's memory on how to accomplish the mission.

Bruxelles, Jan'y 13th 1869

Dear Brother Francis

I am writing again very soon, and probably before I have much of anything new to say. I am writing this in the cafe' where we have so often sat together, and at about the time, I should suppose, that you are arriving in N. York.

I have been well since you left here, and as you can easily imagine, closely engaged in the "ten years of work" which you predicted I had yet before me. If my health continues so good I shall get along rapidly with it, and though many of my pictures will be unfinished, I shall begin my Ex'n and finish up in a private painting room as my Ex'n proceeds. I think I shall put up a temporary building at Ostende for three months, the bathing season, & after that, open in Bruxelles.

I forgot to say a thing in my last letter which I intended to say—that whilst exhibiting in Washington or elsewhere, say as little as you can of my having cartoon copies of my old Collection, but speak as freely as you please of my South American collections, and of my N. Amn's west of the Rocky Mountains, made in my "last Rambles." If the Congress or Institutions knew that I had copied my old Collection it might lessen the value of it, & perhaps check any steps taken for its purchase.

If any enquiries should be made by the Gov't or Institutions about the old Collection, you can easily say that it can be sold *entire & complete*, as it was when the Ex'n closed in London, and that 120 small, full length portraits with many other paintings made West of and in the Rocky Mountains, made in my last voyage, can be added to it, on conditions to be learned from me.

I have got the "Monument" to Fur Company in the Lithographer's hands, and shall lose no time in getting the others chromolithographed and shipped for your Ex'n room and other places where you can sell them, for commission of 33 percent, and I intend also to send you coloured photos of a number of my best portraits, full size of the paintings. You know I have all the materials, and a little time and money are all I now want, to get them ready, and in your hands.

I see by the telegraph just received, that the new Congress

will commence its Session on the 5th of March, but that must not affect your efforts to get my Memorial forward with the present Congress. It will be a good thing for your own Ex'n if the Session commences anew at that time.

I have enclosed a note for D. S. Gregory, which after reading, you will seal and hand to him.

I need say no more at present, but wishing you *unflinching* courage and success.

Your affectionate & loving Brother
George

Bruxelles, 26th Jan'y 1869 [3]

Dear Brother Francis,

I write you again, though I have reason to expect a letter from you in a day or two, announcing your safe arrival in N. York. I suppose you got on board the steamer for which you was aiming (of 30th Dec.) and that you was too much pressed in getting yourself & supplies on board to drop me a line. I am sadly disappointed at not having rec'd as yet a single line from either of my daughters or from Brother Richard. I don't know what to make of it. I fear some illness in the family, in the Gregory branch or my own. I am imagining you about this time in Washington, and Richard, in some way, giving you aid.

On rec't of this (if you have not done it before) find out where Col. Mitchell is, & what he is doing, and how long he held the office of Superintendent of Indian affairs, and let me know. Be moderate and circumspect in all your conversations with members and others, and offend no one—dont speak too strongly of my affairs, but let my works speak for me. You will have a difficult part to act in Washington, where business is done in a way you are not used to, but I have full confidence in your good judgment & prudence.

If in conversation with members or others, you can ascertain

---

[3] Letter by courtesy of the Missouri Historical Society.

about what number of Schoolcraft's great work were distributed, let me know it. If you should see Mitchell—keep cool—dont irritate him, it will do no good. You may tell him plainly that he has done me a great injury, and that now (after he reads Maximilian's letter) he should turn in and help in advocating my cause. Dont *fight* him—*laugh* at him. Tell him that I am coming to Washington in a few weeks, and shall probably see him.

My letter to Richard, of Jan'y 1st, and of which I gave you some account in my last, I should get an answer to in a day or two, and from it, when it comes, I shall be able to judge what interest he is to take in your affairs & mine during the short time that can be allotted to *me*. It will be very strange if, with such ample means as he has, and no children to spend it upon, he refuses to help you through the present pinch—but I trust he will do it. If I had the "needful" he would not have had the opportunity.

I wrote you that my two vols. of drawings were returned from the B. Museum, with (from the librarian) "they are not antique enough." I then sent them with a letter to the richest and most aristocratic Club in London, which is collecting a vast library, and they have been returned by the secretary, stating in his very complimentary letter that "they are works of great historical interest, but *too old*—the Indian subject is getting too old!" How encouraging this—and how droll—not old enough for one library, and too old for another!

I can think of nothing more to write at present, and will close, wishing you all success, and awaiting your letter with impatience.

Your loving Brother
Geo. Catlin

Note. This letter was written last evening in the Cafe, & this moment, just before mailing it, your letter of 29th Dec. came in, having been 27 days coming! I have seen the "arrival of the N.

York all well"—&c. I enclose the cover of your letter, which will explain all.

G. C.

CATLIN'S
NORTH AMERICAN
ETHNOGRAPHS

378 full length *Indian Portraits*
and 5,000 full length figures in
action, in their DANCES—GAMES—
RELIGIOUS CEREMONIES &c. with a
full and descriptive Catalogue

———————

Bruxelles, 17th inst. [1869]

Dear Brother,

I sent you a heavy letter last evening, and forgot to comply with your request as to the form of a "*poster*."

I have sketched off the one above, which I think may be more "taking" than the hacknied "Indian Collection" or "Indian outlines" It should be short, & free from "puffing"—perhaps you may still hit upon a better form than the above, I leave it to you and your son—call it what you please.

Always invite the "Press" & "Big Bugs"—& Millionares; the last are the chaps to subscribe, & also, the Librarians of all Institutions & Literary Societies.

I regret exceedingly that the screen could not have had a place in the Capitol, for an easy access of all the members, however, make the best you can—get them to see the designs if possible.

You can imagine me closely at work, and my sketches fast advancing. My health is yet good, as you saw it. I think of nothing more to write at present.

Your affectionate Brother
George

In Washington Francis got nowhere. He had enlisted the help of his lawyer son, Charley, who had been assigned to the Adjutant General's Office in Washington at the close of the war. Charley, who had returned to his practice in Great Bend, came east to help his bewildered father. But Charley did no better. Permission to exhibit the outlines in the Capitol was denied, and the room they finally found for the display was too far away to entice the uninterested Congressmen to its door. Few came to the exhibit; there were not enough signatures in the subscription book to warrant publication of the proposed Portfolio.

The attendance dwindled to nothing, and Francis was forced to close the show. The memorial was somehow presented to a member of Congress, with the request that it be brought up during the coming Session, but nothing more was heard of it.

Where had George's wits flown to? How could he expect applause for his sketches from a people who still heard the echoes of the war that had split their country and killed their sons and brothers? What an egotism he must have possessed to believe that his tirade against Schoolcraft would be read to a harassed Congress, embroiled in controversial measures regarding the reconstruction of the shattered South. Who in Washington now cared what Schoolcraft had said about Catlin ten years ago!

For forty years "The American Indian" had filled George Catlin's life. To perpetuate the first Americans for future generations was just as vital to him in 1869 as when he mixed the gay colors on his palette on the upper Missouri, long ago. But the subject had become "old hat." His work was ignored in London and the United States; no one was interested in the Indians or George Catlin any more. How sad must have been the old artist's thoughts in his world of solitude and silence.

Bruxelles, 17th Mar. 1869

Dear Brother Francis,

Your last letter was very discouraging, as for your own interest and mine, & I have been delaying to write, daily expecting to hear better news from you. You no doubt are waiting to give me some account of your contemplated trial of the Ex'n and of the presentation of the memorial. A day or two must bring me some report.

Since you informed me that a Room for the screens could not be got in the Capitol, where the members would all have lounged in and become familiar with the interest of the collection, I have felt quite discouraged as to subscriptions, or any chance of an appropriation towards the expenses of publication, & also have believed, that in your Ex'n in another part of the City, in the bustle & confusion at the end of the Session, very few of them would find the way.

On my memorial, they may possibly act, but as for any encouragement from them, all my hopes vanished when I learned that you were defeated in the plan I had confidently counted on, of having the designs shown in the Capitol.

I write this principally to enclose a letter from the Abbe' Brasseur, to you, and also his note to me. his letter, which is very interesting to science, and complimentary to me, is in French, and I send you a *literal* translation, keeping the original in my own hands. I hope that some of the Editors in Washington will insert it for you in their journals, it will do us both good. And send me a copy of the paper.

I dont know what more to write, but must hear from you soon or be compelled to believe that you are ill. Mr. Sanford, whom I called on this morning, is yet in Paris, so I cannot yet send the deed of Conveyance.

Remember me to Charly,
Your affectionate Brother
Geo. Catlin

Naturally George was discouraged over Francis' failure in Washington. He may have thought it the result of sending an untrained envoy on a diplomatic mission; he should have made the trip himself. Francis wrote that he was going back to Hudson and find a job.

His European tour and sojourn in Washington had probably put the poor man deeply in debt. George had told him that he would make a fortune!—one wonders what he now thought about that!

In the following letter, George mentioned that he had made Francis a present of the outlines, and that he had written Gregory to sell them for Francis to some institution.

Bruxelles, 11th June, 1869

Dear Brother Francis,

I rec'd your letter of the 15th may I rec'd in due time, but have delayed answering until the present, hoping to have got a letter from D. S. Gregory ere this, having written to him relative to the outlines. And also I was anxious to learn something from the London man, about publishing the smaller edition.

I have not yet any answer from Gregory, and having made a visit to London, spending time and money, have effected nothing. The publisher is afraid that the Indian subject is getting too old to outlay so much money on; is very willing to publish if I will advance one half the money or advance all the money himself & share profits, provided I will give bonds with security for its safety, and a certain percentum of profits. This is all bosh—he would then have the whole thing in his hands and out of my sight, and account with me for 1,000 copies, when he perhaps he has sold 2,000. this is the shave by which book publishers live, if they can get fools enough in their snares.

I wrote Gregory, as I told you, that I had made you a present of the outlines, by a deed of assignment, and told him to sell them at the best rate he could to one of the Institutions, Smithsonian or Astorian—and perhaps the Boston Free Library would be the most likely; to be sold on his and your joint account. I shall probably have a letter from him ere long, and will at once inform you of his plans. I had a letter from your son Charly a few days since, & shall answer him today.

It makes me sad and sober when I reflect upon the labour and time I devoted to these outlines, and the complete disappointment to us both, which they have produced. And yet, if you manage it right, they will repay you, and if perpetuated in one of these Institutions, will, in a measure answer one of the objects I had in making them.

I am very sorry that you did not get protection at least, for the "slipper" while in Washington, for I am constantly afraid the idea will enter some other person's head who will take it from you. It *is* good—there is no doubt of it—and in the U. States its utility will be vast & valuable. dont lose it—If I had the money to spare I would send and secure the patent *at once*.

I am, as you left me, poor, & daily and hourly at work on my "ten years of work." My health remains good, & if it continues, and I am not disappointed about a Room that is promised me, I shall open my Ex'n here about the 1st of August.

I expect daily to get a letter from Mr. Gregory, and as soon as I do, I will write you again.

I am excessively grieved to learn that my visionary plan has thrown you out, & also your son Charly; but I hope in the end you will not be losers. I trust you will find something profitable to turn your hand to in meantime. Remember me kindly to your good wife and little Boy.

Your affectionate Brother
Geo. Catlin

The outlines and Mr. Steele

E v i d e n t l y Mr. Gregory had no desire to peddle the outlines, and handed the job to an in-law of his, a Mr. Steele, who was also a good friend of George Catlin. This was satisfactory to Francis, who had gone back to a job in Hudson, in order to support his family.

George was satisfied, also, until he found that Mr. Steele had ideas for the outlines that had not been hatched from his, George's, brain. He was not going to furnish apples for a pie made from any recipe but his own!

No doubt Mr. Steele's plan for publishing the outlines had Gregory's approval. And with the backing of the great philanthropist, Ezra Cornell, founder-president of Cornell University, they could have been published. George would have received the honor due him, and Francis would have made some much-needed money.

After all, George said that he was giving the outlines to Francis, hoping that the poor fellow could realize something from their sale. Evidently Francis was satisfied with Steele's idea, and the latter felt that Francis' approval was necessary, not George's. Perhaps George was upset because with Cornell's assistance Steele's plan would succeed, while his had failed.

Bruxelle, 26 Oct. 1869

My Dear Brother Francis,

I rec'd your letter a few days since, in due time, and was much relieved by its arrival, for, from your long and unaccountable silence, I feared some accident had happened to you. I am glad to learn that yourself and family are all well; as for poverty, it is nothing new for you and me, & for *myself*, I have no means as yet, of seeing when I am to get out of it. Certainly though, with me it cant hold on to me much longer. My "ten years of labour," which you predicted, is just finished, and I am trying to get my Ex'n before the world, but as my luck has always been, just as I am ready to go about it, the Ex'n Halls in Bruxelles are all engrossed, and I am at this very moment afraid that I cant make my Ex'n here unless I wait till middle of the winter, or near the spring.

I have incurred expenses of my screens & catalogue & other things, like yourself, and must lie bye with them, or open in some other town. at least it appears so at this time. I may however, succeed in a few days in my last application to the

Bourgmistre, for a grand Hall in the hotel de Ville. if so, in two or three weeks I shall be a showman again.

As to the outlines, which you say my old friend Steele is trying to sell, they should be sent to the Astor Library and to the Smithsonian, and offered, and the Catalogue with them, and the screen, if they should want it, and I shall write by this mail the same thing to Steele. I think he can sell them in the manner proposed, reserving for me the right of taking from them a photograph copy for publication if I should ever be able to do it. As for your proceeding for subscribers in the way you propose, without the drawings, it never will answer at all, it would "cost more than it would ever come to," and I have no faith in it—if the world could have seen the whole collection on a screen as I designed—could see what they were subscribing for, something could have been done with it—but the moment that you informed me that the same could not be put up in the Capitol, I was instantly convinced that my whole plan of publishing would fall to the ground, & I at once gave it up, at least the plan of publishing in that large form. And I almost resolved also that my memorial would be just kicked out of the Congress.

That *may* be however, passed in the coming Session, but it will require some one to be there a short time to get the memorials delivered to the members, & with the Okeepa and paintings & the letter of Max'n properly before them.

How this will be done I dont know—*I* cant be there, and I fear you cannot, and if not, perhaps Mrs. Stevens might do the needful, for the needful. I have no idea how or where the memorials &c were left, or how they are to be got hold of. It would be a great pity if the thing should be dropped, and I allowed to die off with such a Government libel hanging on *my name and my works.*

I shall instruct Mr. Steele what efforts to make with the outlines, & if they are sold—it would not cost you a great deal to run on to Washington for a short time—and *drive* it. no one could *push* it like a Brother, & no other one, (not even myself) would be so attentively listened to. I am sure Mr. Steele *can* sell the drawings for something—a high or a lower price. Get it—*take* it, and dont starve upon them—they have a value, & a great value. I hope you will be able thus to reach Washington—You need not "blaze out"—but economize your dollars—& spend but little.

I want you to get the patent right for the "Slipper"—it *is* a good thing—there is *money* in it—and if rightly managed, a little fortune, even if *I did* make it. Mr. Steele is *not* a rich man —a *good* man, & too good a man to get rich. he married the sister of D. S. Gregorys wife.

My health is still bad, & I think your's the same, write again soon, love to all.

Your affectionate Brother Geo. Catlin

In the following letter George gave Francis his own "recipe" for publishing the outlines.

Bruxelles, 17th Dec. 1869 [4]

My dear Brother Francis,

I received your letter enclosing several letters from Mr. Steele in due time, and your later letters a few days since, and should have answered sooner, but have been waiting with quiet anxiety to hear from Mr. Steele, as he promised in his letter to you to write to me. I can't account for his delay, and having an opportunity today, by Mr. Sanford (resigned), I have written him a long letter, and I have said for himself & you and Mr. Cornell to read and duly consider.

The idea of Mr. Steele's taking up the publication so eagerly was sudden and new to me, and the generous and noble offer of Mr. Cornell, as stated in Mr. Steele's letters. But how strange that Mr. Steele should have gone so rapidly and so far into the thing without giving me some notice of it, or consulting my taste

---

[4] Letter by courtesy of the Missouri Historical Society.

and my wishes as to the style in which the illustrations are to be got out. I have given my ideas and wishes at full length in my long letter, which I have instructed him to send to you when he has read it; and I need not repeat them all in this place.

I have prepared quite a new plan—to publish all in *lithography*—you & he getting a good lithographic lens, and a good experienced operator, and making all the plates yourselves—not from the outlines, but from my paintings, getting the whole effect of my paintings, with every touch of my brush; and on such conditions, with Mr. Cornell to guarantee its completion, to convey to you and Mr. Steele, jointly & forever, the copyright of my whole collection (if you will publish so much), for the U. States. You will find my reasons for this in the letter that Mr. Steele will send you.

As for my coming *"home"* (as you call it) just now, it is out of the question, and I dont know when it may be. If you and Steele push the great work on the plan I have proposed, you will see by my long letter that I am in the right place for it. I should be only a bother and a hindrance if I were with you. I have no funds to move with here, and I should have none to stir with there.

My Ex'n is not opened yet—just when my paintings are all finished, and I am ready, every Ex'n Hall is someway engaged, and as yet it is impossible to get one. You spoke of going to Washington for my memorial, provided Mr. Steele could sell the outlines. If such should be the case at any time during the winter, dont stop long to spend money—long enough to see my memorial distributed to all the members, and some members too engaged to bring it forward. It is not worth lobbying for—my great ambition about it was lost in losing the chance of showing my outlines and plan of my great work to the members in the Library.

If you go to Washington, call on Lippincott in Phila. for several copies of "O-Kee-pa" for members. Trubner has ordered him to deliver to you such copies as you may want, and they will be charged to my account with Trubner of London. I have written so much that I am tired, and I know of nothing more to say at present. I have said all in the long letter.

I am at a loss to know what is the effect of the "Photoliths" you speak of, and Mr. Steele should have sent me one. Certainly he cant be getting out the work without even consulting me. If you and he take up the work on the plan I have laid out, and can have Cornell to back you up, you will have enough to occupy you all your lives & you may both make your fortunes by it. With a photographic establishment of your own, in a cheap place in the country, and all the works of my life to copy, large and small—for sale in the book and for retail sales, if you choose (and coloured if you like), you may fill the American world with them, and the more you spread them the better I shall like it.

I hope this may find you and family all well, and that you get the letter from Steele in a few days.

Your affectionate Brother
George.

Steele finally answered George's letters, probably saying that *his* idea for publishing the outlines was entirely satisfactory to Francis, and that the work had commenced. This would infuriate the artist whose unasked-for advice had not been accepted. George's original plan for publishing the drawings had failed; it galled him to think that another man might succeed, and without including him in the deal.

In George's letter of March 3 (p. 398), he wrote of the "great outline work" being squashed and silent. Either he wrote to Steele, insisting that the publication be stopped, and the outlines returned to Francis in Hudson, or Mr. Cornell, out of patience with George's interference, suddenly washed his hands of the business. Without Cornell's financial help, Steele could not go ahead with the work.

In the following letter to Francis, George tried to convince his brother that the "deal" had been crooked from the start—and that Francis should be grateful that he had a brother wise enough to see through such flagrant deception. At any rate, except for an occasional retrospective sputtering, the case was closed.

Bruxelles, Feb. 5th, 1870

Dear Brother Francis,

Within the last week I have written you two long letters, which you will have rec'd before the arrival of this. Your letters of the 18th of Jany and of the 19th one day later, have both come to hand together, this morning, the Steamer that brought them, coming with one wheel, has been 18 days on her passage.

By my two last letters you will have learned that Mr. Steele *will* have to "back out" of the affair which he has so rashly and so imprudently entered, though he says in his letter to me that he cannot do so. I regret exceedingly the awkward state it leaves you in, but to struggle longer, trying to "push the thing through," and come to the lots of money which the great company, Mr. Steele & yourself have counted on "before it is hatched," might be to place you in a worse condition than you now are in; and I fully believe so, for on the plan that you are "pushing forward," I dont believe that you would have got your 100 good subscribers in one year, nor half that number; you would have worn out my name and fame in putting out a bad work, and forever have prevented me from publishing a better one.

Mr. Steele has most imprudently run himself into unnecessary expenses, and he must get along with them as well as he can —I cant afford to be ruined and allow my works to be condemned and ridiculed that he may make a little money instead of losing a little. I am old and have but a little time to battle with criticisms, and it is barely possible that I may live long enough to publish the works of my cruel life of labour in a respectable & creditable form, & I am not so weak as to allow that chance to be hawked out of me, by a work to be published out of my sight—out of my knowledge, and out of my controul. The remarks in my last letter, and the specimens enclosed, with

393

comments on them will convince you that I am right; and very little time will be sufficient to show you that I can put forth a book that *will sell itself*—put money in my pocket, if I live, and be creditable to me, and soothing to my feelings in old age.

You must be patient, and live along as well as you can; and I trust there will soon be something better for you to do.

When I spoke in my letter to Mr. Steele, of assigning to him and you the copyright of my works in America, that promise was based upon the condition which I then had a right to believe in, that the *great patron* Mr. Cornell would aid in authorizing the negatives to be taken here, in the manner I described—which negatives, remaining in my hands would have had a value, enabling me to have got out an English Edition—by which means you can see, I should have been pecuniarily benefited by the great work in Am. We have neither of us the slightest idea now that Mr. Cornell will ever advance anything, or intended to advance anything towards the great work, and therefore that proposal (which I put expressly upon the condition that the great work was carried through on the new plan which I had proposed) falls to ground, there being nothing to aid me in getting out the negatives here.

If I have to hypothecate everything I have on Earth, and even my own liberty, I shall get them out, and in such case I cant afford to give away the Am'n copyright. I may share it, perhaps with others who may help to push the sales, but I cant afford to pay the whole expenses of the work here and give it away in Am'a, but we will talk about this at a future time.

The Rec't of deposit of title page of my forthcoming book, and also for the outline work came safe in your letter this morning. I told you that I would make you a present of the Am'n copyright of the new book, and as soon as I get a copy or two to send you, I will send with it an authority for you to sell it *in my name,* though to put the money in your own pocket. If you are disappointed in the fate of the "great work," there will be this advantage, it will not be "donated" to the College, and it

394

is still your property, and certainly will be enhanced in value by *not ever being published.*

I have written to Mr. Gregory this day, briefly stating all circumstances, and told him that I advised you to take the outlines and sell them to the Smithsonian or other Institution in the best way you can, and in proposing to do so, it will be better for you to offer them as being sold for *me,* (but putting the money in your own pocket) & for this purpose I herein enclose my authority for doing so.

You need not say it to Mr. Steele, or to anyone else, but it is my opinion, that from the beginning, the company have been regularly planning to swallow Steele so far that *he must* go down, and calculating to swallow some 8 or 10,000 dols. with him; and with Mr. Steele for a catspaw, to get the outlines for the College, leaving you to whistle for any equivalent. Dont repeat this, but to me there is a *clair voyance* in it, and I believe you can also see through it.

Why did not Mr. Steele put your name with his in the circular? his name is not known. the name of Catlin on it might have done some good—given some confidence (though I am glad now that your name was not on it!

You recommend in your last letter that I should apply to Congress for permission to pass my collection duty free into the U. states,—not a word of it. if it is applied for, they will say —"oh, Catlin and his collections are coming into the country —then will be the time, when he is here himself, to take up his "memorial" and to talk about his collection." I have petitioned the Congress enough, and unless they can grant my memorial prayer, they will never be asked for "duty free" whilst my works belong to Geo. Catlin.

You need say no more about a "text," which would have been a hard job—all to rewrite, & with painful labour of 3 or 4 months, not only (as to me) to have been thrown away, and spoiled for a better work. And as for my *portrait,* which you both put so much stress upon, I am thankful that it escapes the destiny which was preparing for it. You have the portrait by Corwin which you brought to me last winter, be careful to preserve it—we shall want it hereafter.

I need not send you any "specimens" of my plan, until this big affair cools down a little. I shall send them soon enough; and if (by the rest of the world) it is supposed defunct, no *matter*.

I feel sorry for Mr. Steele, for though eccentric, he is a good man, and has, I believe, meant well. treat him kindly, and let him not run into further expenses.

Your affectionate Brother
George

P. S. One thing (which you can tell me) I am anxious to know what the great Company were to have for getting up those 220 plates, and for paper and printing the same. The *latter* I dont care so much about—but I want to know what their charge for *getting the tracings, and laid on the stones* ready for printing.

We have all been labouring under an egregious error from the beginning, as to the *size of the book*. one of the leading Book publishers in London told me a little time since, that of the full size, over four feet in length when open on the table, and too large for the shelf in libraries, it would always have to stand on the floor, and that there were not five noblemen in the kingdom that would put it in their libraries, if it were presented to them—& he recommended about half the size.

The glitter of illusion

I N F E B R U A R Y , 1870, the New-York Historical Society asked Francis what price his brother would put on his Indian collection, and Francis immediately wrote the glad tidings to George. This unexpected news would naturally send the artist's ego soaring—common sense forgotten in the flight. He was now suffocating with self-importance.

George was seventy-four years old, and his needs were few. For many years he had prayed that his beloved Indian gallery would find a permanent home in a fine American institution. Here was his chance at last, but he wouldn't price his works at a figure the Society would be willing to consider! His original price for the collection was $65,000. He now asked $100,000! And $120,000 if the cartoon collection was added.

His letter was too long and rambling. A brief note, merely suggesting a price, and asking for their opinion on it, would have brought an answer, and then he could have described what he had to offer beside his old collection. When he asked for $100,000, perhaps he had forgotten that at one time he would have taken $35,000, gladly. Poor old man—he had worked all his life for this; and now that the prize was within his reach, his eager fingers failed to grasp it.

> 8 Rue de Brabant, Bruxelles
> 26th Feb'y, 1870 [5]

Dear Brother Francis,

I rec'd your letter of the 7th. Inst. containing enquiries by the President of the N. York Historical Society relative to my Indian Collection, suggesting conditions so exactly suitable to the ambition with which I have spent a long and toilsome life, that I will not fail to answer in two or three days, and in terms, I believe, which will not be objected to.

In the meantime, present my compliments to the President, and also the enclosed memorial to Congress, by which he will see and understand the shameful way in which Mr. Schoolcraft endeavoured to impeach my veracity, and to destroy the value of my works.

The world as yet knows but imperfectly the extent and interest of my collections, nor will they until they can be

---

[5] Letter by courtesy of the Missouri Historical Society.

brought together. My two collections, including my South American paintings, contain over 1200 paintings in oil, with (besides the portraits) more than 20,000 full length figures in action, in their various games & other customs. You have seen most of them, and I have every confidence in your judicious representations to the President of the Historical Society. I have many letters to write today, and need not at this moment say more.

Your affectionate Brother
Geo. Catlin

Bruxelles, 3d March 1870.

My Dear Brother Francis,

I have this day sent you copies of my forthcoming work on the *"Rocks of America,"* being published by Trubner & Co. 60 Paternoster Row, in London. And I hereby authorize you to make for me, as I should do for myself, such sale of the Copy Right of the same for the United States, or such arrangements there, as in your judgment may best comport with my interest.

Your affectionate Brother
Geo. Catlin.

Bruxelles, March 3d-1870

Dear Brother Francis,

I send you herewith a statement for the President of the historical society of New York, which is the deliberate result of my cogitations on his very friendly enquiries made of you.[6]

This is now the important question for me, and for you; the "great outline work" being quashed and silent. We must accomplish this, if possible, and I have every *confidence in your talking* straightforward with the Society—to the *point*, not with too many words, or words too big. If the arrangement can be made with them, and on the liberal conditions named by the

---

[6] See Appendix XI.

President, it will suit my ambition exactly. He may be too sanguine (like Steele) about raising the money, but let him try. I
think you should copy my letter to him before delivering it.

I have sent you by this mail my catalogue of the Lasalle
paintings, & after he has sufficiently used it, I shall wish to have
it back again (or a *copy* of it, if you have time) as I shall want
it to explain, in my Ex'n—

I send you to day also, a copy of my new book (Rocks of
America), merely stitched together, to enable you to do something with it. And Trubner has just written me that he sent the
day before yesterday, by mail, to the care of D. S. Gregory, two
copies for you. these copies are in sheets, and without the
plates, but I enclose plates for you to put in. And I enclose
my authority for you to sell the Copy Right for me, though you
are to put in your own pocket all you can get for it—If you
find difficulty in getting Copy right, you should make an arrangement with some house to publish it *for* you. And no time
should be lost, as Mr. Trubner writes me it must be published in
both countries on same day, or the Am'n Copy Right will be
lost. the publishers understand this, and whoever buys the Copy
Right, or publishes on shares, must telegraph to Trubner the
day, as he cannot advertise or publish here until he knows the
day fixed upon in N. York.

The copy which I send you has the two maps put in, and also
a slip, part of a note carelessly left out in printing. In the Am'n
Edition that note must be printed in, as part of the work; & the
copy stitched, therefore, which I have sent you, the one for the
Am'n Edition to be printed from.

I can think of nothing more to say at present, but will write
you again in a few days.

Your affectionate Brother
George.

P. S. For the maps in the American Editions, I have ordered the
Lithographers, Messrs. Simoneau and Lowery, to keep them on

the stones, and if required, they can be had, on very short notice, at the trifling price of 20 fran per copy, that is 20 centimes for the two maps.

P. S. encore,

The Lasalle catalogue you may give to the President, I have copied it myself, to day.

If the book on Am'n Rocks be *re*-printed in Am'a, let me know it as soon as possible, as I would make some important addition.

A day later,—after writing the above I have just rec'd your letter of the 17th Feb. enclosing Mr. Steel's letter of nov. 22d— his statements in that, that I had written to him and given him authority to publish &c, are not true. I had written to him, nov 1st—and thanked him for the pains he was taking to sell for you, the outlines, and in that letter distinctly told him that I had resolved not to publish them. And his very modest suggestion that you should *"transfer the outlines formally to him,"* shows clearly what he was aiming at from the beginning. It is well for all hands that the thing has ended so soon as it has.

You speak of "throwing into the trade" the outlines, in case the Society buys my Collections. dont do any such thing, or say another word about it. I *throw in* enough—I give them as you see, my Lasalle collection and one year of service in finishing up the old collection—it has a great many paintings only hastily sketched. Get what you can for the outlines and as soon as possible, that you may live, and feed your little children. Try Astor—and try Professor Henry of the Smithsonian, dont demand 5,000 dols. you wont get it, nor more than half of it.

The two copies of the new book sent by Trubner, he has sent without the maps. I enclose a couple of the maps which can put in—lose no time in getting a publisher for it, as it is all ready (the English Edition) & cant be announced until the day is fixed for publishing in Am'a. The publishers will understand that.

On the 15th of April, 1870, Francis, in Washington or New York, received a long and friendly letter from his brother Richard. It is possible that Richard was giving Francis some financial help. His much loved wife Darwina had recently died, and with Henry and Eliza gone, he was drawing closer to his brother but a few years younger than himself. George and Francis were all the family he had left, and of the former he wrote: "I do hope he will be successful in selling his works and realizing some money. He is advanced in years, & will soon have to lay aside his brushes. He ought to have quiet, and rest. I fear he will not succeed, and he cannot move or get along without means. I don't know anything about the value of his works, but know there is no love for Indians in this country in these times. . . ."

Richard spoke of the hard times and of all the property he owned here and there. He mentioned 760 acres of first rate prairie land in Iowa, and if Francis was interested he thought he might give him half or all of it. Evidently there was some catch in the offer, because in a later letter George wrote: "I was very much surprised, and much grieved at the manner he [Richard] treated you about the land speculation. I hope he will yet think better of it, and *act* better."

A clutch at straws

GEORGE'S "ten years of work," which Francis had predicted, was accomplished in less than two. Father Putnam's "determination and perseverance" held the artist to the seemingly endless task of finishing his cartoons.

In the summer of 1870 George Catlin was a showman again, exhibiting his cartoon collection and LaSalle paintings in Brussels. Old as he was, he put on a magnificent show, highly praised by both the press and noted artists in the city. The passing years had left their mark, but in no way had affected his mastery of the paint brush.

8 Rue de Brabant, 29th Aug. 1870

My Dear Brother Francis,

I rec'd your last letter in due time, but as it came when I was in the midst of excitement and fatigue of body and mind, in getting open my Ex'n, I have neglected it until the present moment.

You will see by the enclosed circular and by my catalogue which I send you, that my works are now before the world. Unfortunately, on the very day that I opened, commenced the public excitement of the first bloodshed in the awful battles about Metz, and the same excitement is still kept up, materially affecting the success of my Ex'n.

The Collection is beautifully arranged in a splendid Hall of 125. feet in length, and covering every inch of the walls, and as far as it has been seen, much praise has been bestowed upon it and on me.

I am glad that you succeeded at last in selling the outlines for *something,* for I can imagine the state to which your unsuccessful labours reduced you.[7] My intention from the beginning was good, contemplating the benefit of both; but from the moment you informed me of the failure to get your screens in the Capitol, and the failure of your running Ex'n, I saw that all was lost. I saw the impossibility of getting a subscription to authorize the publication of such a work as I contemplated, and yet I hoped you would have got a price for the outlines sufficient to cover your expenses.

My loss in the affair is the two years of hard work in my old age in making them; yet they will be preserved in an Institution where they will be honourable memorials of me when I am gone.

---

[7] Francis finally sold the outlines to the New-York Historical Society for seven hundred and fifty dollars.

My contemplated *photo-typographs,* as I wrote you, have so far disappointed me. My Lithographers, Simoneau & Lowery, have produced me nothing yet, of the size I want; and about a month since Mr. Simoneau died of apoplexy, and 10 days after, the young man they had employed from Paris to make all their photographic negatives. But yet another invention has just turned up, of transferring the negatives to plate glass plates, from which the printing is done, and of any size. I am at this moment in the midst of experiments with this, and will report to you in a few days.[8]

I still hope that my great work will be suddenly thrown out and that it will make work for you of a remunerative kind in the U. States. *Live in hope.*

I have had no letter from Richard for 3 months, and fear he may be in a lonesome and drooping mood. And I much fear he will be defeated in his contemplated visit to the Continent by the war—but that should not stop him; the Continent is large enough, even with a desolating war in some parts of it. I was very much surprised, and much grieved at the manner in which he treated you about the land speculation. I hope he will yet think better of it, and *act* better.

I hope this may find you and your family well, & comfortable. Write on receipt.

Your affectionate Brother
Geo. Catlin.

I have not a word yet from the Historical Society. It seems very strange that they should have made such professions to you, and promised to write to me, and now drop the affair thus.

The New-York Historical Society had completely ignored George's letter of March 2, 1870, written at their request. They had

---

[8] These small plates, approximately 3¼ inches square, are beautifully painted replicas of Catlin's originals. They are now in the Bancroft Library, University of California, at Berkeley.

asked Catlin's terms, and he had replied that he would sell his old collection for one hundred thousand dollars, and for an additional twenty thousand would include the cartoons.

Perhaps the price was too high, considering the risks the Society would be taking. They had no idea in what condition they would find the old Indian paintings and artifacts. And for that matter, they could run into legal difficulties in obtaining the collection from Harrison.

They did not have the courtesy to answer George's letter. Apparently they just decided to forget the whole matter. However, George wasn't one to give up easily—he had plenty of paper and ink, and he was now willing to cut the price in half. His ego had come tumbling down from its lofty heights. His second letter to the Society was written by a humbled old man.

> 8 Rue de Brabant
> Bruxelles, Oct. 10th, 1870 [9]
>
> To the Librarian of the "Historical Society of N. York."
> Sir,
>
> The conversation had with my younger brother a year or more since, relative to my Indian Collections, caused me to answer your enquiries at the time, and induce me also, to make to your Society this second communication.
>
> My brother led me to believe that you were intending to correspond with me on the subject; and as I have received no letter from you, I fear the disposition to treat with me for the purchase of my Collection has fallen to the ground. Perhaps the suggestions made in my letter were unacceptable to the members of your Society, and if so, I should have been glad to have learned on what grounds they were objectionable.
>
> The suggestions made to my Brother were so exactly suited to the ambition for which the labours and privations of my long life have been devoted, that in my old age I am more and more

---

[9] Letter by courtesy of the New-York Historical Society.

ready to meet them on terms that may be acceptable to all the members of your noble Institution.

I send you by this mail, a catalogue of my Cartoon Collection, which I have before named to you, and which is now completed, and as you will see by the circular enclosed, is on public exhibition in this city. It has been highly praised by the Flemish artists and the Press, and by the copy of a letter which I enclose, you will be pleased to learn the opinion of one of the most celebrated artists of the present age, as to its artistic, as well as historical merits.

This great (and almost endless) work, which now covers the walls of a splendid Government Hall of 125 feet in length and forty feet in breadth, is now done, and wherever it goes, to Berlin, to Russia, or to my native land, I have the satisfaction of leaving it a *finished work*.

But as to the Old Collection, long known and appreciated in our own country as well as in England and in France, I have anxieties of a peculiar kind which trouble me in the closing years of my life. These are the main objects of this communication, and the explanation of them, which I will make to you, I wish you and your Society to receive (at the present) in strict confidence, for reasons which you will easily understand when you read further.

As I explained to you in my former letter, unfortunate speculations which I was decoyed into in London, brought upon my Old Collection liens which I was unable to pay off, when Mr. Harrison, of Philadelphia, paid off those liens, and shipped the Collection to Philadelphia, where it has been stored in its cases ever since.

Since my return from my South American voyages I have several times written to him for a statement of the amount which he advanced on it, and the accumulated expense of shipment, storage and interest; and, from his vexation that I have not been able to redeem it (or from an idea that he may hold it 'till after my death and then put what claims he pleases on it), he has treated all my letters with contempt, and has answered my children who have called upon him for information, "that I have no claim whatever on the Collection—that he *bought* it outright in London, and that his outlays on it have been more than 40,000 dollars, and that whatever disposition he may see fit to make of it, they need not expect anything from it." And also, he informed them "that he intended to present the Collection to the city of Philadelphia, if they would prepare a Hall suitable for it."

Now the facts are these—I had, in my distress, given three Bills of Sale on the Collection for loans of money which I believed would relieve me from my pecuniary embarrassments until I could get expected aid from N. York.

Mr. Harrison, who had also advanced me some money, paid off these liens and shipped the Collection to the U. States. There was *no sale* of the Collection, and I hold his letter written to me in Paris after he had shipped the Collection, informing me of the shipment, and stating that "if I should not be able to redeem it he would sell it for the best price he could get for it, and after repaying himself for his outlays, he would pay the remainder of the purchase money to my children."

The liens which he paid off, with the amount which he had advanced me, with the accruing expenses on the Collection, cannot amount to anything like 40,000 dollars, and the two things which pain me are—first, that unless I can redeem the Collection I cannot compel him to render me a statement of his claims upon it, and my children and myself may thus be deprived upon any benefit from it if it be sold, or if it be presented to the city of Philadelphia; and secondly, that if it be thus sold, or presented, I shall have the anguish in my declining age to see it thrown into an Institution where I don't wish it to go, jumbled together in the deranged state in which it was probably boxed up in London, and after the Custom's overhauling, and without the finish of all its parts, and its final arrangement which I have been contemplating in case its destination could be that suggested in your encouraging remarks made to my Brother,—an asylum in the noble edifice you are proposing to erect in the city of N. York.

Though I am 75 years old, my painting abilities are yet as good as ever; and as I said in my former letter, if that Collection, the nature and extent, and interest of which is extensively known, should find a resting place in your Institution, I am ready and able (and from ambition disposed) to devote at least one year, at my own expense, in completely finishing and arranging all.

From the above considerations, and the higher value I set on my *name* and *fame* than on money in my old age, I am induced to make the following proposition—that, if the Historical Society of N. York will agree to buy of me that Collection entire, it will enable me legally to demand of Mr. Harrison a statement of the amount of his outlays made on the Collection, and enable me thus to redeem it, saving something, and probably living to see it placed, finished, and arranged, where I would wish to see it perpetuated.

In view of this arrangement, I will agree to take 50,000 dollars for the Collection instead of the price named in my former letter, and if the same be effected, there will be no difficulty in arranging my Cartoon Collection, eventually to be added to it. In his letter to my children, Mr. Harrison states that the Collection has been examined, and that the paintings are in perfect preservation. The costumes, of course, will be damaged, but the other Indian manufactures will be unchanged.

It will be seen that to effect the above arrangements, no intimation of it whatever should reach the knowledge of Mr. Harrison until the same is made, lest he should present the Collection or sell it, and leave me no means of redress.

I am trembling with fear for its fate, and in my old age, by this letter, leave it in the power of your Society to decide where the works of my life (now over 12,000 paintings in oil and many thousand Indian manufactures) shall go. I beg you to lay this communication before the members of your Society, and to advise me as *soon as convenient*, for the chances of seeing my works in a satisfactory resting place are now confined to a very short time, and my present ability for finishing and arranging them cannot last long.

> With high respect
> Your Obedient Servant
> Geo. Catlin

George received no answer to his second letter to the New-York Historical Society. Nevertheless, he was now ready to go "home." His exhibit in Brussels had received so much applause he wanted to show it in the United States. To ship himself and all his belongings to America would be expensive. Evidently he asked Richard to grant his last request: that he talk with Mr. Moore—read the letters George had written to the Society—see some of his work—help him to get home.

The fact that the following note is in the possession of the New-York Historical Society shows that Richard handed it to Mr. Moore, as requested. And it must have been Richard who enabled George to return to his native land.

> 8 Rue de Brabant
> Bruxelles, 29th Oct. 1870 [10]

George Moore, Esq., Librarian of the N. York Historical Society—

Sir,—The bearer of this note, my brother, Richard Catlin of Ripon, I have instructed to call on you, and I beg you will do me the kindness to show him my two last letters, and also the collection of Indian outlines now in your possession.

I have instructed him to peruse them, that he may know my views relative to my Collections.

> In haste, yours truly
> Geo. Catlin [11]

---

[10] Letter by courtesy of the New-York Historical Society.

[11] Thomas Donaldson says that George Catlin returned to the United States in 1870, opening his gallery of paintings at the Sommerville Gallery in New York,

AFTER AN ABSENCE of thirty-two years George Catlin returned to New York. As he stood on the ship's deck and watched the shores of home come closer and closer, a kaleidoscope of form, sound, and color must have tumbled through his mind; tipis and palaces, chieftains and kings. The artist had touched the stars, and groped for a foothold in the pit of despair. Now he had come home with but one desire: to give his life's work a final resting place, here where it belonged.

Francis and three young ladies met him at the pier. Tears must have followed the deep grooves in his cheeks as he saw his dear Clara in the face of his little strawberry-loving Libby, now a grown woman. George was nearly seventy-five, and very, very deaf, but his eyes were bright and alive, and he stood proud and erect.

Another man might have gone home with his daughters and lived in comfort, but not George Catlin! His work was not yet done. The artist was confident that his cartoon collection would receive the same acclaim it had been given in Belgium. Ever hopeful of a call from Congress, or from one of the large institutions in the east, he had a lengthy catalog printed, giving detailed information on every painting in the collection, and then opened his exhibition in the Sommerville Gallery in New York City. It was an excellent showing of the work of a fine artist, but the attendance was small, and the press gave it but slight notice. New York was a noisy, commercial city that lacked the intellectual atmosphere of the old-world town of Brussels with its deep-rooted love for art and beauty. A new generation was

closing it in the fall of that year. It is of small importance, but the date is incorrect. There are many letters from George written in Brussels in 1870. He held his exhibit there in August of that year. The note from George to Mr. Moore, dated Brussels, October 29, 1870, tells us very plainly that George could not possibly have arrived in the United States until very late in 1870. *The George Catlin Indian Gallery*, Annual Report of . . . the Smithsonian Institution, 1885 (Washington: The Institution, 1886), p. 700.

growing up, and what it looked for in New York was amusement and excitement. Who wanted to look at paintings of old Indians, and who was George Catlin anyway?

As the weeks went by, the attendance dropped. George knew he would have to close. But where could he go? It was at this critical moment that help arrived. His old friend Joseph Henry, Director of the Smithsonian Institution, came to his rescue by inviting him to hang his collection in the National Museum in Washington! [12] George came to life again; his worries vanished. Members of Congress would now see his paintings hanging where they belonged, and would keep them there.

George moved to Washington in the fall of 1871, and proudly arranged his cartoon collection in a gallery of the Smithsonian. Mr. Henry gave him a room high in one of the building's turrets, where the old artist could live with his dreams. George spent his days in the gallery, fussing and rearranging his works, explaining them to visitors. As months passed, however, he realized that he was here only because of his friendship with Joseph Henry; and if Congress did not act in his behalf he would have to leave. And Congress chose to ignore the issue.

It is true that the Indians had caused a lot of trouble since those halcyon days George had roamed among them on their native soil, before our government seriously tried to make farmers of buffalo hunters. The Indians could never adopt the white man's civilization, and so they fought it. They preferred death to being fenced in.

The United States government was well aware that the red man was doomed; that the days of war-whoops were over. But it should not have forgotten that this country had been populated for centuries before the white men arrived, and that future generations would want to know as much as possible about their country's background. Congress must have been composed of men disturbingly lacking in foresight if they could not see the ethnological importance in Catlin's paintings.

---

[12] Harold McCracken, *George Catlin and the Old Frontier* (New York: The Dial Press 1959), p. 207.

In October, 1872, George became ill and was taken to his daughters in Jersey City. No doubt he recalled the healing power of Mother Nature in the past, for Donaldson, in speaking of the artist's last illness, said that George would walk the floor until his strength gave out, saying 'Oh, if I was down in the valley of the Amazon I could walk off this weakness.' He constantly referred to his paintings, and almost the last words he spoke were, 'What will become of my gallery?' " [13]

George Catlin died on December 23, 1872, at the age of seventy-six, and was buried beside his wife and little son in Brooklyn's Greenwood Cemetery. No marker graced his resting place. The following item appeared in the *New York Times* for May 18, 1961: "A little group made a pilgrimage yesterday to Greenwood Cemetery and the grave of George Catlin, America's first great painter of American Indians. There they dedicated the first tombstone it has ever had. A gray granite headstone standing on a grassy knoll, ringed with ivy, is inscribed simply: 'George Catlin 1796–1872.' Beside it stands a weathered stone, believed to mark his wife's grave, on which the only legible words are 'to the memory of.' The headstone was a gift of the 'Westerners,' a society of historians and others interested in Western Americans, and Catlin's collateral descendants."

George Catlin's death did not bring to an end the many pleas to Congress to purchase his Indian collection. In 1874, the following letter, signed by George's three daughters, was received by the University of California, at Berkeley:

Washington D. C. Feb. 10th 1874 [14]

To the President and Faculty of the University of California
Sirs
The Collections of the late Mr. George Catlin illustrative of the Indian race, a description of which is herewith enclosed, are now offered for sale to the government to be preserved as a

---

[13] *The George Catlin Indian Gallery*, pp. 716–717.
[14] By courtesy of the Bancroft Library, University of California at Berkeley.

foundation for a national museum. If not secured at this time it will not be possible to retain them in this country. We desire to obtain from those who appreciate the importance of their possession such testimonials as will carry weight to the mind of Congress in favor of their purchase. The letter enclosed has been given as the testimony of Professor Henry of the Smithsonian who empowered us to use it. We desire such learned bodies as the faculties of colleges of the different States should give their voice in recommendation of the measure to retain them among the scientific treasures of Country. We have already obtained the signatures of many distinguished men to a petition in its behalf.

We request from your influential college a letter expressing in such a manner as you think best a concurrence in this project addressed to the Chairman of the Library Committee of Congress, and enclosed to the address designated below, so that it may be presented as soon as possible with the documents.

As the daughters and sole representatives of Mr. Catlin we naturally desire his own country to possess these Collections as a memorial of his life's labors, but it is to the interest in the cause of American art and science that we appeal for an expression of your opinion in favor of this object.

(signed)   Elizabeth W. Catlin
Clara G. Catlin
Louise Catlin Kinney

Address E. L. Kinney, 1321 New York Avenue, Washington D. C.

Congress ignored the pleas. The original Catlin Indian Gallery finally went to the Smithsonian Institution in 1879, a gift from the heirs of Joseph Harrison who died shortly after Catlin. In 1912 the American Museum of Natural History in New York City purchased the cartoon collection from the artist's daughter, Elizabeth, who had taken possession of it at her father's death.

The paintings of George Catlin are the most important and complete pictorial record ever made of the American Indians, and have been copied over and over. They have been used as illustrations for thousands of publications dealing with the subject of Indians and the early years of America. His books are used for research by countless ethnologists.

Catlin's road, like that of many before him who pursued the elusive bluebird in the field of art, was a hard and lonely one a good part of the way. He swung high in adulation and popularity during interludes of success; poverty brought him shame and condemnation. Perhaps this may explain his ultimate success, not attained in his lifetime. A softer life might have lessened the intense demand of his spirit to reach his goal, perhaps even the reason for his long life. The struggle for survival in the wilderness gave him back his health, and his inner drive to make his name honored in his own country carried him along. It is a pity that the dream of his youth could not have been realized before he died, but his works will go on through the years to come, and be both inspiration and education to all who are, and ever will be, interested in the first Americans.

With George's death, Richard and Francis alone remained of the Catlin family. Richard passed away in 1874, and Francis, the youngest of Putnam and Polly's brood, was alone. It is said that he was a happy, jolly old gentleman, whose long, white, Santa Claus beard shook up and down with every chuckle. He was splendid company, and never lacked listeners. He liked most to talk about the past; about the early days of Wisconsin, about the wilderness and the wild life. He would perhaps give a deep chuckle and begin: "I remember one time when—."

The nineteenth century came to an end, and when the last echoes of the bells had hushed, Francis Catlin, eighty-five years old, slipped quietly through to the greener grass beyond. The Catlin family was together again.

APPENDIXES

APPENDIX I

The Collection of Catlin Letters

1. June 5, 1798: The Hon. Samuel Sitgreaves, Philadelphia, to Putnam Catlin, Great Bend, Pa.

2. July 12, 1817: Charles Catlin, Wilkes-Barre, Pa., to brother George, Litchfield, Conn.

3. Aug. 4, 1817: Putnam Catlin, Montrose, Pa., to son George, Litchfield, Conn.

4. Nov. 27, 1817: Charles Catlin, Wilkes-Barre, Pa., to brother George, Litchfield, Conn.

5. Jan. 3, 1818: Charles Catlin, Wilkes-Barre, Pa., to brother George, Litchfield, Conn.

6. Jan. 24, 1818: Putnam Catlin, Montrose, Pa., to son George, Litchfield, Conn.

7. Aug. 10, 1818: Charles Catlin, Wilkes-Barre, Pa., to brother George, Litchfield, Conn.

8. Dec. 31, 1819: Timothy Pickering, Wenham, Mass., to Putnam Catlin, Montrose, Pa.

9. Dec. 2, 1820: Joseph Horsfield, Bethlehem, Pa., to Joseph Meister, Governor of Pennsylvania, Harrisburg, Pa.

10. Dec. 14, 1820: Charles Hall, Sunbury, Pa., to Putnam Catlin, Montrose, Pa.

11. July 25, 1824: Putnam Catlin, Montrose, Pa., to son George, Owego, N. Y.

12. Jan. 8, 1827: Geo. Griffen, New York City, to Jonathan Thomson, Esq., Collector of Port of New York, New York City.

13. May 11, 1827: Putnam Catlin, Montrose, Pa., to Abra Bradley, Esq., Washington, D. C.

14. May 27, 1828: Julius Catlin, Easton, N. Y., to brother George, New York City.

15. May 30, 1828: Putnam Catlin, Montrose, Pa., to son George, New York City.

16. June 5, 1828: Julius Catlin, Morristown, N. Y., to brother George, New York City.

17. June 6, 1828: Julius Catlin, Morristown, N. Y., to brother George, New York City.

18. July 3, 1828: Julius Catlin, Morristown, N. Y., to brother George, New York City.

19. July 8, 1828: Julius Catlin, Morristown, N. Y., to brother George, New York City.

20. Feb. 15, 1830: Putnam Catlin, Montrose, Pa., to son George, Richmond, Va.

21. Jan. 21, 1831: Putnam Catlin, Great Bend, Pa., to son George, Washington, D. C.

22. June 23, 1831: Putnam Catlin, Great Bend, Pa., to son George, New York City.

23. July 3, 1833: John Catlin, New Bernville, N. Y., to brother Francis, Lockport, N. Y.

24. July 26, 1833: Putnam Catlin, Great Bend, Pa., to son Francis, Lockport, N. Y.

25. Nov. 24, 1833: John Catlin, New Bernville, N. Y., to brother Francis, Lockport, N. Y.

26. Apr. 10, 1834: John Catlin, Delta, N. Y., to brother Francis, Great Bend, Pa.

27. Apr. 29, 1834: John Catlin, Delta, N. Y., to brother Francis, Great Bend, Pa.

28. Oct. 31, 1834: Anson Dart, Delta, N. Y. to Francis Catlin, Great Bend, Pa.

29. Jan. 1, 1835: Putnam Catlin, Great Bend, Pa., to son Francis, Delta, N. Y.

30. Jan. 13, 1835: Polly Catlin, Great Bend, Pa., to son Francis, Delta, N. Y.

31. Feb. 5, 1835: Polly Catlin, Great Bend, Pa., to son Francis, Delta, N. Y.

32. Apr. 25, 1835: Eliza Catlin Dart, Delta, N. Y., to brother Francis, Great Bend, Pa.

33. Dec. 16, 1835: Putnam Catlin, Great Bend, Pa., to son George, Pittsburgh, Pa.

34. Mar. 18, 1836:   Polly Catlin, Great Bend, Pa., to son Francis, Pittsburgh, Pa.

35. Mar. 18, 1836:   Putnam Catlin, Great Bend, Pa., to son Francis, Pittsburgh, Pa.

36. June 10, 1836:   George Catlin, Albany, N. Y., to brother Francis, Lockport, N. Y.

37. Aug. 1, 1836:   George Catlin, Prairie DuChien, to brothers Henry and Francis, Buffalo, N. Y.

38. Sept. 11, 1836: Polly Catlin, Great Bend, Pa., to son Francis, Buffalo, N. Y.

39. Sept. 11, 1836: Putnam Catlin, Great Bend, Pa., to son Francis, Buffalo, N. Y.

40. Sept. 19, 1836: Eliza Catlin Dart, Delta, N. Y., to brother Francis, Buffalo, N. Y.

41. Oct. 12, 1836:   Putnam Catlin, Great Bend, Pa., to son Francis, Buffalo, N. Y.

42. Nov. 25, 1836:   Putnam Catlin, Great Bend, Pa., to son Francis, Delta, N. Y.

43. Dec. 3, 1836:   Putnam Catlin, Great Bend, Pa., to son Francis, Delta, N. Y.

44. Dec. 21, 1836:   Putnam Catlin, Great Bend, Pa., to son Francis, Delta, N. Y.

45. Dec. 28, 1836:   George Catlin, Utica, N. Y. to brother Francis, Delta, N. Y.

46. Feb. 23, 1837:   Putnam Catlin, Great Bend, Pa., to son Francis, New York City (to the care of Dudley Gregory)

47. Apr. 11, 1837:   Putnam Catlin, Great Bend, Pa., to son Francis, Navy Yard, Pensacola, Fla.

48. June 17, 1837:   Putnam Catlin, Great Bend, Pa., to son Francis, Navy Yard, Pensacola, Fla.

49. Aug. 7, 1837:   Polly Catlin, Great Bend, Pa., to son Francis, Navy Yard, Pensacola, Fla.

50. Oct. 16, 1837:   Putnam Catlin, Great Bend, Pa., to son Francis, Navy Yard, Pensacola, Fla.

51.   (No date; contents place letter as written in Jan. 1838) Polly Catlin, Great Bend, Pa., to son Francis, Navy Yard, Pensacola, Fla.

52. Jan. 21, 1838:   Putnam Catlin, Great Bend, Pa., to son Francis, Navy Yard, Pensacola, Fla.

53. Mar. 7, 1838:   Theodore Burr Catlin, Great Bend, Pa., to Francis, Navy Yard, Pensacola, Fla.

54. Mar. 18, 1838: Putnam Catlin, Great Bend, Pa., to son Francis, Navy Yard, Pensacola, Fla.

55. Apr. 22, 1838: James Catlin, Pensacola, Fla., to brother Francis, Navy Yard, Pensacola, Fla.

56. May 4, 1838: Putnam Catlin, Great Bend, Pa., to son Francis, Navy Yard, Pensacola, Fla.

57. May, 1838: Eliza Catlin Dart, Utica, N. Y., to brother Francis, Navy Yard, Pensacola, Fla.

58. July 12, 1838: Putnam Catlin, Great Bend, Pa., to son Francis, Navy Yard, Pensacola, Fla.

59. Aug. 21, 1838: Polly Catlin, Great Bend, Pa., to son Francis, Navy Yard, Pensacola, Fla.

60. Sept. 8, 1838: Putnam Catlin, Great Bend, Pa., to son Francis, Navy Yard, Pensacola, Fla.

61. Sept. 19, 1838: James Catlin, Pensacola, Fla., to brother Francis, Navy Yard, Pensacola, Fla.

62. Sept. 23, 1838: Putnam Catlin, Great Bend, Pa., to son Francis, Navy Yard, Pensacola, Fla.

63. Oct. 15, 1838: Putnam Catlin, Great Bend, Pa., to son Francis, Navy Yard, Pensacola, Fla.

64. Nov. 16, 1838: Polly Catlin, Great Bend, Pa., to son Francis, Navy Yard, Pensacola, Fla.

65. Dec. 20, 1838: James Catlin, Pensacola, Fla., to brother Francis, Navy Yard, Pensacola, Fla.

66. Jan. 4, 1839: Putnam Catlin, Great Bend, Pa., to son Francis, Navy Yard, Pensacola, Fla.

67. Jan. 8, 1839: Richard Catlin, Apalachicola, Fla., to brother Francis, Navy Yard, Pensacola, Fla.

68. Mar. 12, 1839: Putnam Catlin, Great Bend, Pa., to son Francis, Navy Yard, Pensacola, Fla.

69. Mar. 30, 1839: Richard Catlin, Apalachicola, Fla., to brother Francis, Navy Yard, Pensacola, Fla.

70. Apr. 15, 1839: Putnam Catlin, Breat Bend, Pa., to son Francis, Navy Yard, Pensacola, Fla.

71. June 7, 1839: Putnam Catlin, Breat Bend, Pa., to son Francis, Navy Yard, Pensacola, Fla.

72. June 22, 1839: Richard Catlin, Pensacola, Fla., to brother Francis, Navy Yard, Pensacola, Fla.

73. Nov. 12, 1839: Putnam Catlin, Great Bend, Pa., to son George, New York City.

74. Nov. 31, 1839: Abigail Catlin, Pensacola, Fla., to Francis Catlin, Navy Yard, Pensacola, Fla.

75. Jan. 10, 1840: George Catlin, London, to parents, Great Bend, Pa.

76. Feb. 17, 1840: George Catlin, London, to parents, Great Bend, Pa.

77. Feb. 22, 1840: Eliza Catlin Dart, Utica, N. Y. to brother Francis, Great Bend, Pa.

78. Feb. 29, 1840: George Catlin, London, to father, Great Bend, Pa.

79. Apr. 23, 1840: Putnam Catlin, Great Bend, Pa., to Clara Catlin, Albany, N. Y.

80. May 11, 1840: Putnam Catlin, Great Bend, Pa., to son George, London.

81. May 20, 1840: Putnam Catlin, Great Bend, Pa., to son George, London.

82. June 3, 1840: George Catlin, London, to parents, Great Bend, Pa.

83. June 23, 1840: Putnam Catlin, Great Bend, Pa., to son George, London.

84. June 29, 1840: George Catlin, London, to parents, Great Bend, Pa.

85. July 9, 1840: Putnam Catlin, Great Bend, Pa., to son George, London.

86. July 17, 1840: Abigail Catlin, Pensacola, Fla., to Polly Catlin, Great Bend, Pa.

87. Aug. 13, 1840: E. Smith Sweet, Owego, N. Y., to Francis Catlin, Great Bend, Pa.

88. Aug. 24, 1840: Eliza Catlin Dart, Great Bend, Pa., to Clara Catlin, London.

89. Sept. 30, 1840: George Catlin, London, to father, Great Bend, Pa.

90. Oct. 17, 1840: Putnam Catlin, Great Bend, Pa., to son George, London.

91. Oct. 29, 1840: Clara Catlin, London, to Putnam and Polly Catlin, Great Bend, Pa.

92. Nov. 7, 1840: Mary Dart, Green Bay, Wis., to Francis Catlin, Great Bend, Pa.

93. Nov. 10, 1840: Eliza Catlin Dart, Green Lake, Wis., to brother Francis, Great Bend, Pa.

94. Dec. 28, 1840: Eliza Catlin Dart, Green Lake, Wis., to Elizabeth Catlin, Great Bend, Pa.

95. Jan. 4, 1841: Putnam Catlin, Great Bend, Pa., to son George and Clara Catlin, London.

96. Jan. 11, 1841: Anson Dart, Green Lake, Wis., to Francis Catlin, Great Bend, Pa.

97. Feb. 7, 1841:   Theodore Burr Catlin, London, to Francis Catlin, Great Bend, Pa.

98. Feb. 28, 1841:   Clara Catlin, London, to Putnam and Polly Catlin, Great Bend, Pa.

99. June 19, 1841:   George Catlin, London, to his father, Great Bend, Pa.

100. July 3, 1841:   George Catlin, London, to his father, Great Bend, Pa.

101. July 18, 1841:   George Catlin, London, to his father, Great Bend, Pa.

102. Aug. 24, 1841:   Putnam Catlin, Great Bend, Pa., to George and Clara Catlin, London.

103. Oct. 4, 1841:   Putnam Catlin, Great Bend, Pa., to son George, London.

104. Nov. 3, 1841:   George Catlin, London, to his father, Great Bend, Pa.

105. Nov. 21, 1841:   Eliza Catlin Dart and daughter Mary, Green Lake, Wis., to Elizabeth Catlin, Great Bend, Pa.

106. Nov. 29, 1841:   Putnam Catlin, Great Bend, Pa., to son George, London.

107. Dec. 24, 1841:   George and Putnam Dart, Green Lake, Wis., to Francis Catlin, Great Bend, Pa.

108. Jan. 22, 1842:   Mary Catlin Hartshorn, Delta, N. Y., to brother Francis, Great Bend, Pa.

109. Feb. 3, 1842:   George Catlin, London, to father, Great Bend, Pa.

110. Feb. 16, 1842:   Richard Catlin, Brooklyn, Ala., to brother Francis, Great Bend, Pa.

111. Mar. 3, 1842:   George Catlin, London, to father, Great Bend, Pa.

112. Mar. 9, 1842:   Mary Catlin Hartshorn, Delta, N. Y., to brother Francis, Great Bend, Pa.

113. Mar. 11, 1842:   Eliza Catlin Dart, Green Lake, Wis., to brother Francis, Great Bend, Pa.

114. Mar. 21, 1842:   Henry Catlin, Lockport, N. Y. to brother Francis, Great Bend, Pa.

115. Apr. 3, 1842:   George Catlin, London, to father, Great Bend, Pa.

116. Apr. 21, 1842:   Last Will and Testament of Putnam Catlin

117. May 19, 1842:   Benjamin Armitage, New York City, to Francis Catlin, Great Bend, Pa.

118. June 13, 1842:   James Catlin, Jr., Philadelphia, to Francis Catlin, Great Bend, Pa.

119. June 21, 1842:   Henry Catlin, Lockport, N. Y., to brother Francis, Great Bend, Pa.

120. Aug. 14, 1842:   The Dart family, Green Lake, Wis., to Clara Catlin, London.

121. Aug. 20, 1842: Henry Catlin, Lockport, N. Y., to brother Francis, Great Bend, Pa.

122. May 14, 1843: The Dart family, Green Lake, Wis., to George Catlin, London.

123. Aug. 16, 1843: Eliza Catlin Dart, Green Lake, Wis., to mother and brother Francis, Great Bend, Pa.

124. Sept. 5, 1843: The Dart family, Green Lake, Wis., to Francis Catlin, Great Bend, Pa.

125. Sept. 16, 1843: George Catlin, Manchester, England, to Charles Dimon, Esq. and Francis Catlin, Great Bend, Pa.

126. Sept. 16, 1843: George Catlin, Manchester, England, to his mother and brother Francis, Great Bend, Pa.

127. Sept. 21, 1843: Mary Catlin Hartshorn, Delta, N. Y., to brother Francis, Great Bend, Pa.

128. Nov. 4, 1843: Eliza Catlin Dart, Green Lake, Wis., to brother Francis, Great Bend, Pa.

129. Nov. 28, 1843: Theodosia Catlin, Pensacola, Fla., to Francis Catlin, Great Bend, Pa.

130. Jan. 12, 1844: Anson Dart, Green Lake, Wis., to Francis Catlin, Great Bend, Pa.

131. May 18, 1844: George Catlin, London, to brother Francis, Great Bend. Letter forwarded to Green Lake, Wis.

132. July 2, 1844: Polly Catlin, Delta, N. Y., to son Francis, Green Lake, Wis.

133. July 24, 1844: Mary Catlin Hartshorn, Delta, N. Y., to brother Francis, Green Lake, Wis.

134. Aug. 5, 1844: Eliza Catlin Dart, Green Lake, Wis., to George and Clara Catlin, London.

135. Oct. 27, 1844: Mary and Putnam Dart, Green Lake, Wis., to Clara Catlin, London.

136. Nov. 11, 1844: Henry Catlin, Niagara Falls, N. Y. to brother Francis, Great Bend, Pa. (letter forwarded to Green Lake, Wis.)

137. Jan. 24, 1845: Mary Catlin Hartshorn, Delta, N. Y., to brother Francis, Green Lake, Wis.

138. Feb. 23, 1845: Eliza Catlin Dart and daughter Mary, Green Lake Wis., to Clara Catlin, London.

139. May 15, 1845: The DuBois family, Great Bend, Pa., to Elizabeth Catlin, Green Lake, Wis.

140. Oct. 30. 1845: Nicholas DuBois, Great Bend, Pa., to Francis Catlin, Green Lake, Wis.

141. July 17, 1846:   Joseph DuBois, Great Bend, Pa., to Francis Catlin, Green Lake, Wis.

142. Dec. 29, 1848:   Nicholas DuBois, Owego, N. Y., to Francis Catlin, Fond du Lac, Wis.

143. May 3, 1849:   Nicholas DuBois, Owego, N. Y. to Francis Catlin (no address)

144. Aug. 26, 1849:   Eliza Catlin Dart, Dartford, Wis., to brother Francis, Stillwater, Minnesota Territory.

145. Feb. 6, 1852:   Eliza Catlin Dart, Milwaukee, Wis., to brother Francis, Hudson, Wis.

146. Dec. 19, 1852:   Eliza Catlin Dart, Dartford, Wis., to brother Francis, Hudson, Wis.

147. July 9, 1854:   Eliza Catlin Dart, Washington, D. C., to brother Francis, Hudson, Wis.

148. July 26, 1857:   Eliza Catlin Dart, Ripon, Wis., to brother Francis, Hudson, Wis.

149. Dec. 2, 1857:   Fannie DuBois Chase, Great Bend, Pa., to Francis Catlin, Hudson, Wis.

150. Sept. 12, 1858:   Eliza Catlin Dart, Ripon City, Wis., to brother Francis, Hudson, Wis.

151. Apr. 17, 1859:   Eliza Catlin Dart, Ripon, Wis., to brother Francis, Hudson, Wis.

152. Feb. 21, 1860:   Eliza Catlin Dart, Paterson, N. J., to brother Francis, Hudson, Wis.

153. Apr. 25, 1860:   Eliza Catlin Dart, Paterson, N. J., to brother Francis, Hudson, Wis.

154. Oct. 9, 1861:   Eliza Catlin Dart, Dartford, Wis., to brother Francis, Hudson, Wis.

155. Dec. 29, 1861:   Henry Catlin, Dartford, Wis., to brother Francis, Hudson, Wis.

156. July 11, 1862:   Eliza Catlin Dart, Dartford, Wis., to brother Francis, Hudson, Wis.

157. Feb. 9, 1863:   Eliza Catlin Dart, Dartford, Wis., to brother Francis, Hudson, Wis.

158. June 7, 1868:   George Catlin, Brussels, to his brother Francis, Hudson, Wis.

159. Sept. 9, 1868:   George Catlin, Brussels, to his nephew Burr Catlin (no address)

160. Sept. 9, 1868:   George Catlin, Brussels, to his brother Francis, Hudson, Wis.

161. Sept. 18, 1868:   George Catlin, Brussels, to his brother Francis, Hudson, Wis.

162. Oct. 31 to Dec. 30, 1868: Francis Catlin's Diary on his trip to Brussels.

163. Jan. 4, 1869:   George Catlin, Brussels, to brother Francis, Hudson, Wis.

164. Jan. 9, 1869:   George Catlin, Brussels, to brother Francis, Washington, D. C.

165. Jan. 13, 1869:   George Catlin, Brussels, to brother Francis, Washington, D. C.

166. Feb. 17, 1869:   George Catlin, Brussels, to brother Francis, Washington, D. C.

167. Mar. 17, 1869:   George Catlin, Brussels, to brother Francis, Washington, D. C.

168. June 11, 1869:   George Catlin, Brussels, to brother Francis, Hudson, Wis.

169. Oct. 26, 1869:   George Catlin, Brussels, to brother Francis, Hudson, Wis.

170. Feb. 5, 1870:   George Catlin, Brussels, to brother Francis, Hudson, Wis.

171. Mar. 3, 1870:   George Catlin, Brussels, to brother Francis, Washington D. C.

172. Mar. 3, 1870:   George Catlin, Brussels, to brother Francis, Washington D. C. (or New York City)

173. Apr. 15, 1870:   Richard Catlin, Ripon, Wis., to brother Francis, Washington D. C. (or New York City)

174. Aug. 29, 1870:   George Catlin, Brussels, to brother Francis, Hudson, Wis.

Included in this collection of letters are two genealogical lists of the Catlins since the Norman Conquest, 1066.

APPENDIX II

Wenham, Mass., Dec. 31, 1819

Dear Sir,

On the 28th instant, I received your letter of the 16th. Mr. Willing will of course advise me of the presentation of the order on the merchant at Baltimore, as soon as the result shall be known—as did of the receipt of the $650 you sent him last May.—I feel under great obligation for your attention to my interest, that of my orphan grand-children, and of the heirs of General Hamilton. . . .

Our army is twice as large as it ought to have been, subsequent to the last peace with G. Britain, and so Mr. Calhoun admitted in a conversation with me just before the close of the last Session of the last Congress, of which I was a member; but observed that there was not then time enough left to bring the matter, if entered upon, to a proper conclusion. The principal ground of my opinion was, that the Northern Army was absolutely useless, as to any service eastward of Detroit. And to this opinion, expressed by me to General Swift, he readily assented, when he accompanied Mr. Monroe on his Eastern & Northern tour;—with a single exception of a post near the Northern end of Lake Champlain, to facilitate any future operations against Canada. This I presume is the place (Chary, I think) where a fort has been begun at a great expense; but which now, it seems, falls within the Canada line; and fortunately for the U. States, in my opinion, to avoid a further large & permanent but useless expenditure of money, because we do not want a single fortress on our whole northern frontier, eastward of Detroit, & *there* only on account of the numerous tribes of Indians in its vicinity. The grounds of my opinion, a few words will describe—

The British will never invade the United States from Canada, *because they cannot expect to hold possession,* and certainly they will never make any *predatory incursions,* because *these would be easily retaliated, with aggravation.* And if we should hereafter decide to invade Canada, surely the St. Lawrence may be crossed in various places without any previously formed permanent fortifications to guard the passage of an army. If indeed such fortifications were established, the British would defeat their object by erecting counter-works. The reported population of the state of New York will soon open road to the St. Lawrence, wherever convenient crossing places shall be formed, to facilitate the friendly & commercial intercourse which during a peace, will always take place. On the same ground, all our armed vessels on the lakes Champlain & Ontario had better be sold, if of value enough to bear the expense of brushing them up,—or burnt, rather than pay a single man to look after them. For the same reason, all the existing fortresses should be dismantled.

Were it not for the projects of our government in relation to Florida, the deficit of the revenue, to the amount of five millions of dollars, might happily induce Congress greatly to reduce the army, and as a few troops will suffice for the taking & occupying of that country, I hope a reduction may be provided for, before the close of the present Session.

But we must have some regular troops & officers, with *military educations,* and there is no one whom it will give me more pleasure to serve, in this case, than you. I have therefore written a letter to my friend Mr. Calhoun, Secretary for the Department of War, recommending the admission of your son to the military academy at West Point, agreeably to your request. I avoided asking it as a *favour;* because I considered it but an act of *justice* toward you. For your satisfaction I subjoin a copy.

> I remain, dear sir, your friend,
> Timothy Pickering

P. S. Would it not be well for you to address a letter to the Secretary of War?

[COPY OF PICKERING'S LETTER
TO MR. JOHN CALHOUN]

Wenham Mass'tts, Dec. 31, 1819

Dear Sir,

You will not have forgotten my sentiments in regard to our military peace establishment, and therefore may not expect that I should take an interest to introduce any man into the army. Buy our army [illegible] vastly greater than has ever seemed to me necessary for a *peace* establishment, yet whatever force shall be [illegible] up, so far as individual citizens can be benefitted by the employment, the advantages should be apportioned among those of all the States, with an impartial hand. I entertain no doubt that such a distribution of offices, where there is equal merit, corresponds with your views and feelings. I therefore venture to recommend to your notice, Julius Catlin, a youth of sixteen years, the fifth of nine sons of my worthy friend Putnam Catlin, Esquire, of Pennsylvania. The father informs me that this son "has a strong bias for the army, with an ambition which will not fail (he thinks) of rendering himself useful to his country." If Revolutionary services in our war for Independence entitle to any preference, my friend Catlin may justly urge them. He served through that war. His father also, who lives with him, and whom he supports, was likewise engaged in that Service. Mr. Catlin is a native of Connecticut, but has lived in Pennsylvania above thirty years; during all which time I have been well acquainted with him.

The son I do not know; but the father is too judicious and too honest to propose for the son an employment uncongenial to his character, or in which there was not a well founded expectation of his public usefulness. Mr. Catlin is desirous that his son may be admitted to receive his military education at West Point. I add my request that you will place him on the list of candidates, and give him as early an entrance as shall be practicable.

With sincere respect and esteem,
I am dear Sir
your obed't Servant
Timothy Pickering

John Calhoun, Secretary of War

APPENDIX III

FROM THE *Rochester Daily Advertiser*, SEPTEMBER 22, 1828

OBITUARY

An Ill-fated Artist

Considerable excitement was produced here yesterday by the sudden death of a young gentleman named Julius Catlin, brother of the celebrated artist of that name.

He arrived here on Saturday from New York for the purpose of delivering to the Franklin Institute the portrait of the late lamented Clinton, painted by his brother for that Institution. On the following morning he proceeded to the lower falls of the Genesee (at Carthage) two miles north of this place, for the purpose of taking a sketch of the principal Cascade and the romantic scenery adjacent.

With the object probably of obtaining a full view of the Cataract, he descended the precipitous bank which is nearly 200 feet high, and after taking some sketches on the margin of the river, swam out to obtain a view from the center of the stream leaving his clothes and sketch-book on a rock. A person named Thomas Munn was fishing within a short distance (a rod or two) of Mr. Catlin, say's that he swam with much ease, that he was an expert swimmer, but that when a few moments in the water he suddenly shouted, "Help! for God's sake help," and stretching out his hand sunk to rise no more with life.

The clothes were taken to Judge Strong's. Munn, when interrogated, stated that Mr. Catlin had an elegant watch establishment, chain, seal, etc. That he (Munn) had on first seeing Mr. Catlin, asked him the time of day, to which Mr. Catlin replied, "Just twelve." Yet in examining his clothes neither watch, chain or seal were found, and no other money than a solitary cent in his pocket, Munn declaring he knew nothing of what became of them, although he admitted that he saw the watch establishment, and was told the time of day by the ill-fated Catlin before his melancholy end. It is not for us to attempt to reconcile circumstances so apparently contradictory.

The face of the deceased had some slight bruises, occasioned probably by rubbing on the bottom, and the body had somewhat the appearance of cramp spasms. Considerable part of yesterday was spent by many of our citizens in fatiguing search for the body. The inquest, after a protracted investigation, returned a verdict of death by drowning.

Mr. Catlin was educated mostly, we understand, at West Point, was an intelligent and accomplished gentleman, and proficient in the Arts in which his brother is such a distinguished master. His untimely fate, falling literally a martyr to his favorite study, in the very rigour of manhood, has created a deep sensation through the village.

APPENDIX IV

BRITISH REVIEWS OF GEORGE CATLIN'S *Letters and Notes on the Manners, Customs, and Condition of the North American Indian* (1841) [1]

Westminster Review: "This is a remarkable book, written by an extraordinary man. A work valuable in the highest degree for its novel and curious information about one of the most neglected and least understood branches of the human family. Mr. Catlin, without any pretension to talent in authorship, has yet produced a book which will live as a record when the efforts of men of much higher genius have been forgotten . . . ."

Dublin University Magazine: "Mr. Catlin's book is one of the most interesting which we have perused on the subject of the Indians, . . . and his faithful and accurate observations may be considered as the storehouse from whence future writers on such topics will extract their most authentic statements . . . ."

Literary Gazette, London: "Catlin's book on the North American Indians.—An unique work! A work of extraordinary interest and value. Mr. Catlin is *the* Historian of the Red Races of mankind; . . . We need not recommend it to the world, for it recommends itself, beyond our praise . . . ."

---

[1] As quoted in Catlin's *Eight Years of Travel and Residence in Europe* (2 vols.; London: published by the author, 1848), I, 53–58.

Art Union, London: ". . .The book is exceedingly simple in its style; it is the production of a man of benevolent mind, kindly affections, and sensitive heart, as well as of keen perceptions and sound judgment. . . . no library in the kingdom should be without a copy."

United Service Gazette, London: "Mr. Catlin is one of the most remarkable men of the age. Everyone who has visited his singularly interesting gallery at the Egyptian Hall, must have been struck by his remarkable intelligence on every subject connected with the North American Indians; but of its extent, as well as of his extraordinary enthusiasm and thirst for adventure, in which hardly any work is published that is not founded more or less on other volumes which have preceded it . . . it is refreshing to come across a book which, like the one before us, is equally novel in subject, manner, and execution, and which may be pronounced, without hyperbole, one of the most original productions which have issued from the press for many years."

APPENDIX V

Last Will and Testament of Putnam Catlin

Susquehanna County

By the tenor of these presents, I, Hiram Finch, Register for the probate of Wills and granting Letters [illegible] Administration in and for the County of Susquehanna in the Commonwealth of Pennsylvania——

Do make known with all men, That on the day of the [illegible] at Montrose, before me was proved, approved and [illegible] the last Will and Testament of Putnam Catlin, late of the township of Great Bend in the County of Susquehanna, aforesaid,—deceased. (A true copy whereof is to these presents annexed), having whilst he lived, and the time of his death, [illegible] goods, chattels, rights and credits, within the said Commonwealth, by reason whereof the approbation and intimation of the said last Will and Testament, and the committing the Administration of All and Singular, the goods, chattels, rights and credits, which were of the said deceased, and also the auditing the amounts, calculation and reckonings of the said Administration, and a final dismission from the same, to me are manifestly known to belong, and that Administration of All and Singular, the goods, chattels, rights and credits of the said deceased, in any way concerning his last Will & Testament was committed to Francis P. Catlin————in the said testament, named he—having first

434

been duly sworn, well and truly to administer the goods, chattels, rights and credits of the said deceased and make a true and perfect Inventory thereof, and exhibit the same into the Register's office at Montrose, on or before the twenty first day of May next, and to render a true and just calculation and reckoning of the said Administration on or before the twenty first day of April Anno Domini, one thousand eight hundred and forty three, or when thereunto lawfully required, and also, diligently and faithfully regard and well and truly comply with the provisions of the law relating to collateral Inheritances.—

In Testimony whereof, I have herewith set my hand and affixed the Seal of said office at Montrose this twenty first day of April—in the year of our Lord, one thousand eight hundred and forty-two.

Hiram Finch—Register

TESTAMENT AND LAST WILL OF PUTNAM CATLIN
DECEASED.

Copy

The last Will and Testament of Putnam Catlin of Great Bend Township in the County of Susquehanna, and State of Pennsylvania.——

I, Putnam Catlin, considering the uncertainty of this mortal life, and being of sound mind and memory, do make and publish this my last Will and Testament in manners following.—I will and direct that immediately after my decease, that one Inventory be made by my Executors herein mentioned, of all my Estate, real and personal (excepting wearing apparel and household furniture, which I bequeath to by beloved wife, Polly Catlin) being duly appraised and recorded by them. I will and direct also, that all just debts owing by me at the time of my death, together with my funeral expenses shall in the first place be fully made and paid.——

First. I give and bequeath unto my beloved wife Polly Catlin, (on condition of her release of dower) three hundred dollars for her im-

435

mediate expenses, in case she remains a widow. Also a milch cow for her use. Also the wearing apparel in the house, and the whole of the household furniture at her disposal.——

Item. I give and bequeath to my son Henry Catlin, three hundred dollars.—

Item. I give to my son George Catlin three hundred dollars.

Item. I give to my sons James and Richard Catlin, *each* three hundred dollars which they have recently received from me in Bonds and mortgages assigned to them with satisfaction.

Item. I give to my son Francis P. Catlin six hundred dollars in addition to Town lot recently given and Conveyed to him by myself, estimated at six hundred dollars.—

Item. I give to my daughter, Eliza Dart four hundred dollars.

Item. I give to my daughter Mary Hartshorn eight hundred dollars.

Item. I give and bequeath to the orphan children of my deceased son, Charles Catlin, namely Theodore B. Catlin, Theodosia Catlin and James Catlin jr. cash, the sum of one hundred dollars, which several sums of money above mentioned, I *will* and direct to be paid to the respective and beloved Legatees within one year after my decease.— And lastly, as to all the rest residue and remainder of my real and personal estate, after payment of my just debts, the cost of administration, and the several sums herein before mentioned, and a residue of my estate still left, I give and bequeath such residue to my seven beloved children herein before mentioned, Viz: Henry Catlin, George Catlin, James Catlin, Rich'd Catlin, Francis P. Catlin, Eliza Dart, and Mary Hartshorn, in proportion to their former sums.—

And I hereby appoint my son Francis P. Catlin and my esteemed friend Charles Dimon Esq'r, both of Great Bend, Penna, Executors of this my last Will and Testament, hereby revoking all former *Wills* by me made.

In Witness whereof, I have herewith set my hand and Seal this sixteenth day of September in the year of our Lord, One Thousand Eight hundred & forty-one.

Putnam Catlin   (Seal)

Signed, sealed and delivered by the above mentioned—Putnam Catlin to be his last Will and Testament in presence of us who at his request and in his presence . . . thereunto, the day & year last mentioned.

Wm Wales
Samuel Wales

Susquehanna County pr—

Hiram Finch, Register for the probate . . . Wills and granting Letters of Administration . . . and for the County aforesaid . . . is an . . . copy of the last Will and Testament of Putnam Catlin . . . proved and registered in the Register's office at Montrose, in and for the County aforesaid. In testimony whereof I have herewith . . . my hand and caused the Seal of the said office to be hereunto affixed at Montrose—the twenty first day of April, Anno Domini, 1842.

Hiram Finch, Reg'r.

APPENDIX VI

Extract from Daniel Webster's Senate
Speech, 1849[1]

Extract from the speech of the Honorable Daniel Webster, on a
motion in the Senate of the United States, for the purchase of
Catlin's Indian Collection, in 1849:

Mr. President—The Question is, Whether it does not become us,
as a useful thing, to possess in the United States this collection of
paintings &c, made amongst the Indian tribes? Whether it is not a
case for the exercise of large liberality—I will not say bounty, but
policy? These tribes, sir, that have preceded us, to whose lands we
have succeeded, and who have no written memorials of their laws,
their habits, and their manners, are all passing away to the world of
forgetfulness. Their likeness, manners, and customs are portrayed
with more accuracy and truth in this collection by Catlin than in all
the other drawings and representations on the face of the earth.
Somebody in this country ought to possess this collection—that is
my opinion; and I do not know how there is or where there is to be
found any society, or any individual, who or which can with so much
propriety possess himself or itself of it, as the Government of the

---

[1] As quoted in George Catlin's *Last Rambles Amongst the Indians of the Rocky
Mountains and the Andes* (New York: D. Appleton and Company, 1867), pp.
47–49.

438

United States. For my part, then, I do think that the preservation of 'Catlin's Indian Collection' in this country is an important public act. I think it properly belongs to those accumulations of historical matters respecting our predecessors on this continent, which is very proper for the Government of the United States to maintain. As I have said, this race is going into forgetfulness. They track the continuation of mankind in the present age, and call recollection back to them. And here they are better exhibited, in my judgment, better set forth and presented to the mind and the taste and the curiosity of mankind, than in all other collections in the world. I go for this as an American subject—as a thing belonging to us—to our history— to the history of a race whose lands we till, and over whose obscure graves and bones we trod, every day. I look upon it as a thing more appropriate for us than the ascertaining of the South Pole or anything that can be discovered in the Dead Sea or the River Jordan. These are the grounds, sir, upon which I propose to proceed, and I shall vote for the appropriation with great pleasure."

APPENDIX VII

GEORGE CATLIN'S REPORT OF JEFFERSON DAVIS'
SENATE ACTION ON THE CATLIN COLLECTION, 1849[1]

Mr. "Jefferson Davis," at that time (previous to the Rebellion),
a member of the Senate, before giving his vote, made, in a speech of
two newspaper columns in length, and now matter of record, the
most complimentary eulogy that has ever been passed on my works,
stating that I was "the only artist who ever had painted, or could
paint, an American Indian; that he had been a campaigner with me
for several months amongst the Osages, the Comanches, Pawnee
Picts, &c, whilst he was an officer in the 1st Regiment of mounted
Dragoons,—that he had sat by and seen me paint many of my
portraits from the life, and knew their accuracy, that the collection
was one of great interest and value to our country, and that it would
be a shame if it were sold in a foreign land." And yet, when the
stage of the voting showed that his vote was to turn the scale,
stated that, "from *principle*, he was bound to vote against the appropriation," which he did, and defeated the bill.

---

[1] As quoted in Catlin's *Last Rambles Amongst the Indians of the Rocky
Mountains and the Andes* (New York: D. Appleton and Company, 1867), pp.
50–51.

APPENDIX VIII

6 Waterloo Place Pall Mall
London, 4th April, 1852

Dear Sir,

I have long since intended to acknowledge my thankfulness for the kind and independent manner in which you advocated the motion for the purchase of my Indian Collection in the Senate, and hope it may be in my power personally to thank you for it at some time in my life.

An extract from your appropriate remarks I have had printed and circulated in this country, and the intelligent English people are all surprised that a Government so able as ours should hesitate to secure memorials so full and so peculiarly interesting to them.

I have held my Collection here at almost ruinous expense, in the confident hope that the Congress would make the appropriation for it, and I do not despair yet in that hope. Few people in the U. States know how my Collection looks now; the paintings, to the number of six hundred, all completed, and several collections which I have met in England added to it, at an expense of more than three thousand dollars, with the view to

---

[1] By courtesy of the New-York Historical Society.

restore them to the country to which they belong. So much I am doing for the history of our country, and I do think the government, from which I never yet have had a shilling, should call my collection home and pay me for my labours. I have devoted the best part of my life to it, and twenty five thousand, the expense of procuring it.

The latter part of my life in this country has been unprosperous, and besides afflictions of the most painful, protracted and expensive kinds in my family, I have been led into unfortunate speculations which have brought my affairs to a most trying and alarming state, and the heavy expenses of my Collection running on while I am struggling to keep it together for a place in the annals of our country.

I am now, my dear Sir, communicating to you what I would not tell to the world, nor would I ever trouble *you* or anybody on earth with my alarms if they were only for *my own liberty* or *my own property*, but for *a collection* such as I have made, unique in itself,—incapable of being reproduced, intended as a monument to a dying race, and a monument to myself. I cannot reserve the truth of my position from one so nobly advocating the preservation of my works. My liabilities here are such at present that I much fear I shall not be able to reach Washington this Session, as I had designated, and I actually tremble for the security of my works.

I am fighting at this moment with the most unfeeling wretches, which the civilized world, I have just learned, is made up of, to protect my Collection for my country. I don't know that you can appreciate the position I am in, and the feelings under which I am stung at this time, but I trust that you will excuse me for naming them (in confidence) to you.

If my Collection comes to the hammer it would not more than pay my debts,—and would inflict an indelible disgrace on our country in the estimation of English people. If it can get the approbation of Congress, it will have the benefit of my future in adding to its extent and interest, and produce something for the maintenance of my three little, now motherless, children.

I have sent today a circular to the members, praying for the last time that some efforts may be again made *without* delay—not to be too late.

I remain Dear Sir, with highest admiration,

Yours Sincerely
Geo. Catlin

APPENDIX IX

The 1850 census for Oregon Territory is the only one indexed. It is the first federal census (which goes by 10 years) which lists every member of a family by name. There were some earlier county censuses taken in Oregon, but they listed heads of families only, with the number of other members . . . . The information as given in the 1850 census for Clackamas County, Oregon Territory, is as follows:

House No. 210: Gideon Millard, age 45, born New York
Elizabeth Millard, age 34, born Ky.
Wm. T. Lagg, 16, born Missouri
Elizabeth A. Dart, 10, born Illinois
Aaron H. Lance, age 6, born Iowa
Owen A. Lance, age 4, born Iowa
Squire B. Millard, 1 year, born Oregon Ter.

It appears Elizabeth was living with the Millard family and two other children they were caring for.

House No. 314: E. Hamelton, age 45, lawyer, born Va.
Catherine Hamelton, age 40, born Pa.
St. Genevive Hamelton, age 19, F, born Ohio
Catherine Cox, age 19, born Ireland
Guadalupe Delacrux, age 13, M, born Mexico
Anson Dart, age 50, Superintendent of Indian Affairs, born Vermont.

---

[1] From a letter to the author from the Oregon Historical Society.

APPENDIX X

SUBSCRIPTION BOOK AND PROSPECTUS
FOR GEORGE CATLIN'S *The North Americans,* 1869

The subscription book is a black leather-covered scrapbook, with "*The North Americans*" printed in gold on the cover. Inside the book, in Catlin's clear, graceful calligraphy, is his "Prospectus," and many pages for the needed signatures:

THE

NORTH AMERICANS

IN THE

MIDDLE OF THE NINETEENTH CENTURY

FAST PASSING TO EXTINCTION,

AND LEAVING NO MONUMENTS OF THEIR OWN

BEHIND THEM.

by Geo. Catlin

The author designs publishing under the above title the results of 12 years labour amongst the Indian tribes of North America, the works to contain the illustrations on the accompanying screen, which will be published in the same form and of the same size as now seen, and executed in the best style of Modern Art; and facing each plate, and intervening, letter-press in bold types, fully explaining the illustrations, and all the modes practiced by the North American Tribes.

The publication of this work which will contain the portraits and customs of nearly every tribe (and remnant of tribes) now existing in North America, has been the ultimate ambition of the Author during a long and laborious life in which he has visited these tribes without Government or individual aid, and all his earthly means exhausted, and his life nearly so, he submits his designs and plan of publication to the Government, the Institutions and individuals of his Country, in the hope and confident belief that subscriptions will be tender and sufficient to authorize him to assume the expenses of the publication, the illustrations and text for which are now in readiness, and arrangements made for its rapid production, conditionally.

The full-length portraits, 377 in number, reduced from his original oil paintings by a photographic lens (to add to their interest), have been grouped into families and tribes, exhibiting every mode of dress worn by the North American Indians, and in their hands, every variety of weapons of war and of the chase, their pipes & other manufactures; and in the groups, their games, Religious Ceremonies, hunting scenes, &c, in which more than five thousand full-length figures are in action.

In addition to the portraits formerly exhibited in Washington, N. York, London and Paris, there are added, as seen in the designs exhibited, 120 full length portraits made amongst the tribes in & west of the Rocky Mountains, both in British and U. States Territory, during the author's last voyages in 1852 to 1857.

Not to make the price of this complete work too great for its successful circulation, it is intended to render the illustrations in outlines, as seen in the designs on the screen, leaving the colouring to be given in the descriptive text, in which will be found the name of each individual in his native language, and its translation into English; and every article of costume & ornament, as well as weapons, will be minutely explained.

In the front of the work will be a map of the Indian localities in

446

North America, and a full Glossary of all the Indian terms and phrases used in the descriptions of costumes and customs.

The work will be delivered to subscribers complete in two volumes, of the size and form of the model (rough) volume lying on the table, handsomely bound and lettered, and susceptible of any mode of further ornamentation which the purchaser may fancy; and the paper, both for plates and text, of the usual quality used in similar large and elegant works.

The cost of an Edition of 400 copies, besides the expenses attending their sale and distribution, it is estimated will be 20,000 dollars, and the subscription price £20 per copy, payable on the delivery of the work complete; and my Brother Francis P. Catlin, who has charge of the designs and of this prospectus, is duly authorized to solicit subscriptions, (and Donations, if any should be kindly made), in support of the heavy outlays necessary for so expensive a publication; and from him, at the time of subscribing, each subscriber will receive a printed list of all the illustrations engaged to be delivered in the work.

(signed) The Author
George Catlin

[Following the Prospectus comes a page headed]

DONATIONS*

* If the Government of the U. States, or State Governments, Institutions, or Individuals should feel disposed to subscribe in aid of the publication, their subscriptions will be entered only as *guarantees*, to be paid, like the subscriptions for the work, when the work is completed.

(signed) The Author.

[The page is blank.

Another page is headed "Subscriptions," and the following names appear:]

H. F. Sanford, Minister Resident Brussels. *One copy*

His Majesty the King of Prussia, (by letter to Mr. Catlin, of Baron d' Olfens, Director for the Royal Museum, Berlin).

D. S. Gregory—Jersey City. *One copy*

John Armstrong. Presd't Hudson Co. Nt. Bk. Jersey City. 101 Madison Ave., New York. *One copy*

G. E. Wynants, 464 West 23rd. New York City

W. H. Gregory, Jersey City

George B. Edwards, Bergen, N. J. *One copy*

J. Panemier, Jersey City. *One copy*

Chas. E. Gregory, *One copy*

Wm. H. Horton, Jersey City, *One copy*

Abbe' Brasseur-de Bourbourg, Paris. *One copy*

Ezra Cornell, Ithaca, N. Y. *Two copies at $100 each*

Cornell University, Ithaca N. Y. *One copy at $100*

Cornell Library Association, *One copy at $100*

F. O. Matthiessen, J. City. *One copy—$100*

J. H. Santier. N. Y. *One copy $100*

W. A. Wrickers, Staten Island. *One copy*

Frank D. Philes, Owego, N. Y. *One copy*

Charles M. Catlin, 45 South St. New York. *One copy*

Mrs. Arm. S. Stephens, St. Cloud Hotel, New York. *One copy*

Geo. Haseltine, 12, Southampton Buildings, London. *One copy* [This was all. Three more pages for signatures were left blank.]

APPENDIX XI

GEORGE CATLIN TO THE PRESIDENT OF THE
NEW-YORK HISTORICAL SOCIETY[1]

8 Rue de Brabant
Bruxelles, 2nd March 1870

Sir,

As I promised a few days since, I will now endeavour to give you a statement in answer to the very friendly enquiries you made of my Brother, relative to the possible appropriation of my Indian collection for your noble institution.

My works are all contained in two collections my *old* (or first) *collection*, (which was exhibited in N. York, in Washington, in London and in Paris, all canvass paintings), and my Cartoon collection, also painted in oil colours, but on cartoons manufactured for the purpose.

The two collections, about equal in numbers, contain over twelve hundred paintings, and in addition to the portraits, over twenty thousand full length figures in action illustrating the games and other customs of the Indians.

The Cartoon collection contains a great proportion (but not all) of the portraits of the old collection, grouped into families

---

[1] By courtesy of the New-York Historical Society.

449

and tribes, to add to their interest, and painted full length, showing their whole costume to their feet.

This I had anticipated from the very commencement of my labours; and with that in view, had, in nearly every instance, after painting the bust portrait life size, made a sketch of the figure and costume from head to foot from the life; and with these, and the bust portraits reduced by a photographic lens, I had been several years employed in London, (before my London disasters commenced) in grouping and copying my portraits as they now are, on the cartoons, and these being in my private painting room in another part of the city enabled me to remove them to Paris, and in my subsequent campaigns from 1852 to 1860, in South America and on the Pacific Coast of North America, I carried cartoons of the same size which were more portable than canvass, and all my portraits, landscapes and other paintings in those voyages were painted from nature, as they now are, on cartoons. These cartoons altogether, constituting my "Cartoon Collection" are over six hundred, and all precisely of one size, two and one-half by two feet, designed to make a neat, handy and agreeable exhibition.

If the two Collections were put together into one, it would contain the greater portion of the portraits of the Indians east of the Rocky Mountains *twice* painted, but certainly all the better for that; for in the copies where they are grouped three, four, or five on a cartoon, and at full length, they get a new interest by showing the whole costume and the handling of all their weapons, pipes, etc.

I feel therefore, a decided reluctance to sever the two Collections, if they can be kept together.

As works of art, these Cartoon paintings (studied and elaborated infinitely more than the first Collection, both in the portraits, landscapes and custom) will do me vastly more credit than the works in the old Collection. The two collections might possibly be separated; but on no account, nor for any consideration, would I be willing to sever the Cartoon collection. It has been the ambition of my life, and may be said, (as it has been here called) the "poetry" of my works.

I should prefer to see both collections (my whole works) perpetuated in one Hall, and certainly should prefer the conditions which you so kindly named to my Brother before any other that could be offered to me in the world. Such a position in the city of N. York, in a hall to be shaped and lighted as I may direct, and with my privilege of finishing and arranging them therein, for perpetuity.

In London my collection attracted great crowds and gained me much applause, and money also; but unfortunate speculations which I was enticed into ultimately brought liens on my collection which separated me from it, and a Mr. Joseph Harrison of Philadelphia paid off the liens, and shipped it to Philadelphia. I saw the impossibility of my redeeming it, and started on my South American voyage. The advances which he made on it, the shipment of it to America, the interest for seventeen years, and warehousing will amount to something like forty thousand dollars.

When opened, the Indian drapes, &c., so far as they were covered with fur or hair, will undoubtedly be pillaged by moths; but the paintings and Indian manufactures, such as pipes, weapons, &c., will be found unchanged. And as for the drapes in furs and hair, they are of little account, for in any collection or museum they fall to pieces in a very little time, and become a nuisance.

Now as to the Cartoon collection, (which is all completed, and for which I am just now getting the catalogue printed and screens to uphold the whole, and an expensive Hall engaged for its approaching Exhibition in this city), I have an offer of eight thousand pounds (about forty thousand dollars), for which I can take at any moment, by an English nobleman who came from Paris a few weeks since, expressly to see it, and spent two entire days looking it over. But where to go? Into the perpetual imprisonment of a nobleman's mansion, to be seen by side lights only, and to be visited perhaps by fifty Americans in fifty years!

Now the running exhibition of it, which I have been designing to make for a year or two, to Artists—to men of Science and Historians (and perhaps without other profit) I shall value much more than the eight thousand pounds. And if an arrangement be consummated with your noble Institution for it, you will certainly not deny me that privilege whilst your building is being prepared to receive it.

When dollars were much more valuable than they now are, a Committee of Congress reported that sixty five thousand dollars was a moderate price for the old collection; and after the above explanations, I believe you will justify me for the following statement of the terms on which I would part with one or both of the collections; to wit—for the old collection, entire—paintings and Indian manufactures, &c., and one year of my exclusive labour which I would give in finishing them up and arranging them for perpetuity, the sum of one hundred thousand dollars. Or, for the two collections, complete, arranged and catalogued, the sum of one hundred and twenty thousand dollars. And in which event, allowing me to exhibit in several principal cities of the Continent the Cartoon collection (though affianced), and to be paid for when the whole should be entirely finished arranged in the Hall of the Historical Society's buildings.

My life has been one of toil and exposure, and of privations in making these collections, and in case of the completion of the above arrangements, the small remainder of it will be given to extend, if possible, and increase the interest and value of this, my self-raised Monument.

I know of nothing more to add at this moment, and will await any suggestions you make make.

Very Respectfully Yours, &c.

Geo. Catlin

In addition to the collections already named, I have twenty seven oil canvass paintings illustrating the voyages of discovery by Lasalle and Father Hennepin, and of the same size exactly as the Cartoons, which, from a desire to see all of my works perpetuated together under the protection of so honourable a Society, I would add, as forming a part of the Cartoon collection, and to be included in the price above mentioned, of one hundred and twenty thousand dollars for the whole collection, complete.

These twenty seven paintings, containing over four thousand figures, cost me one year's labour in Paris during the reign of Louis Philippe. He said to me one day while in my Exhibition: "Mr. Catlin, you are the only man on earth to illustrate the discoveries of Lasalle, which I want done for the Marine Gallery at Versailles." I told him that I had visited every tribe of Indians that Lasalle saw, and that I could show him landscape views of every place that Lasalle had visited. He sent for me the next day, and I found him with "Lasalle's Voyages" in his hand, with many leaves turned down, and we soon, together, decided on the twenty seven points to be illustrated and the size of the paintings to be made. He said: "As soon as they are done, send them in a case to Mons. de Cailleux, Director of the Louvre, and I will meet you there and examine them. Unluckily for me, they were sent to the Louvre only three days before the Revolution broke out, so that the King never saw them, and it was five years before I could learn anything of them, and then I got them only at some expense, and they have been boxed up ever since.

These paintings, which are French as well as American, history, I have valued at least at three thousand dollars, and I should be proud to show them in Paris in my Cartoon collection, and enabled to write on them "Sold to the New York Historical Society."

I send today to my Brother a descriptive catalogue of them, by which you can form some idea of them. I forgot to say in my estimates given above that if my Cartoon collection alone (which itself would require 100 by 30 or 40 feet) should be preferred, its price including the Lasalle (27) paintings would be sixty thousand dollars.

G. C.

When I spoke of *twenty thousand* full length figures above, I should have said the *Cartoon collection* alone (including the Lasalle paintings) contains that number.

G. C.

INDEX

INDEX

Albany, N. Y., 32, 53, 87, 90–91, 99, 103, 108, 110, 114, 160, 162, 163
Alzar, Jose, 328
American Fur Company, 48, 57, 59, 61, 123, 147
Arkansas River, 71
Arkansas Territory, 71–75
Art Union, The, 156 n.
Assinaboin Indians, 57, 61

Baltimore, Md., 133 n.
Barstow, Darwina. *See* Catlin, Darwina Barstow
Beall, Mr., 177, 186, 190, 200, 201, 203, 227, 229, 230, 263
Blackfoot Indians, 60, 61, 62
Black Hawk (Sauk chief), 47, 65
Bodmer, Charles, 64, 150
Bolla, Caesar, 327
Boston, Mass., 133 n., 136, 137, 138–140, 250
Botocudo Indians, 328
Bradley, Abra, 24–26
Brazil, 319, 356, 359
Breath of Life, The, 343
British Museum, 382
Brooklyn, Ala., 187, 211, 238, 239
Brooklyn, Penn. *See* Hopbottom, Penn.
Brussels, Belgium, viii, 306, 329, 343–408
Buenos Aires, Argentina, 328, 329
Buffalo, N. Y., viii, 31, 54, 67, 87, 90–98 *passim,* 164, 169
Burr, Amanda. *See* Catlin, Amanda Burr

Cantonment Leavenworth, Mo., 48
Cass, Lewis, 72
Catlin, Abigail Sayre (James' wife), 27, 79, 115, 124, 138–140, 160, 164, 179, 182, 195, 330 n.
Catlin, Amanda Burr (Charles' wife), 10, 15, 17, 18, 45, 134
Catlin, Anna (James' daughter), 330, 331, 334, 339
Catlin, Burr. *See* Catlin, Theodore
Catlin, Caroline (Carry; James' daughter), 330, 331, 334
Catlin, Charles, 8, 10, 13–15, 17–21, 33, 43, 45, 51, 54, 65, 69
    Letters by, 14–15, 17–18, 20–21
Catlin, Charles (Francis' son), 284, 292, 297, 320, 339, 354, 384
Catlin, Clara, 8, 9, 88
Catlin, Clara (Francis' daughter), 287, 320
Catlin, Clara (George's daughter), 154, 163, 172, 195, 210, 214, 318, 409, 411–412
Catlin, Clara Gregory (George's wife), 5 n., 32, 34, 43, 46, 49, 50, 53, 75, 76, 78, 81, 82, 84, 87, 89–92, 94, 96, 99, 102, 107, 109, 112, 113, 116, 124, 130, 134, 136–141, 145, 148, 154, 156, 158–161, 163, 166, 170–172, 175, 183–185, 192, 195–197, 207–210, 214, 215, 217–223 *passim,* 233, 243–244, 246, 248–249, 255–261, 264–269, 273, 278, 279, 280, 287 n., 289–290, 295–309, 316, 345
    Letters by (to Abigail), 138–140; (Polly), 195–197, 207–210, 223, 290

Catlin, Clara Gregory (*Continued*)
Letters to (from Putnam), 159–161;
(Eliza), 183–185, 248–249, 256–
258, 296–298, 303–304; (Mary
Dart), 258–259, 267–269, 298;
(George Dart), 259–260, 264–265;
(Putnam Dart), 260, 265–267

Catlin, Darwina Barstow (Richard's wife),
69, 88, 90, 95, 103, 111, 113, 115, 117,
137, 195, 209, 211, 215, 219, 220, 223,
224, 226, 227, 238, 239, 248, 304, 309,
324, 329, 333–335 *passim*, 400

Catlin, Eli, 4 n., 5, 10, 25, 32, 42

Catlin, Elizabeth. *See* Dart, Elizabeth Catlin

Catlin, Elizabeth (George's daughter), 90 n.,
124, 138, 163, 172, 195, 210, 213–214,
221, 260–261, 265, 267, 278, 318, 409,
411–412

Catlin, Elizabeth DuBois (Francis' wife),
161, 164, 165, 178, 187 n., 198, 199, 201,
202, 224, 226–229, 235, 237–242 *passim*,
269, 274, 275, 277, 281, 282, 287, 291,
297, 298, 309, 320–321

Catlin, Francis Putnam, viii, ix, 10, 27, 34,
42, 49, 51, 52, 66, 67–70, 75, 77–81,
83 n., 87–146 *passim*, 158–254 *passim*,
257, 263, 268, 269–299 *passim*, 307–309,
312, 320–324, 326, 330–340, 345–404,
409, 413
Letters to (from Putnam), 67–69, 89–
90, 94–97, 98–99, 103–105, 107–
113, 117–118, 121–122, 125–131,
133–135, 137–138, 140, 143–146;
(Polly), 77–80, 87–89, 97–98, 113–
116, 124, 131, 135–136, 141, 290–
293; (Eliza), 80–81, 132–133, 162,
242, 281–284, 308–309, 322–324,
330–336, 338–340; (George), 90–
91, 102–103, 279–280, 288–289,
345–347, 350–353, 376–400, 402–
403; (Anson Dart), 203–204, 276–
277, 284–286; (Putnam Dart), 204–
205, 230; (Burr), 206–207;
(George Dart), 229–230, 286–287;
(Richard), 238–240; (Henry),
246–248, 249–254, 270–272, 294–
295, 337–338; (Mary), 293–294

Catlin, Frank (Francis' son), 320, 330,
339 n.

Catlin, Fred (Francis' son), 320, 330, 354

Catlin, George, vii–xi, xv, 3–415 *passim*
Letters by (to Francis), 90–91, 92–93,
102–103, 279–280, 288–289, 345–
347, 350–353, 376–400, 402–403;
(Putnam), 154–155, 156–159, 170–
176, 192–195, 197–198, 211–215,
216–217, 221–224, 233–238, 243–
245; (Richard), 217–218; (Polly),
278–279; (Burr), 348–350; (To
N. Y. Historical Soc.), 404–408

Catlin, George (Francis' son), 187, 202,
205, 238, 241, 242

Catlin, George (George's son), 262, 290,
309, 311, 345

Catlin, Henry, 8, 14, 16, 19, 27, 33, 45, 51,
54, 66, 67–69, 79, 82, 83 n., 87, 91–95,
99, 104, 105, 107, 110, 116, 117, 125,
130, 144, 148, 165, 187, 209, 215, 217,
219, 243, 245–254, 270–272, 286, 287 n.,
294–295, 308, 324, 325, 329, 332, 335,
336–340, 346
Letters by (to Francis), 246–248, 249–
254, 270–272, 294–295, 337–338

Catlin, Henry (Henry's son), 213, 215, 295

Catlin, James, x, 8, 16, 21, 27, 33, 42, 45,
51, 52 n., 54, 67, 69, 76, 78–79, 80, 88, 91,
99 n., 103, 104, 106–108, 110, 113, 115,
117, 124, 125, 128, 134, 137, 140, 142–
143, 145, 166, 178, 182, 187, 209, 211,
239, 240, 242, 291, 309 n., 330 n.

Catlin, James (Charles' son), 134, 136, 137

Catlin, John, 10, 27, 42, 51, 54, 69–70, 80,
144

Catlin, Juliet, 8

Catlin, Julius, x, 9, 21–22, 31–32, 34–37,
43, 68

Catlin, Julius (Putnam's cousin), 115

Catlin, Lynde, 9, 27–29

Catlin, Lynde (Putnam's uncle), 24, 25

Catlin, Mary. *See* Hartshorn, Mary Catlin

Catlin, Mary Grubb (Henry's wife), 27, 66,
68, 83 n.

Catlin, Mary Weed Tolbert (Francis' second
wife), 331, 336, 338, 339

Catlin, Polly, viii, 7–10, 33, 49, 66–68, 77–80, 87–89, 91, 96–98, 111, 113–116, 121, 124, 126, 128–141 *passim*, 159, 178, 181, 185, 192, 194, 199, 202, 212, 214, 224, 226, 235, 246–252 *passim*, 268–270, 272, 273–280, 282, 283, 287–298, 303, 304
    Letters by (to Francis), 77–80, 87–89, 97–98, 113–116, 124, 131, 135–136, 141, 290–293
    Letters to (from Eliza), 273–276; (George), 278–279; (Clara), 290
Catlin, Putnam, viii, ix, x, 3–55, 65–69, 75–248 *passim*, 269–270, 278–280
    Letters by (to George), 15–17, 19–20, 27–29, 32–34, 44–46, 50–51, 52–54, 75–77, 82–84, 163–170, 178–182, 185–188, 201–202, 219–221, 224–226; (A. Bradley), 24–26; (Francis), 67–69, 89–90, 94–99, 103–105, 107–113, 117–118, 121–122, 125–130, 133–138, 140, 143–146; (James), 142–143; (Clara), 159–161
    Letters to (from George), 154–159, 170–176, 192–195, 197–198, 216–217, 221–223, 233–238, 243–245; (Clara), 195–197, 207–210, 223
Catlin, Richard, 9, 27, 42, 51, 52, 54, 68, 69, 80, 88, 98 n., 103–121 *passim*, 134, 137, 140, 145, 166, 182, 209, 211–227 *passim*, 238–240, 248, 282, 283, 291, 304, 309, 324, 325, 329, 331–353 *passim*, 376–379, 382, 401, 403, 408, 413
Catlin, Sally, 9
Catlin, Theodore (Burr; Charles' son), 18, 114, 125, 134–141 *passim*, 149, 158, 159, 166, 172, 174, 182, 205–209, 215, 267, 268, 335, 339, 345–353 *passim*, 375
Catlin, Theodosia (Charles' daughter), 114, 136, 141, 166, 182, 207, 209, 244, 267, 291, 304
Catlin, Victoria Louise (George's daughter), 216 n., 255, 318, 409, 411–412
Catlin, William (Henry's son), 131, 134, 136, 137, 250, 253, 295, 337
Catlin, William Weed (Francis' son), 336, 338

Catlinite. *See* Pipestone Quarry, Red
Catlin's North American Indian Portfolio, 262, 299, 305
Chaco Indians, 328
Chadwich, Joe, 72, 74
Charleston, S. C., 125
Chittenden, Hiram Martin, 58, 65–66
Chouteau, Pierre, 48, 57, 59
Cincinnati, Ohio, 55
Clark, Sally, 136, 138, 141
Clark, General William, 46–49, 55, 57, 63, 119
Clayton, Senator J. M., 310
Clinton, Governor De Witt, 36
Clinton Hall, N. Y., 121, 122
Comanche Indians, 71–74
Congress, U. S., xvii, 126, 130, 133, 146–148, 177, 220, 288, 310–312, 314–317, 321, 324, 325, 333, 344, 347, 349, 376, 378, 380–381, 384, 395, 397, 410–411
Cornell, Ezra, 388, 390–392, 394
Coteau Des Prairies, Wis., 100–101
Crow Indians, 56 n., 60–62

Dart, Anna C. Tichenor (George's wife), 330 n.
Dart, Anson, xviii, 27, 45, 50, 51, 54, 69, 75, 78, 80–82, 88, 95, 105, 107, 110, 127, 131, 132, 137, 138, 141, 145, 160, 162–205 *passim*, 208, 219, 226–230, 239, 240–242, 256–257, 260, 263–265, 272–277, 282–286, 288, 290, 292, 296, 297, 307, 308, 321–326, 333–334, 336, 338, 339, 340
    Letters by (to Francis), 203–204, 276–277, 284–286; (George), 263–264
Dart, Charles (Anson's son), 164, 169, 185, 241, 242, 257, 304, 324, 326, 329, 330–333, 336
Dart, Elizabeth (Anson's daughter), 114, 164, 169, 185, 241, 257, 269, 281, 296–297, 323, 333
Dart, Elizabeth A. (Anson's daughter), 325
Dart, Elizabeth Catlin (Eliza; Anson's wife), xviii, 8, 17, 27, 33, 50, 75, 80–81, 91, 97, 105, 107, 110, 114, 116, 118, 131–133, 136, 139, 153, 162, 164–208 *passim*, 219, 224–230, 239–243, 248–249,

Dart, Elizabeth Catlin (*Continued*)
256–258, 263, 268–284 *passim*, 287 n.,
292–313, 322–326, 329–340
Letters by (to Francis), 80–81, 132–
133, 162, 242, 281–284, 308–309,
322–324, 330–336, 338–340;
(Clara), 183–185, 256–258, 296–
298, 303–304; (Elizabeth Catlin),
226–228; (Polly), 273–276
Dart, George (Anson's son), 103, 131, 132,
164, 169, 186, 191, 201, 205, 229–230,
256, 257, 259–260, 264–265, 276, 282,
283, 286–287, 296, 324, 330, 332, 333,
334, 336–338
Dart, Mary (Anson's daughter), 164, 185,
187, 228–229, 241, 256–259, 265,
267–269, 273, 274, 277, 281, 296–297,
298, 323 n., 325, 326, 329, 330, 332–333,
338–339
Dart, Olivet, 227, 230
Dart, Putnam (Anson's son), 68, 76, 132,
164, 169, 186, 200, 201, 204–205, 230,
256, 257, 260, 265–267, 273, 274, 276,
281, 282, 286, 296, 303, 309, 322–323,
324, 332, 334, 336, 338
Dart, Richard (Anson's son), 105, 132, 164,
169, 185, 189–192, 228, 241, 257, 260,
265, 266, 281, 282, 286, 287 n., 297, 307,
324–325, 334, 338, 340
Dartford, Wis., 307–309, 323–340
Davis, Jefferson, 314 n., 315
Delaware Indians, 48
Delta, N. Y., 69, 70, 75, 77, 80, 89, 91, 95,
97, 103, 106, 114, 132, 137, 140, 141,
202, 270, 283, 287, 290–292
DeVoto, Bernard, x, xi, xv, 61, 122
Dimon, Charles, 270, 278, 280
Dodge, Henry, 72–74, 165, 177
Donaldson, Thomas, vii, 5 n., 9, 21 n., 22–
23, 31, 43 n., 55, 150, 121 n., 408 n., 411
Dragoons, U. S., xvii, 72–75
DuBois, Elizabeth. *See* Catlin, Elizabeth
DuBois
DuBois, Joseph, 106–107, 108, 110–115
passim, 128, 131, 136, 140, 161, 287
DuBois, Nicholas, 287, 296, 324, 354

Easton, Penn., 34, 35

Egyptian Hall, London, 153, 155, 157, 171,
196, 254, 261–262, 300
*Eight Years of Travel and Residence in
Europe*, 313

Falls of St. Anthony, Minn., 81, 100
Faneuil Hall, Boston, 137, 139
Farnham, Thomas, 61
Flathead Indians, 57
Fort Cass, 61
Fort Clark, 63
Fort Crawford, 47–48
Fort Gibson, 71, 72, 74, 75
Fort Laramie, 55
Fort McKenzie, 61
Fort Pierre, 58–60
Fort Snelling, 81, 82, 100, 101
Fort Union, xvii, 57, 60–63
Fox Indians, 47, 48
Franklin Institute of Rochester, N. Y., 36

Gazette, United States, 147 n.–148 n.
George Catlin Indian Gallery, Annual Report of. *See* Donaldson, Thomas
Goodrich, Mr., 348, 351, 353, 356, 359,
361, 364
Great Bend, Penn., 11 n., 49–54, 66–69,
75–80, 82–84, 87–90, 93, 96–99, 106,
110, 115–116, 121, 129–131, 135, 137,
143 n., 146, 158, 161, 163, 167, 178, 183,
212, 214–215, 219, 221, 224, 236, 242,
250, 268–270, 281, 287, 288–291, 320,
354, 384
Green Bay, Wis., 82, 100, 105, 160, 164,
166, 169, 177, 186, 187, 188, 190, 199,
200, 257
Green Lake, Wis., 177, 179, 181, 186–192,
198–205, 219, 224–230, 240–242, 256–
261, 264–269, 270, 273–277, 281–287,
295–298, 303–304
Greenwood Cemetery, Brooklyn, 411
Gregory, Clara. *See* Catlin, Clara Gregory
Gregory, Dudley, 32, 43 n., 67 n., 95, 103,
106, 107, 110, 130, 159, 207, 211, 214,
223, 225, 234, 263, 318, 377, 381, 386,
387, 395, 399

Grubb, Mary. *See* Catlin, Mary Grubb

Haberly, Loyd, xv, 13
Harrisburg, N. Y., 45
Harrison, Joseph, 318–319, 369, 404, 405, 406–407, 412
Hartshorn, Asa, 50, 54, 69, 70, 75, 107, 127, 132, 162, 163, 165, 166, 169, 170, 178, 179, 180, 202, 219, 272–273, 287, 291, 292, 297
Hartshorn, Mary Catlin, 9, 27, 75, 80, 107, 114, 118, 132, 162, 165, 169, 195, 219, 267, 270, 272–273, 280, 282, 283, 290, 292–294, 297, 309 n.
Henry, Joseph, 410, 412
Hopbottom, Penn., 10, 11, 51, 130, 144, 168 n., 180
Hudson, Wis., 330, 335, 337, 338, 385, 387
Humboldt, Baron Alexander von, 305, 327, 343–344, 345

Indian Collection (Gallery), ix, xvi–xviii, 122–123, 125–127, 129–137 *passim*, 145–149, 155–157, 167, 170, 173, 175, 180, 184, 193, 194 n., 196, 206, 207, 225, 254, 256, 261, 305, 306, 309–319 *passim*, 344–353 *passim*, 357, 358, 370–371, 380, 383, 396–397, 401, 402, 404
Iowa Indians, 47, 48, 58, 299–300, 305

Jackson, President Andrew, 104
Jefferson Barracks, Mo., 65
Jersey City, N.J., 130, 263, 411
Johnson, Mr., 323, 324, 332

Kansas Indians, 58
Keene, Augustus, 323 n., 336
Keene, E. A., 332
Keene, James, 322
Kee-o-Kuk (Sauk chief), 47, 65, 125 n.
Kickapoo Indians, 48
Kidder, Rev. Samuel T., 177 n.
Kiowa Indians, 71, 74
Kipp, James, 63, 64, 123

Lane, Senator, 325, 333
La Salle paintings, 311, 312, 370, 399, 400, 401

Last Rambles Amongst the Indians of the Rocky Mountains and the Andes, 343, 346, 352
LeRoy, Pete, 189, 191, 199, 200, 260
Letters and Notes on the Manners, Customs, and Condition of the North American Indians, 209–210, 212, 213, 215, 217, 221–223, 234, 236, 313
Life Amongst the Indians, 343, 346, 352
Litchfield, Conn., 3, 4, 6, 12
Litchfield Law School, 14, 16, 19, 20
Liverpool, Eng., 245, 254–256, 263, 354
Lockport, N. Y., 33, 45, 51, 54, 66, 68, 91, 93, 95, 99, 104, 127, 137, 209, 246, 249–254, 270–272, 294
London, Eng., xvi, xvii, 3, 81 n., 127, 148, 149, 153–159, 170–176, 180, 184, 192–198, 206–226, 233–238, 243–245, 256, 261–262, 279, 288–290, 299–300, 305, 310, 311, 312–318, 327, 345, 386, 406
London Quarterly Review, The, 156 n.
Louis Philippe, King of France, 305, 306, 309, 311–312
Louvre, 306

McCracken, Harold, xv, 55, 149
McKenzie, Kenneth, 48, 61
Manchester, Eng., 256, 261, 278–279
Mandan Indians, 48, 49, 61, 63–64, 123, 344, 357
Maximilian, Prince of Wied-Neuwied, 48, 58, 61, 64, 150, 345, 378
Melody, G. H. C., 299–300, 305
Menomonee Indians, 177, 189
Miller, Alfred Jacob, 150
Milwaukee, Wis., 322–323
Miner, Mr., 24, 25
Minnetaree Indians, 61
Mississippi River, 47, 81–82, 101, 179
Missouri Indians, 47
Missouri River, xvii, 47, 48, 49, 56 n., 57–60, 62, 63, 65, 101, 150
Montrose, Penn., 10, 11–13, 15–18, 24–26, 27–29, 32–34, 43, 76, 114, 144, 160, 166, 180, 182, 209
Moore, George, 408
Morgan, Dale L., 55–56

Morristown, Penn., 35–36
Murray, Charles Augustus, 81 n., 153–154, 155, 158, 174, 206, 209, 234, 313

Naya Indians, 328
New Brenville, N. Y., 69
New Orleans, La., 79, 143
New York City, N. Y., xvi, 27, 32, 35, 41, 52, 99, 102, 105, 106, 107–114, 121–129, 133, 136, 142, 148, 165, 187, 219, 220, 288, 322, 331, 354, 376, 409–410, 412
New-York Historical Society, 396–397, 398, 400, 402, 403, 404–408
Niagara Falls, N. Y., 34, 127, 294, 295
North American Indian, Letters and Notes on the. See Letters and Notes on the Manners, Customs, and Condition of the

O'Fallon, Major Benjamin, 48
Ojibway Indians, 61, 81, 82, 261–262, 306, 307
O-Kee-pa ceremony, 64, 123, 344
O-Kee-pa: A Religious Ceremony, 344–345, 378, 391
Omaha Indians, 55, 58
Ona-qua-gua Valley, N. Y., 8–9
Oneida Indians, 9
Oregon Territory, 321, 324, 325
Osage Indians, 72
Osceola (Seminole chief), 125, 127
Otoe Indians, 58
Overton, Edward, 16, 18

Paraguay River, South America, 328
Paris, France, 300, 305–313, 316, 318–319, 329
Patterson, N. J., 332–333, 339
Pawnee Pict Indians, 55, 71, 72, 74
Payagua Indians, 328
Pearce, Mr., 316–317
Pensacola, Fla., 67, 70, 76, 78–79, 89, 91, 95, 99 n., 103, 105–108, 110, 111–115, 128, 129, 131, 137–140, 166, 178, 211, 212, 219, 222, 239, 240
Philadelphia, Penn., ix, 23, 49, 110, 123, 124, 129, 133, 136, 137, 140, 141, 142, 144, 145, 219, 318, 319, 369, 405, 406

Phillipps, Sir Thomas, 314
Pickering, Colonel Timothy, 7, 22
Pipestone Quarry, Red, Wis., xvii, 91, 100–101
Pittsburgh, Penn., 87
Platte River, 55
Ponca Indians, 58
Portfolio. See Catlin's North American Indian Portfolio
Prairie du Chien, Wis., xvii, 47, 92–93, 177

Rankin, Arthur, 261–262, 299
Red Jacket (Seneca chief), xvi, 31, 45
Red River, 71
Reeves, Judge Tapping, 14
Richmond, Va., 44, 46
Ripon, Wis., 324, 329, 330–333, 336
Rochester, N. Y., 36–37
Rocks of America, 398, 399, 400
Rocky Mountains, 55, 56, 60, 61, 65, 71, 150
Roehm, Marjorie Catlin, xv, xvi, xviii
Royal Institution, London, 157

St. Louis, Mo., xvii, 44, 46–47, 49, 55, 57, 64–65, 75, 81, 82
Sanford, H. S., 348, 351, 353, 362, 364, 365, 376, 378
Sanford, Major John F. A., 57, 63
San Francisco, Calif., 324, 326, 327, 336, 338
Sault St. Marie, Wis., 91, 93
Sauk Indians, 47, 48, 58
Sayre, Abigail. See Catlin, Abigail Sayre
Schoolcraft, Henry Rowe, viii, 312, 344–345, 357, 358, 370, 382, 384, 397
Scrap-Book, 344, 357–358, 371
Seminole Indians, 125 n.
Senate. See Congress, U. S.
Seneca Falls, N. Y., 51, 54
Sentinel, The American, 148 n.
Seward, William Henry, 316, 317
Shawnee Indians, 48
Simmons, Mr. and Mrs., 200
Sioux Indians, 59, 60, 101
Smithsonian Institution, ix, xviii, 310–311, 410, 412

Sommerville Gallery, N. Y., 408 n., 409–
410
South America, xvii, 326–329
Steele, Mr., 387–395, 396, 400
Stone, Colonel William, 31, 45, 64
Stuyvesant Institute, N. Y., 121, 122, 148
Susquehanna County. *See* Montrose, Penn.
Susquehanna River, 8, 49, 53
Sutton, Polly. *See* Catlin, Polly

Taylor, President Zachary, 307, 308
Tecumseh, Mich., 97, 98
Thompson, Jonathan, 24, 26
Tichenor, Anna C. *See* Catlin, Anna C.
Tichenor
Tichenor, Captain William, 330 n.
Tit-tee, 329
Tolbert, Mary. *See* Catlin, Mary Weed
Tolbert
Towanda, 136, 137
Treadway, John, 80
Trowbridge, Oliver, 112, 144

United States Dragoons. *See* Dragoons, U. S.
Uruguay River, 328

Utica, N. Y., 97–112 *passim*, 132–133, 136,
137, 145, 162, 178, 189, 265, 280

Victoria, Queen, 153, 158, 175, 206, 233,
234, 255

Waco Indians, 71, 74
Wallace, Mary M., 168–169, 188, 220, 224,
225, 233, 236, 279–280
Warner, Mr., 76, 79
Washington, D. C., 44, 46, 49, 51, 124,
127, 129, 130, 133, 147, 214, 297, 307,
308, 322, 323, 326, 330–333, 336, 338,
340, 345, 376, 378–380, 384, 385, 410
Webster, Daniel, 133, 314, 315
West Point, 22, 31
Weston, N. Y., 45, 51, 52
Wilkes-Barre, Penn., 6–8, 13–18, 20–21
Willamette Valley, Ore., 321–322. *See also*
Oregon Territory
Willow River, Wis. *See* Hudson, Wis.
Winnebago Indians, 177, 189, 241
Wood, Robert, 100–101

Yankton Sioux Indians, 81–82
Yellowstone (steamship), xvii, 57–60
Yellowstone River, xvii, 57, 58

Bruxelles. 11th June 1849.

Dear Brother Francis,

I rec'd your letter of the 15th May I rec'd in due time, but have delayed answering until the present, hoping to have got a letter from O. S. Gregory on this, having written to him relative to the outlines And also I was anxious to learn som— —— ——— —— London Mean, about publishing the Small edition.

I have not got any answer from Gregory; And having made a visit to London, spending time and money, have effected nothing. The publisher is afraid that the Indian Subject is getting too old to out =lay so much money on; is very willing to publish if I will advance one half the money